Hazel's Story

A gripping, compelling, true story

Hazel Lakeland

Published by Shakspeare Editorial, England

ISBN: 978-0-9929731-8-6 (pbk)
ISBN: 978-0-9929731-9-3 (ebk)

Cover image: Peter Vinten
Design and typesetting: www.shakspeareeditorial.org

Dedicated to my sons

Contents

Acknowledgements

To my whole family for their support.

In particular to my wonderful husband for his insistence that I write this story and to his daughter, Alice, whose initial editorial guidance and encouragement was invaluable.

My biggest thanks should go to my mother because without her sharp memory and friendship with Lieselotte there would not have been a story. It is sad that she died before it was completed.

Hazel's Family Tree

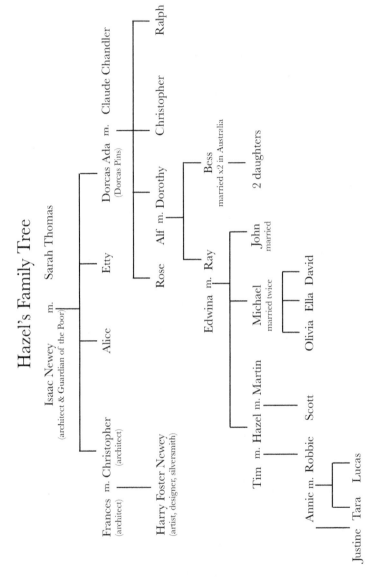

CHAPTER 1
1923 ◊ My Grandmother

I am Hazel, and I feel that the time has finally come to make this story available. Over the years I have divulged various parts of it to friends, family, even close work colleagues, and have ended up being swept up by their incredulity. However, when I fit the story together in my head it both frightens and uplifts me and I hope it is not interpreted in an inappropriate way.

Also, the man whose almost fatal error is vital to this story, was my neighbour. I had the highest regard for him and did not wish him to suffer because of what happened. He has now retired and I hope that he will not be blamed in any way as the full story emerges.

So, this has been my conundrum: to tell in full or not to tell at all. My conclusion is that this story – although it is all true – should be read simply as a remarkable tale that could have happened to anyone, anywhere, regardless of their country, situation or religion. While I was born to Western parents, this is a global story.

Although this is essentially my story, and unlocks the mystery surrounding my paternal grandmother's death, a second drama emerges that twists to the present day and ends with a question.

I'll lay out my family background and my history to allow you to reach your own conclusions regarding what happened to me. But please imagine this as no more than a story. To this end, I have changed many of the names, including my own. My father had wished that I, his firstborn child, should be named Hazel. My mother wouldn't allow it as she thought I would be nicknamed Nut! So, I will honour my father and call myself Hazel. My father's Christian name was actually Raymond and I see no reason not to call him Ray.

◊

Ray's parents met in Birmingham. His father, Alf, after the end of World War I, was working as an architectural designer in London for a company that decided to spread its wings to the growing city of Birmingham. Alf, whose family had originally come from Liverpool, was not unhappy to find himself moving to this thriving hub. When looking for lodgings he was instantly drawn to a double-fronted, three-storey Victorian house called Armscot. It overlooked a small park in what was one of the more pleasant streets in the city. He soon became aware of the strong, tall, willowy beauty of one of the daughters of the house. Alf thought it strange that, although Dorothy must be nearing her early thirties, she had not married. Her older sister Rose had inherited her mother's less attractive features but was a gentle accommodating woman, unlike her mother Dorcas, who was known as a bit of a dragon.

It seems clear that Dorothy found Alf very attractive and commanding with his long, curled moustache. During dinner the family listened as he related his time during the First World War in France, when the 2nd Dragoon Guards he had enlisted in joined the 1st Calvary Division. He was a natural, clever, story teller, so may have embellished his tales a little to highlight the dashing officer upon his horse – and to hide the goriness of it all.

Dorcas owned the house and appeared to have no husband but there were two brothers, Christopher and Ralph. Ralph was the youngest and spent most of his time strapped into a wheelchair, even though he appeared quite capable of walking. Alf had witnessed him having a severe fit and concluded that the wheelchair was for Ralph's own safety.

Several days later Alf came across Dorothy alone in the warm kitchen, arranging flowers. She looked up as she heard him enter.

"I'm sorry you had to see poor Ralph the other day. He has endured these fits since a small child. Unfortunately, they have become increasingly more frequent and violent. The wheelchair is necessary for his own protection," Dorothy confirmed.

"I had presumed as much. It cannot be easy for your family and Ralph is such a likeable fellow. Did your father fall in the war?"

Dorothy hesitated. "It's rather a long and onerous story. Shall I make some tea?"

Alf took a seat, happy to spend some time in her company and watched as Dorothy elegantly prepared tea in the best Spode teapot and laid out matching cups, saucers, small plates and a freshly baked cake. She finally sat down, poured the tea, cut and placed on their plates a generous portion of cake for Alf and a smaller piece for herself.

Dorothy became still and thoughtful and then began.

"My grandfather was Isaac Newey, a successful architect and surveyor, who also belonged to a group called Guardians of the Poor, so was generally well-known and respected in Birmingham. Unfortunately, he died of bronchitis when only fifty-one, but my grandmother skilfully managed the various properties and wealth he had accumulated."

She paused to take a bite of the moist cake.

"On her death, my mother, who had been nursing her, inherited the family home, and from its sale she purchased this more modern house. It is ideal, with the whole of the top floor perfect for lodgers. My father, Claude, first came to the house as one such lodger. By all accounts he was a charming man, a salesman by trade, who, in his spare time, loved amateur dramatics. It was his idea, while wooing my mother, to turn the large sitting room into a theatre on occasion, to perform plays for all my mother's family and friends to enjoy. It meant my mother was also able to display her dressmaking skills in the wonderful costumes. It was not until after their marriage that my mother discovered his other loves. Gambling and entertaining women. Over time he not only frittered away his own salary but he began taking my mother's earnings as well. This was no small amount as she not only had regular lodgers but, as an accomplished dressmaker, her abilities were sought out far and wide. Throughout my childhood my parents argued about money, but as I grew older I realised that my father was also spending money on other women and I watched as my poor mother became increasingly unhappy. The arguments became constant and were having such a detrimental effect on us all, particularly poor Ralph, that I spoke to my mother and we agreed that my father no longer really cared for any of us and so we had to do

3

something. He had once, previously, been ostracised from the house and had spent some weeks in a hotel."

Dorothy paused for some more cake, then rose from the table.

"I have a photograph and a letter."

She returned and handed Alf a picture of a moustached man in breeches and a fancy tunic.

"My father in costume, for one of their plays."

Then she passed Alf a neatly written letter.

"I was only seven at the time. My mother showed it to me years later. He was to go to London for his work and my mother discovered that a woman was going with him."

> *"Fife" Hotel*
> *19 and 20, Ely Place,*
> *Holborn Circus, London 8*
> *Aug 16 1898*
> *My dear Wife.*
>
> *You will by this time have had my express letter. I hardly know what I said in it, in fact I scarcely know what I am doing at all this week. I have only seen 5 customers yet I ought to have seen 25 by this time. What Mr W will think I am doing I don't know or care much. Now let me say that 11 years ago I took you as my wife to love and cherish, which I shall do today, and can live my life more devoted to my dear children and you, if you will only let me. And not again bring accusations against me, to which there is not the least foundation. I have been a true husband to you and never done anything to bring dishonour upon you, my children or myself. This statement can be published to the world and I can face all and prove it. I know full well I am not perfect, in fact I know I have many faults. The truth will never hurt me. It is the lies. How well you tell me your idea of a husband's devotion to his wife and children, also a wife's devotion to her husband, and I will do my part, try my best to carry it out. For any more of this kind of life will finish me. It is enough to have business worries, but the two combined is too much. The human frame can only stand a certain strain. I can willingly forgive all past differences, even the last, would only be too pleased to know that we could live in the bonds of love and peace and bring our darlings up to be a credit to us and themselves. Thank God Rose was away on Sunday and God forbid*

4

that any of our children should ever witness such a scene. If you can see the matter in the same light as me, and I wish you could, for I swear I have never had a thought of anyone (beyond a thought of friendship) but yourself. How can I prove it to you? Tell me. Because you do not seem to believe a word I say. I did not know I had quite such a character of a liar as I have. Now this is the last letter of this description I am going to write, so let the matter be settled once and for all, if only for the sake of the children. We must love, for them, and try to train them up alright. I will finish my writing and it will then be 9 p.m. Shall catch the 9.30 post and it shall not be long before I am in bed and will try to get some sleep.
Your still loving husband Claude.

"He was never able to have just 'friendships' with other women but my mother was compelled to take him back that time to allow him a chance to prove his word. And perhaps for a while he may have tried. This time though we all agreed that he could no longer be considered any part of our family. This may sound dramatic, but to my mind there was only one solution. The following day I went to see the local locksmith and arranged for him to change the locks on the front door in a week's time. My mother then asked my father to move out. This time he refused, and did nothing to change his behaviour. So, on the morning that the locksmith had arranged to change the lock, my mother and I waited until my father left for work and then systematically put all his belongings into suitcases and boxes and laid them out in the front garden. He obviously had a shock seeing everything he owned there for all the neighbours to see, and his anger when he found that his key could not open the door was profound to say the least. He banged and hollered for over half an hour before I opened an upstairs window and told him that this was final and that none of us wanted any more to do with him. With no money we knew he was in no position to take any legal action and my mother was sure he'd find some woman to take pity on him. Although pity her! It wasn't until the following day that he took his belongings away. It was such a relief when everything had gone. My mother did receive a couple of pleading letters but burnt them, and that, amazingly, was the last we heard from him."

"May I ask your age at that time," enquired Alf.

"Only nineteen. But certainly old enough to understand my mother's suffering."

"To evict one's own father in that way is a credit to your strength of character. I had best endeavour not to displease you!" he smiled.

Dorothy considered, "I have had proposals of marriage, but have chosen to stay and help Rose and mother and maintain my independence. Although, perhaps it is also through fear of how even charming men can be so false."

The home Alf now blended into was happy and cultured. Putting on plays at home had become a part of Dorothy's life and through the years they had attracted ever-swelling parties of friends and family. Dorothy's cousin, Harry Foster Newey, belonged to the Royal Birmingham Society of Artists and would often bring fellow associates to watch and make merry.

Alf confided to Dorothy that his father's sister and her husband had been childless, so had brought him up, as his mother had been an alcoholic and had proved unable to cope with a baby. His father had been a cartographer and had illustrated some of the latest Encyclopaedia Britannica. His mother had died as a result of her addiction when he was still young. So, to now be part of such a family home was wonderful and, in time, Alf convinced Dorothy that he could never be like her father and they fell in love and got married.

They remained at Armscot and Ray was born less than a year later. He was a lovely baby with a mass of blond curly hair, brown eyes and a ready smile. Two years later Alf's company gave him the option of permanently relocating to London. He and Dorothy had enjoyed holidaying in the bright, busy, seaside town of Southend-on-Sea, with its miles of beaches and the longest leisure pier in the world and decided that it was within a commutable distance.

Life during those early years was good. Alf and Dorothy were fortunate enough to find au-pairs always willing to help around the house. They entertained their gorgeous and appreciative son by pushing his pram along the seafront, cliffs and parks. But Hazel's grandparents were both strong characters and, according to Dorothy's cousin Jean Brown, who would occasionally stay with them, the atmosphere could become strained and argumentative, but she also saw that Dorothy was a good, warm and loving mother.

Ray was five when his sister, Bessy, was born. Hazel has a beautiful family portrait of the four of them, with Alf sitting on the right and Dorothy on the left, a handsome couple, with just enough room for six-year-old Raymond to stand in between, looking out with large eyes that Hazel can only describe as doleful. A little baffled, Bessy sits on Dorothy's lap in her baby chubbiness, looking straight at the camera. She certainly looks a sturdy child but was very lucky to have survived two bouts of pneumonia, which might explain why her parents became over-protective and tended to spoil her. Hazel's aunt remembers one example of this when, just before her fifth Christmas, her father brought home three doll's prams for Bess to choose the one she preferred. She chose the largest. When she was officially presented with it on Christmas day she found that she was too small to actually push it but wanted to take her doll out for a walk, immediately. Alf therefore instructed Raymond to push his sister's pram for her. Imagine poor Ray, ten years old and having to take a doll's pram, plus doll, with little sister also attempting to push it, round and about until she was able to manage it herself. The relationship between Ray and his sister continued rather uncomfortably, with Bess always getting her own way.

Then Alf's job took him on a visit to Germany, where he was privileged to stay in the house of the Burgomeister of Bad Bodenteich. During this stay the Burgomeister (literally, the master of a town, borough or fortress) asked Alf if he would kindly take his daughter, Lieselotte, back to England with him as his au-pair, to enable her to refine her English. She was an attractive young lady from an aristocratic family; Alf was more than happy to do so.

Dorothy immediately recognised real intelligence in this quiet girl and a strong bond formed between them. Lieselotte also fell in love with Ray and Bess and soon realised how Bess' dominating nature had been nurtured. Lieselotte sensitively turned Ray's life back into the happy, balanced childhood he had enjoyed before Bessy's birth, without making an enemy of this feisty little girl.

When Lieselotte finally returned to Germany she was sadly missed by the whole family.

But Dorothy was beginning to have health problems. She was finding it increasingly difficult to get about with painful legs that had to be heavily bandaged. Without Lieselotte's companionship she became increasingly unhappy and frustrated. Alf eventually decided to contact the Burgomeister and ask if Lieselotte would be happy to return as companion to Dorothy and nanny to the children. Her return to England was so welcome.

The family were now living in a large, chalet-type house in a prestigious part of Leigh-on-Sea, a fishing village eight miles up the Thames estuary from Southend. While Dorothy became unhappy with her deteriorating health and more difficult to live with, Ray and Bess thrived.

Then one terrifying morning it all changed.

Dorothy became quite ill. The doctors, because of various other problems she had, were unsure of the cause, and this was before antibiotics. Lieselotte was kept very busy caring for both her and the children. After more than two weeks in bed, Dorothy worsened and began to slip in and out of delirium. Lieselotte summoned the doctor during the night but nobody remembers what treatments or medicines were administered. After the doctor left, Alf went to work. Seven-year-old Bess, who had not been allowed to see her mother for weeks, slipped into Dorothy's bedroom, understandably concerned. But Dorothy became very agitated and suddenly got up out of the bed, grabbed Bess and began screaming, "The house is on fire, the house is on fire."

The bedroom window was open a little and Dorothy rushed over to it with Bess gripped tightly in her arms and began to try to push her out of the window, still screaming, "Help, help, the house is on fire, it's all burning."

Lieselotte rushed up the stairs to Bess' screams as she frantically tried to fight her mother's unexpected strength. In her terror Bess found enough strength to jam herself against the window frame, which gave Lieselotte time to cross the room and wrestle Bess from her mother's hold. After managing to calm Dorothy, Lieselotte carried the traumatised girl downstairs and asked Ray to run to the phone box, dial 999 and ask for an ambulance, which arrived quickly.

Lieselotte attempted to hide from the distraught children the fact that their mother was taken out to the ambulance in a straitjacket. She then rang Alf at work to give him the disturbing news. He arrived home later that evening, after visiting his wife in Rochford Hospital and explained to Lieselotte that he'd had to sign a form allowing her to be 'sectioned' in the psychiatric unit. The distress he felt for the wife he loved so very dearly can only be imagined.

Alf wrote to Dorothy's mother and he must have visited Dorothy but, some weeks after she was admitted, her brother Chris was the last person to see her alive. He reported to Alf that her eyes had been bulging and that same evening Alf received the news of her death.

Because Dorothy had taken so little part in the life of her children over the preceding few months, very little changed for them when their mother was taken into hospital. They loved Lieselotte and her caring security remained unchanged. Bess appeared to miss her mother the most and kept asking when she would be well enough to return home. Alf instructed Lieselotte not to tell Ray and Bess of their mother's death. They were not told until almost six months later, although they were never told how or why she had died.

Hazel has an old exercise book that once belonged to Dorothy's sister. Across the front is written:

Rose Chandler
'Diary' Starting from
"1935"

Poignantly, it begins:

June 15th 1935.
Dorothy was taken very ill and Alf Lawson put her in Rochford Hospital,
then he wrote & told us she got much worse & Chris had to go over
and see her, she knew him & that was all, he had to come back the next
morning because of business & she died in the night with no one by her
side poor Dorothy. The first time I really felt ill and it did something to
me as we were always so fond of one another although Dorothy was very
awkward at times, but she was my sister & that is all.
She was brought to Handsworth Cemetery & we had a grave for 3 and
she was buried in July. Alf Lawson came up and went with Chris. I

stayed at home with mother & Ralph. The death of Dorothy upset my mother quite a lot & she died in the June 1936 and was buried with Dorothy. We were all very upset & Ralph very much. Then in January 1938 Kathleen died (my help) from meningitis, she was well and dead in 4 days. It was an awful shock, then Chris, Ralph and I went to Weston for a week's holiday and stayed at Mrs Bellinger's & it was very nice & Ralph seemed to be much better. Then in the August of 1939 Ralph started to lose weight & did not seem so well, he started a cough & coughed & was ill, very ill for 2 1/2 years & in 1942 Ralph died, which quite finished me, also Chris. We will never be the same again, although we have to keep going, our lives changed from this point.

About a month after Dorothy's death Lieselotte walked into the sitting room to find Alf burning all Dorothy's records in the grate, including her birth, death and marriage certificates. As she began to voice her astonishment, Alf turned to her and said, "I must forbid her name to be mentioned again. Please leave the room."

As Lieselotte had become such an intricate part of their lives, her marriage to Alf just a year following Dorothy's death seemed natural. At the outbreak of World War II the family remained in Leigh-on-Sea. Alf and Ray joined the Home Guard and were involved in the fire watch. This meant spending nights on the roofs of tall buildings ready to alert the fire service during night raids. The end of the war heralded the birth of Alf and Lieselotte's son Arthur in 1946, an event that was welcomed by all.

CHAPTER 2
1940s ◊ Ray

As Ray went through adolescence, the distance between him and Bess grew. Their relationship was not entirely without affection but, as with many siblings with an age gap, they had little interest in each other's life and friends. However, Bess had formed the opinion that her brother needed strong guidance or he would daydream through life.

During his final years at school Raymond was undecided about a career. His father attempted to steer him towards the architectural profession but Ray's love of art meant he wanted to study at Central Saint Martins. When war seemed unavoidable, the fear of conscription pushed him to sign up for the RAF as soon as his schooling was finished because he would far rather be in the sky as a pilot in control of a plane than on the ground and powerless. But Alf knew that his marriage to Lieselotte, a German, would concern the authorities. Determined to keep it a secret, he refused to allow his son to fill in any forms. He secured a place for Ray at Moss Brothers, who had been commissioned to make army clothing. As this was necessary war work he avoided conscription, so this and fire watching was all he was able to contribute to the war effort, initially.

Ray's yearning to fly and to fight for his country did not lessen and eventually he was able to lay his hands on a conscription form without his father's knowledge. He discovered that all he needed to put on the form was that his mother had died. He'd been fortunate to have had a private education and so, to his father's fear and anger, he was accepted into Cranwell. But by now it was 1943. Raymond's greatest disappointment was discovering that he was unable to hold his eyes in a cross-eyed position, which was vital when lining up an enemy plane in combat. One eye, it appeared, continually bounced around. This affliction did not affect Ray's ability to read but it did turn out to be genetic and manifested itself in Hazel's elder son and grandson.

Ray did learn how to fly but was unable to pass the medical requirement for a fighter pilot, so he began navigation training and passed as an air gunner and wireless operator (technically WOP/AIR). He was then sent to an officer training school in Vancouver, Canada, to complete his navigational training and final grade WOP/AIR. His dream of flying the skies as a pilot was over. Then fate intervened and before he could complete his training and join the war he fell ill with rheumatic fever. He thought it may have been caused by sitting on damp grass! So he spent nine months in Canada recovering but, while he came to love the country, he was tormented by the awful news of the loss in combat of so many of his friends. By the time he was fully recovered and fit enough to complete his exams, the navigation courses had all closed and he was only able to complete his final WOP/AIR requirements. By which time the war was virtually over.

He joined 96 Squadron Transport Command flying Dakotas in Burma in 1945. His log book shows that he did get to be second pilot on various occasions and flew to and from such places as Bangkok to Mingaladon, Hmawbi to Dum Dum and Butterworth to Kallang. In 1946 he became part of 110 Squadron based in Kai-Tak, China. The last date in his log is 11.8.46.

Most squadrons made up their own code for communicating while in flight and Ray devised the code, set within a song, that his squadron used. He returned home with a leather suitcase that had his name and address printed in black letters across the top, to which his crew had added 'Squadron Leader' at their leaving do. This shows the immense affection and respect that had built up for this tall, dark, slim man who was never able to call himself a fighter pilot.

Because he had lost so many friends Ray rarely spoke of that time, but he had a passion for photography and compiled an album. Hazel remembers her mother giving it to her to look at when she was recovering from a now-forgotten childhood illness. It was both fascinating and tragic. A good half of the photos cover his time in Canada and many depict the beautiful snow-covered Rocky Mountains around Alberta, including The Great Divide between Alberta and British Columbia, Hell's Gate in Fraser Canyon, Stoner Creek Bridge, the Royal Canadian Mounted Police Station in Banff, the frozen Bow River at Calgary and Lake Louise (which he captioned

'Famous Honeymoon Spot !!'). Also photographed in August 1944 are Stanley Park, where he says he spent all his Sunday afternoons while he was convalescing, and Alexandra Park, where he was obviously strong enough to go rowing on the lake. Both parks are in Vancouver and the Convalescence Hospital looks both grand and beautiful, with a wooden veranda overlooking the splendid gardens. By September 1944 he was fit and able to enjoy a mid-term leave before starting at the Air Operating Section (Shepard) #2, Wireless School, Calgary – where he took pictures of the Harvard F.E. 988 (which he flew) in formation flight and as 'Documentary Evidence of Low Flying!'

There are two mysterious photos of Wichita High School, dated May 1943 and January 1944, and a third showing floods in a Wichita street. Edwina remembers Ray mentioning an engagement to a girl he had really cared for but, because he was sure his father would disapprove, he had kept it a secret. Tragically, when paying a short visit to her family somewhere in the north of England, she had died during a bombing raid. Aunt Bess says he certainly kept it a secret as she has no knowledge of it.

Ray took photos of his home in Winnipeg, followed by a page titled 'LEAVE FOR BURMA 30th SEPT 1945' and pictures of Hmawbi Airfield, including a makeshift cinema – rows of barrels lying flat in a field in front of a canvas screen with the comment, 'Spent many an hour in the lap of luxury at our celebrated open-air cinema!!' He included photos of the inside of his tent, 'The boys constructing a chair' outside a row of tents, and a Dakota KN 579 by which he has written, 'We "pranged" this aircraft two weeks after this was taken'. Further pages show scenes in Rangoon and then India, featuring Calcutta, the Taj Mahal, the Maharaja's Palace in Agartala, Lui Lake in Kashmir and the Central Assembly Hall in New Delhi. Two photos were taken 'From our bedroom window at the Majestic Hotel showing river scenes'.

Ray clearly enjoyed Hong Kong and there are three pics of him in swimming trunks on the beach and six of him with native girls in 'Ray's Cafe'! Next is a photo of '110 Squadron dispersal strip, Kai-Tak aerodrome 19th June 1945', together with photos taken as they flew over the mountains of Kowloon Island.

It is the next page that wipes away what appears to be Ray's rather glamorous image of his time in the RAF:

'HIROSHIMA. BOMB DAMAGE FROM THE SECOND ATOMIC BOMB. TAKEN FROM 500FT ON 27TH APRIL 1946.'

Four pictures. Total black devastation. So very awful.

Facing these is a 'Mustang Fighter which flew alongside us while taking pictures of Hiroshima'.

The final section of the album is labelled 'Homeward Bound 1946' and shows photos of Hong Kong, Shanghai, Japan and the Middle East, including: 'Bombed out submarine factory Kure and the Japanese aircraft carrier "Katsuragi"'; 'Paradise Island in Miyajima and its Sacred Temple'; 'A snake charmer and magician in Singapore'; 'A street in Aden'; and 'Along the Suez Canal'.

To end on a pleasant, pretty note Ray filled the last pages with photos of all the girlfriends he'd had during that time, some of them signed with love and best wishes. He included one of ice skater Barbara Ann Scott, captioned 'Went skating with her at the Arena ice skating rink Calgary 1944'.

After all his experiences he found it impossible to contemplate the thought of seven years' study for the full architectural training Alf still wanted for his son, or even of going to art college. So he accepted a position as an apprentice architectural designer with a shopfitting company in London's West End and honed his draughtsman's skills at night school.

One Monday morning he was standing on the platform at Leigh-on-Sea station with Alf (who still worked in the City) when he noticed a pretty young lady waiting for the same train. As the steam train clanked, screeched and hissed to a stop, Ray stepped up and neatly opened the door for her. He entered the carriage after her, with Alf close behind, to discover there were only two vacant seats next to each other (I would like to remind readers that those were the days when chivalry still mattered). So both men waited for the young lady to settle into her chosen seat. It would have been disrespectful of Ray if he had forced his father to stand all the way to Fenchurch Street and so he allowed him to take the remaining seat. Edwina still remembers the embarrassed discomfort she felt as Alf attempted to chat her up on his son's behalf, painting Ray and his time in the RAF in brilliant, glowing 'over-the-topness'. However, she displayed suitable, intelligent responses, with appropriate laughter at the older man's conversation, while Ray had no option but to stand by, raise his eyebrows and roll his eyes. On arrival at Fenchurch Street Station Alf ascertained that she would be catching the same train the following morning.

Edwina lived with her parents on a council estate in Leigh-on-Sea, in a home and garden that were immaculately and lovingly cared for. Edwina's mother Rosemary had enjoyed various interesting pursuits prior to meeting her husband Reginald. Photographs show her holding a gun in the midst of a group of men at a rifle club and sitting astride her bicycle in a mixed cycling club. The pair had met while both were working in the railway offices and subsidised fares meant they were well travelled and knowledgeable about many things, as was their daughter. Edwina also had a brother, Jack, five years her junior, whose quiet determination to follow his own path from a young age presented some difficulties. For instance, he hated going to school but every weekday Rosemary would watch Edwina and Jack walk to the end of the road. The second Jack knew he was out of his mother's sight, he would refuse to walk any further, so every day Edwina had to drag him to school. Most embarrassing was the day the headmistress called her out of class and asked her to find her brother, who had taken to hiding in the playground after morning playtime and was refusing to return to his classroom. Jack had a succession of childhood illnesses during his first term at school, which had put him behind his classmates. He was eventually given extra help as it became obvious that he was struggling with even basic concepts. However, it was given too late to build up his confidence.

Reginald served in France with the army during the war. Edwina and Jack were evacuated to Quorndon, a village in Derbyshire, with their mother who volunteered as a helper, and they lived happily together on a farm. While there Edwina won a scholarship that had been organised by Southend but which allowed her to study at Mansfield College. Jack disappeared when he was due to sit for a scholarship but returned to the farm at the end of school time, so it was a few days before Rosemary found out.

There was also the incident of a soldier reported to be walking over the fields towards the village. Word spread very quickly. From a distance it was impossible to tell if he was a 'shot down German'. It was late afternoon and the children were home. Rosemary gathered up Edwina and Jack and, with most of the village, they tentatively made their way to the end of the village, in the direction he had been seen. To their absolute amazement and delight the soldier appearing over the hill was Reg, with kit bag slung over his shoulder. He'd unexpectedly been given a week's leave. By July 1942 Rosemary felt it was time for them all to return home and take their chances in a war that had begun to feel endless.

Their evacuation was an enjoyable time for all and Jack helped with some information for a book about the village during the war. He and Edwina visited Quorndon for a book signing in 2008.

Echo was a well-known radio manufacturing company based in Southend and Edwina, who had completed her studies, began work in the goods-in department, checking and collating the paperwork. Nine months later she was offered a position in London to train as an auditor – a great opportunity that she accepted. But she hated London during the blackout when even road signs had been removed. Then in June 1944 the V-1 flying bomb was used. It was the world's first cruise missile; an unmanned gyro-guided plane, able to deliver a ton of high explosive. A total of 2,419 exploded in London between 13 June 1944 and March 1945. The pulsing noise of their jet engine would suddenly cut out and they hurtled noiselessly to their final destination. They were nicknamed doodlebugs and terrorised London's population.

At least Edwina was able to escape home at night, where only one bomb had been dropped on a nearby house that, luckily, was empty. The office she worked in during the day was cold and dark and in winter they were only allowed to burn one lump of coal at a time – she was often reminded of Dickens' story about Scrooge. After her eighteenth birthday in September 1944 she was able to enlist in the Women's Royal Naval Service as a Wren, although it was not until May of the following year that she was finally called up – and took the position of paymaster, sorting out sailors' pay. She really enjoyed the work for twenty-seven months, until she was 'demobbed'. It was while she was working as a bookkeeper for a company who imported goods from abroad, mainly floor coverings and crockery, that she met Ray.

Jack cleverly managed to never sit an exam in his whole life, but somehow wrangled an apprenticeship in the engineering department of Avery, who made scales. At eighteen, when required to do his two years of National Service, he joined the Royal Engineers. It's not clear exactly what he did but, as he had been driving officers around, he was granted a driving licence on completion of his National Service.

Alf had sought to elevate himself above the status of his alcoholic mother and, to this end, after his marriage, he had added his mother's maiden name of Blake as a prefix to his own surname and bestowed this double-barrelled name on Dorothy and their children. It also enabled him to say that he was related to William Blake. We later discovered that there was indeed *a* William Blake in his ancestry – but not *the* William Blake he had insinuated it was. If Alf had hoped for a daughter-in-law from a middle-class family he never voiced it, but Bess believed her brother was making a mistake and that he needed a woman who was stronger and more assertive to help lead him in an open-minded, intelligent way. Although this may have been more to do with Edwina not being able to warm to Bess, rather than their slight class differences. Lieselotte simply hoped for Ray's happiness and Reg and Rosemary were delighted when he formally asked Reg for his daughter's hand in marriage.

Ray instructed Edwina to finish her job in London and look for a local job and a flat to rent in Leigh-on-Sea. She duly found a small, downstairs, two-bedroom flat with a little garden. Work was harder to find as most companies still expected employees to work Saturday mornings and, while he had to work two Saturdays in every month, Ray believed his future wife should not. She was still unemployed when a date was set for the wedding in May 1950. Unfortunately, just two weeks before this date they were told the flat would no longer be available. Edwina rushed around to find an alternative but was unable to find anywhere suitable that they could afford, so it was agreed that they would live temporarily with her parents.

The wedding, at Crowstone church in Leigh-on-Sea, went well. The sun shone and five-year-old Arthur was almost as stunning in his ivory silk pageboy suit as Edwina was in her slim, figure hugging, ivory silk wedding dress that was extended by a long train. Her cousin Anita was bridesmaid in a long, lilac silk dress. Rationing was still in force but by pooling resources they had a wonderful day.

A year later Bess decided she had had enough of the long, grey, wet English winters and secured a cost-assisted passage to Australia.

CHAPTER 3
1950s ◊ Hazel's Early Childhood

I believe that many things help to mould a new life. The genetics of the parents, their diet, the stresses and quality of their lifestyle are all being proven to affect their chemical balance, which can, even slightly, alter their genes. Likewise, a mother's chemicals and her mental state during pregnancy can all have an effect, however tiny. Breastfeeding, beyond passing on essential fatty acids and natural immunities, also helps to form a good bond and improves childhood health. Good nutrition as a baby goes through early life must also be significant in ensuring an optimum chemical balance for sound mental and physical strength, which is almost as important as providing a loving and secure environment.

To this end, to understand what truly made Hazel into the adult she became, I have attempted to be as observant and as fulsome as possible.

◊

Three months after the marriage Edwina secured a bookkeeper's position with a local pipe manufacturer and found a gardenless, first-floor, one-bedroom flat. As a first home together, it was passable. The ground floor was occupied by another young couple, Irene and Ronald, who were expecting their first baby. The women were befriended by a dear, cheerful, Scots neighbour, Mrs Gardiner. Her husband had died quite young, leaving her with one daughter, Patricia, who was married to a young, extremely good-looking singer, Jim Dale. He was becoming nationally well-known and Mrs Gardiner loved telling everyone about "my Jimmy's" antics. Edwina occasionally looked after Patricia's firstborn by taking her out in her pram.

Mrs Gardiner was a cat lover and her home was full of them since any stray was welcome. Ray, who came from a dog-owning family, felt cats were unworthy of house space, although Edwina's parents had two black cats. So, on the day that her ever-smiling Scottish neighbour offered Edwina a kitten, it was not without trepidation that she took the little ball of black and white fluff up to their flat. As soon as Ray saw it he told her to return the kitten, but Edwina decided to ignore her husband. It was mainly white but had a black blotch above each eye, two black ears and a black nose – so they named him Panda.

That evening Ray put on his slippers and, just as he settled down for a quiet evening with the paper, the fluff ball appeared and gently patted a slipper. He grumpily shook his foot, causing the kitten to jump into the air and dash behind the chair. But the slipper was intriguing, so it couldn't resist slinking out to tap it again, then skittered off as soon as it moved. Edwina was amused to observe that her husband soon became as absorbed in the game as the kitten.

Mrs Gardiner felt that such a wee young thing should not be left in the flat alone during the day so it was agreed that Irene, who was now at home during the day with her baby, would look after Panda in her flat when Edwina was out. This arrangement worked well until Panda practised his bird-catching skills on the couple's canary, Barney. His cage hung from the lounge ceiling and he was regularly allowed to stretch his wings when Irene was in the room. Generally, the bird remained high in the air or perched on the curtain pole or the top of a cabinet. One day Irene went to check on baby Graham, asleep in his pram in the garden. He cried a lot, so any period of quiet bothered her. Squawking brought her rushing back to find Barney firmly clenched in Panda's mouth. She carefully prised him out. He appeared unhurt and fluttered back into his cage. But an hour later shock got the better of poor Barney and he lay dead on the cage floor. Panda was not welcomed into that flat again, but was now old enough to amuse himself or sleep when his own flat was empty.

Ray and Edwina were delighted when they discovered they were soon to be parents. Panda was about a year old when Hazel was born in March 1953 in Rochford Hospital. The birth was straightforward and Edwina had heeded all her mother's advice. Rosemary considered childbirth a natural process and felt that simply relaxing and allowing your body to achieve what it was designed to do was the best way through it. A ten-day stay in hospital after a first birth was normal and breastfeeding was seen as the mother gifting immunity and essential nutrients to this new life, if she was able – but at Rochford Hospital no help or tuition was given, one was simply expected to get on with it.

This, as for most mothers, was a challenge for Edwina. Offering sore nipples to a hungry mewling infant with a ferocious sucking reflex is almost as bad as offering your hand to a flame. But it is what nature intended and mothers have achieved the hardest part: giving birth.

The only help to hand were 'nipple shields'. But less nipple to chew on only caused more frustration in Hazel. Edwina, experiencing the overwhelming sensations of a nursing mother as her tiny being draws out its precision-balanced milk, hoped that perseverance would be rewarded. Some mothers are lucky enough to have a baby who, with very little encouragement, manages to grasp the mechanics of suckling and calmly gets on with the business. Hazel was not one of those. She felt she had to play and experiment to discover the most successful way to acquire her sustenance. She chewed, bit, rolled Edwina's poor nipples all around her mouth and was intent on spending as long as she could before she was replete. Of course Edwina's nipples suffered and, when not in use, were coddled in soft pads and tucked into a nursing bra. Towards the end of her time in hospital she dropped a pad on the floor. A nurse duly retrieved it and handed it back to Edwina. Did that pad now harbour some germs?

Edwina received home visits from her family doctor, the midwife and the health visitor, who were all happy with the baby's progress, but she continued to struggle with feeding and began to feel quite ill.

After less than a week at home, Dr Quinn realised she had developed an abscess in one of her breasts and immediately sent her back to the hospital to have it cauterised. This was a simple procedure that, although done under a general anaesthetic, meant she was able to go home the same day. A tube was left in place to act as a drain. Edwina had to accept defeat on the breastfeeding front and Hazel, who had spent that day with Rosemary, did not take kindly to being offered a bottle by her grandmother, nor from her father when he returned from work.

This was not quite the wondrous entry into parenthood that Ray and Edwina had expected. It took a visit from the midwife, who advised Edwina to heat a pin and use it to enlarge the hole in the glass feeding bottle's rubber teat, to bring much-needed peace. But Edwina continued to feel unwell even though her breast appeared to be healing. Dr Quinn concluded that the abscess had grown again and needed to be completely removed, which was likely to mean two weeks in hospital. Paternity leave was frowned upon in those days, so Rosemary and Lieselotte worked out a rota to care for Hazel during the day. Ray, though, was besotted with his tiny, rather ugly, first offspring and insisted on collecting her from wherever she had spent her day, to bathe, feed and tuck her into her own cot every night. After night feeds, washing, changing and feeding again first thing in the morning, Ray had a brisk walk with the pram to that day's house. Rosemary's was closer to the flat and Chalkwell Station, Lieselotte's was further from the flat but closer to Leigh Station.

He was a proud father as he pushed his daughter in her grand Silver Cross pram that he and Edwina had chosen together. At only five feet two inches tall Edwina thought it would be important to be able to see over the pram when the hood was up, but Ray had declared that the largest model, with plenty of shiny chrome, was the one they were taking home.

By the time Edwina returned from hospital a strong bond had developed between father and tiny daughter. Edwina was soon fully recovered and Hazel grew into a sturdy, happy, beautiful baby who, like both her parents, had a ready smile for everyone – unlike dear baby Graham downstairs, who grew from a crying baby into a screaming, grizzly toddler. Ray and Edwina were relieved by the peace after Irene, Ron and little Graham moved out and Ted and Joyce Dipple moved in. Even when the Dipple's were at home Ray and Edwina heard nothing and they only met during general comings and goings. But they were a warm and genial couple who had not been married long and they both worked. Ted was a local police constable who trod the 'beat' and his presence added an unconscious sense of security.

As they had no garden Edwina would take Hazel out every day, regardless of the weather, to Chalkwell Park, down to the beach or to the library gardens. One of the fields in Chalkwell Park was used by Essex 1st XI cricket club for their county championship matches. Another field contained a series of ponds linked by short streams full of newts, sticklebacks, frogs, toads and, in spring, tadpoles. Young children were free to clamber around with their nets and to fill their buckets. Old Chalkwell Hall sat in the middle of the park with rose gardens to left and front. A café with a large wooden terrace was enjoyed by many. Nestling next to the Hall, under a canopy of trees, were cages with outdoor enclosures. All were small, apart from a larger one at the end that housed the peacocks. The first cage was home to a black honey bear, the second to a gorilla, the third was filled with rabbits and guinea pigs who were allowed to spill into the safety area between the cages and the wire fencing – erected to ensure that small arms weren't eaten.

Hazel, in her pram, was mesmerised by these animals. The male honey bear was quite young and agile, he played with his tyre and various balls, he climbed up the front of his cage, displaying his full size, or simply slept in the sun. He had enormous paws with claws that were so long they'd touch anyone stupid enough to force their arm through the safety fence. The female gorilla was older but she enjoyed climbing through her hanging tyre and lumbering around her cage to applause and holding her hand out for the food that was thrown to her. Quite regularly a male peacock would fan out his magnificent iridescent tail with a shimmering vibration. Nowadays, such small cages would not be acceptable, but to a very young Hazel the animals appeared to be equally entertained by the antics of the adults and children. Certainly, the close proximity of such majestic animals, allowing one to gaze into the depths of their brown, watchful eyes, helped forge in her a love and empathy for all animals.

It was in this park, one warm weekday, that Edwina laid out a blanket on the quiet cricket field and sat Hazel down for a picnic. She was fourteen months old and, while she regularly walked around at home holding on to the furniture, she had yet to take any unaided steps. This day, though, she suddenly decided to stand alone and, seeing the vastness of the open park, she ran and ran and ran. How to stop? A hedge loomed. She knew how to sit, so she did. Fortunately, with a bottom cushioned by a nappy, this proved painless. No need for tears. An early lesson though – think in detail before acting!

Ray subscribed to *Amateur Photography* magazine and he submitted a photo of Hazel on Chalkwell beach for a competition entitled 'Children'. In those days it was normal for very young girls to wear just slightly frillier versions of boys' swimming trunks, and she was no exception. At sixteen months, climbing over the wooden groynes that stretched out across the beach was not allowed and the picture captured her pensive look as she was halted in her exploration by Ray's voice. One of his large white handkerchiefs was tied across her shoulders to protect her from the sun. The caption he gave his photograph was 'Who said Cover girls'. It was awarded a Certificate of Merit and was displayed, with all Hazel's chubby charm, on the front cover of the magazine.

That same summer Hazel enjoyed her first holiday. This involved catching a train to Southend Pier, then clambering on the small wooden enclosed carriages of the pier train, which trundled them to the end of the pier to wait for a paddle steamer to ferry them across the Thames Estuary to the Isle of Thanet. She is sure she remembers seeing the enormous paddles churning the water as the ship pulled in alongside the pier, but Edwina later assured Hazel that it was one of the steamers, either the two-funnelled *Daffodil* or the single-funnelled *The Royal Sovereign*, that took them across the estuary that time. Hazel had enjoyed riding in her pram or pushchair quite a few times to the end of the pier, so she would probably have seen the paddle steamer then. Once across the water they hailed a taxi to take them to a family-run hotel, Green Roofs at Westgate. On the ground floor, once past the entrance hall, a wide corridor ran to the dining room. The corridor was filled with toys, including a small child's table with chairs, shelves stacked with games, story books, colouring books, crayons and boxes of wooden bricks. Hazel instantly fell in love with the beautiful, large rocking horse. Once in the saddle, she could rock away to her imagination's delight. Shoe shops often had rocking horses to encourage families in, but there was never enough time. There was also a pedal car that she soon worked out how to move by pressing each pedal down smoothly as it rose towards her.

The owners, Mr and Mrs Mann, were impressed that, at two years old, Hazel sat at the dining table, on a cushion, and ate with a fork and pusher (a child's blunt knife bent a little to push food on to the fork) and did not get down until her meal was finished. Most toddlers were offered a high chair with spoons and forks in an attempt to hold them long enough at the table – although children running around in the middle of a meal was acceptable to some parents. Mr Mann called the pretty, well-behaved Hazel "a chocolate box baby". Mrs Mann provided a babysitting service to allow parents the luxury of enjoying their evening without the encumbrance of young children and added to her husband's praise by saying that once Edwina put Hazel in her cot, she lay down and didn't get up or make a sound.

Westgate's beach seemed endless to little people. No mud when the tide went out, just a larger expanse of fine golden sand, not spoilt by lots of pebbles. Ray was used to rising early, even on holidays, so to allow Edwina, now pregnant for a second time, an unspoilt lie-in he carried Hazel down to the still quiet beach to hunt for long razor shells, limpet shells, pretty little pink shells and lumps of chalk. They stared into clear rockpools at deep red anemones slowly waving at darting shrimps and watched for shy little fish venturing out of their hiding places. Large crabs with equally large pincers could be safely inspected, magnified by the water. Ray bought a canvas-covered rubber lilo, so that later that day, after a picnic lunch on the beach, Hazel could have a nap in the shade of her parents' deckchairs, after which she was treated to a ride on the lilo with her father, in the shallow waves. On some days she was lifted onto the saddle of a real live donkey. She loved the gentle sway of its slow walk along the sand and the soft warmth of its muzzle as Ray lifted her to stroke the donkey that had carried her so carefully. For her first Christmas she had been given a toy donkey, whose grey fur lightened realistically around his nose. He was set on a red frame with four wheels and a handle that rose up behind him for toddlers to hold on to. Hazel could sit on him and scoot along but, as he had no mechanism for steering, it was far easier to just push him everywhere, which she often did as she loved him so much. Seeing the real live version was a little incomprehensible at first. "Where's their 'andles?" she asked her parents. But she loved them anyway and could have spent all day riding them.

A week after returning home they moved out of their one-bedroom flat into one with three bedrooms, situated only 500 yards from Chalkwell Station, just one stop from Leigh-on-Sea. An open wrought-iron bridge next to the station stretched over the train line, then sloped down to the seafront in two long sweeps. To the right, sheltered by the station, was Jocelyn's Beach, which became their regular beach. The station deflected chilly east and north winds and only needed a little sun to warm up the sand, even in the spring and autumn. It often had a seaweedy high tide mark showing how windy it had been, which made the tide heights and times easy to plot. It was also the first of the beaches that stretched along the coast to Shoeburyness and it was the sandiest, as it received all the sand that was washed along the muddy edge of the estuary from the single beach at Old Leigh.

Their new flat, like their previous one, was neither self-contained nor had access to a garden. A wide, winding stairway led from the ground-floor hallway up to their first-floor landing, opposite a lounge, and then narrower stairs rose from a little further down the landing, up to a top-floor flat. There was no bathroom or toilet on the top floor, so occupants had to share with the first-floor residents. Ray and Edwina didn't know their upstairs neighbours, nor their friends and family who often visited. This meant that one did not always know who was passing along the landing to use these essential amenities, by night or day.

Hazel was given the smallest bedroom, next to the stairway from the downstairs hall. It overlooked the back garden and her bedroom door was always shut at night, which gave her a sense of security. She could also see the wooden stairs that ran down the outside of the house from a door on their landing to give them access to the back gate, through which the coalmen came, who filled their coal scuttle at the bottom of the stairs, and Panda, who had settled in well. But Hazel loved the bright, sunny, west-facing bedroom that had a balcony attached and where a cot appeared, later to be filled by her new baby brother, Michael. Ray painted the lower part of one wall in this bedroom with blackboard paint so that she could use the chalk she had gathered on holiday, together with purchased coloured chalk sticks.

Ray began to believe Hazel was ambidextrous as she showed no preference for drawing with either right or left hand. This may not be too unusual at that age, but she was equally skilful with both hands and simply used whichever was best positioned for whatever creation she was engaged in, whether on the board or on paper. This was not a problem until she came to cut out some coloured paper. Ray had to explain that most tools, including scissors, were generally designed to be used in the right hand and that when she was older and used an ink pen at school, using your right hand meant you didn't smear the wet ink.

Hazel had a small wooden cart filled with coloured bricks that she trundled out on to the balcony to build castles with her dear donkey, who offered a ride to her large blue teddy bear. His unusual colour did perplex her but his deep rumbly growl when he was leant forward more than made up for it. After she'd been given a toy china tea set her dolls would join her for a tea party and Edwina helped her make tiny sandwiches. Ray's half-brother Arthur had a blue pedal car that, at nine years old, he had long grown out of, so Ray brought it to the balcony. Hazel felt great satisfaction pedalling the car from one end of the balcony to the other but was frustrated by not being able to pedal it around in such a narrow space. She either had to shunt it round while standing up or pedal it backward – and she can't remember why it was never taken out on walks.

The hours she spent playing on the balcony were made memorable by the wonderful sights and sounds of the old steam trains, the sea gulls crying over the waves on the beach just the other side of the track, and the amazing sunsets that blazed across the estuary, reflected in iridescent pools in the mud when the tide was out. In the mornings she often watched the milkman making his way carefully down the road with his white and grey horse, Sea Surf, tethered in the arms of his cart. The lower part of their road was steep and Hazel watched in tender fascination as the horse knew exactly when and where to stop. In winter, as his hooves slithered on the ice and snow and white steam snorted from his nostrils, her little heart was wrung. It was a few years until she felt brave enough to stand beside his colossal body and offer him a biscuit from her open hand. But she was rewarded by the gentle warmth of his muzzle as he carefully lifted the biscuit away between his yellow teeth and chomped appreciatively.

The large kitchen on the east side of the flat had an open fireplace and she remembers sitting on her potty in front of a glowing fire after her midday dinner, enjoying *Listen with Mother*, a fifteen-minute radio programme with a story, songs and nursery rhymes. It always began with, "Are you sitting comfortably? Then I'll begin." The kitchen had a pale-blue bench seat built into a bay window, in front of which was the breakfast table where Hazel would spend long periods watching the sunrise in winter, the light changing over the water through the seasons and following the many ships as they made their way down or up the estuary at their different speeds. Occasionally, a particularly large ship or one of the steamers disappeared from sight as it went up to London and it could be picked up again by running down the landing and on to the balcony. Garden birds and sea gulls often swooped right by the window when food was thrown into the garden for them. She was enthralled by their grace in flight and their vehemence as they fought over the pickings. Ray would often bring home rolls of paper, pencils and crayons and lay them out on the table for his little daughter to express her growing artistic nature.

During antenatal clinic visits expectant mums were advised that, to minimise jealousy in older siblings, parents should explain that the new baby was to be a companion. Ray and Edwina were particularly concerned as Hazel had a strong character and already believed that she could organise both her parents and Panda. With this in mind Edwina sat her on her lap, read her a story and then explained that she (Hazel) was going to have a baby! And that Mummy had to go into hospital for a short while to bring the baby home.

Hazel enjoyed a few days with her father and Rosemary before Daddy said, "Mummy is coming home from hospital tomorrow with a little baby boy."

She was so happy and eagerly took her tiny little brother into her arms. She sat on the sofa and cuddled him for a long time until Mummy came and gently went to lift the newborn out of her arms, "to feed him and change his nappy."

"No Mummy, i's my baby. You go back to 'ospital an get a novver one."

From that moment on she saw her mother as a challenge and more as an elder sister who was insisting on taking something away that she had promised to Hazel. Edwina lived to regret informing her intelligent little toddler that Michael was her baby. The toddler attempted to do everything for him but was happy to accept advice and share her baby at bathing and nappy-changing time.

After watching Edwina breastfeeding her brother, when he next cried Hazel fetched her little stool, sat down, pulled up the front of her dress and said to Edwina, "Here, now, I'll feed him."

Edwina had to admire the strong love and intelligence of her very young daughter when caring for Michael, and she did nothing to discourage her from being involved in every step of his nurturing. Hazel even cleaned out his ears and nose with cotton wool, which Edwina only discovered when she found a piece of cotton wool lodged in a nostril. Hazel did discover that Michael hated having anything sticky or sandy on his hands, which was the only thing the little girl found irksome. Once he could sit up, he was put in a small lowchair (as opposed to a highchair) in the lounge and the large tray in front formed a table that Hazel sat at on her stool, where the children would eat their tea. The corridor in their flat was long and she seemed to have to go and get a flannel and towel to wipe Michael's hands far too often. Jam sandwiches were a nightmare!

"Why, Mummy, does Michael not like sticky hands, when I don't mind mine being a bit sticky for a while?" But Edwina had no idea.

By allowing Hazel to supervise her brother at meal times and whenever they were together meant that a little pressure was lifted from Edwina. Such was Hazel's natural care and tuition of Michael that during those early years it was often only Hazel that needed the occasional reprimand. Edwina and Ray knew that they must not spoil their children and Edwina had been brought up by a generation who believed that a sharp smack was sometimes necessary. Hazel's desire to assert herself would now and again step over an acceptable level, so she knew a sting on her leg from her mother would be forthcoming if she pressed a poor point! Ray preferred not to smack and, certainly with his daughter, diplomacy always won.

On the whole, apart from the weird dynamic that Edwina had unwittingly produced between her siblings, they were good, intelligent, practical parents. Edwina had chatted away to Hazel as though she was a small adult since the day she was born. Hazel never heard 'tah' ("Sounds like tar, which is what they put on roads and flat roofs isn't it?" said Edwina) and managed 'tank oo' very early. She was understood by her parents so no temper tantrums were needed. If she was told something she disagreed with, she was allowed to voice her answer. If this got her nowhere she went to a corner, clenched her fists and stamped her feet and her frustration soon evaporated. Michael on the other hand, at two, would throw himself on the floor and sob uncontrollably for so long that he forgot what he was crying about! Was that because half of his mothering came from a four-year-old or was it simply his character?

As the youngsters got older Hazel enjoyed putting hair clips in Michael's unruly curls, but was concerned when the hairs on his legs grew darker than hers. She found a razor in the bathroom, just within reach, that she knew Mummy used on her hairy legs. Michael was happy enough to have his legs roughly scraped, until small beads of blood appeared from little scratches. His cries quickly brought Edwina, so no great damage was done. Hazel never displayed any jealousy towards Michael so Edwina had not been wrong.

When Hazel was not tending to or playing with Michael, Edwina encouraged her to help in the kitchen, to use round fluted pastry cutters and then carefully tuck the pastry into baking trays with nine round shallow cups, then slide a teaspoon of jam into the centre of each using her little finger. No licking until the job was complete and definitely not involving Michael! She learnt how to stick smaller circles on top of sweet fruit mix for little mince pies, using a little water. She absorbed all the basics of her mother's cooking, who had learnt the importance of what was then considered a healthy diet from Rosemary. Breakfast always began with cereal, such as Cornflakes or Weetabix, with hot milk on Shredded Wheat in the winter or hot porridge, followed by something cooked, such as toast topped with eggs, either poached or scrambled, tinned tomatoes, baked beans or crispy streaky bacon. They then had to endure, every day, a teaspoonful of cod liver oil, washed down with a teaspoon of deliciously rich, treacly sweet malt.

When they were young Hazel and Michael had their main meal in the middle of the day. This might be mutton stew, stewed lamb with lentils and pearl barley, liver and bacon, hearts, poached plaice, cod or smoked haddock, rabbit, veal, stewed oxtail, minced beef cottage pie, steak and kidney with beef suet dumplings, sausages with mashed potato or 'toad in the hole'. Beef marrowbones were boiled and used as a gravy and as babies they were both given the soft marrow to eat. There were always plenty of fresh vegetables. Hazel's favourite was spinach with a small knob of butter, even cabbage was tolerated like that. Dessert was some form of fruit, such as stewed apple, lemon meringue pie, banana and custard, blancmange or junket. Tea might be something on toast. Hazel's favourites were soft cod's roe or sheep's brain, which had a similar texture and flavour. Or corned beef or ham sandwiches. Cake, jam tarts or jelly might finish it all off.

Ray generally worked on Saturday morning but would get home in time for midday dinner. Tea on Saturday evenings was usually tinned pilchards and salad, even in the winter. On Sunday it was always a traditional roast dinner, enjoyed while listening to *Hancock's Half Hour* on the radio, and dessert might be rhubarb crumble or syrup sponge or bread and butter pudding, with either cream or custard. Hazel was a rather fussy eater when young, so was often made to sit until most of her small portion was eaten – except for the sweet stuff. That always disappeared rapidly, with the exception of suet pudding, which left a fatty coating all around the inside of her mouth.

Edwina often baked a chocolate cake for tea on Saturday and Hazel loved to scrape out the remains with a spoon. When Michael was old enough Hazel would run a spoon across the bowl to mark equal halves so they would not squabble. And they were always equal.

Monday was always wash day and the kitchen housed a boiler with a mangle that consisted of two rollers and a large wheel with a handle. Edwina let her little daughter help fold the boiled and rinsed sheets and offer them to the mouth of the rollers. Hazel was fascinated by the large amount of water that cascaded out and how flat the sheets were when they came out on the other side. She then knelt next to her mum on the bench seat as Edwina lifted the large sash window and pushed her left hip against the window ledge to enable her to hang out the washing on a rope that ran in a taut band from a pulley in the wall by the window to a post at the far end of the garden below. The squashed large sheets would be pegged on and slowly unfurl and billow in the wind as Edwina inched the line along, followed by their clothing, which had also been through the mangle. It was such fun on windy days.

In the winter Hazel watched as Edwina laid a sheet of newspaper out on the floor. She then placed a knitting needle on one corner and began rolling the paper tightly around the needle. Edwina removed the needle before it was all covered, then continued rolling with just her hands. Once the sheet was all rolled up, she bent the long thin roll at six-inch intervals into a concertina shape and wrapped the end into a knot. This 'twiddler' was laid on some loose newspaper in the fire grate. Only a few thin strips of wood were then needed before it was piled up with coal. Usually the fire caught quickly once it was touched by a lighted match, but occasionally the flames died. Edwina would grab another sheet of newspaper and stretch it across the fireplace. Gradually a crackling sound could be heard and a glimmering, dancing light would show through the paper. Edwina instantly removed the newspaper to display the bright flames.

But whenever Ray was home, Hazel was usually by his side, watching as he hung wallpaper, painted woodwork, drilled holes, fitted shelves, mended their chiming clock, carefully glued together and painted model aircraft then soaked and fitted their transfers. She was even fascinated when he steamed his bowler hat and tenderly brushed it in sweeping strokes.

In a back corner of their lounge, Ray had a large aquarium filled with gently drifting angelfish, who had silver and black striped markings flowing from the top of their long slender dorsal fin, over their flattened disc-shaped body, down through a long anal fin. Their grace was completed by two low, long ventral fins that trailed around the many green plants. Silvery guppies with waving orange tails and bright little neon tetra fish with an iridescent blue horizontal stripe above a bright-red stripe, proved lively companions as they played around the bubbles that aerated the tank. Ray would lift up Hazel at feeding time to drop in a pinch of food. Then graceful angelfish became shooting stars among blue and orange fireworks as the surface churned. Within minutes though fishy life regained its calming normality.

In the alcove next to the open fireplace stood a cabinet that housed a black and white television set on which *Watch with Mother* came to life. Hazel loved Andy Pandy, his friend Teddy and rag doll Looby Loo, who danced and sang only when she was alone; and Bill and Ben the flowerpot men, whose strange language was understood only by little Weed and Slobberlob the tortoise; and The Woodentops family, with Spot the dog, who lived in a farmhouse in the countryside. Later in the day other favourites were enjoyed, such as *Lassie, Crackerjack, The Adventures of Robin Hood* and *The Lone Ranger*. The News was watched in the evening, just before Hazel went to bed, and on Saturday *Dixon of Dock Green* reinforced the affection and respect she already had for the police. This had come from Ted Dipple, who occasionally called in at their flat for a cup of tea when he'd finished his shift because Joyce was still working. He would allow Hazel to put on his very heavy helmet, so she had no fear of him or his uniform and knew that if she ever got lost, a friendly policeman would always help her.

Hazel found the *Black and White Minstrel Show* a little boring, but their black-painted faces with large white eyes and large red lips produced a warm, inviting ambience exactly as the 'golliwogs' on Robertson's jam were designed to do. This friendliness made an impression on her as, even from a very young age, she disagreed with the occasional bigoted comment about people with darker skin, made by her mother and others of her parents' generation. She simply believed all human beings were equal and was unable to see why this should not be so.

At weekends Hazel would sometimes join her father as he watched 'wrestling' on the television. This was funny as the men would attempt to make the audience laugh while they pulled each other about. However, men kicking a ball around a field soon bored her. Listening to the list of match scores being called out so that Ray could fill in his 'Pools form' felt a little exciting, just in case they won a large amount of money. But they didn't. Hazel felt frustrated when Ray occasionally wanted to go out at the weekend, without his daughter.

"Daddy, where are you going, I want to come."

"No dear, Daddy has to see a man about a dog and you can't come."

She never understood why he never brought a dog home!

Family walks in nearby Belfairs woods were a regular treat. Much of this ancient woodland is more than a 1,000 years old, making it the earliest woodland recorded in Essex. Ray had enjoyed exploring them throughout his childhood and had often camped there as a scout, so was able to impart a good understanding and love of nature to his children: kicking around in the autumn leaves and finding rich mahogany coloured conkers, then spying one that was shiny and new as it just poked out of its case; the thrill of squeezing it out between their little shoes, or in mitten-covered hands, in the hope of finding the largest one; staring at the intricate patterning, a conker's own individual thumb print, so obvious when they are fresh; watching squirrels chasing around under the trees, digging for acorns they were sure they had buried; finding dormouse nests cleverly woven around bracken; little tunnels in the base of trees and in the ground that might lead to the tiny homes of mice, or fairies.

Afterwards they might call in on Alf, Lieselotte and Arthur for tea. On warm days they would all take a picnic down the road to Leigh cliffs. Arthur was happy to crawl around on all fours so that Hazel and Michael could take turns riding on his back, although Hazel wasn't too happy when their boxer dog, Jasper, wanted to lick her and join in the fun. His rough tongue was okay but the strings of saliva that hung from his drooping jowls and clung to her hair were not. Hazel quite liked dogs, as long as they didn't dribble.

Jocelyn's Beach, protected from north winds and situated by Chalkwell station, was privately owned but open to the public. Edwina often took Hazel and Michael on to this beach, even in the winter, to play with their buckets and spades and generally run off steam, as they had no garden. It was even more fun at weekends during the summer months when Ray would join them. He'd dig car or boat shapes in the sand, with two seats for his children to sit in. He showed them how to build a tall sandcastle and, using a tennis ball, would gently carve out a helter skelter for the ball to roll down. Sometimes, if the sand was damp enough, he would dig out a tunnel all the way underneath for the ball to roll out the other side. In the afternoons a permanent little hut would open for Punch and Judy shows. The children loved watching them and shouting at the policeman to tell him Punch was behind him with his truncheon. Then Ray would indulge his children with dripping ice creams.

When the tide was out, the uncovered mud was hard and any shallow holes that were dug would quickly fill with warm water. Little canals were engineered to join them up, so toy boats or lolly sticks could travel between them. Baby crabs that scuttled about could be caught and kept for a short while in salt water-filled buckets, to be gently emptied back on the mud or the water's edge before going home.

In winter they would crunch along the damp sand in wellies. On windy days listening to the foaming white surf crash against the pebbles and then the rumble as they tumbled together, caught in the undertow. They would climb and jump over the groynes that often housed whelks and cockles and stones caught in the cracks. Finally, they would arrive at a long row of cafés in identical arches under the road that swept up from the seafront. The cafés were owned and named individually, but were collectively known as The Arches. If the family were passing at lunchtime they would huddle in the warmth and sit down to plates of ham, egg and chips, Hazel's favourite. After an afternoon walk Ray would order hot chocolate for the children, a pot of steaming tea for himself and Edwina, and a plate of mixed Kunzel cakes. These delights were deep, hexagonal-shaped chocolate cases, filled with chocolate or vanilla sponge and topped in a piped swirl of thick, rich butter-icing with flavours to match their colours.

Hazel soon learnt that Christmas was an exciting time, heralded by a visitation from the fairies, who arrived when she was asleep and busied themselves in the lounge. Narrow twisted streams of red and green crepe paper were strung between the picture rails, rising up and over an almost invisible line that had been pinned right across the centre of the ceiling. From this line also hung about a dozen twisted, shining, coloured foil decorations that swivelled around in the slightest breeze. In the corners coloured balloons dangled. In the lounge bay window stood a large real Christmas tree adorned with small coloured lamps glinting through shiny tinsel. Fine silver strands hung like icicles among bright red and green baubles. Perched on the top of the tree, turned to china by day, was one of the fairies.

Hazel ran in amazement to Michael's bedroom, dropped the side of his cot and scooped him up in her arms. This he must see. She slowly opened the lounge door and gently put her brother on the floor. He was so excited he flapped his arms and blew raspberries as he toddled all around the room. His face and pyjama top ended up quite wet.

On Christmas Eve Ray explained that they needed to put a drink out by the fireplace for Father Christmas, together with biscuits for his reindeer. He gave Michael and Hazel one of his large socks each, to hang at the bottom of their beds. Because there were sometimes strangers traversing their landing, Hazel always wanted her bedroom door firmly closed, so the thought of a fat, hairy, red-clothed stranger entering her bedroom did not go down well.

"No, please, I don't want him down the chimney! Can he leave our presents by the front door? We've been good so he must have a present for us. Please, Daddy put the drink and biscuits outside."

It was so rare for Hazel to display fear that Ray and Edwina did not hesitate to comply. So, for Michael's first Christmas, a pillow case was left for each of them, apparently outside, but brought up by Ray in the morning. They were filled not only by a present and chocolates from Father Christmas, but Mummy's and Daddy's relatives also contributed and their labelled parcels were always acknowledged as being from the named giver and not from Father Christmas. Stockings were never again seen in their home. Pillowcases held so much more!

The following year Hazel was happy for Father Christmas to come down the chimney to enjoy his refreshment in the lounge, fill the pillow cases they had laid out on the carpet in front of the fireplace and take the biscuits for his reindeer.

For Hazel's third Christmas her parents gave her a pop-up book of the nativity story so she understood that Christmas was really all about celebrating the birth of baby Jesus. She particularly loved the scene in the cattle shed with the little baby lying tightly swaddled in the animals' manger, as there was a dear donkey with the cattle and the sheep brought in by the shepherds. Mary and Joseph were clearly very proud of their new baby and they all looked warm and comfortable among the animals.

Once Hazel and Michael were old enough, 'thank you' notes for their gifts were painstakingly written.

Another date in the calendar the whole family looked forward to was the fifth of November, bonfire night. When Hazel was tiny, Ray had got permission to let off some fireworks in the garden below the flat while Edwina held her daughter up at the window to watch. Not wishing to frighten his little daughter with her first experience Ray had been careful not to buy any that made a noise, apart from the whizzing of some Catherine wheels that he nailed on a post. Edwina was able to encourage a feeling of awe in Hazel with lots of ooooh and aaaah sounds that helped to make it fun.

Then Edwina's longstanding friendship with her school friend – intelligent, round, warm Ruth – evolved after Ruth met Lionel. Ruth was a secretary in a branch of the Ministry of Defence on Foulness Island where Lionel worked as a photographer. Ray and Lionel became firm friends with a mutual interest in photography. Lionel had mistakenly got married while visiting Las Vegas during the war and was still waiting for his divorce to be finalised. In the meantime, a pair of very small semi-detached cottages came up for sale, nestling in four acres of land in Wakering, not far from their work. With their well-paid jobs Ruth and Lionel were able to negotiate a mortgage. They moved in to the cottages to 'live in sin', while converting it to a single house. Their smallholding came with stables that they decided to let out as neither of them had the time for riding. They purchased pigs and white rabbits to breed and geese to act as guard dogs, which they did so brilliantly that when visitors where expected they had to be rounded up into a pen. Hazel was then able to toddle around and look for their very large and sometimes warm eggs. She stroked the rabbits, was lifted up to tentatively run her hand over a horse's nose and delightedly watched the pigs and their squealing piglets.

Lionel's birthday was on the fifth of November, so they hosted a bonfire party in one of their fields. The bonfire was always enormous and if rain had dampened it on the day, Lionel threw some paraffin over to assist it – needless to say, well before it was lit! Each invited family brought along their own fireworks to blend in with the monster ones Lionel purchased. Sparklers were passed around, even to little children. The well-wrapped women explained to their equally warmly wrapped children the dangers of the bonfire and fireworks and year after year passed without mishap. After a magnificent display of fireworks, ignited by the men in turn, bread and marshmallows were roasted around the bonfire before everybody made their way inside the cottage, warmed by a log burner and open fires. The buffet banquet that Ruth and friends mustered completed a wonderful evening.

Hazel's early formative years were filled with many happy experiences, with many people who smiled back at her (even the strangers encountered on their landing were friendly), so she developed no insecurities, no fears. Except she did have nightmares about one thing. Cats! Not gentle, tolerant cats like Panda. Although, she did wonder whether, as a toddler, she had pushed and poked him just too far and got swiped as a consequence. But it was more likely that she had witnessed cat fights in the garden and had heard them at night. Their ferocity may have become embedded deep in her subconscious, ready to rear up in her dreams. Usually only one cat featured and it could be any type of moggy, although generally it was a tabby. She'd dream she was walking innocently along outside when, with a hiss and a scream, a cat would jump out at her with its sharp little teeth bared and all its claws extended, intending to harm her. At which point she would wake up and know it was simply a bad dream. She didn't even bother to mention it to her parents. It did not happen too often and did nothing to lessen her love of cats.

The only negative occasion was when Hazel was four. Edwina had walked the children up the road to a garage owned by Maureen and Jack Grisley. They had two young daughters, Debbie and Susan, and the four children had become good friends while playing on the beach.

The Grisleys lived in the flat above the garage that was reached by walking through the garage and going up a wooden stairway to the front door. One whole side of the garage was large, green-painted doors with small windows that Jack would fold open when he was working, as he was on this cold winter's day. The floor was dark, greasy and slippery and care had to be taken when walking to the stairway. Around the walls hung tyres, exhausts, even engines. Hazel found the strong smell of oil and petrol not too unpleasant, even though it permeated the warm flat above.

Once tea was made Maureen excitedly told Edwina that Jack had been offered a job in Canada as a mechanic and that he was leaving in a month's time to stay with his brother and family, who now lived there, while he looked for a house. As soon as he found somewhere suitable she and the girls would move out to join him. Edwina knew Ray had loved Canada and thought emigrating was something he might consider.

After a pleasant few hours playing with their friends, Edwina told the children it was time to go home. Hazel slowly buttoned up her new, thick, red corduroy coat. Edwina was attempting to get Michael into his coat but the two-year-old had a temper tantrum at the thought of leaving, so it was taking a while.

In the meantime, Debbie was useful and opened the front door at the top of the stairs. Hazel's red coat had a white, fur-lined hood that she pulled over her head as she stepped out on to the platform to the stairs. Debbie reached out to feel the soft fur just as Hazel moved and her finger accidentally went into Hazel's eye. Hazel jumped away, missed the first step and fell backward. Everything whirled around as she rolled down the stairs – tyres, black floor, engines, sunlight, stairs, balustrade, a blue car, more tyres, more stairs. Then blackness. Seconds passed until Jack's concerned face came into focus. Then there was her mother. With help Hazel struggled to her feet, still rather dizzy, but everything felt fine. It had been a shock, but she wasn't hurt and didn't cry. Her new coat was not quite so pristine, but Edwina assured her that the 'cleaners' would sort that out.

When Ray returned from work he checked Hazel to make sure she really wasn't hurt, but no, not even bruised. Thank goodness for her new thick coat. He then listened with interest as Edwina explained that their friends were emigrating to Canada.

Living in a flat without the freedom of a safe garden for her two lively, energetic, young children was proving a strain for Edwina, and Ray would come home from his long day up in London to find his wife understandably tired and the flat untidy but, like a lot of men of that time, expecting his dinner to be on the table. Friction was building between the couple. A chance to begin again in Canada seemed like a great idea at first.

Jack and his brother had an advantage in that the garage business, begun by their father, had been very successful and their father was able to give both sons enough money to use as a deposit for a house or business premises in Canada. Ray had no savings. His Uncle Chris was his only possible answer. Whenever work necessitated a visit up north Ray would call in on his Birmingham family home and spend the night with his Aunt Rose and Uncle Chris and he was close to them both.

Ray decided that he would catch the train one weekend to see them and sound out his uncle for a loan. Unfortunately, and inexplicably, his uncle said no. But within weeks Ray was offered a shopfitting position in Vancouver and the whole family travelled up to London, to the Canadian Embassy, to arrange visas and have vaccinations.

Ray was hoping to find somewhere to live through some business contacts before they moved out. Many people were taking the opportunity to move to Canada and that year the numbers were the highest yet, totalling around 282,100. Family homes in Vancouver were selling fast. With Uncle Chris refusing them a loan, Edwina began to worry that they would be travelling with two small children to a country with no NHS and with no money to secure living accommodation. She tried to encouraged Ray to do as Jack had and move out first, to find a home, but despite his time in the RAF he lacked an adventurous spirit and was reluctant to leave his family. Edwina thinks now, with hindsight, that Ray may have felt that his wife might change her mind and not follow him!

As a consequence of delaying, Ray's job offer was withdrawn and then the Canadian economy took a downturn, so Canada no longer seemed so inviting.

Edwina's cousin Anita got married and they moved into the now-vacant flat upstairs, meaning there were no longer strangers to bump into on their landing.

CHAPTER 4
1958 ◊ Starting School

It was time for Hazel to think about school. Edwina had prepared her by explaining that school was fun, with plenty of painting and drawing, cutting out and pasting, singing songs and listening to stories. One of her beach friends, Louise, would also be there. Edwina took Hazel to buy her school uniform. She would start after Easter so a summer dress of blue gingham, a navy cardigan and a smart navy blazer with the school badge on the front pocket was the accepted uniform. How grown-up.

Easter came with its usual multitude of eggs, which the children were encouraged to ration, and Hazel was looking forward to her first day at school. But she didn't feel too good when she went to bed on the Sunday. Edwina came to wake her on Monday morning only to find her covered in spots. Dr Quinn called in and confirmed it was chicken pox. That meant no school for two weeks and pink calamine lotion splodged all over her itchy spots. It was a long two weeks as she felt fine after a couple of days.

At last, her first day. Hazel proudly put on her uniform and, after breakfast, Edwina, with Michael in his pushchair, walked her up their road, over the zebra crossing, along the main road, past the corner of the much-loved Chalkwell Park, then through the school's large, wrought-iron archway. The playground was full of noisy children running around, some playing chase. Large skipping ropes swung over jumping girls. More girls bounced over hopscotch chalked on the ground. Boys kicked balls and played marbles in the grooves of drains. Groups of children laughed together. Oh, it did look fun. Edwina steered Hazel to a corner of the playground dominated by a large, drooping cedar of Lebanon. Smaller children were playing here and hidden in the shadow of the great tree was a green-painted, corrugated tin shed. A slim, smartly dressed lady came out to greet Edwina, and after a few words turned to Hazel.

"Hello, Hazel. My name is Mrs Wilkinson and I'm your teacher," she gently said as she took Hazel's hand. "Mummy will come back at lunchtime. Now I'll show you your seat."

Hazel very happily held the hand of this nice lady as she blew a whistle. Once the smaller children had formed a line in front of her she led them all into the tin shed. Not even a backward glance to Mummy. It seemed larger and brighter inside and had all sorts of interesting pictures hung around the walls. The children clambered in around Hazel, finding their seats. Mrs Wilkinson showed Hazel an empty desk, "This is your own desk and you are next to Linda. She will be your friend and help you if you are not sure what to do for the first few days."

Hazel looked into Linda's round, rosy, smiling face and smiled back. Her first morning went well. Small bottles of milk with a straw were given out by a child called a milk monitor and Linda showed her how to push her thumb into the foil top to make a hole for the straw. Hazel liked her milk very cold, this milk was tepid, but she made herself drink it as everyone else seemed to. Right through junior school she found it difficult to drink tepid milk without gagging, but she obediently forced herself. At playtime Linda showed her the white line painted on the ground that separated their playground from the 'big' playground and explained that they must not cross it.

All too soon it was lunchtime and when Mrs Wilkinson opened the door of the tin shed, there was her Mummy with Michael in his pushchair waiting with just a couple of other mummies.

"Let's go and look at the dining room," urged her mother. "Most children don't seem to be going home."

They crossed the 'big' playground to a separate hall. The door was open and the first sitting was already queuing up with their plates. Hazel was not impressed by the smells wafting out and told her mother that dinner at home would be best. Lunch break was an hour and a half. But with a twenty-five-minute walk home and the same back, dinner at home was not leisurely! But Ray told Edwina that evening that if his daughter wished to come home for lunch then so be it.

Although Hazel had not attended the first two weeks of term she was unaware that she had missed anything and with so many new interesting activities, she didn't miss home too much. That is, until one morning when all the class went in ahead of their teacher and took their seats. However, instead of Linda on her right, her brother Michael was insisting that it was his seat. Hazel had no idea how to deal with this and burst into tears. Mrs Wilkinson immediately saw the problem and encouraged Michael to take her hand so they could find his mummy, which he happily did without any argument. As Hazel watched her brother obediently take her teacher's hand and leave the classroom, she stopped crying and normality returned. She did sometimes think of home and Panda and wondered what Michael was up to now that he had his mother's sole attention. She didn't have the slightest problem with that, she trusted her now to do a reliable job!

They practised writing their letters on rectangular tablets of slate set in a wooden frame that were handed out to everybody along with a small felt and wood rubber and a piece of white chalk. To Hazel this was simply drawing shapes and she greatly enjoyed it. Counting was learnt with wooden sticks and small wooden squares. Again, enjoyable. Was she remembering much though, when the sheer enjoyment of copying and drawing well was paramount to her? Painting with diluted powder paint in jam jars and using big paintbrushes was wonderful and Mrs Wilkinson soon recognised that Hazel had a natural talent. Even cutting out intricate doilies from carefully folded paper was a breeze. Linda really struggled with scissors, so Mrs Wilkinson asked Hazel to help her – and she was pleased and proud to be able to do so.

Louise was a very pretty, olive-skinned, brown-eyed, wavy black-haired, little girl who lived with her parents and older brother Paul across the road from Hazel. Their large house was separated from the next two smaller semi-detached houses by a short narrow road that led to three garages that belonged to their houses. Louise and Paul were part of the group of children who regularly enjoyed the freedom and fresh air of Jocelyn's Beach. Their mothers, including Edwina, would all sit together and chat, as mothers do, as they watched over the children – rather like mother and toddler and nursery groups all rolled into one. Hazel and Michael were wary of Louise and Paul, who refused to share their buckets and spades, balls or other beach toys. If other children attempted to join in digging holes or any other games they were playing they ran the risk of being pushed over or having sand thrown in their face. Hazel concluded that it was best to just sit next to Louise and try to engage her in simple conversation about what they were playing.

It was dear little, silver-blonde Carol, who was a year younger than Hazel, that they most enjoyed playing with. She was so gentle and happy and, as an only child, greatly enjoyed their company. Her parents Barbara and Alf rented the semi that sat the other side of the three garages. The two families became firm friends. Once a week the children would play and stay for tea at each other's home and they all got on splendidly. Carol and Hazel became especially close. That first year at school, though, it was Louise who was in her class and Hazel dealt with her in the same way that she did on the beach. However, the other children in their class had yet to learn!

Hazel learnt to skip in PE (she discovered that she could run fast, climb ropes, jump over horses, do front rolls and cartwheels and swivel a hula hoop around her hips with the very best of them) and at playtime would sometimes join in with a row of girls who took turns jumping through a long rope held by two other girls, or played hopscotch.

Linda remained her best friend that year and they would sit chatting on the benches that lined the playground. But, as those infant years passed, Hazel realised that her greatest enjoyment and relaxation came from simply sitting and observing the interactions between all her classmates. Linda gathered other friends, which Hazel was more than happy for her to do, and from the bench she watched Louise taunting others. There was one particular little girl in a younger class who wore glasses, called Kathy. Her mother was a bright, bouncy, attractive Belgian lady with a strong accent, but Kathy – who as far as we knew was her biological daughter – seemed to have inherited nothing from her mother except her warm, welcoming smile. Louise, unfortunately, quickly saw that Kathy's simple, happy nature was an easy target.

"Owl face, why can't you skip?" taunted Louise regularly.

One day, while Hazel was playing hopscotch she noticed that Louise was teasing Kathy to tears. After finishing her go she went over to Louise. Many of her classmates stopped to watch how this was going to work out.

"Please Louise, leave Kathy alone. She's doing nothing to you. Just go away and play something else."

Hazel stared severely into Louise's eyes, determined to stand her ground. Louise stared back then pushed Hazel, not very hard, who moved one foot back to secure her strength and pushed back harder, correctly gauging that it would not quite push her over. Louise was clearly surprised. She stared back briefly then turned and walked away. 'Phew,' thought Hazel. She was shaking because if Louise hadn't backed down it could have meant a fight and that was too serious to contemplate. Hazel suggested that Kathy come and join in the hopscotch. Kathy's coordination was not good and, even after Hazel's patient tuition, she could not master hopscotch or skipping. Although Hazel and Louise would have many altercations during their school life, Louise came to respect Hazel's strength of character and body. She suspected that Paul, who always treated Louise and her friends with incredible disdain, may have bullied his younger sister. She surely learnt it from someone!

During the last term Hazel was invited to various classmates' sixth birthday parties. These were the days of small parties, with no more than ten children, held in their own homes. She enjoyed pass the parcel, musical chairs, statues and other games, little sandwiches, ice cream, wobbly jelly and always a cake with candles. Party bags had not yet been invented. A balloon and a piece of birthday cake to take home were occasional, unexpected bonuses.

Andrew Kerr was a sweet boy, smaller than most of his age, who got on well with everybody. Invites went to about eight of his favourite classmates, including Hazel and Linda. When Edwina left her at the school gates after lunch on the day of the party, she thought her mother instructed her to meet her at the front gate as usual.

Afternoon classes finished and, as Hazel and Linda were putting on their coats to leave, Linda said she was meeting her mummy at the back entrance as it was easier to reach Andrew's house from there.

Hazel thought 'What exactly had Mummy told her? Which entrance to meet at?' She was sure her mother had mentioned he

45

lived on the other side of the park so she supposed she should meet her by the back entrance too. Her mother surely would not have said anything if they were meeting at the normal entrance. Hazel quickly ran to the front entrance to check her mother wasn't there then ran to, hopefully, follow Linda, down to the back entrance. There were plenty of mothers there but she couldn't see hers. Nor could she find Linda. She waited. Everyone else drifted off.

'Where was her mother? Was she supposed to have gone with another mother?' She remained calm. She knew the party was on the other side of the park. Hazel decided to run and catch up with the last straggling family at the crossing to the park. Once in the park she hoped to see at least one classmate going to the party, but it was quiet. No young children. She ran on through the main path. A few older children. She knew her mother would not have forgotten her so another mother must have been meant to take her.

'Would they not remember once they got to the party. Would they not come looking for her?' She reached the gates at the other end of the park. She had no idea where to go from here, so she waited. And waited. It seemed no one was coming to find her. She would just have to search the streets and hope she might hear or see a party through a front window. She ran through all the roads around that side of the park until she was exhausted. She had hardly seen anyone at all and knew she must not ask strangers. She began to cry, the party would be finished, she was hungry and now had no idea what to do. Where was a friendly policeman when you needed one?

Eventually an elderly lady came up to her and asked if she was lost. Hazel was not sure about speaking to this strange woman but she'd run out of options.

"I'm meant to be at a party but I don't know where it is."

The woman asked whether she knew the name of the child whose party it was.

"It's Andrew Kerr. Do you know him?"

She didn't but said, "There's a phone box in the next road. We could look up the surname in the phonebook. Come with me."

What else could Hazel do? Children weren't taught the alphabet song then and when she'd looked through the phone book at home it appeared quite intimidating. She followed the woman and waited outside the phone box. The phone book soon offered an obvious address.

"It's just down the road," the woman said. "Let's see if we can find your party."

Hazel's tears had dried by now and it was her own mother who opened the door. She hugged her daughter as tears of relief poured down her face.

"I've searched everywhere for you. The party has almost finished."

Edwina could not thank the elderly woman enough but she declined an offer to come in for a cup of tea. Andrew's mother took Hazel's hand, "All the sandwiches have gone but there's some jelly and cake left. We are so pleased you finally got here." Hazel later discovered that she should have gone with Linda's mother.

Hazel was also six when Ray drew a road on the blackboard to explain perspective. The road began at their feet and was very wide. Its two edges converged to finally touch near the top of the board, which he called the horizon and ran a horizontal line across the board. He then lined one side of the road with electricity pylons, beginning with a tall one at the bottom of the board and a tiny one near the horizon. He drew a faint line joining the tops of the pylons and another joining the bottoms, then drew in more pylons that got closer together and reduced in size as they sat within these faint lines. The cables he added further demonstrated perspective as they too converged at the horizon. On the other side of the road he laid out a house, with two visible sides, roof, a front door, windows and chimney, all drawn within faint straight perspective lines. Hazel was then able to add two trees on either side of the house, following the rules her father had shown her so brilliantly.

That year Father Christmas brought scooters. A two-wheeled one for Hazel and a three-wheeled one for Michael. On Boxing Day they excitedly set off for a scoot along the seafront with their parents. Michael tired quickly, while Hazel alternated evenly between legs, as each one tired.

"Swap your legs over Michael, use your other one to push with for a while," helpfully instructed Hazel.

Michael tried but it just wouldn't work, he couldn't coordinate his left leg and it kept catching on the brake that sat across the back wheel. He gave up after a while and Ray carried his scooter until he wanted to scoot a bit more.

"Why can't Michael use both legs like me?" enquired Hazel.

"I think you might be ambidextrous. Most people are either right- or left-handed. In right-handed people the left side of their brain dominates the right side of their body. In left-handed people the right side of their brain dominates the left side of their body. Ambidextrous people have no dominance on either side of their brain so can use their body equally."

"How do you say that word again, Daddy?"

"Am, bi, dex, trous."

"Oh."

Hazel had no idea, until she was about forty, that this phenomenon was quite rare.

Back at school, while sitting and 'children watching' she decided that there were a couple of boys she enjoyed watching more than others. Andrew Stanton was in her class and seemed very good at everything. Mummy had told her that he could already read a proper newspaper. He was quiet, very polite and he lived down Hazel's road in a large house. Their mothers would sometimes walk home together and Hazel and Andrew would saunter behind them shyly, making very little conversation and he would occasionally smile at her. The other boy was in the juniors, two years above her, so was very unapproachable. Both lads were quite tall and slim. Sadly, neither of them showed any interest in Hazel.

During a parents' meeting to discuss preparing their children for school, the parents had been advised not to attempt to teach their children to read as it might conflict with the teacher's phonetics method and cause confusion. So an obedient Ray and Edwina followed this advice. Unfortunately, whether due to missing those first weeks, or whether Hazel would have learnt more easily at home if her parents had ignored the school's advice (as Andrew's parents had done) the outcome was that by the end of her first school year her parents were told she was struggling with her reading. However, Mrs Wilkinson presented her with a proper paint box with lots of separate squares of colour and two quality paintbrushes. She was so pleased that she was unaware of the information her teacher had given her mother. That is until Edwina sat her daughter down at the kitchen table and showed her the first *Janet and John* reading book and explained that she needed to be able to read book four by the time she returned to school after the six-week holiday. Hazel was happy to begin this challenge. However, mother and daughter became frustrated at her inability to quickly grasp phonetics. It seemed the teaching style Edwina adopted did not work well for Hazel and, coupled with the fact that this was holiday time and there were so many other things that she wanted to enjoy, the daily lessons always ended in tears and shouting. Somehow, Hazel made it to the end of book three, but reading at home continued to be a fraught occupation.

A week's holiday at Green Roofs in Westgate brought a respite. Hazel was able to infect Michael with all the excitement of chugging down the pier on the wooden train and waiting with a crowd of noisy people at the pier end. Then Daddy pointed to a small dot on the horizon that grew slowly larger until a faint stream of smoke became visible, then two funnels above a white ship. As it approached the pier the *Daffodil*'s engines went loudly into reverse and churned up the water as it slowed and the gap shrank between ship and pier. Ropes were thrown and gangplanks cranked out. Families, groups of female friends, laughing men with arms slung over mates staggered up the gangplanks off the ship. Once it was empty, the two orderly queues waiting to alight, slowly began showing tickets and stepping onto the gently undulating planks. As Hazel stepped on the deck a sour, pungent smell rose above the normal coal and steam smell she remembered. She turned to her father as she wrinkled her freckled nose, "Daddy, what is that horrible smell?"

He replied, "Sweetie, that's beer. Is it really that awful?"

"Yes," was her curt reply.

After a tour of the top deck they went below for a drink and a cake and she slowly accepted the pervading beery scent. Unknown to her, her father had, like most men during the war, drunk a lot and in Burma had lost his way one drunken night, fallen into a ditch and drifted into unconsciousness. In the morning he was found in such a poorly state that he decided he would never again have more than a single drink, two at most. He stuck to that resolve, apart from his children's weddings, when he needed to lose some inhibitions before the speeches! But he never again got drunk.

It was a great holiday. The rocking horse and pedal car were still in the corridor. Hazel was very pleased to rock for ages on her familiar friend, unless Michael wanted a go, but he was mostly happy enjoying the car. His sister's use and the elements out on the balcony had worn out Arthur's old pedal car, so it was a novelty. He did need a little instruction from his sister about where exactly the pedals should be before you pushed one down! More chalk was gathered for the blackboard at home – where Michael did attempt the odd drawing, but he found it difficult to replicate his sister's lifelike works of art, even slightly, so his offerings were rather half-hearted.

All too soon the school holidays ended. The winter gymslip that had been rather too large the year before still fitted and, as September remained mild, Ray carefully cut off the upper-front leather of her sandals so that they were effectively open-toed and didn't cramp her growing feet. This meant that they could delay buying winter shoes. Hazel noticed that she wasn't the only child with home-remodelled shoes, so thought nothing more of it. She enjoyed hearing all about what the other children had got up to during their six weeks off and straightaway slipped naturally back into school life.

Hazel looked out for Carol in the playground. She spied her playing chase with her next-door neighbour, who was called John. They were the same age and had lived next door to each other all their lives, so were particularly close. Johnny's parents were both coaches for the Leigh tennis club and his older brother David was on his way to professional standard. David had once passed Carol and Hazel playing outside his gate and had completely ignored the girls. "He's like that!" whispered Carol to Hazel. Johnny and his younger brother Tony were far more approachable and their older sister Ann would smile over the fence. In the playground though, Johnny was rather shy when he saw Hazel and ran off to continue his game while Carol stopped to say hello. Hazel realised Carol wanted to continue playing with Johnny. He was a great-looking chap, with hair only a little darker than Carol's and tanned skin from the large amount of time spent on the tennis court. She felt a little disappointed that her best friend outside of school might prefer to spend school time within her own year group, but without resentment.

Hazel got on well with all her classmates, with the exception of the bullies, such as Louise and Roslyn who felt they had the right to push children around. Hazel found that she had to be incredibly diplomatic with them both to avoid conflict, which was both wearing and a little scary and she attempted to steer away from them. Having observed the angst, distress, arguments and, at times, tears aroused by fighting for friendships among some of the girls, she concluded that she was happiest not relying on close friendships.

At the beginning of her final term in the infants her teacher introduced a new boy, Christopher. The class sat with eight chairs around a square table and Christopher was led to an empty chair at Hazel's table. He was a pleasant-looking boy with mid-brown hair and was quiet in the unfamiliar surroundings. She gave him a reassuring smile and he responded by smiling back.

Later that week the class were told to line up in the playground, in pairs, for a stroll across the main road, via the zebra crossing to the park. The teacher, an assistant and the caretaker were laden with bags and boxes full of balls, hula hoops and bean bags for games on the grass.

"Hold hands tightly with your partners and keep close together in the line as we cross the road," the children were instructed.

Christopher looked on shyly as they all quickly partnered up. Hazel went up to him and took his hand. He smiled at her gratefully. After a great time in the park she found him again as they lined up to walk back to school.

Their friendship deepened and, while they often spent time playing separate games at playtime, they always found each other as they lined up to go back into class. At the end of the day they put on their coats in the cloakroom and then came together on the step of the doorway and it seemed natural to give each other a kiss as they went their separate ways.

One day a teacher from another class spotted them and remarked as she walked past, "Stop that! It's not allowed."

But they felt it was not wrong, after all they both kissed their parents and siblings when leaving them. So the following day they continued this reassuring parting, unchallenged for the rest of term.

During the final week Christopher told Hazel that he was moving to London in the holidays and would be going to a new school.

"Will you come back? Will I see you again?" asked Hazel.

"No, I don't think so," he replied sadly.

On the last day of term, they gave each other one final kiss and Hazel never saw him again.

CHAPTER 5
1960 ◇ A Junior

Aged seven the world grew a little larger for Hazel; she was given a watch for her birthday and she became a Brownie, the entry stage to the Girl Guides Association.

The Brownies met in the hall of the newly built St Michael's and All Angel's Church, just up on the main road. Louise and Hazel went together for a few weeks' trial at the start of their new school year as juniors. Hazel noticed that Louise had matured a little during the holidays and was certainly easier to be with at Brownies.

Both girls were up for the new challenges that guiding offered them and quickly integrated with girls of varying ages and from different schools. Brown Owl presided over the group with a caring firmness. Hazel was enrolled into Pixie patrol, which suited her quick, petite, cheeky nature. She learnt how to play new games, especially ones involving running, how to iron and fold clothes and sing campfire songs in readiness for her first camp the following year. She also learnt how to tie knots (her winter shoes and plimsolls had elastic laces to facilitate speedy changes for PE), such as the rabbit running around a loop and diving into a hole to form a knot.

She and Michael sometimes stayed overnight with Grandma and Grandpa Dorrit (Rosemary and Reg), where they were spoilt a little, but camp sounded like a real adventure.

In an effort to encourage Hazel to read, Edwina had shown her where to find Enid Blyton's 'Famous Five' books in the library. Hazel had loved the 'Noddy' books she had been given when she was little and had been reading them to Michael, so the 'Famous Five' series from the same author were a good next step and she devoured them. The freedom these stories afforded the five characters was really appealing. She had no real worries about going somewhere completely new without her family, living in a tent, cooking and eating outdoors, it just sounded exciting. Pictures of past camps were displayed in the hall to encourage discussion and help alleviate any fears the new girls might have.

Hazel soon discovered the one downside to being a Brownie, church parade. Both Edwina and Ray had been baptised into the Church of England and had followed that tradition by christening both children when they were babies. But religion and going to church was something they only undertook for marriages, christenings and Mothering Sundays (the children, fortunately, hadn't yet attended any funerals). So Hazel found attending a church parade one Sunday a month a little tiresome.

She loved weekends, particularly Sundays, as her father was there all day and it usually began with the children snuggling into their parents' bed to listen to a story made up by Daddy. This she had to miss out on. In fact, the whole morning just disappeared in ironing her uniform, neatly folding her tie and polishing her shoes. In the days before hair conditioner it was painful when Edwina brushed Hazel's long hair and pulled it into a ponytail. Even though it happened every day it seemed even more torturous on Sundays, when it took up time that she could spend playing with her toys.

Hazel's favourite toys were: a magnetic driving-test game that required deep concentration and skill to ensure the car stayed on the cardboard road; a magic robot game that answered general knowledge questions simply by swivelling and pointing to the correct answer; and a little metal cooker with real burning lumps that were designed to be used in camping burners. She could cut up fine chips of potato to fry or cook a little scrambled egg and bacon. She had puppets, jigsaw puzzles, books, two dolls with a twin pram to ride in, and more. There was always drawing and painting. And gonks (round, stuffed, soft toys) were in fashion and had given her an idea for an illustrated children's book. She called them the Egglets and they lived in a home set in a grass hillock – very similar to a Hobbit hole from J.R.R. Tolkien's books, an author Hazel was not yet aware of.

Unfortunately, Ray and Edwina had decided to honour the promise made at their children's christenings to bring them up with knowledge of the Christian faith. This meant adding Sunday school to Hazel's curriculum. Bad idea.

Sunday school was from nine until ten on Sunday morning each week, followed by church parade at ten-thirty once a month. If Hazel was chosen to carry a flag or read the lesson for church parade she was proud to do so. At Sunday school she enjoyed attempting to wrap her brain around the physics of such stories as the parting of the waters, how such a small number of loaves and fishes could feed so many and how sick people could be healed simply by the laying-on of hands. All this knowledge was supplemented by visits to the Science, Natural History and British Museums, sometimes as a family or occasionally just with Daddy.

She decided that a higher power, which she was happy to call God, probably did exist and heaven was a comforting thought. It was religion itself that posed a problem. Her thinking was that the world entertained many different religions and that as the Bible had been collated by many people, often long after the event, and then translated, she preferred to read it as an ancient history book whose accuracy could not always be taken literally. And, if God was everywhere, why did she have to go to church? Yes, churches were amazing feats of architecture (another of her father's loves was to visit churches, specifically to admire their beauty and wander around the graveyard reading the inscriptions), and it was great to have such immense and magnificent buildings as meeting places. She came to understand the brilliant acoustics when she climbed into the pulpit to read a lesson from the enormous Bible. She had practised at home, with her parents encouraging her to 'project' her clear voice. They was no microphone in the church at this time but she did not need one.

But, as she listened to the gossip between her mother and grandmother about certain neighbours, she concluded that going to church did not necessarily make you a good person. So, with God apparently everywhere, why could she not close her eyes, put her hands together, concentrate her mind and pray anywhere that was quiet.

She really resented Sunday school and not only for losing part of her precious Sunday. She accepted that she had to wear a uniform for school and Brownies, but wearing skirts or dresses at other times was becoming hateful. Jeans weren't in the local shops yet, but Hazel felt so much more comfortable in corduroy trousers or stretch slacks. She couldn't climb or crawl around comfortably, or play with Michael's cars, train set and Meccano with her usual abandonment if she was made to wear a skirt or a dress. They kept getting in the way and Mummy disapproved of her showing her knickers. So she developed a dislike for skirts and dresses.

Hazel was happy to be called a tomboy. After all, she seemed able to do everything the boys could do and she discovered that if a football occasionally came her way in the playground she was able to dribble it and kick it reasonably skilfully with either foot and without any practice. Having to put on a dress for tea or dinner with her grandparents led to drawn-out arguments that Edwina would not tolerate and would often end in a smack and tears.

Thus, Hazel's view that religion messed up her Sunday became ingrained and hearing her father berating the bigotry surrounding the Roman Catholic church only added to her dislike.

Ray, through Edwina's contact with Louise's mother, was asked if he would take official photos of the local ballet and tap group that Louise belonged to. They were to be taken during and after a concert, so Edwina suggested the whole family went to watch.

Hazel was impressed by Louise's abilities on stage but when Edwina asked if she would like ballet lessons, she retorted with no uncertainty that prancing about in a tutu just wasn't for her. Her parents had also mentioned piano lessons but she felt that the studious practice required would be too tedious. She also held the belief that there was something underlyingly sissyish about both pursuits! When she imagined a child pianist it conjured up an image of a child with a perfect haircut, glasses and a mind that was not able to see much beyond music. Her world was boundless and she wanted to absorb as much of it as possible.

As a pre-Christmas treat, Ray took the family up to London to visit the large stores – Gamages, Selfridges, Liberty – finishing at the amazing Hamleys, where you could touch many of the toys on display and watch them being demonstrated and where Father Christmas was hiding in a grotto. They stayed until all the beautiful lights in Regent and Oxford Streets were lit.

Hazel's best fantasy though was remembering their yearly autumn visit to Never Never Land on Southend seafront. These were the days before Disneyland and visitors flocked through the cranking metal turnstiles to enter a world that was best visited at night. There were gently lit fairy castles, goblins and dragons, and a model railway transporting dolls and teddy bears to picnics and parties. It was set in The Shrubbery, a part of Southend cliffs with magical waterfalls. Perfect for fairies. Hazel found it hard to believe she might not spy a real live one.

That Christmas, Hazel and Michael were given roller skates and the tarmacked seafront promenade was perfect for learning on. They also carried their skates on the bus to Priory Park in Southend, where there were lakes with ducks and swans to feed and a small museum with a beehive fitted to an outside wall – with a glass side to display all the activity inside.

Occasionally they caught a bus to Maldon, home to some of the old Thames sailing barges, or they took a small, diesel-smelling, open boat from Wallasea Island across the River Crouch to Burnham-on-Crouch. It was captained by 'dirty Ted' who wore diesel-ingrained clothing, so that the change he gave Ray smelt likewise. Burnham was quaint, it had been a ferry port, then a fishing village known for its oyster beds, and contained many listed buildings. A stroll along the riverside, past the listed Royal Corinthian Yacht Club and the permanently moored house barges with their bright containers full of colourful plants, was engaging. Apart from Sunday school and dresses, life was great.

During February 1960 Edwina surprised her children by informing them that they were going to have another brother or sister. It was also a surprise to Ray and Edwina! But other than the occasional chance to touch Mummy's moving lump the children thought little of it and life carried on as normal for the next few months.

For Hazel's eighth birthday Ray purchased a swing from Gamages. He rented a small piece of garden at the bottom of their wooden steps to put it on and Hazel watched excitedly as her father bolted it all together and slowly raised it in place. She stayed as he dug holes around each of its four legs and was fascinated as he explained how to mix cement to fill the holes and hold the legs firmly. Hazel had to be patient and allow the cement to set before she could use it. It was worth a day's wait.

She'd loved the swings in the park, now she loved her own. Time became meaningless when she was racing through the air. She was easily able to push it to its maximum height, then relax while gently keeping up the momentum and allowing her mind to wander. Sun or clouds, summer warmth or winter chill, and always the twittering birds to keep her company – at least when Michael wasn't around. When he was, they took turns. For the one not on the swing, boredom was relieved by running across between the frame legs as the swing reached its full height.

Until the time when Michael was just not fast enough and the seat caught his lip and his teeth went through. Hazel jumped off in dismay at his cry and the sight of blood, and rushed up the steps calling for her mother. They decided they wouldn't play that game again.

They had been told sternly by their parents that they were not to stray into the rest of the garden, in particular the old, falling-down shed against the house, because it was dangerous. It could not be seen from any windows though and Hazel had to test her climbing skills. She told Michael not to follow her up until she had checked out the strength across the whole of the roof. Once she had worked out where it felt soft, she let him join her and pointed out where he must not go. They did this quite often. Only once or twice were they caught and chastised.

Occasionally they ventured inside and one winter discovered a hedgehog curled up in a leaf-filled box. Sadly, when they looked in the spring he was dead.

They were granted the freedom to play in the alley through the gate at the bottom of the garden. It was a maze that threaded past back gardens, around and out at various places to the roads on either side, and was filled with a wonderful variety of weeds or, more exactly, wild flowers. They soon learnt to tell dead nettles from stinging nettles, but there were so many of the stinging ones that it was easy to be touched by their venom when running away while playing hide and seek. So Hazel experimented and discovered that the large hairy burdock leaves could be screwed up and the sap used to soothe the rash. Although she realised it was invasive, she found the white simplicity of the convolvulus flower beautiful as its stem twined around whatever was in its way as it followed the sun. She gathered daisies and made a chain.

Hazel was now allowed the extra freedom of walking down the road to the zebra crossing opposite the station and onto the open wrought-iron bridge to wait for her father's train. A whistle heralded its approach and there was no health warning about standing in the smoke from the train as it steamed under the bridge. The excitement of running to the station entrance to greet her father was especially great on Fridays, as he always brought home a bag of sweets.

Edwina sometimes saw Michael and Hazel across the road to the piece of wasteland that stretched from the bottom of their road along to the station. It had a steep grassy slope dotted with hawthorn and crab apple trees and led to a more wooded area at the bottom. A path stretched through the grounds from the station to a white fence with a white gate that blocked the path to a long row of houses facing the railway line. A notice nailed to the gate said 'Undercliff Gardens. Private property. Trespassers will be prosecuted'.

They were left to please themselves on The Undercliff and Hazel loved climbing the trees. She got a feel for the strength of the branches and could gauge just how close to the ends she could go. Sometimes they met up with Louise or some boys in Michael's year at school. Hazel had to admit to feeling a satisfaction at being able to climb higher than any of them.

Louise declared a dare one time to find out who would go the furthest through the white gate. Hazel was scared. 'Trespassers will be prosecuted' sounded incredibly serious. However, Louise went through first and Hazel couldn't face being called a coward. No one appeared to be about and Louise crouched behind a shrub next to the path just past the second house. She beckoned to Hazel, Michael and a friend of his to follow her. Hazel suggested the two boys wait until she had reached Louise before venturing past the gate. Hazel had only got past the first house when a lady appeared in the window of the second house. Hazel's heart was thumping. She was certain she could be seen, so made the decision to turn around and walk purposefully back to the white gate, hoping the woman might think she was returning from a friend's house further down. All the while, though, she waited to hear a shout, but no one called so she went through the white gate and didn't bother to wait for Louise. She wouldn't 'trespass' again.

One spring she discovered a robin nesting in a shallow hole in the ground in the woody area. There was a clutch of small featherless babies. She advised Michael that they keep it a secret. She was worried that boys and cats might not care much for the babies' welfare. It was a couple of weeks before Hazel went back. The nest was empty. Could the young have grown and flown in that time? She felt they hadn't, but hoped otherwise. Not a clever place to put a nest!

As the summer holiday dawned, a sleeping bag was purchased for camp. Ray painted Hazel's initials on a plastic plate, bowl, mug and set of old cutlery; while her name tag (already compulsory in her school and Brownie uniforms) was added to a drying-up cloth. Everything was bundled into her, already named, PE bag.

Two weeks after school closed, Ray, Edwina and Michael walked with Hazel and all her kit up to the hall. The other excited Brownies and their families congregated just inside the walled front garden to await the coach. There were shrieks of delight from the Brownies as it pulled up. Their kit was piled into a separate van with all the tents and necessary stuff for a week outdoors. They only had to hold on to plastic bags with their lunch in.

Hazel hugged and kissed her family before taking her seat next to Jill, who had straight, cropped, blonde hair and went to the local Roman Catholic school. She was also in Pixie patrol and it was her second camp.

They travelled up to Diss in Norfolk and if any of the girls suffered from travel sickness Hazel wasn't aware of it. Brown Owl, her second-in-command and a couple of helpers could be relied upon to sort out any problems.

It was a warm dry day, perfect for stopping at a picnic site for lunch. At last they arrived at the campsite, a large clearing surrounded by light woodland. The Brownies were assigned to their tents, each with a coloured square pinned to the front pole. These were still in the process of being erected by various helpers. All camps were themed and this year's theme was Toyland from the 'Noddy' books. Brown

Owl was Mrs Tubby Bear. Her two assistants were Tessie Bear and Pink Cat and a third mischievous helper was Bumpy Dog!

Jill and Hazel were in the same tent and while they were helping by handing out tent pegs, Mrs Tubby Bear came up holding a white envelope with Hazel's name and the camp address on the front. Hazel took it, surprised. She seemed to be the only Brownie receiving one of these. She quickly opened it. Her home address was on the top. Then:

Dearest Hazel,

After kissing you 'good night', the other night, Daddy thought he would write a you a little note, just to let you know that we will be missing you, and there will be no one for me to tuck into your bed for a whole week. What a big girl you are now and you are going to have so much fun. I think the weather will keep fine for a few days. I hope it lasts until Tuesday, because I shall be on holiday too! Then we really all look forward to visiting you on Wednesday and hearing all about what you have been up to. Don't forget to do all the jobs you are given, be careful, and be a good girl.

I think Grandpa and Arthur are going to call in and see us tomorrow. Grandpa rang this evening and was very surprised to hear that you had gone off to camp by yourself, as he didn't think you were big enough. Isn't he silly!!

Well, I will write again when I have some more news, so goodbye for now. God bless you dear, and be a good girl and look after yourself and remember 'Brown Owl' is there if you have any worries.

We all send lots and lots of love. Michael already wants to know when you are coming home and we look forward to seeing you on Wednesday. Lots and lots of love, and huge big kisses from us all.

Daddy

xxxxxxxxxx from Mummy

xxxxxxxxxx from Daddy

xxxxxxxxxx from Michael

Hazel felt a spreading warmth inside as she read and was so proud to have had this waiting for her. It made her feel very loved and special, and Wednesday didn't feel too far off.

'My tent looks ready. I must join in,' she thought as she saw Jill getting her kit ready to put inside.

The smell of frying sausages that evening, the delicious porridge that had been left soaking overnight (just as Daddy did) for breakfast the next morning, followed by big pots of scrambled eggs and bacon, toast and butter all served to rev up Hazel's appetite. For breakfast they could queue for freshly fried eggs. Large cooking barrels completed the great Brownie circle and the food was passed around as they sat on groundsheets on the dewy ground. The odd bit of grass or leaf or other outdoor detritus that blew in only caused her to exclaim, "Just a few extra vitamins!"

By the end of that week Hazel's fussy eating had been transformed. All food seemed to taste good from then on (except for tripe and onions, her father's favourite; just the smell was stomach curdling).

Everything about camp was great. Even sleeping on hard ground among girls who snored wasn't a problem. The fresh air, continuous physical exercise and fun meant they all quickly fell into a pleasantly exhausted sleep.

Hazel was pleased to discover that fire could be started two other ways if your matches had run out or were damp. The first was using a magnifying glass to concentrate sunlight into a tiny pinhole of hot light held over paper or dry straw. She was amazed at how easy it was. If the sun was not out, the other option was to whittle a fine point on a stick, using the knives they were all allowed to carry on their belts, then dig out a furrow in a thicker stick, add a little, very fine, dry straw or dried grass and then twizzle the fine stick in the furrow. It was hard work, but when Hazel finally saw a tiny waft of smoke she gently blew as Mrs Tubby Bear had shown them and, wow, a flame. She carefully laid a few dried sticks on top and watched with satisfaction as the little flames licked around them and grew. She'd achieved her fire-making badge, a great confidence builder. Even some of the older girls had given up when their muscles flagged.

Of course, Hazel thought about home and how lucky she was to be so happy there, but it became apparent to her that, generally, if any of the girls felt homesick it was their mother that they missed the most. This caused her to reflect on her own mother.

Edwina was great when her children were ill. She would tuck them into bed with a hot-water bottle and a bowl by their side if their tummy was upset and regularly checked to see if there was anything they wanted. At night a little paraffin lamp would be lit for comfort. She brought fizzy Lucozade to aid recovery, made toast with their favourite jam, soup to help build up their strength and, Hazel's favourite, a poached egg on mashed potato. They were allowed to get out of bed as soon as they could to curl up on the sofa with the television or radio on. While looking through photo albums pleasantly passed some time. Fortunately, Hazel did not often feel ill, but felt secure knowing that because her mother didn't work she would always be there for her.

She also appreciated that her mother's practical, no-nonsense approach to things such as injections and the dentist helped Hazel to have no fear of them.

"Just a tiny prick and if you don't look at the needle and concentrate your mind on something else, it will be over before you know it has been done."

Hazel's dentist was very gentle. He carefully navigated his fingers around her mouth and, while the noise of the drill and the smell (sometimes of burning), were not pleasant, he was careful not to induce any real pain. This was just as well, as the dentist explained that when she was about twelve they would extract four teeth and fit a brace to pull in her two front teeth. Edwina described how a black mask would be placed over her mouth and nose and a (not unpleasant smelling) gas would put her fast asleep and she would be completely unaware of anything. She might even wake up laughing, as it was called 'laughing gas'. And that was exactly what happened.

Beyond this practical help, though, Hazel still found her mother a challenge! Although that was all forgotten when Wednesday arrived and excited girls showed their families a little of their camping life.

CHAPTER 6
1961 ◊ *School and Life*

A crossing lady had finally been supplied for the crossing just along from the top of their road. Just in time, thought heavily pregnant Edwina. Hazel was happy to take Michael's hand and walk them both to school. Now was also the time to insist on them staying for school lunch. After some moaning the children accepted it. Michael soon considered it was not cool to walk with his sister and before long they made their way separately. One morning Michael had left ahead of Hazel. As she daydreamed along the main road she passed a dead tabby cat on the pavement, tongue lolling out of a blood-filled mouth. It turned her stomach and really saddened her. Panda was such a part of their family life, to lose him like this would be heartbreaking. Someone or some family would be bereft tonight. She thought of Michael and hoped fervently that, just for a change, he had taken the other, slightly longer, route she had shown him round the back streets. But when she returned that afternoon she found he had been sent home as he'd been sick after seeing the poor animal.

Her mother regularly asked Hazel to walk up the road to the general store, just opposite what used to be the Grisley's garage, to get such things as a quarter-pound of butter and a half-pound of bacon. Once a week during her final year in the infants they had to play in a specially erected hardboard 'shop' with a doorway and counter, in a corner of their classroom. They were given realistic plastic money to buy goods, and scales weighed out the purchases. They had to check they had been given the correct change. This was the only time Hazel felt any real anxiety at school. She had not played with money at home and found it confusing that there were twelve pennies in a shilling and twenty shillings in a pound, compounded by weights of sixteen ounces in a pound and fourteen pounds in a stone. When it was time for the teacher to choose shopkeepers and shoppers Hazel would duck down under a desk and managed, most of the time, to evade the excruciating embarrassment of not knowing what the hell she should be doing!

But now it was not the money side of the transaction that bothered her. It was her memory. She left the house with a quarter-pound of butter and a half-pound of Cheddar cheese in her head but would see a cat sitting on a wall waiting to be stroked. She loved to hear a throaty purr before she carried on up the road, but then realised she couldn't remember whether it was half-pound of butter and a quarter-pound of cheese, or vice versa. So many times she had to return home to ask her mother what exactly she was buying before eventually making the correct purchase. How long did it take before Hazel insisted her mother write down what she wanted, even though it was usually only two items? That was when Hazel thought she had a butterfly mind. In fact, watching butterflies or seeing a pretty wild flower poking out of a crack in a wall were all great distractions.

Edwina's bump was now noticeable, even to the children, and they were told that it would not be long before they had a brother or sister. Hazel was never reminded that she had been told that Michael was *her* baby and her maternal instincts towards him had long been replaced by sisterly affection. No one considered, though, that Michael might be put out by no longer being the focus not only of his mother's affection but also of his sister's.

Hazel, who had always preferred her father's affection (Mummy was only for practical stuff and arguing with), declared, "I've got a brother. So now I'd like a sister."

A bunk bed appeared one day in Hazel's bedroom and Edwina explained that the new baby would have a cot in Michael's bedroom and Michael was moving in with her. As the eldest she got to choose the top bunk, with a ladder. During the first night sharing the room with her brother she made an awful discovery; he snored incredibly loudly. It was made worse by the fact that Hazel was a light sleeper. Loud sssssssssshhhhhhhhh noises were a waste of breath and had no effect. She descended the ladder and gave him a gentle push. He rolled over but within seconds was snoring again. That night she had little sleep. She complained to her mother. In desperation, some nights she would hang from her ladder and kick him hard before the snoring momentarily stopped and allowed Hazel to fall into an exhausted sleep. Edwina gave her a glimmer of hope when she explained that Michael would be having his tonsils and adenoids out, which would ease the problem. In reality it made little difference. Relief came for Hazel eighteen months later when the new baby's cot was dismantled and the bunk beds were moved into his room and Michael went with them. Finally, peace at night as the room became her own once more.

Edwina felt her contractions begin not long after the children had left for school one day, so she rang her mother at work (Rosemary had returned to work with the railway after the war). Fortunately, Rosemary was able to leave early to pick the children up from school on her way up from Chalkwell station and to take them home with her. It wasn't until Ray was home that the contractions really strengthened. With the help of a midwife, Edwina gave birth at home without any problems. Ray was with her throughout, helping by bathing her forehead with a cool flannel. The following morning, he rang Rosemary and asked her to inform his son and daughter that they had another brother. Another brother! Nevertheless, Hazel was looking forward to going home to see the new infant.

Rosemary took them home that morning. Their front door was opened by a lady they'd not seen before. Slightly overweight, middle-aged and wearing a colourful apron, she introduced herself.

"Hello, my little darlings, come in and see your Mummy and her new bairn. I'm Auntie Gladys and I'm going to look after you all for a couple of weeks."

She wasn't a real aunt, just a home help, but she fed them well, apart from the white gravy that was made only from meat juices and flour, without the Oxo stock cube they were used to. She also made a large fruit cake at the weekends.

As soon as Hazel saw the baby her natural maternal instinct kicked in once more. This time she asked her mother why she did not have breasts that were capable of producing milk, as she wanted to feed him. Edwina explained that the mammary glands that produced milk would not develop until puberty, at around twelve years of age, and that they wouldn't actually be triggered to produce milk until she had a baby herself and that wouldn't happen until she was married. So, no sex education.

Hazel was old enough to fold the nappies and fit them carefully using two safety pins. She tried to avoid smelly nappy changes but did learn that baby boys could wee indiscriminately, right into the air. She soon forgot that she had wished for a girl. Baby John was gorgeous and she loved playing mum with a real live doll. He, fortunately, was happy to have a bonnet put on him and to ride in Hazel's doll's pram and to be pushed by Michael. Edwina and Ray had not differentiated between their eldest son and daughter regarding gendered role playing and were happy for Michael to play with Hazel's dolls and all her toys, just as Hazel equally enjoyed playing with all of Michael's toys. Sharing was the most important criteria. Interestingly, in this time before feminism, and before scans were able to determine the baby's sex in the womb, pink toys for girls were unheard of. There was no reason for Hazel not to believe that, as the eldest and two years older than Michael, she should also be two years better than her brother, at everything. She wasn't trying to prove it, it simply seemed to be.

Back at school after Easter they began trials for sports day. Even though Hazel was quite short for her age, her little legs could pump hard, which meant her running speed was good enough to qualify her to represent her school at both the hundred-metres and relay races in the county sports day. It was also discovered that she had spring enough to practice for the high jump.

Hazel found herself at weekly lunchtime practices with three others from her class. Jane was a tall, fair-haired, very quiet girl who had only joined her class that year. Simon Ash and Colin Brown both played football for the school and were still at the stage of paying scant attention to girls. It was during these weekly practices that Hazel found herself drawn to Jane's quietness and to Simon's physical attractiveness. She saw grace in the lithe movements of his tall slim body. His brown eyes were gentle, his nose slim and neat, ending with a slight point. His lips, although not thick, appeared sensitive, both at rest and in speech. His hair was the pale brown that was described as mousy, but it was stylishly cut and flopped gently over his forehead.

A friendship immediately developed between Jane and Hazel and they remained close for the rest of their time in the juniors. Jane was generally happy to spend lunch and break times engaged in a game of Hazel's choosing, who would check that Jane was happy with her choice as she had no wish to dominate. She watched Simon with interest from afar.

Hazel was comfortable with herself and wasn't overly aware of how she appeared to others. Her baby-blonde curls had darkened to a long straight brown, with only slight golden highlights where they had been touched by the sun. Her mother's insistence on scraping her hair into a ponytail emphasised her sticking out ears. Her large blue eyes and long lashes still prevailed but her two front teeth were crowded into protrusion and freckles spread out from a spattering over her nose. Her body was very slim, with a hint of muscle. Hazel felt confident but knew that beyond her cheeky nature there was nothing that might intrigue a boy.

Unfortunately, Hazel couldn't achieve the extra inches in the high jump that the others could, so she only took part in the running events that year. She did wish for an extra inch on her legs as she came fourth out of six for the hundred-metres sprint. She, Jane and two other girls fared no better in the relay. Sports Day took place in Southchurch park, just off the seafront at Southend. Hazel was familiar with the park, it was another pleasant place where the family went to sail Michael's small wooden yacht on a large lake, on the side especially set aside for such enthusiasts. The other side, separated by a bridge, was for rowing boats and pedalos. A visit to a café for snacks and ice creams finished a lovely day. The sun shone for Sports Day and it meant a day off school. Mummy came on the bus with John in his pushchair to watch and take her daughter home afterwards.

In 1962 Hazel's parents were able to fund a family holiday at a Butlin's holiday camp. These had become increasingly popular and a million people enjoyed the hospitality of the Redcoats at sites across the country. At Cliftonville in Kent, not far from their previous holidays in Westgate, Butlin's had a complex of four hotels – St George's, Queen's, The Norfolk and The Florence – which felt a little more upmarket than the camps of separate cabins. Again, taking the train up the pier and crossing the estuary by steamer was all part of the holiday experience, with the added bonus that Michael and Hazel could explain the associated delights to their baby brother.

Ray continued his early morning forays to the beach, with whichever combination of children wished to accompany him, sometimes including a little friend the children had made. Fishing nets were part of their beach 'tools' and Hazel became adept at catching little fish to watch in their buckets of water until they gently returned them to another pool.

Next to the promenade was a roller-skating rink with skates for hire that, unlike their own, had a round, rubber brake block underneath the toe. Hazel had to relearn her skating skills. If she tipped her skate too far forward when building up speed, she caught the brake block and almost lost her balance. Ray had shown his children how to stop without brakes simply by swinging one foot in an arc and slowly placing both feet in a 'T' shape. Brake blocks were just a hindrance, nevertheless it was good practice and Ray encouraged Hazel to try skating backward, a lot of effort on hired skates.

Ray had taught Hazel and Michael to swim by walking out into the water up to their waists, turning to face Jocelyn's beach, then doing a rapid doggy paddle to keep them afloat until they touched the sand at the water's edge. As their ability grew they walked in deeper and learnt to use their arms in a crawl. The children being able to swim brought peace of mind to Ray and Edwina who, once home from their holiday, gave them the freedom to ride their lilo in the shallows, using their spades as paddles and, when they tired of it, to wander over the rocks that edged the thin width of sand beneath the raised pathway that led to the beach at Old Leigh. They carried their nets and buckets of water to find crabs, shrimps and, occasionally, little fish. Green algae and 'popping' brown seaweed covered the lower rocks, so it was a skill to manipulate little feet to balance and grip. Some children had rubber beach shoes, but Hazel and Michael, having grown up on the beach, had no need for them.

In later years, to Hazel's dismay, the council poured black tar over the whole length of rocks right to Old Leigh. The rocks were large and it took an enormously rough tide to dislodge a few low ones, so it is not known exactly why this was done. Another feat of balance Hazel practised was along a permanent wooden frame on the other side of the beach from the rocky edge, used by sailing clubs to store their dinghies. The children knew they should not climb over the boats, but they all did. The wooden beams were over one and a half yards tall but only about three inches wide and, while some children fell off, Hazel was able to walk along them with ease.

If the tide was out the family would put their towels around their necks and, with John in Ray's arms, would 'mush' across the mud. After the first few firm yards it became squashy and they had to take care there were no sharp shells or crabs underfoot before putting weight on each bare foot. The reward was wonderful undulations of firm mud to run over without a care and lovely warm little pools to splash in. A creek of fast-flowing water had to be crossed that was usually no more than knee deep, its depth could be used to work out how long it was to low tide. More firm, undulating mud slowly levelled out to the edge of the Ray, a large channel of water parallel to the main estuary. Its water was mud-coloured but warm and since few people made this journey it meant they were in a large and eerily quiet space. Ray taught them how to keep an eye on the water's edge to note when the tide settled at its lowest ebb by marking the mud with a sweep of one's toe. Then, as it began to turn and the little wavelets stretched forward again they knew it was time to head back. Rounding up three reluctant children and making them dry themselves before 'mushing' back, took time and they often waded the creek at waist level. With their complete trust in their father, though, it only added to the excitement of the day.

The strain of living in the flat with two lively children and now a baby had escalated for Edwina. John was rather late to walk, perhaps because his sister spent hours supporting him under his armpits up and down the landing – and anywhere else he wanted to be taken. One Saturday morning Ray was at work and Michael went down to join his sister by the swing. He forgot to close the back door and John crawled out to follow him. Edwina was alerted by his screams as he tumbled down the flight of wooden steps and hit the concrete at the bottom. She rushed down the stairs, grateful that he was still crying and that all his limbs were moving. Carefully, she gathered him up and rang Dr Quinn, who arrived within minutes and checked him over. Thankfully, apart from some bruising, he appeared to be unharmed. The doctor instructed Edwina to keep him quiet and said he would return that afternoon to make certain there was no concussion. John got over the shock of his tumble so quickly that after lunch Edwina had to take him out in his pram simply to comply with the doctor's instruction as John did not want to stay quiet, anywhere. They missed the doctor's visit but fortunately John was fine.

That incident could so easily have ended in tragedy and it made Edwina more insistent about finding a home with their own garden. Ray's income depended, to a large degree, on commission, and meant they could not rely on a regular monthly income. Hazel hated hearing her parents arguing when they thought the children were out of ear shot, mainly about money and their flat.

Hazel and Michael did not have many chores to do at home, just washing-up and drying the dishes and sweeping the stairs with a dustpan and brush (Edwina had a cylinder vacuum cleaner, but it didn't stretch very far). Hazel sometimes helped with the ironing. The children were responsible for keeping their bedrooms tidy, which was difficult for Hazel. Her mind was naturally unmethodical, she loved daydreaming and allowed her thoughts to wander unchecked. When she tired of one game, thoughts of another distracted her completely and it did not occur to her to clear away the first one. Edwina made it a rule that on Saturday mornings, after breakfast, one chore must be completed followed by bedroom tidying. One particular Saturday morning it had been arranged that Hazel would meet Carol at ten to go shopping with her mother. Hazel was so looking forward to it she forgot about the state of her room. At nine forty-five, after sweeping the stairs, she put on her shoes and went to get her coat.

"Is your room tidy?" her mother called out.

Irritation flooded through Hazel. She stepped back into her room and quickly thrust armfuls of clothes, books and toys under her bed, just as Edwina put her head around the door.

"You're not going anywhere until this mess is all put away and that includes everything under your bed."

Hazel's eyes filled with tears. "I'll never get this tidied in time, I'll have to do it when I get back."

"No, you'll do it now. I'm fed up constantly having to nag you on a Saturday. Perhaps this will be a lesson."

Hazel stamped in frustration.

"I was really looking forward to going shopping with Carol. I have to spend all week learning lessons at school. Then Sunday school tomorrow. This is just so bloody, bloody stupid."

"That's it, I've had enough and I won't have you swearing. You can stay in your room now until your father gets home. I'll let him deal with you." And Edwina slammed the door on her crying daughter.

Hazel sat on her bed and let the tears of disappointment flow. She knew that swearing was not allowed, although it seemed okay for her mother to say bloody, even bugger occasionally (not that Hazel had any idea what that meant, and had heard her father remonstrate with her mother once when she used it). She wondered what her father was going to do. She didn't expect it to be too bad. It was hours before he got home. Plenty of time to slowly sort out her room. She watched the time tick by. Grandparents Dorrit had recently bought her a cuckoo clock from Switzerland. The sound of its pendulum ticking and the cuckoo popping out every hour was comforting, even at night. Her bedroom was tidy by the time she heard footsteps on the stairs, then go along the length of the landing to Edwina in the kitchen. She could just discern her mother giving her father an account of their argument. Her mother concluded by saying that she would not have swearing and it was up to Ray to teach his daughter that lesson. Then Hazel heard her father's voice.

"I'm sorry, but I will not have any child of mine waiting in fear until I get home. It's up to you to deal with the problem at the time."

"Good old Daddy," thought Hazel.

It was some minutes before a subdued father opened her door and told her she could come out now. He refrained from giving her his normal hug and kiss. That was enough for her to realise he was not happy with either his wife or daughter. Edwina still had to nag about tidying her room but Hazel had learnt to do it without swearing.

During the school holidays Louise and Carol rode their bikes around the short road between their houses that led to their garages. One day Louise left her bike propped up against her fence and was playing Two Balls against the garage wall. Hazel asked if she would mind if she had a go on her bike. "No, that's fine," replied Louise. Hazel had seen photos of herself riding a tricycle when she was about three but her parents had not been able to afford to buy bikes for two children. She had watched Louise and Carol enviously as they rode around with such apparent ease. If they were able to, surely she could.

Carol was a little taller than Louise and Hazel, so her saddle had felt too high when Hazel sat on it. Hazel decided she would feel secure if she could put the balls of both feet on the ground while her bottom nestled on the saddle, which she thought she would be able to do on Louise's bike. She walked up to the red bike, took a firm hold of the handlebars, lifted one leg over the low bar and planted her bottom on the saddle. Yes, she was able to balance the bike with both balls of her feet firmly on the ground. She squeezed the brakes together, then separately, to determine which hand controlled the front brake and which controlled the back brake. Both locked quite tightly around each wheel. Hazel knew that if she wanted to slow down she should just use the back brake. She was aware that if she only applied the front brake at speed, she was likely to go over the handlebars. There were only about fifty yards of road behind her to the garages. In front was about the same distance to the end before Hazel's road crossed in front of it. She turned the bike to face the garages.

She hoped she would be able to balance well enough to follow the pavement as it bent around ninety degrees and then went down the run-in, on to the road. For someone who had never ridden a bike before this was rather ambitious. Her only stabilisers were her feet! But she was confident and, as she pointed out to herself, if she felt the bike tipping over she simply had to put a foot on the ground.

She straightened the bike so the frame was completely vertical while the left handlebar was against the fence, she moved the right pedal up with her right toes and put her foot on it. Still against the fence, she felt the weight of her foot and the balance of her body as she pushed against the pedal and squeezed both brakes to ensure she didn't move at this point. She let her brain settle into this upright balancing position. When she was happy that she could sustain this balance, she released both brakes and gently pushed the pedal. Keeping her head up, she quickly glanced down to check that her left foot found the left pedal. She was cycling! It really was that easy. But, as the garages loomed closer, she wasn't sure she could turn that tight corner. She squeezed the back brake, slowed right down and, as the bike wobbled, put both feet down. 'Phew, that was close!' she thought as she stopped just in front of the garage. She got off the bike, wheeled it past the garages and leant it against Carol's fence.

Louise had disappeared into her house before Hazel had begun her cycle, so there were no onlookers. She was alone. Again, she mounted the bike as it balanced against the fence. This time she was facing her road and noticed that there was a slope off the pavement into the road just before the junction. As this short road was still quite wide she thought she should be able to go down the slope and gently turn around. She perched on the saddle and settled her mind again until she felt ready to move off slowly. She kept a reasonably straight path along the pavement and carefully squeezed the back brake when she felt she was going too fast. She approached the slope quite slowly and managed to keep her balance as she carefully turned the handlebars and steered the bike down the slope. She continued at the same speed until she had turned in a gentle arc on the road and was now facing the garages. She was so happy. She felt in charge of the bike and confidently cycled towards the garages, gently squeezed both brakes and put both feet on the ground. Next, she turned the bike in the road and made her mind relive the sensation of balance as she pushed off completely unaided. She stopped expertly before the end of the road. She was quietly excited. Perhaps now her parents might buy her a bike.

That winter brought the big freeze. They'd had light falls of snow most years, in fact, the previous Boxing Day they'd trudged through a few inches of snow on their way to dinner at Alf's and Lieselotte's. When Ray was a child, Alf had visited Davos in Germany on business and had brought home a toboggan. Its slatted wooden seat had room for three at a push and was lifted high on wooden legs strengthened by metal brackets from the two ski-shaped runners, each finished with a shiny metal strip that allowed it to glide easily through the snow, with little effort from someone pulling it along by the rope at the front. Arthur rarely used it now so Ray pulled Hazel and Michael home on it while Edwina pushed John in his pram. The following morning Ray took his two eldest children across the road to the hill leading down to Undercliff Gardens and joined other families on a variety of toboggans. With the weight of Ray and both Hazel and Michael tucked in front, they sped down at an exhilarating speed. They were all disappointed by the end of the following day when the slope was worn down to mud.

So Hazel and Michael were very excited to see some snow in the middle of December 1962 but disappointed that it had melted by the weekend. Their wish for more was granted. On the morning of 27 December the scene through their frozen windows was wrapped in total whiteness. After their usual hot breakfast, Ray told Hazel and Michael to put on plenty of thick clothing, two pairs of thick socks, wellington boots, warm coats, woolly hats, scarves and mittens so they could take the toboggan down to Undercliff Gardens. The snow had drifted against the front door so Ray, after managing to force open the back door, had to carefully negotiate his way down to the coal bin, clear the top hatch, give it a good thumping to break its icy seal and retrieve the coal shovel. It took him a while to clear and open the back gate and make his way through the alley to the front of their flats. After clearing the worst of the snow from the front door to let the children out so they could hurl snowballs at each other, Ray cleared the front path. Sea Surf had somehow managed to deliver the milk that had frozen in the bottles – following that winter the milkman decided to retire his faithful old horse.

It was not easy to discern exactly where the pavement ended and the road began but it hardly mattered as they trudged over to the slope. The pure, white snow was deep, perfect for their Davos toboggan; those that sat lower had to wait until the snow had been trampled a little. Ray demonstrated how to steer it by putting his foot out on the side he wished to turn towards. It allowed one to manoeuvre away from looming trees and other toboggans. Ray and Hazel took turns to pull it up the hill, which was probably why Michael got cold and bored after a while. Hazel persuaded her father to let her stay and toboggan without them.

She flew and bumped down the snow and missed the trees and other toboggans time and time again. She got hot and thirsty. There was plenty of pure unsullied snow among the trees to each side of the main sledge run. Hazel plunged her mittened hand into the crisp, white, clean, gleaming softness. As an experiment (she'd not seen anyone else do it), she gently pressed the tip of her tongue and lips to the snow. It instantly melted. She bit a little and felt the coldness spread to liquid in her mouth. She took in a larger mouthful and drank. Oh, fresh water straight from the clouds. Later she saw her father waving from the top of the hill. Lunchtime. She trudged up and greeted him with a glowing smile. He grinned back. She loved this Davos and the snow as much as he did.

Unfortunately, it was Monday the following day and Ray had to return to work. The steam trains may have run a few minutes late but they did run. The children still had another week before school began. Monday was always wash day. Edwina hung it out as usual, but it froze quickly. The fires in the kitchen and lounge had not been allowed to go out over the whole Christmas period, so, as on any wet Monday, washing was dried over a clothes horse and chairs in front of them. A hot iron and then everything was ready for the airing cupboard by the end of the day.

On Tuesday they needed to go up to the shops. Once more the children wrapped up warm. Fresh snow had fallen and it was not easy to push the large pram up the hill, they had to walk in tracks in the road, perhaps made by a coal lorry, certainly made by Sea Surf's milk cart. Buses also managed on the salted main roads. They were fortunate to have all the shops they needed just at the top of the road. A butcher, a baker, a greengrocer and the general store that roasted fresh coffee beans every other morning. The wonderful aroma wafted out of the ducting at the top of the large glass corner window. All were open for business as the shopkeepers either lived directly above their shop or within walking distance. They all knew Edwina's family by name. It was bitterly cold but, clothed in so many layers, Hazel and Michael loved it.

The biting wind was worse on Friday but the family made it further down the main road to the clothing shop, Knights and Pollards. It was Ray's birthday that Sunday. His worn slippers had been replaced by fur-lined ones at Christmas, together with a new jumper, but Edwina knew that warm woollen socks and gloves would be appreciated. Clothes for the children always came first, so Christmas and birthdays were when Edwina and Ray treated each other to new essentials. Several times during that week, the children took the toboggan over the road to the snowy slope. On Saturday Ray pulled both children up the road on it to get fresh bread and rolls and they all slithered back home again.

On Sunday afternoon Alf managed to drive Lieselotte and Arthur in his black Sunbeam Talbot, very slowly round the slippery roads, to their house for Ray's birthday tea. Rosemary and Reg walked. The sandwiches, trifle and chocolate cake Edwina had baked all went down well. Some of her homemade, marzipanned and iced Christmas cake was left (Edwina always added a squeeze of lemon to her icing, which added a zing that set it above plain icing). It was a shame that Ray always had to take the Christmas decorations down the night before, as that was Twelfth Night.

That year the snow continued its seasonal shroud right up until the first week of March. School began as usual since teachers and pupils all lived within walking or bus distance. Wellington boots, each pair kept together with a named peg, were lined up in front of radiators and plimsolls from PE bags were put on feet. Mittens and gloves, made damp by snowball fights were laid on top of radiators. The relentless snow had not stopped life from proceeding much as usual.

Hazel was ten when she experienced what amounted to sexual abuse. Her innocence and naivety meant that she didn't realise it was wrong, nor could she have said that she either disliked or liked what happened. Perhaps she accepted it because no one had ever caused her harm. It was not a concept she understood.

At the beginning of her third year in the juniors she waited outside her new classroom, with Jane and most pupils from her previous year, to see who would be teaching them. Mr Godfrey, who'd been at the school for years, opened the classroom door and directed them to choose their desks. Hazel took Jane's hand and held her back until Simon and Colin passed them. Hazel quickly jumped in behind to ensure that she and Jane got the desk directly behind the two boys. She was determined to make Simon notice her this year.

Mr Godfrey was a big man in his late fifties. His large wooden desk at the front of the class was on a raised platform with sides and front completely enclosed so the class were unable to see much more than his head and shoulders. He was not too unpleasant a teacher who seemed comfortable in his position. He was known to throw the board rubber with brilliant accuracy to land right next to talking boys, but it was never aimed at girls. This didn't appear unusual as the boys generally misbehaved more. Reading up at Mr Godfrey's desk was done on a regular basis, with each child in the class taking turns throughout the week.

During Hazel's second reading session she felt Mr Godfrey's fingers gently touching the elastic of her navy school pants, just around the lower edge of her buttock. The passage she was reading was designed to stretch her ability and so she continued to concentrate on the words in front of her. When she'd finished reading and stepped down off the platform to make way for the next child she thought no more of what had happened, other than to conclude that her teacher must like her. On other occasions she even attempted to guess how many other girls might be afforded this attention.

Taking up far more of her thoughts at this time was Simon. One morning he had brought an accordion into school and Mr Godfrey invited him to play in front of the class. Simon had taken to greasing his hair back, something Hazel was not sure about, but as he eased himself into the straps of his instrument with such confidence, she felt herself adjust to this minor change. Exactly what he played she had no idea except it sounded more like the classical music her father listened to on his gramophone than the modern pop she heard on the radio. As Simon squeezed his accordion, the wonderful tune he produced squeezed her heart. It was brilliant. The class clapped and he played a second piece of music. Hazel was enthralled. Was there nothing this boy couldn't do well. She so wanted him to really smile at her, to laugh with her, to hold her hand, to be a best friend.

Hazel and Jane had started flicking a tiny rolled up piece of paper or a little corner of rubber at Simon and Clive during the odd boring lesson. All four of them happily participated, but that was as far as any attention went.

During the final term of that year, Hazel, in a desperate attempt for Simon's attention, concocted a plan to get him alone. She wrote a note on a small piece of paper: 'If you would like to meet me in the cloakroom in five minutes, put your hand up and ask to go to the toilet. I'll wait a few minutes and do the same. Hazel'. She screwed it up, leant forward, touched his arm and passed him the note. He unscrewed it and read. Her heart pounded. This had to work. She waited and waited. He put up his hand.

"Please Sir, may I be excused?"

Mr Godfrey nodded. As Simon left the classroom she checked her watch. Two minutes slowly went by, then she put up her hand.

"Please Sir, may I be excused?"

Mr Godfrey nodded again. Hazel left the classroom and walked down the corridor. She passed two more classrooms before the corridor opened out into a larger space. The cloakroom filled one half of this space, with benches below the metal frames filled with coats on hooks. Two doors in one wall were marked 'Boys' and 'Girls'. The corridor continued through the space to further classrooms. There was Simon sitting on a bench at the back of the cloakroom, half hidden by hanging coats. Hazel went and sat next to him. To this day he maintains he has no memory of this meeting or of what took place. Shamefully, Hazel remembers perfectly. He had a sister, two years younger, in Michael's class, who shared Simon's perfectly balanced facial features, his brown eyes, his neat, straight nose that ended with a point and his fine mobile lips. With long, straight, blonde hair she was warm and friendly. Hazel was sure that, like Michael and herself, when they were small, they would have shared a bath together, so she opened the conversation that day in the cloakroom with,

"You probably know that girls don't have willies, Simon."

"Yes, I do," he sheepishly replied.

"Would you like to see what I have instead?"

Simon hesitated. Hazel watched as his mind computed this possibility.

"Okay."

"But can I see your willy first?"

"I want to see you first."

"This was my idea, so please go first."

"No, you go first. Otherwise how do I know you'll let me see."

"I promise, I really promise, but it's easier for you. You just have to unzip your fly."

They wrangled back and forth, but Hazel held out and Simon finally capitulated. Still seated he unzipped his fly and carefully pulled out his penis. Hazel was now standing up and she looked down at it. It was probably a couple of years since she had seen her brother naked and, apart from accepting that sometimes it looked a little larger than its normal floppy state, she knew an erection was just part of being a boy, probably after asking her mother why it varied in size. Seeing Simon's felt a little different and drew her to say that while she had seen her brother's willy, she'd not seen him have a wee.

"Could you do just a little wee?"

"What, here?" asked Simon incredulously.

"Just a little drop."

Simon looked down at his engorged penis and said, "I don't think I can, like this."

"Oh please, please, just try. Just a drop."

Simon concentrated. In a minute or so Hazel was delighted to watch as a drip of liquid rolled out of his penis and plopped on the floor. Simon then quickly pushed it back into his Y-fronts and zipped up his trousers.

"Now it's your turn."

Hazel looked at the clock on the far wall. It showed, to her shock, that she had been out of the classroom for almost twenty-five minutes. So far, no one had walked by but she felt a rising panic. Surely someone would come and check up on them, or the headmaster might walk past. She would have to lift up her skirt and pull down her pants. It felt far more obvious than undoing a zip. To keep her promise meant they might be caught. She'd heard of children being expelled. She couldn't bear the thought of being in separate schools and not seeing him again and it wasn't fair on Simon, this was all her idea. Fear raced through her.

"Sorry Simon, we've been here too long, someone might walk past. We must get back to class." She turned and ran.

She heard, "You promised."

Simon returned a minute after her.

It changed nothing between them. With hindsight Hazel thinks keeping her promise would have made little difference, but she had to acknowledged to herself that, actually, she'd had no intention of keeping it. Either way, she now hated herself for both not intending and not keeping her promise. It had gained her nothing and probably dropped her even further down Simon's list of interests. Not that she had ever been on such a list! She pledged to herself that, in future, she would only ever make a promise if she knew she could keep it.

A welcome distraction then occurred at home. They were moving. Not far. No longer within sight and sound of the sea, although only a fifteen-minute walk away. It was a three-bedroom terraced house with a seventy-foot garden. Moving day was a Saturday so the children spent Friday night and the following day and night at Reg and Rosemary's.

The new house was closer to her grandparents and on Sunday afternoon they walked them to it. Michael and John shared a bedroom overlooking the back garden, with the separated bunk beds now on a carpeted floor with space between. They would later each have a bedside table with a shelf underneath. Hazel had the small box room, very similar in size to the one she had left. Its small leadlight window looked on to the road and one of the flowering cherry trees that lined its pavements. She didn't mind the size. It was large enough for a small wardrobe and a dressing table. Their beds were already made up and their clothes hanging in their wardrobes. Boxes with their toys and books were under their beds.

Mummy and Daddy were exhausted. The move had run smoothly but not without an incident involving Edwina's engagement ring. It was a vintage one, with three diamonds, that she had chosen from a shop in London. At £37 this had been the maximum the couple felt they could stretch to. As the band around her finger was a little worn she did not wear it all the time, but hung it on an ornate ring holder on her dressing table. One day, as she was getting ready to take the children, then aged four and two, down to the beach, she noticed it was not on the hook. She didn't panic at this point but decided to search as soon as they returned. As she helped Michael into a bright summer shirt that Reg and Rosemary had brought home from one of their holidays in Italy, subconsciously something tweaked a cord in her brain and she put her fingers into the little pocket and there, with relief, she found her ring. Edwina was aware that Michael loved her jewellery so when she mentioned the incident to Ray that evening, he hammered in a nail inside their wardrobe, well out of young children's reach. With all the stress of packing up Edwina had not given her ring a thought. When everything had been offloaded into their new house and the removal men were getting ready to leave, one of them came back and asked Edwina if a ring he had just picked up off the road was hers. What an honest man. Edwina was obviously delighted not to have had their new home blighted by such a loss.

It was truly wonderful to finally own a house. The kitchen was small but led off a separate dining room that had plenty of room for a fold-out dining table and chairs, a television, a two-seater sofa bed and an armchair. This sunny room had French doors that opened on a sheltered patio and the garden had a rectangular lawn surrounded by flower beds. This room became the living room, allowing the lounge to remain tidy and toy-free for visitors. At the bottom of the garden, Hazel's swing was re-erected and ready to use by the following weekend. They had moved just at the right time of year: to be able to simply open a door and run out into their own garden; to have picnics on their grass; to put up deckchairs and sunbathe. John was happy to share his play tent with his siblings.

A woman living up the road asked Edwina whether she would take their guinea pig. She had bought it for her daughter only to discover she was allergic to it. Ruth and Lionel dropped in to see the new home and when Lionel was shown little black and tan Gerty in a small hutch, he mentioned he had some ammunition boxes that could be converted into more spacious accommodation. That was soon accomplished and a young ginger Gerry was purchased from the pet shop as Gerty's mate. A large pen was attached to the hutch to allow the guinea pigs freedom to run around on the lawn. Ray regularly moved the hutch to ensure fresh grass. The furry couple got on well together and gave Edwina a chance to discuss the basics of reproduction as they went on to have many litters of babies, all freely given away to loving homes when they were old enough. Michael and Hazel were meant to share cleaning out the hutches. Michael wasn't too bothered by a dirty cage but Hazel was. So after some subtle nagging from her mother she usually did it alone.

Alf and Lieselotte also moved that year. They swapped their large semi just off the Leigh cliffs for a detached chalet that sat on the main road into Benfleet, the next town on the coast towards London. It had views over the Benfleet Downs to the estuary. Jasper dog had sadly come to the end of a long life the year before and once they had moved they decided to buy a white Scottish Terrier puppy. They named him Puck. Because he was so sweet and playful he made visits to their grandparents a delight.

Hazel and family now needed to catch a bus to visit. Arthur was very rarely there. He was playing tennis or taking a girlfriend out for a spin in his red MG Midget. Hazel missed him. She found her grandfather rather overbearing and they weren't allowed to play on his perfect lawn, only to sit on a rug while the adults sat on deckchairs.

When she was a young child, Lieselotte's strong German accent had been intimidating, but now Hazel glimpsed the real warmth she obviously felt for her father and them all. Every Christmas she presented the children with a Hansel and Gretel house she had made from a cardboard box. She cut out a front door, leaving one side attached so that the witch could stand menacingly in the doorway. The witch had a beautiful German, carved wooden head, with tiny wire glasses perched on her large, hooked nose. Lieselotte had stitched a black cloak with hood to cover her wine stopper body. Peeping out of the cloak, a hint of a plasticine hand held a wooden walking stick. The windows were covered in clear cellophane. A large cauldron hung over a fire opposite the door and Lieselotte placed a small light inside the house. Cotton wool smoke poked out of the chimney. The whole house was covered in sweets of all shapes and sizes, including candy walking sticks on either side of the door, chocolates, toffees and biscuits all stuck on using flour and water paste. The little Hansel and Gretel dolls held hands as they approached down a winding path. A well and a papier mâché cave sat in the garden. The cave had a large door made to imitate a rock that could be rolled in front, and actually hung attached so it didn't get lost. Inside, sticks were piled over red cellophane that hid a flickering bulb. When this wonderful model was plugged in and switched on the story was brought to life.

Lieselotte had given four-year-old Hazel a German fairy story book that had been translated into English, so they knew the story.

She had first made the model for Ray and Bessy, remade it for Arthur and it was now being enjoyed by a second generation. Edwina had told the children that Alf's first wife, their real grandmother, had died when their father was twelve. Hazel imagined how desolate a loss this must have been to a seven-year-old girl and a twelve-year-old boy. But Edwina explained that, due to their grandmother's ill health, Lieselotte had become close to the children and was much like a mother.

Aunt Bess paid a rare visit from Australia that year. She was pleased to see her brother settled in his own house. Bess had married an Australian and they lived just outside Sydney with their two daughters. The families exchanged tapes each Christmas filled with tales from their different lives. Hazel recoils a little now from the thought that they each sang a song for those first tapes. Great for her father, his deep baritone voice moved something deep inside Hazel; and her mother had an uplifting, pretty voice. At five Hazel had sung her favourite hymn for the tape, *God Made Little Robin* (written by Florence Hoatson, 1881–1964).

Her voice sounded cutely acceptable, but she was disappointed that, as she aged, it appeared to deteriorate. She had two parents who, with training, could have had singing careers. What had happened to those genes? Hazel loved singing hymns in church but she would never be able to sing like a robin.

Then began another wonderful six-week summer holiday, including a week at Brownie camp and a week at Butlin's. The days floated past in warmth and pleasure and it was with reluctance that Hazel returned to school for her final year in the juniors.

Her school streamed all children according to ability every year in four classes. The top class in its final year was always taught by Mr Jeffrey and everybody was meant to pass their eleven-plus. Hazel was in the second class, taught by Miss Wyatt, and about three-quarters of the class were expected to pass the eleven-plus. Miss Wyatt was grey-haired and overweight. She was the PE teacher who had coached Hazel, Jane, Collin and Simon for the high jump, so Hazel felt happy with this familiar teacher and lessons proceeded with ease.

Hazel was disappointed to discover that during the holidays Simon had taken pretty, blonde, curly haired Lynda to the cinema. Lynda's round, fair, smiling face (not splattered with freckles) and with 'rosebud' lips, charmed everyone. Hazel was not surprised and cursed her stupid behaviour last term. While her feelings for Simon did not diminish she knew she now stood no chance of winning his affection. He deserved pretty Lynda.

One Monday morning, about six weeks into their first term, they entered the classroom to find the headmaster at the desk. He told them that Miss Wyatt had been taken ill and would not be returning for a while. Lessons with the headmaster that week did not flow from where Miss Wyatt had left them and Hazel struggled to tie it all together. The following Monday a new teacher sat behind the desk. Again, it took her a while to settle into another teaching style. During that final year her class had six different teachers and Miss Wyatt did not return. Each time Hazel entered the classroom to find a new teacher, her heart sank. Maths in particular became all jumbled up as some teachers went over stuff they had already learnt but in a different way. It was just so confusing.

On Friday afternoons throughout the junior years the children were allowed to play board or card games, but not until they had completed copying a piece of text taken from whichever book they were reading. Hazel always had a problem with this. She really concentrated hard, copied it slowly, checked it and was often one of the last to hand it in to the teacher. It was always returned to her marked 'careless, rewrite this'. Not once, regardless of how much she cared (and she seriously did), did she copy it correctly first time. She only occasionally got the second copy correct, by which time most of playtime had slipped away. It frustrated her terribly. Six weeks before Hazel was due to sit her eleven-plus Edwina found an advertisement from a retired headmaster who offered to coach children for the eleven-plus exam in their own home. Mr Vernon was a large man with drooping cheeks and long wild eyebrows, but his wisdom and gentle, caring patience, brought a clarity and understanding to maths and to English grammar in that short time. So she was able to sit her exams with some understanding of the papers in front of her.

Then there was the wait for the results. A letter addressed to Hazel's parents arrived. She was anxious. Edwina agreed they would wait for her father to return that evening before opening it. They all stood in the lounge as Edwina opened the letter. Silence as she read it. Then, "You achieved a borderline pass."

"What does that mean?" asked Ray.

"It says that because of the numbers passing this year you cannot be offered a grammar school place. However, you have been offered a place at St Bernard's. They hold a number of placements for pupils who've passed the eleven-plus."

"A Roman Catholic school!" retorted Ray.

"Let's have a few days to think this over," suggested Edwina, knowing her husband only too well.

Hazel was not surprised. Her parents didn't appear to be too surprised either. Her final year had been a struggle. She was disappointed though. She imagined herself in a school with nuns as teachers. Might she be happy to sit quietly and listen to their religious teachings? Probably not.

A few days later Hazel sat at the table in the bright dining room, drawing a picture of some trees, Edwina sat on the chair opposite her.

"Daddy does not want you to go to a Roman Catholic school. It seems your second-best option would be Belfairs High School for Girls. The headmistress, Miss Wiseman, expects a high standard from her pupils and teachers. Like St Bernard's it offers O-levels in maths, English, art and the sciences. Belfairs doesn't have a sixth form though, so you would go on to college for A-levels. What do you think?"

Hazel had lain in bed over the previous two nights thinking. Having spent years watching *Dixon of Dock Green* she seriously thought she would make a good detective. Gathering facts, weaving them into possibilities. Deducing from all angles. But her height that was not cooperating. Women had to be five feet and six inches tall to enter the police force. Her father was almost six feet but her mother was only five feet two inches and, unfortunately, her mother's genes were dominating so far. That was her greatest disappointment. Perhaps there was a tiny chance of a growth spurt. She loved art but she knew that to teach it would be full on, with no time to daydream, so she discounted it. Artists and illustrators in general earned very little. By the time she reached sixth form, and if her height had not complied, other possibilities may have arisen.

"Do either school teach technical drawing? If I can't join the police force I might like to study to become an architect."

"Your father asked this question, but no, it's a subject only taught at boy's schools."

"Jill said they do a lot of religious study in all years at St Bernard's. I think I would find that just boring and unnecessary. Jane is going to Westborough High School for Girls, that's about the same distance from here. What's that like?"

"Belfairs girls seem to leave with higher O-level grades."

Hazel digested this.

"Oh, well, perhaps Belfairs is best."

Ray and Edwina attended the final parents' evening to find Miss Wyatt presiding as Hazel's teacher. She apologised for her long absence and said she would return next year, although conceded that this was now irrelevant.

"I feel Hazel has great potential. I'm happy she has been offered a place at St Bernard's, it's a good choice. I think she will do well there."

Hazel's parents didn't enlighten her.

Via the mums' grapevine Edwina discovered that only three children from Hazel's class had passed the eleven-plus and received grammar school places. She also heard that Mr Godfrey had been sacked and was being prosecuted, although it was uncertain exactly what for. When Edwina passed this on to her daughter Hazel described what he had done to her.

"He didn't go inside my pants though."

Hazel also explained that, while it was not discussed among her friends, she was sure she was not alone.

"I wonder who told. I suppose it didn't bother me enough to mention it," she said to her mother.

After Hazel went to bed she heard an argument between her parents and, while she got the impression it was to do with reporting her abuse, she was unable to discern any details. But nobody mentioned it again. Certainly, Mr Godfrey he was no longer allowed to teach and that's all that seemed important to Hazel. She had not been damaged by it. In fact, she thought it was probably no bad thing for her to be aware that she should now be tuned to the fact that trust must never be presumed.

Jane did go to Westborough High School for Girls. Louise, Linda and Lynda were going to Belfairs so Hazel was happy enough. She heard that Simon was going to Belfairs High School for Boys. While the schools were completely separate they were joined by the hall and canteen, but the students were never allowed into these shared spaces together. It meant she might occasionally catch sight of him outside. Apart from a special morning assembly dedicated to the school leavers, there was no party or special concert that Edwina or Hazel can remember. At the end of every year there was a prize giving and one year she was presented with a wonderful book on English birds. The illustrations were perfect paintings, depicting each bird and a life-size, perfectly detailed painting of their egg. Inside the cover a golden award sticker proclaimed that Hazel had won this award for 'Perseverance'. To this day it still holds a cherished position on her bookshelves and was the only prize she received throughout her schooling.

That summer holiday, while at camp as a Girl Guide, her father wrote to say he was wallpapering her bedroom with pink rosebuds. This bedroom became a beautiful sanctuary where she allowed her mind to soar to the very heights of her imagination. To assist her she decided to practise whistling. Her father was able to whistle even better than a bird. So, in the peace of her bedroom, usually while lying in bed waiting for sleep to engulf her, she practised among the rosebuds. With the perseverance she was blessed with, she could soon whistle well.

But it was in this sanctuary that she had her first experience of real fear (apart from the nightmares she'd had as a child, in her previous bedroom, about a ferocious cat jumping out at her). With hindsight, Hazel realises that because she was naturally a lark, who was always most alert in the morning and struggled to stay awake in the evening, she presumed she needed to go to bed early and get as much sleep as she could. Even as a toddler, once tucked into her cot she was just happy to lie there, daydreaming, until sleep claimed her. That quiet, undisturbed time helped Hazel's vivid imagination to blossom as she lay with her eyes closed and allowed her mind to wander freely. She would watch coloured patterns like rainbows shimmering on oil, swirl behind her closed eyelids. She made a cave out of her pillow as she found putting her head inside it was soothing. She didn't know that the carbon dioxide she was breathing out has that effect. But one night she was having a particularly difficult time finding sleep and was lying on her back staring at the shadow of light from the street lamp outside, when she watched in sudden terror as a silent, black, human-shaped shadow moved across her window, behind her curtain. Her heart was pounding as she struggled to understand what this shadow was. Was it someone trying to find a window to climb in at? She froze and watched it disappear. It took about twenty minutes to convince herself that it was only her lack of sleep that had made her brain manufacture the apparition. She just couldn't accept that it might be a ghost. She was sure they didn't exist. It was just her overactive mind.

It was also in this bedroom that she tested her belief that, while God may or may not exist, it was only she who could really control her mind. She had suddenly developed a feeling of nausea whenever she went to the pictures. Probably triggered by a slightly upset stomach on one occasion. It developed again the next time she went and she spent the whole time worried about throwing up in the cinema. The following film the whole family were going to see was *Zulu*. They were all, bar Hazel, excited to be going to see this epic film. Nausea swirled in the pit of her stomach for hours before they caught the bus to the cinema. Once seated and the film began she was so certain she was going to be sick that she told her dad. After a whispered discussion with his wife over Michael's and John's heads, Ray agreed to take his daughter home and leave the rest of the family to enjoy the film. Hazel was upset, knowing how much her father had wanted to see the film and, in her distress, on the bus home her stomach still churned. Her father swept aside her apologies saying she couldn't help it. Once home, a teaspoon of bicarb dissolved in a glass of warm water helped her nausea to subside.

That night she questioned herself about why she was allowing her mind to cause this problem because she'd been going to the cinema for years without any mishap. Even that first time she had experienced it, when it was most likely to have been a naturally occurring upset tummy, she hadn't actually been sick. She was sure that the large screen itself was not a problem. It had to be her mind. 'I must take back control.' She began by telling herself repeatedly that it was her mind causing her problem and not her stomach, meaning that she must be able to persuade her mind it was manufacturing the problem. And virtually overnight she convinced herself that it would not happen again and it never did. She had regained control. Simply by talking to herself.

Hazel and Louise moved up into the Guides and midnight feasts and midnight rambles were secretly organised by some tents that summer. Not all the occupants were happy to partake and this was always accepted. Hazel thought Louise had matured and their friendship felt closer. As Guides they were learning to understand and respect each other and the two were drawn together by their shared need to test the boundaries of their courage. Exploring the wood alongside their campsite at night was flouting the camp rules and viewed as an adventure. They were in separate patrols and separate tents, but Hazel and Jill arranged to meet up with Louise and Barbara at midnight, under a large oak tree on the boundary between their field and the wood. No moonlight assisted them that night and they daren't turn on their torches in case the light was seen by a patrolling leader.

They met up by the oak tree and decided it was best to hold hands and slowly inch their way into the wood with their torches off. Hazel, as a regular visitor to Belfairs woods, was used to all the natural daytime woodland noises but Jill and Barbara weren't so much. At night it was scary. Every footfall seemed to snap a twig and they could hear what they hoped were normal nocturnal animal noises. But what animals? And how big?

Jill and Barbara decided to go back to their tents, unable to face these unknown fears. Louise and Hazel decided they were now far enough into the wood to be able to switch on their torches and hold them very low so the beam only lit up a small area in front of their feet and they no longer needed to hold hands. They were hoping to pick up a path that would lead them through to the other side of the wood. It seemed hopeless. Perhaps there simply wasn't one. They were curious as to how far the wood went. They both held their compasses and, as she had been checking their direction at regular intervals since leaving the oak tree, Hazel felt confident she could go further. Louise suggested they move out in a V-shape to fan the area more affectively. They agreed on a signal – an 'owl' hoot and three quick flashes with their torches – to communicate across the expanding distance. This worked well until Hazel could no longer hear or see Louise responding. Hazel's heart sped up as she called Louise's name and waited in the following silence, then a clutch of fear as she felt herself alone.

Then annoyance took over. How could she have stupidly presumed Louise had grown up? She decided to turn and try to follow her path back. After only about ten yards she felt the hairs on the back of her neck rise as she became aware of a flash of movement in the trees above. As she swung her torch up, a terrifying screech tore through the wood. The enormous eyes and face of an owl with a massive wingspan swooped down so fast towards her head that she was sure its talons were meant for her. Then, with a great rush of air, it vanished. Her heart was really pounding but more in sheer wonderment and relief. She knew, from visits to London and Colchester zoos with her family, exactly what the various English owls looked like in cages. But the round, white, ghost-like head with its large eyes and wings so wide that the ends seemed lost in the low tree canopy as it swept so close to her head, not with the sound of flapping wings but with a rush of wind, had been so real! Was this where the word banshee came from? She guessed it must have been a barn owl, but so much larger than she expected. Well, that was Louise's loss. Had she expected Hazel to be frightened and lost on finding herself alone?

She followed her memory of the way back. She had taken note of each unusual bend of a tree trunk, the leaves and shapes of certain shrubs, the pattern of clumps of bracken and the long arms of prickly brambles that she had had to avoid. It probably wasn't much more than 250 yards. It was the denseness of the woodland that made it appear endless. She switched her torch off as she spied the edge of the wood and slowly, silently crossed the field. Her eyes had to adjust to the almost complete darkness. No glow of lights in any of the tents. She wondered if she should check that Louise had made it back to her tent, but she believed she knew her well enough to be almost certain that she had. In the morning, she described to Louise her encounter with the owl and nonchalantly said she couldn't understand what had happened with their signalling but had been sure Louise was able to take care of herself.

CHAPTER 7

1964 ◊ A Senior

Belfairs High School for Girls dictated that the new students begin their first term a week after the rest of the school. Hazel, with her brand new, tan-coloured leather satchel, containing only her new PE gear, slung diagonally across her body had to catch a bus from the bottom of her road. Another girl was waiting there, also in what appeared to be a new Belfairs uniform, but as the girl was quite a bit taller Hazel thought she might be older so she just gave her a smile that was weakly returned. They chose separate seats as they travelled about six stops along the London Road to one that was named 'the Highlands'. On the south side of the road was the expensive Marine Estate that sat above the Belton Hills that climbed up from Leigh Station. Hazel's new school was nestled just up an adjoining road into the, almost as expensive, houses of the Highlands Estate. Belfairs School for Boys shared this frontage and the buildings ran back in parallel, joined only by the kitchen and dining hall. All the new girls gathered in the playground at nine-thirty. Hazel saw Louise's dark hair and swarthy face through the crowd. She also picked out Linda and Lynda talking together, but decided to retain her independence as they were instructed to follow a teacher, file into the hall and take a seat.

Miss Wiseman, the headmistress, was standing in front of a small podium on one side of the stage. She gave a short welcome speech and then explained that each of the four teachers for their year would call out the names of the girls in their class. As they heard their name they should come and line up at the foot of the stage. Hazel did not recognise any of the girls who queued up for the first and second classes and watched as they were led out of the hall by their respective teachers. She knew that they were being streamed according to the results of the final exams they had all sat in their junior schools. She then heard the third teacher call out both Linda's and Lynda's names and then Louise's. The teacher completed her list and led her queue out. 'Does this mean I'm in the bottom class,' thought Hazel, 'or have they just forgotten me?' Hazel noted that the fourth teacher's name was Miss Speed. Hazel heard her name and joined the last queue. As they all marched behind Miss Speed, Hazel noted the neatness of their knotted ties and their new, shiny shoes and, from the few intelligent whispers that she overheard, concluded that this might not be the bottom class. She was pleased to discover that it was the top class in her year.

Miss Speed was a young, neat, pretty, petite lady, possibly not long out of teaching college. She needed to wear glasses, but only for reading. When she was standing up in front of the class or slowly walking among them as she talked, she held one of the arms of these glasses and twirled them around. Her initial strict manner became a little gentler as her confidence with the class grew and she would smile occasionally when it was appropriate. Hazel watched her with wary respect for the first few weeks but as the term progressed her teacher seemed to return a respect for the girls who were attempting to meet her expectations, which included Hazel.

Hazel quickly settled into the school routine with the help of their timetable and the very acceptable food at lunchtimes. The girls in her classes were all pleasant enough. During the first month one girl stood out. The sound of her perfectly executed English, which Hazel later discovered came from elocution lessons, was enough to draw Hazel to listen to her. She was about Hazel's height, but a hint of curves suggested her blossoming puberty. With her naturally straw-coloured hair, full lips and green eyes, she was very attractive. Hazel found herself standing next to her one day, while they were waiting for a teacher to arrive for class, and got chatting. Her name, Danique, was Dutch, and her Dutch father was a merchant sea captain. Her mother was English and a dressmaker, which explained why Danique's skirt looked and fitted so much more stylishly than everyone else's. She had a similar bouncy disposition to Hazel's but Danique had a way of drawing one in, even girls, with a seductive gaze and a tongue that regularly flashed across her lips. The boys must love her, thought Hazel. A natural openness developed between them and they became firm friends. Hazel had also made friends with Mirren, the girl at the bus stop, as it turned out they were in the same class. Mirren was friends with a short, dark, slightly plump, smiling girl called Lee. During school hours the four became inseparable, but Hazel always felt a closer bond with Danique.

Miss Speed was their class tutor throughout Hazel's time at Belfairs and taught the top class for English. Mr Vernon's home lessons had prepared Hazel for entry to this top class and she found that almost everything Miss Speed taught made perfect sense. The same could be said of maths, taught by another young woman, Miss Delderfield. By the end of the first term Hazel sensed a mutual liking and both teachers always made sure their pupils knew they should not hesitate to ask if there was anything they were not clear about. Hazel was happy to oblige with sensible questions when necessary. In fact, she discovered that a sense of humour could, occasionally, be drawn from both teachers if the right question was put. For science, Hazel had an older lady, Mrs Broughton, who also added a little humour to help step up attention, so again Hazel felt an empathy. For their first French lesson she was amused to see a tall, dark, very ugly woman with an enormous nose and large pouting lips, standing next to the blackboard. Miss Dench's humour, though, could be very dry and often quite sarcastic. Hazel was able to appreciate this, so it was not long before she happily settled into this class as well. Clearly, Miss Wiseman, when selecting teachers through the interview process, was being very wise! RE (religious education), however, was boring. The only interesting part was when the teacher asked the girls if they would like to make a model of the Garden of Gethsemane at home.

That evening Hazel mentioned this to her father. He explained that it would not be difficult and that they could make the landscape out of papier mâché. Hazel found a picture and description of the garden, as it was presumed to have been in the time of Jesus, in an encyclopaedia at the library. She wasn't allowed to take it home and photocopying machines were not seen outside hi-tech places such as government buildings. But she was able to rely on her visual memory. Ray cut up a piece of hardboard he had in the shed to about eighteen inches by just under two feet and bought a pack of balsa wood from a model shop near where he worked. He showed Hazel how to cut it into narrow lengths with a sharp scalpel, with each one at a different height so they could be glued to the hardboard base at intervals to give an impression of uneven sloping ground, as the garden, which still exists, leads up to the Mount of Olives. Hazel was then able to cut and stick strips of cardboard to the tops of the balsa pillars to join them all up. She mixed up a flour and water paste and began the laborious job of tearing up strips of newspaper and pasting them to build up a solid papier mâché slope for the garden. She carried it upstairs and placed it on the top of her chest of drawers and left it to dry out.

Hazel bought some powder paint. After some thought she had decided that the colours she would need could all be mixed from red, yellow, blue, black and white. Even a dusty path could be achieved by mixing a little yellow and black into the white and she'd have plenty of colour for some wild flowers.

Ray then gave her a pack of green, fine, soft, spongy material that was designed to look like fine branches covered in leaves and was used by model makers for trees. He suggested finding some small, dry twigs in their own garden that could be used as tree trunks. He showed Hazel how to use a bradawl to make a hole to glue the sticks into. Then it was a matter of sticking on little pieces of the green stuff. This could also be used to make small shrubs and even tiny sprigs of it as wild flowers, when touched-up with colourful paint.

On the beach Hazel searched for tiny stones and sand that would make good representations of rocks and natural rubble that might have lain around and edged the paths. She carefully glued them all on. She knew that water paint would not adhere to glue so she had painted in the path first and ensured that the glue under the sand and rocks was as invisible as possible. Hazel felt a sense of satisfaction as she painted in the scrubby dry landscape, mixing and blending dry, sandy colours with patches of green and added colour to the some of the trees. She had discovered at the library that the leaves of olive trees were a grey-green. Decisions on the type and colour of shrubs and wild flowers were taken from photos of dry Mediterranean landscapes. The 'burning bush' that appeared to Moses was most likely to have been some kind of bramble or thorn bush (the experts decided), so Hazel endeavoured to add grey branches underneath the green leaves of the odd shrub.

Hazel was very proud of the final model. Ray found a box and adapted it to fit. Fortunately, Mirren was at the bus stop to help her manoeuvre it on to the bus. Miss Speed suggested she took it straight to the RE room. The RE teacher, Miss Jacks, said nothing as Hazel wrestled to get her model out of its box and place it on a table at the front of the room. She did walk over and look, once it was in place. A nod and a weak smile were all the model elicited and with that came the realisation that her teacher probably cared more about Hazel's uninteresting RE written work and that this model was not going to change that. Hazel was disappointed at this reaction though, after all her hard work.

When the girls entered the classroom later that day for their lesson, Hazel saw another small, less well-made model, sitting next to hers. As the girls gathered around to look at the only two models that had been produced, she had very mixed feelings. She hadn't intended to eclipse any competition and now felt she had been too 'big headed' in her attempt, just because she could. She'd only wanted to convey to this teacher that she did care about a lot of things, which she now suspected she had not achieved.

Okay, Hazel concluded, it was her religious spirit that this teacher cared about. Another minus point for religion in Hazel's book. The smaller model had disappeared by their next lesson but Miss Jacks let her model remain until the end of term and it was on display again on parents' evening, so it hadn't been completely pointless. If nothing else, Hazel had learnt three very different lessons outside of the curriculum: first, her reward might not be equal to her hard work; second, consider the feelings of the competition; third, should she take any notice of the conclusions to the first two? In this instance she was satisfied that she had done the correct thing.

Neither Hazel nor Danique had any interest in their music lessons so they always chose a table together at the back of the class and Danique regularly brought in her *Jackie* magazine. Hazel had not been allowed comics and was definitely not allowed teen magazines. Louise had loved her *Beano* comic with Dennis the Menace, but then she loved all cartoons on the TV. Apart from *Tom and Jerry*, *Popeye* and *The Flintstones*, Hazel wasn't too bothered. But Ray and Edwina had set up a subscription for *Look and Learn* that Hazel had received since she was about eight and had always enjoyed. Michael had it now and Hazel still found it full of great articles. But *Jackie* was so worldly and the girls kept their heads down in class and giggled their way through the stories, anxious letters and articles such as 'How to be more kissable!'

That year, Ray's work colleague, Alan, decided to move his family up north to be closer to his ailing mother and Ray was able to take over his client list. It meant he now had to make occasional trips abroad for conferences or fairs, for instance to Brussels and Scandinavia, but he always sent postcards home to Edwina and the children to let them know what he was up to. To facilitate all the extra travelling in the UK he was offered a company car. He was annoyed that he didn't pass his driving test first time but managed on the second attempt. One evening he proudly drove home a Morris 1100 in dark racing green. No more walking to and from the station. He bought a Reader's Digest *Places of Interest* and Sundays became adventures consisting of air shows, Colchester and Whipsnade Zoos, fishing trips to Danbury Lakes and walks around pretty villages and churches to admire the architecture. They visited Uncle Jack and his wife Audrey and their younger two cousins, Karen and Paul, in their new home in Woodham Ferrers, where they spent one great day clearing the back garden of overgrown shrubs and brambles and burning it all on a smoky bonfire. They visited quite often and Hazel, Michael and John were impressed by their cousins' Siamese cat, Willow. He was taken on walks across the fields and on picnics in a collar and lead. One day, as distant rumbles of thunder became a sudden deluge of rain, they had to make a mad dash to an old barn for shelter. Needless to say, Sunday school became a distant memory.

During the middle term at school that year, after they'd all piled out of class for break, Hazel left her friends to make a toilet stop and, in usual Hazel style, hurtled across the playground to meet them on the surrounding grassy area. She tripped and put her hands out to break her fall. She quickly got up and, apart from a slight pain in her right wrist, was fine. As it slowly stiffened up she presumed she had sprained it. At Guides they had been taught how to bandage a sprain, but it wasn't too painful so Hazel couldn't be bothered, although she mentioned it to Edwina, who agreed it was just a sprain. However, at the end of the second week following her fall it had become so stiff that she had to run it under cold water to be able to use it. When Hazel explained this to her mother, they waited until Ray got home and he drove them to the A&E at Southend Hospital for an X-ray, which revealed a fracture. The doctor was not impressed that it had taken two weeks to do anything. It was plastered up and finally Hazel felt some relief from what had become a constant ache. Making a fuss wasn't in Hazel's nature so she felt her mother was rather unfairly blamed for not suspecting the real problem.

Her father wrote a note for her to take to school the following day, excusing her from PE. She handed it to Miss Speed first thing at registration. Later that day they had their usual double period of English, during which Miss Speed always gave them dictation from a book or play they were working on, probably to ensure complete concentration and spelling proficiency. Miss Speed had been reading clearly for almost ten minutes when she registered that Hazel was having to write with her left hand. With mild shock their teacher put her hand to her mouth.

"Oh, Hazel, I'm so sorry. I had completely forgotten about your plaster."

"That's fine, Miss Speed, really. I'm writing all right with my left hand. It's not a problem at all. My Dad always thought I was ambidextrous."

She held her book up to show her mystified teacher.

Ray's Aunt Rose had died of heart failure at Armscot in Birmingham and Ray invited his Uncle Chris to came and stay with them for a week, but he could only be persuaded to stay for a weekend. He drove down in his white Mini. The sofa in the lounge was pulled out into a double bed for Ray and Edwina and Uncle Chris had their bedroom. During his short stay the children found this elderly gentleman pleasant and humorous. Ray was hoping that he might consider selling the large family home and moving down to live near them. But Chris wanted to stay in the only home he'd ever known. He was hopeful of finding a live-in housekeeper. His will was also discussed. As his only living relatives, the house and contents would be left to Ray and Bess in equal share. Chris asked his nephew whether he would be happy to be executor. However, Ray decided that, because of the distance between them, it might be more prudent to name a local solicitor. He could have no idea what a mistake that would be. They all hugged and kissed him goodbye and promised to visit soon. It would be another year before Ray saw his uncle.

At Easter the following year, the girls were offered the chance to take a trip to French-speaking Montreux in Switzerland for ten days to help tune their ears to French pronunciation. It wasn't cheap but Ray and Edwina thought it was worth scraping the money together for. Not many of Hazel's year were able to afford it but Danique was able to go. She was in the top class for French with Mrs Head as her teacher. Mrs Head had arranged the trip and Miss Dench came to help. It was Hazel's chance to experience flying and they boarded a flight from Southend to Ostend. She so appreciated her parents paying for this trip as she was sure it had meant going without something. The thrill she got as their plane soared up into the sky, the landscape shrinking beneath them, was tremendous. Through and above the soft white clouds. Then glimpses of minuscule buildings on the land, just like a model. Then they were over the sea. She completely understood why her father had wanted to be a pilot. Nothing on land brought quite such a sense of wonderment and awe. Hazel was blown away, fortunately not literally, and they landed safely. They had a few hours to wander around and enjoy some lunch in a café before picking up a coach for the long drive to Montreux.

The only thing that had slightly bothered Hazel was a girl in her class called Belinda. She was not unpleasant and she did appear to have a few friends and perhaps it was just that she had a very sensitive nose, but Belinda smelt! And it wasn't just 'BO' because it reminded Hazel of wet nappies. If Belinda happened to come close it seriously took her breath away. She hoped that at some point a teacher might think it worth mentioning to Belinda's parents. To date this seemed not to have happened. Hazel mentioned to her father that the prospect of being in a dormitory with Belinda for a whole ten days was difficult to bear. So, Ray wrote his daughter a note to give to Mrs Head if she felt it might be necessary. Fortunately it wasn't, as Hazel and Danique were not in the same dormitory as Belinda.

Hazel was again delighted to find a letter waiting for her at their Hotel Joli-Mont when they arrived. From her father, of course:

Hello Darling,

I bet you didn't think that your Daddy would remember to write so that you had a letter waiting for you when you arrived!

Well, dear, we all hope that you had a lovely journey and enjoyed all the things you must have seen on the way. We all hope you that you were not sick on the plane! How do you like flying? Daddy thinks it's super! Did you wave to Southend Pier as you flew over?

How did you like Ostend? I thought it was quite a nice seaside town when I passed through on my way to Brussels. I expect it was too cold to sit on the beach and anyway I bet you spent all your time looking around the town. When I spent the night there, I stayed in a hotel right on the sea front.

By the time you read this I expect you will have been given your room in the Hotel and are settling down to really enjoying yourself. Don't forget to write a card to us as soon as you have the time. Don't forget to send a card to both Grandmas and Grandpas and don't forget to put England on all your cards!

Well darling, have a really lovely time, behave yourself always and be very careful and don't try and do anything silly. Try and remember all the things you see and do, as we all expect a full report of your holiday when you get home. As you come back on Saturday I expect we will be at the airport to meet you!

God bless you dear, and Daddy sends you a goodnight kiss – here – (a drawing of some lips).

Love from
Mummy, Daddy, Michael and John
xxxxxxxxxx

Hazel touched her lips to those her father had drawn. Dear Daddy. He never forgot her. A few days later another envelope arrived and inside were letters from both her parents.

She didn't tell her parents, though, about the night that she, Danique and a couple of other girls decided to climb out of the window (they were only on the ground floor) to go exploring after they were supposed to be tucked up in bed. There was a small-gauge railway line running near the perimeter of their hotel and they followed it into the heart of Montreux and down to the lakefront before making their way back again. It was exciting, trying to stay hidden from the few people still about. Fortunately, nothing unusual happened. It was great to tumble, exhausted, back under the wonderful, thick, soft, feather and down continental quilt. Hazel thought they were so luxurious and it was so much easier to just shake them in the morning. Why could they not dispense with the many layers of sheets, blankets and bedspreads that they had at home?

They visited Lucerne to see Chapel Bridge, the oldest wooden bridge in Europe. The medieval town of Basel was fascinating. They wandered around the chateaux at Gruyères and visited the cheese shop, passing through the Rochers de Naye mountain peak on their way back to Montreux. But it was the mountain train that took them through thick, snow-covered pine forests on the way to Chamonix that remained most firmly in Hazel's memory. Just how amazing would it be to toboggan down those mountains?

She did find time to send postcards home to her family, including both sets of grandparents, but it was a task that she always found onerous, even as an adult. It seemed a waste of valuable time, both thinking exactly what to say and how to spell it all correctly and there was always at least one crossed out word on each card. She could tell it all with far more animation when she got home. But postcards were what everyone expected. It was a brilliant holiday. Hazel quite enjoyed learning French at school, but on their holiday there actually didn't seem to be many opportunities to practise the language as most of the time their teachers spoke for them. But as an experience of a different country it was invaluable. Hazel was very happy, though, to see her family eagerly awaiting her at Southend airport.

When Hazel got home she opened the letter addressed to Mrs Head from her father, just to see what he had written:

Dear Mrs Head,
It would be much appreciated if you could arrange for Hazel not to be billeted with Belinda Bilton.
Thanking you for your understanding and co-operation & I hope that you all have a thoroughly enjoyable trip.
Yours Sincerely
Ray's signature

Mrs Head, for some reason, did not appreciate Hazel's cheeky nature and Hazel was glad she had not had to hand her this note. But she loved her father for writing it.

That summer the lease expired on the house Carol's parents were renting. Hazel was sorry to hear that her best friend would be moving to live in Benfleet and would not be going to Belfairs. Within weeks of them moving, though, Hazel was invited to stay for a week during the holidays. Carol was lucky enough to have a double bed. Curled up side by side at night they spent hours discussing life and giggling. Their laughter would occasionally bring one of Carol's parents up the stairs to knock on their door and tell them it was late and that they needed to sleep. Both girls wore pyjamas in the winter but on these hot summer nights just a vest and pants was cooler and, for relaxation in the heat, they would gently stroke each other's back or arm or outer leg. Hazel was aware that sex between the same gender was not really accepted but she felt that this was more about a gentle, pleasurable experience to help maintain their closeness, rather than a precursor to something sexual. And she was sure her friend felt the same.

Carol's new house had a garden and they played skipping and ball games, often throwing two or three balls against the wall of the house in a juggling fashion. It frustrated Hazel because, unlike Carol, she wasn't consistent and some days she could keep the balls in motion for a fair time but on others she was rubbish and kept dropping them. She didn't give up but she had to accept she would never be as good as Carol at juggling. They explored Benfleet, walking up the steep Vicarage Hill and wondering at the large houses set back behind a little grassy green, dark and heavy with large trees. They walked down to the station and along to the wasteground named The Wreak. It was nothing more than a large expanse of scrubland with a few small trees. Hazel felt it all lacked the atmosphere of Leigh-on-Sea but Carol seemed happy and Hazel looked forward to visiting.

During their second year Hazel, Danique, Mirren and Lee began to go out for lunch. It was not technically permitted to leave school premises at lunchtime, but the rule was rarely enforced, which was a good enough excuse for them to go to Danique's house when her mother was out and her father away. They bought hams, cold meats or cheese from the delicatessen on the way. There was always bread and butter in the larder to make sandwiches. Danique received generous weekly pocket money from her mother and, since she made whatever stylish clothes Danique wanted, her daughter could spend her money on other things, including the records she played on their expensive gramophone – John Mayall, Cream, Fleetwood Mac, the Rolling Stones. Just as well Danique's house was detached, Hazel could feel the beat vibrating through the floor.

The girls never met up outside school hours and had not really discussed their private lives but Danique's large house and lavish furnishings did elicit a conversation about what jobs their fathers did. Mirren said her father drove lorries and was rarely at home. Hazel felt sad for her initially until she explained that she was very close to her mum and was happiest when her father was away as he only upset their routine. Lee's father also spent a fair bit of time travelling. She was not clear about exactly what he did but thought it may have something to do with insurance. Hazel knew Danique preferred her father to be away at sea and, as she listened to the three of them conferring about the very close relationships they had with their mothers, she considered how it was a complete reversal for her.

She loved her father deeply and, for some strange and inexplicable reason, she thought that calling him 'an architectural designer' didn't reflect how special he felt to her. Their house felt very cheap compared to Danique's, so Hazel knew she could not say her father was an architect. In her head Hazel still had a strong desire to become a detective so how all these feelings got mixed up and came out in such an outrageous lie she still does not understand. But, as she accurately explained her feelings for both her parents, she concluded by saying her father was a detective who was not allowed to talk about his work but that most of it was in London. In Hazel's mind this added a glamour that almost matched Danique's life. She thought there was very little chance that her friends would ever speak to her parents. But why this lie? At the time she didn't think to question her motives. Perhaps it had something to do with the large difference in their fathers' incomes and possibly Hazel's underlying sense that Danique enjoyed believing she belonged to a higher class. Through being around her friend for thirty-five hours a week Hazel's speech had naturally picked up Danique's perfectly clipped, eloquent English but perhaps now, for the first time in her life, Hazel felt outdone. Growing up as the eldest sibling in a family where they were praised and encouraged to be their own person, she didn't think it could have anything to do with insecurity. But for once here was someone who felt well beyond her equal and envy was not an emotion Hazel had had to deal with before. Or was it a reflection of her competitive nature? These seemed to be her only excuses.

Hazel was not able to get away with lying to her sharp mother and would not have wanted to lie to her father. She had thrown the occasional small white lie at her brothers, which they had believed, but lately she seemed to be able to make acceptable, fictional excuses for not doing or giving in homework on time or for being late to class. Maybe she was helped by her good imagination, in that she could easily live the lie in her head and appear convincing, even though she knew it was false. It certainly wasn't a characteristic she was proud of but neither did she consider it one she should be ashamed of. Perhaps she simply needed to grow up.

CHAPTER 8
1966 ◇ A Visit to Birmingham

While Ray had visited quite often, Hazel had only visited the family home in Birmingham twice. Great-Uncle Chris had employed a housekeeper after his sister died and her husband and son lived on the first floor and had requested their own private kitchen, even though the ground-floor kitchen was extensive. The top floor was leased to a spinster who lived a quiet and very private life, never bothering Hazel's great-uncle. As Chris only lived on the ground floor and had put a bathroom in the only spare room on that floor, there was no longer a bedroom for Ray if he was up north on business. As it had been a year since his uncle's visit, Ray decided to drive up on one of his free Saturdays during the school holidays. Ray asked Hazel if she would like to come. Michael was at Cub camp and Edwina thought she would like to enjoy a day with just John rather than all of them enduring the long drive to Birmingham.

She slept part of the way and happily daydreamed when awake with the radio playing quietly. They did stop a couple of times at cafés so it was not too tedious a drive. Ray parked in the driveway next to Uncle Chris's white mini and they walked around to the front gate and up the black and white chequered path. Ray explained to Hazel a little of the family history.

"The house had belonged to my grandmother, and her family actually had a family crest," he said, while they waited for the front door to be opened.

It duly was by a very sour-faced woman who said nothing as she directed them through the dark, large, square hallway and motioned them to the door on the left. But Hazel stopped, as hung on the wall facing the front door, was a large, commanding painting of a knight in black armour on a black horse. Hazel had visited both the National

Gallery and the Tate Gallery in London and was trying to decide whether this was an actual oil painting or only a print. It was too high for her to touch but she concluded that it was most likely a print as she could not discern any brush strokes. Her father called her name and she entered a large room with a wide, open fireplace. French doors opening on to the rear garden let in light to brighten a room that appeared spacious because it only contained a little furniture.

On further inspection Hazel saw that some of the brightness was due to old, faded and threadbare furniture and furnishings, including a Persian carpet that looked as though all the colour had been scrubbed out of it. There was a heavy oak sideboard, a grandfather clock with two small clocks above the main face, one showing pictorial phases of the moon, the other pictures of the sun, sunrise, sunset and night-time stars with a moon. A slow, deep tick resonated around the room as the pendulum swung. Two armchairs sat either side of the fireplace and a worn sofa faced them. Great-Uncle Chris sat in the armchair nearest the French doors with a small side table next to him. Hazel greeted him with a hug.

After ten minutes of chat the housekeeper brought in a tray with tea and a cake, placed it on the side table and left without a word. Chris invited his nephew to 'play mother', so Ray poured tea for them all and handed Hazel a large piece of Victoria sponge. She had to put her cup and saucer on the floor while she ate. When she had finished her great-uncle suggested she go and explore the garden.

The garden was about twice the size of theirs with a brick outbuilding close to the house with two green, rotting wooden doors. Hazel opened the first to find an old, dirty, musty smelling toilet that had not been used for years, full of cobwebs, spiders and wood lice. The second door hid a lawnmower and a few garden tools. She wandered around slowly, smelling and touching the surrounding shrubs. She presumed that her father and his uncle needed to discuss things and wondered how long she should stay outside. There wasn't anything else to amuse her so, in the absence of a bench, she sat down on the dry grass to watch and listen to the birds. She guessed that after half an hour she could go back in.

When she did return the room was empty so she was able soak in the aged and faded atmosphere. On one wall there was an old gilded mirror with the silver backing breaking down around the corners, next to this were a couple of small watercolours on which she recognised her grandfather's signature. He had some of his watercolours hanging in his house and they had one at home. They were okay but probably wouldn't win any prizes. Hazel secretly hoped that as an experienced adult she would be able to do better. She stopped by the grandfather clock and got lost in its timeless tick-tock, trying to imagine her grandmother hearing this in the background of her life. But even this beautiful piece needed renovating. She heard a door open in the hall and the two men returned. Her father suggested she use the bathroom as they were about to leave. That, at least, was quite modern. Chris was once more seated in his armchair when she returned and gave him a farewell kiss. They made their way back through the hall. Hazel asked her father about the large painting.

"It's the Black Prince," her father replied, "My mother's family came over from France with him. He was the son of King Edward III and father of King Richard II. Although he was never King himself he was one of the original Knights of the Order of the Garter and is said to have been a great military leader. His actual name was Edward of Woodstock, then Prince of Wales. He was called the Black Prince because of his black armour. He's buried in Canterbury Cathedral."

Walking round to the car Hazel's imagination took her again to thoughts of her grandmother passing that picture each day, and then to a family she was descended from who lived in medieval times. She forgot to ask whether *The Black Prince* was an actual oil painting.

CHAPTER 9
1967 ◇ A Teenager

As a thirteen-year-old Hazel rolled over the waist of her school skirt to shorten it and wore long black socks to her knees, but her mother still insisted on scraping her hair into a pony tail, so her ears still stuck out a little. At least her teeth had been straightened. She sometimes saw Simon walking to the bus stop with Lynda. She knew that both Lynda and Danique were more curvaceous and attractive than her. She had no sign of even tiny breasts. She wasn't deeply bothered though. Her mother assured her that she was just a late developer and she knew things would happen at some point. Simon still owned a part of her heart, though.

It was the following year that she became certain she would never be of any importance to him. Two years above Hazel were a group of fifth-form prefects who were close friends of Vanessa, the head girl. One of them, Lisa, was a slim, blonde, petite girl who had developed in all the right places. She had such a stunningly beautiful model's face with high, chiselled cheekbones and large, brilliant blue eyes. It was her character that Hazel questioned. She appeared to treat anyone outside her immediate circle of friends with total distain, especially the younger girls. The only time Hazel ever saw her smile was when she watched another prefect deliberately put out a foot in the corridor as a younger girl ran past. The poor girl fell. Fortunately, she picked herself up and appeared unhurt. Okay, she should not have been running indoors, but Lisa clearly approved of this cruel method of discipline.

After leaving school one afternoon with the usual hordes of boys and girls, Hazel had just settled into a window seat on the top of a double decker bus when she saw Simon walking towards the bus stop. He had his arm around Lisa's shoulder and, with an attentive smile, was watching her face as she spoke. There may even have been a slight smile on Lisa's lips. Hazel felt, as she watched them together, that their relationship would be long term. Why, she had no idea. But she was sure. And she wondered whether Lisa would really make Simon happy. She sincerely hoped so. She cared that much for him.

School routine for Hazel and her three closest friends was becoming boring and an afternoon without an important lesson was open to occasional truancy. They were aware that more than one of them out together during school time might draw attention so they left school separately and met up in St Clement's churchyard in the heart of Leigh-on-Sea. It stands on the upper cliffs overlooking Old Leigh. A church had been on the site since the thirteenth century, the present one dated from the fifteenth century. The ceiling of the north aisle resembles the inverted hull of a ship and may have been constructed by the medieval boat builders of Leigh. While it's only a village church, its position and eighty-foot tower is a beacon on the river, en route to London, standing watch over its thriving fishing community and its history. Smuggling prospered in Essex and secret tunnels were rumoured to run from the old town and up under the cliffs. Certainly, the Peterboat pub had a warren of secret storage chambers.

Directly outside the church porch is a brick tomb with a sandstone top named the 'cutlass stone' as it has a deep fissure worn by the sharpening of knives. The girls, as they gathered to decide what to do during their truancy, felt the long groove and imagined the stories about smugglers sharpening their cutlasses. Or the navy press gangs sharpening knives while waiting to snatch men leaving church for an enforced career at sea. The inscription on the tomb reads: 'Here lies the body of Mary Ellis, daughter of Thomas Ellis and Lydia his wife of the parish. She was a virgin of virtuous courage and very promising hope, and died the 3rd of June 1609, aged 119.' It provoked discussion between the friends on the virtuosity of remaining a virgin and whether you had a better chance of living a longer life if you remained single. Danique and Hazel thought not and promised to be bridesmaids at each other's wedding.

Hazel, standing in the churchyard of this beautiful little church in which she had been baptised, felt that she was also part of this speck of history. She may never be famous and, as she had decided she wanted to be cremated (just in case she was not totally dead and awoke to find herself buried underground), she would not have a gravestone here, but this town was where she felt she truly belonged.

They gathered in a phone box a few times and made some strange phone calls. Hazel ran her finger down the list in the phone book and discovered there was a piggery in Purley. She rang a random number and a woman answered. While she didn't sound too young Hazel decided she wasn't too elderly either and so told the lady she was ringing from Purley Piggery to let her know that her two pigs would be delivered first thing tomorrow morning. The very surprised lady denied any knowledge of this, of course, and advised Hazel that she had the wrong number. Hazel repeated the name by the number she had rung and said that two pigs had definitely been paid for, with delivery to the said lady at her address, so she hoped she would be there to take delivery in the morning, thank you, goodbye. She put the phone down and they all left the phone box in fits of laughter mixed in with plenty of swearing. Their swearing had developed to such an extent that most sentences contained at least one or two expletives. These were kept purely for their own ears and rarely used within range of any adults.

Inside school they regularly raided the over-ordered cartons of milk that were waiting to be returned to the dairy – not too terrible. However, waiting on the bridge over the main walkway with a plastic bag full of water to drop on teachers as they went underneath at break time was stretching it. The first time, Lee held the bag and dropped it just as Mrs Head was passing under them. They immediately ducked and tore down the nearest stairway so were unable to witness what actually happened. They'd not heard a scream so after five minutes ventured out to the path. There was a damp patch but no bag in sight. Danique told her friends later that her French teacher appeared completely dry with her hair still beautifully coiffured. Maybe they'd missed. Later that week Miss Jacks was not so lucky. In assembly the following morning Miss Wiseman reported that dropping water from bridges would not be tolerated and any girl discovered doing this would be expelled. Ha, so they didn't know who had drenched Miss Jacks!

At home problems were brewing between Michael and John. When John was small he had become used to his sister looking after his needs if she was around, as his brother had. But during his first couple of weeks at school John discovered his own strong identity. Hazel, while being surprised to find that he no longer needed her help with anything, was not overly upset by this total change and concluded that this was fine and normal.

However, Michael was not happy that his little brother was no longer compliant around him and that he wanted to play by himself. He couldn't accept it and presumed he could play with any of John's toys whenever he wished, regardless of whether his brother was in the middle of playing with them himself. Arguments between the two brothers began to erupt regularly. Hazel did hear her parents arguing occasionally and it was something she hated. Edwina generally sorted the boys arguments if she was about but, with a mortgage to pay, she had returned, part-time and still as a bookkeeper, to the pipe manufacturer that she had worked for before Hazel was born. The job was perfect as they allowed her to choose her hours to suit school time. Rosemary had now retired so was able to look after the children during the holidays but every now and then Edwina asked Hazel to watch over her brothers for a short while. Michael took advantage of his mother's absence by tormenting his younger brother. Hazel heard their raised voices coming from her brother's bedroom. She crept quietly up the stairs to listen outside the door.

"I'm going to pull off his head and stamp on it if you don't let me play with him," Michael shouted.

Hazel opened the door just as he was snatching John's Action Man by its head from his brother's hands. John had tears pouring down his face. She was furious.

"Give it back to him and leave him alone, Michael."

He wouldn't so, since she was still taller and stronger, she managed to wrestle the toy from him intact, but he snatched it back as she handed it to John. It led to a real fight, with Hazel finally retrieving it and running downstairs. Michael followed her and the fight continued at the bottom of the stairs. But he was no longer a small child and she thought that if she was going to end this, the cupboard under the stairs was her only option as her brother was refusing to listen or to accept he was in the wrong. She was not happy about bundling him in and shutting the door. He kicked it a couple of times before going quiet.

Hazel said he was not to treat his brother in that bullying way and she would let him out when he calmed down. Which she did and no more was said between them about the matter.

It wasn't always Michael she had to chastise. Sometimes it was John who started their scraps but at least he conceded to his sister's authority. One time, though, when Hazel had to break up a fight between her brothers, she ended up fighting desperately with Michael at the top of the stairs until she managed to shove him off her and run down the stairs. He didn't follow but John appeared downstairs a few minutes later and told her she must have a magic touch as Michael had fallen asleep. Worried by the thought that she had rendered him unconscious, she immediately went to check. But he had gone. She opened his bedroom door and, to her relief, he was sitting at his desk, occupied with a model.

The second time Hazel had to shut Michael in the cupboard to end a fight she told her mother. But when their mother was not there he was not frightened enough of the cupboard and continued to fight his sister with all his strength whenever he felt she was getting the better of him. These fights continued for a few years, with the cupboard being the ultimate end, until she had to accept that her brother was her equal in strength. She still shouted or intervened whenever an argument was not quickly resolved, but she refused to fight and John now seemed to be old enough and wily enough to manage his own disagreements.

The following Christmas Hazel's parents bought her a secondhand red bike. It looked almost new. This allowed her to sign up with the newsagent at the bottom of her road to do a newspaper round. At the time all the rounds were covered but a spare person was needed to turn up each weekday morning and wait in case someone didn't turn up. She was paid a little less than those assigned to a round but it was topped up whenever she filled someone's place. She was happy to earn her pocket money this way. The quietness of the early morning roads felt calming before the onslaught of school.

Sadly, Grandpa Alf died of a heart attack that spring. The funeral was during the week and her parents felt that the children did not need to go as it necessitated taking them out of school. They were not close to their paternal grandfather. He had not been a warm, cuddly grandfather like Grandpa Dorrit. So, while Hazel was sad it was more for her father, although he seemed to bear it well. She had been more upset when, a year previously, someone had left Grandpa Alf's gate open and Puck had run out into the road and been run over. He had been replaced by a yappy, snappy Jack Russell named Skippy that their grandfather had adored. But Hazel thought Skippy was a poor replacement and he continued to irritate the children for his long doggy life. It was strange now to visit with her grandfather's dominant presence absent, and not having to worry so much about what she was doing. It was great that Arthur was there more often. This may have been to keep his mother company. However, he often had one or other of his girlfriends with him, so didn't think to play with his niece or nephews anymore, which saddened Hazel.

Another holiday, this time to Pontins in Brixham. They left early and went by car. Edwina had packed a breakfast of hard-boiled eggs and sandwiches, which they ate while sitting among the giant stones at Stonehenge. There were no restrictions around the stones then. As it was still early and only a few other people were there Hazel was able to get a sense of a long ago time. She took her mind back to an utterly different age. She put the sun behind a stone just enough to block out its blinding light, and raised her voice.

"Good morning, Sun," she shouted. It echoed. She was not aware of having read about the circle's acoustics, but as she heard her echoes she felt that acoustics were somehow very important to this place.

At Pontins, Michael and Hazel had their own wooden cabin just opposite the one shared by their parents and John. They didn't misuse what felt like a grown-up privilege, so no midnight feasts or secretly slipping out.

Having a car meant they could visit local villages and Dartmoor. But what was most memorable for Hazel was dropping her Ilford camera, a birthday present from her parents, in a rockpool. She and Michael were enjoying their usual clamber over the rocky coastline, investigating any fish or creatures in the pools, when the camera, that had felt secure over her shoulder, dropped with a splash into the water. She grabbed it and quickly ran to her father. He said he would have to open it, which meant destroying anything on the film, to see if it could be dried out. He took it back to his cabin, gently dried out what he could with one of his clean large white handkerchiefs and left it on a sunny windowsill to dry out completely. A couple of days later he put a new film in but the winder would not wind on after the shutter had been pressed. Her father told her there was nothing that could be done. It ruined her holiday. It had been such a cherished, valuable camera and she had mindlessly destroyed it. She daren't ask for another one.

Panda was now fourteen and losing control of his bowels. It was distressing for all the family to see and Panda was upset by it too. The vet said it was simply old age and no pills would help. After a sad discussion it was decided that the kindest thing would be to let the vet put him to sleep. He'd had a happy and loved life. Hazel cried that night in bed. He had always been there. It was the first time that death really had a direct impact on her. She wanted so much to believe in heaven because surely she would find him there. His presence in her life had given so much pleasure and loving company, she couldn't imagine a perfect place without him.

At fifteen Hazel was working towards her O-levels in maths, English with English literature, history, geography, biology and art. By now she was resigned to the fact that she would not reach five feet six inches, which meant no chance of joining the police force (her lie about her father's profession had remained undetected). Architecture was her next passion. Seven long years of study. To date she had scraped through senior school lessons and all her homework with the minimum work possible but had managed to climb from near the bottom of her class in her first year to a passable twelfth place in her fourth year. Now she knew the rest of her life might depend on the work she put in, so began to study more seriously.

Guides had been replaced by Rangers. Hazel belonged to a small group, including Louise and Jill, who were practising club swinging. The clubs were large wooden batons that the girls held, one in each hand, and twirled around in time to music. Their leader was Jackie, who had been an assistant through Hazel's Guiding years. Her sister Lynn was a few years older than Hazel and now acted as helper to her older sister. Hazel liked them both. There was a club swinging competition at Butlin's in Bognor Regis and Jackie organised a three-day trip to stay at the camp and enter the competition. They practised quite intensively for the first two days but nerves affected them a little during the competition and they came fourth. But it had been an enjoyable few days and a party was arranged for their final evening at the camp. They'd been aware that a rugby team was also staying, a group of well-behaved, well-muscled, good-looking lads. They were also invited to the party.

Hazel had brought her favourite dress with her. The top layer was a fine voile, deep green with a softly blended pattern of lighter green and bluish leaves and sleeves finished with gentle ruffles. It was lined with a dark-green, silky material. It was slim and short, showed off her shapely legs, hugged her slim waist and accentuated her little curves. Her mother had bought her some bras a while ago but she still had to fill them with the cut-off legs of some old tights! Her look was completed with dark tights and ankle boots with heels. She'd bought some dark green and grey eye make-up and discovered her eyes were actually a greeny-blue.

She gathered with her Rangers group in the hall. She loved to dance and the DJ had a great selection of contemporary music that got her swaying and bouncing along almost immediately. She persuaded Jill and Louise to join her on the dance floor. They weren't as enthusiastic and after a few dances left her to enjoy herself with Jackie, Lynn and girls from the other groups. The rugby guys joined in and danced among them. There was no pairing off though. One amazingly handsome, tanned, golden-haired, young man politely danced near and around Jackie and Lynn. They clearly enjoyed the attention. Hazel was surprised that he also threw her a couple of smiles, which she returned. At the end of the evening as the music was winding down he stepped up to Jackie to speak to her. Hazel presumed he was choosing his favourite lady to spend the last few minutes with. Jackie nodded in agreement but he walked over to Hazel.

He had to bend right down to whisper in her ear, "Please may I walk you back to your cabin?"

Total shock and pleasure swept through her. Really? The best looking guy there was asking her! She composed herself instantly, lifted her face to his very blue eyes and said, "Yes. Thank you."

With a hand gently against her back he guided her to a glass door that led out into the gardens. Hazel pointed out the direction to her cabin and they walked slowly side by side. Outwardly, she was calm and easily entered into conversation. Inwardly, she was overwhelmed and honoured to be walking alongside this stunning man. They exchanged names and Allen said he was twenty-two. If he was surprised when Hazel announced she was only fifteen, he didn't show it. Too soon they reached her cabin. He turned towards her and gently took her hands. He drew her into his arms, then cupped her chin as he bent softly to kiss her. Lips to lips. Then she felt his tongue as it began to very slowly brush across them. She parted her lips and his tongue slid tentatively into her mouth. She melted into his body, his subtle masculine aftershave enveloped her heightened senses and she felt the hardness of his erection. After a timeless moment he withdrew his mouth. He still held her and she raised her eyes to his, wishing time would freeze.

Seconds later he broke her wish and said, "You are a lucky young lady. You'll have many admiring men in your life. Thank you so much for your company."

He released her and gave her hands a final squeeze before turning and walking away. Attempting to swim back to reality, Hazel let herself into her cabin. She silently thanked *Jackie* magazine's preparation and hoped he hadn't realised it wasn't all her in her bra.

Danique had been spending Friday evenings at the Leigh Youth Club since she was fourteen but Hazel's parents insisted that she was too young to be out alone in the evening. Because of this, she sensed a distance growing in their friendship. She also knew that the other three smoked regularly and at lunchtime was happy to enjoy the odd herbal tobacco rolled up in liquorice paper with them but refused to add anything else. She made it clear to her friends that she had no intention of even experimenting. She hated the idea of something other than her own free will taking control. But one lunchtime at Danique's house she accepted a cup of tea and as she drank it she thought the taste was slightly odd but concluded it was probably just the sterilised milk Danique's mother bought. As they were leaving to walk back to school, though, her legs felt wobbly and her eyesight began to blur. She was livid with her friends and told them so. They had drunk alcohol at Danique's occasionally and Hazel had drunk a large glass of sherry at home once when no one was about, but whatever they had put in her tea felt stronger than that. She remained with her friends only because it felt safer given the weird state she was in. She concentrated hard on walking as naturally as she could. Somehow she managed to get through the afternoon without anyone questioning her, so she couldn't have appeared too bad. By the time she got home she felt almost normal. Not the best way to discover your friends weren't to be trusted. She concluded that it was possibly human nature and the only person one could trust was oneself.

Hazel decided to continue to sit with Danique for most lessons (and face the 'devil' she knew rather than discover it in someone else) and her friend began to enthuse about a boy. Tim was two years older and went to the Leigh Youth Club. His father was manager of the off-licence opposite the Youth Club and they lived in the flat above. He went to Belfairs boys' school and Danique pointed him out one day as they walked out of school. He was quite short and rather stocky but had long, pale brown, curling hair that was bleached almost golden on top by the sun. With a tan to match he wasn't unattractive. Hazel listened politely to Danique's constant chatter about him. Then, unexpectedly, after more pestering her mother agreed that Hazel could go to the Youth Club. She had learnt to use a sewing machine at school and sewn up a couple of short, well-fitting skirts and had bought two fine-knitted, tight-fitting jumpers to go with them. She decided that with make-up, dark tights and knee-high boots she wouldn't look too shabby next to her stylish and voluptuous friend.

Danique was disappointed that Tim didn't appear that week. Hazel actually found it boring. The boys played pool and darts but the girls just sat around chatting and giggling. It felt like a long evening but she agreed to go the following week. After an hour or so Danique excitedly nudged Hazel. Tim had just walked in. He acknowledged Danique with a slight smile and disappeared among a group of boys. Clearly there was not much there that interested him as he left not long after. Hazel thought she was not going to be able to endure many more weeks of this boredom. Rangers was more exciting.

Danique suggested they got some chips from the fish 'n chip shop over the road. It was empty, so they were served immediately. Just as they stepped away from the counter with their open bags of chips, Tim walked in and asked, "Which of you lovely ladies has got a chip for me?"

Hazel glanced at Danique. What was she doing? Danique appeared to be fluttering her eyelids and licking her lips, but saying nothing. Hazel's natural desire to share took over and she held out her bag.

"Please, have one of mine."

Tim took a chip, thanked her and they followed him outside. He stopped and turned to them.

Hazel said, "You're welcome to have another chip."

As he took another Hazel was lost as to why Danique was not trying to enter into conversation with him. After an awkward silence Danique finally said she was walking home. Tim asked where she lived. She told him as she roughly gestured in the direction she was going. Hazel, presuming Tim would walk with Danique, said goodbye and turned to walk in the opposite direction. Just as she did so, she heard him exclaim, "Hang on. Can I follow your chips?"

They slipped into easy conversation as they walked. She laughed at the light humour that peppered his observations on life. As they reached the top of her road he asked if he could take her to the pictures next week. It wasn't without a conscience that she said yes and wondered later whether, if the roles had been reversed, Danique would have done the same. She spent the following week floating in happiness. He hadn't kissed her but she was sure it would happen. Oh dear, what should she do about the tights in her bra! She did have small mounds there now. She decided that she'd dispense with the tights and hope he didn't notice the discrepancy in size.

Once comfy in her relationship with Tim, she asked him why he had chosen her over a girl she'd always believed was much more attractive. He replied that she had sparkling eyes, a lovely smile and a naturalness that had really drawn him. While this was not such a glamorous explanation, it held an honesty that did not disappoint her. Surprisingly, Danique appeared to accept defeat. As to why she had not said anything on that fateful day at the chip shop, she told Hazel she had been "trying to think of something witty to say!"

Growing up so close to her father and brothers, Hazel fell into a deep, seemingly equal partnership with Tim. He loved the outdoors, in particular fishing up and down the coast – from the pier, from beaches and from boats. He soon made it clear that Hazel was his preferred companion on these trips, although they were both happy to be joined, occasionally, by his fishing mates.

The only one unhappy with this relationship was Michael. He knew Tim from school and explained to Hazel how, as a dinner monitor, Tim would hand out smaller portions to younger boys and keep the best bits for himself, something that other monitors didn't do. Michael decided this demonstrated an unfair nature. Hazel could not see this in him and was shocked one day to find the front door open and her brother and boyfriend fighting on the front path. She ran out and broke it up. She never did discover the cause of the fight. Later, she sternly told her brother he had to accept Tim as a boyfriend who treated her with great care and not at all unfairly. She even thanked him – although she didn't tell her brother this – for stopping her smoking. Tim had come around one afternoon after she'd returned from school. On giving her a welcoming kiss, he smelt on her breath the herbal cigarette that she'd smoked as she left school with her friends. Both his parents smoked but he actively didn't and told Hazel her breath smelt off-putting and she must stop. After a short argument, with Hazel trying to convince him that herbal cigarettes were different, she acquiesced.

The following summer her parents booked a family holiday in Zeebrugge, Belgium, for a week. Hazel was spending most of her spare time with Tim and the thought of a week away from him felt unbearable. Emotionally and physically they were tied together far more tightly than her parents might have wished. Sex had been an adventure for them both as Tim was also a virgin when they began their relationship. She had only been fifteen when they started dating and they decided to wait until she was sixteen, although it wasn't easy. They had discussed it in depth and only days after her sixteenth birthday she said she was happy for them to indulge fully as long as she could be on top and have control. They chose an afternoon when they knew his parents would be out. He showed her how to fit a condom. Relax, relax, Hazel told herself and it had all been surprisingly easy and quick. Not actually painful.

It is a peculiar transition in that it happens instantly. One minute you're a virgin, the next you're not! A little blood on her knickers had confirmed that she was a virgin no more. The revelation that she could now use her unproblematic, regular, monthly cycle to produce a baby was astounding, and left her childhood firmly behind her.

After a few months of fumbling around with condoms Hazel booked an appointment to see Dr Quinn. She explained that she and her boyfriend had been together now for almost a year and cared deeply for each other and that she really felt that it would be safest to go on the pill. At the time there was controversy over whether doctors should inform parents if young girls asked to go on the pill. Hazel was confident her doctor would treat her request with confidential respect as he'd known her all her life. He instructed her that regular check-ups were important as he handed her a prescription and to see him immediately if she had any problems. Fortunately, she had none.

Getting up early to stand around at the newsagent, waiting to see who might not turn up for their paper round was becoming tedious and, after Tim had a chat with his father, Ron offered Hazel a Saturday morning job, working behind the counter of the off-licence. It was a valuable experience on how to be pleasant to everyone and, as a lot of customers bought more than a single bottle, Ron taught her how to add the items up in her head.

Hazel suggested she stayed with her grandparents while her family went away. The answer was a definite no. She was not happy. Adolescent love had devoured her so completely she had no use for her family if it meant not seeing Tim, regardless of the fact it was only for a week.

Edwina says she thought Hazel did enjoy the holiday a little. All Hazel remembers is wandering behind her family alongside a river in Bruges, staring into the dark green murk, thinking of Tim and trying to imagine his thoughts at that moment. Her family may have thought she was enjoying herself but, really, she felt empty.

Back at home Hazel continued to attend weekly Rangers meetings. One dark evening after a meeting, she was walking home down her road, deep in thought but vaguely aware of a man in a hooded sweatshirt and jeans running down the other side of the road. She thought nothing of it as he stopped to tie up his shoelace. Moments later she felt a hand go up her skirt. Rage made her swing round and roar out, "What the bloody hell do you think you are doing?"

Possibly not what he had expected. He turned and ran up the road. Hazel quickly walked home, sure he had disappeared. It wasn't until she opened the front door that she started to shake. She called out to her parents that she was tired and going to bed. She sat on her bed and digested what had happened. Had she unnerved him or was a hand up her skirt all he would have attempted? With his hood pulled up she had seen no more of his face than an impression that he was probably not much older than her. She didn't believe she would recognise him if she saw him again. As she began to calm down, she went downstairs to the telephone in the hall, rang Tim and told him exactly what had happened. He said he would go out straightaway to look for him. She dissuaded him, saying that by now he would have gone. She later questioned whether she should have reported it, in case it saved someone else from the experience, but her gut feeling was that rape was not his intention. But who was she to make such an assumption?

She continued to walk to and from Rangers for a few more weeks without incident but then decided that her time would be better spent on homework or with Tim. But for many years after, the sound of footsteps behind her when she was out at night, or occasionally during the day, would elicit a rising fear. This only calmed down if she stopped and allowed whoever it was to pass.

Around this time, her father received the biggest disappointment imaginable. In February of that year the whole family had visited Uncle Chris in Birmingham. He'd had a minor heart attack and his bed had been placed in the lounge while he recovered. The housekeeper had again made them all tea and supplied a cake, still without a word or smile. Chris assured his nephew that she was looking after him well. They stayed until the old man was obviously tiring and all kissed him goodbye.

Ray visited him again in April and although his bed was still in the lounge, Ray reported he'd been up and sitting in his armchair. Chris once more assured his nephew that he was being well looked after. Sadly, in May he had a fatal heart attack. Ray wrote to inform his sister and knew that, although she had occasionally written to her uncle from Australia, she would not fly over for his funeral. Ray went alone as it meant staying overnight in Birmingham.

Days later a letter arrived from the solicitor informing Ray that the house and most of the contents had been left to the housekeeper. All their uncle had bequeathed to Ray and Bess was the family bible and some Spode crockery. Edwina explained this to Hazel and said that her father was going to discuss contesting the will with a solicitor. Hazel watched hopelessly as her pale, drawn father attempted to carry on as normal. Unfortunately, as Chris's GP could only say that he had been of sound mind right up to his death, the solicitor concluded that the time and cost involved in attempting to overturn such a will would be great and that they would most likely lose. Ray had presumed he would have inherited enough to have been able to at least pay off their mortgage, even perhaps purchase a semi-detached house. But he was more upset by the fact that the uncle that he had loved dearly had so totally dismissed him. Hazel knew he was affected deeply, but the joy he felt about his children did not dim, so on the surface nothing seemed to change.

All too soon O-level exam time closed in. They had one small common room for the whole of their year to revise in. It was always noisy. Someone even brought in a radio. Hazel couldn't concentrate. Since her previous occasional truancy had never been found out she now went home on most of her free afternoons to revise seriously. Usually out in the garden, lying on her stomach on a towel, elbows bent to allow her hands to support her chin. So peaceful, with only birdsong to distract her.

It may have been Miss Jordon who reported her absences. As their geography teacher she had taken most of the class on a week's field trip to Wales. The majority of the trip had been very enjoyable. They stayed in a youth hostel. A group of younger boys were also there. A couple of them hung around Hazel and Danique and the girls didn't discourage them, rather to Miss Jordon's disdain. However, one night towards the end of the week Hazel was ill. It began with severe stomach pains and soon she was having to dash to the portaloos across a yard from the cabin she shared with Danique and a couple of other girls. She spent most of the night running across the yard. The stench from these toilets was enough to turn the stomach of even a healthy person. That night was deeply etched in her memory. By morning she felt very weak but at least the pains had subsided. She asked Danique to let Miss Jordon know she had been up all night with bad diarrhoea and wouldn't be able to come on the twenty-mile walk they were to do that day. Danique returned to say Miss Jordon insisted she came on the walk. Hazel was shocked and said surely her teacher must come and check on her. She certainly wasn't able to eat any breakfast. How could she walk twenty miles on an empty stomach, feeling this weak? Danique returned to say Miss Jordon wouldn't change her mind. How she managed that walk she's not sure. Later in the day she did struggle through a bag of crisps but that was all. She somehow found a robotic state that allowed her to put one foot in front of the other and straggled behind the others. She should have complained to her parents when she returned home but didn't. She was not able to forgive her geography teacher and hardly bothered to go to any more lessons with her. Miss Jordon said nothing so she ceased going altogether. She did worry a little about this but as the teacher appeared to allow it to happen, Hazel did nothing.

Her parents were obviously very unhappy to receive a letter from the headmistress stating that Hazel was playing truant and had been seen with a group of boys and that consequently she was going to do badly in all her exams. Hazel was upset by this lie. Tim was now working for May and Baker in Dagenham and fortunately her parents did seem to believe her when she assured them that she had not, at any time, met with any boys and only came home because it was impossible to revise in the small common room, especially as someone usually brought in a radio. However, the accusations did add extra impetus to her revision. She would fail geography but she was determined to get the, very acceptable in those days, five O-levels. The marks for her English mock were a shock to both Hazel and Miss Speed as this and geography were her only low marks in the mocks. She couldn't understand it since her general school marks were more than passable. Her teacher suggested she shouldn't sit the exam until November of the following year. The school was offering A-level art with art history that year and, to fill a little more time, Hazel decided to do craft O-level, which in this case was weaving on tabletop Harris looms. Learning how to mix textiles and colours seemed interesting. An easy final year. In total she achieved six O-levels and one A-level, so a year for a diploma in art at Southend Technical College was next. Then the lengthy path to architecture.

Hazel had discussed this all with Tim but as the time came to sign up at the college he voiced his displeasure, to the extent of issuing her with an ultimatum. If she was seriously going to follow a laborious path towards such a career, he could see no point in them staying together. Did she not want to get married, buy a house and eventually have a family? She considered this in depth over a couple of days and, yes, this was ultimately what she wanted. She had helped Tim to get an HND in chemistry by explaining to him how brackets worked in algebra. He had failed in his first attempt due to being unable to get his head around what to do. He now had a well-paid job with Shell. It meant shift work but Hazel had no problem with that. They loved each other deeply, didn't they? Spent all their spare time together. She knew he was reliable. What more could she wish for? He suggested they went on holiday together to help dispel any doubts she might have.

Hazel got on brilliantly with Tim's parents, Ron and Audrey, and they asked if she could go with them for two weeks in a caravan to their regular holiday destination, Portland in Devon. Ray and Edwina were okay with this arrangement but sad that it coincided with their holiday to Italy. She would miss Florence, the Sistine chapel, all the art she loved. However, they could not dissuade her. Wherever Tim was going she had to go and she fell in love with the wildness of Portland and even more deeply with Tim. She sketched the rocky coastline dotted with old derricks and fished with Tim during the day and by gas lamp at night and most times caught at least a pollack or codling or some mackerel. She was equally happy just sitting next to him and reading. They visited Weymouth and the Swannery at Abbotsbury, went for long walks and watched the sun set over Chesil Beach. There was a large go-cart track on the road to Portland. The four of them went one morning as soon as it opened and were the only ones there. Hazel and Tim's dad definitely had the fastest cars and fought each other ruthlessly to win. His dad did. Just.

Once home it did seem pointless to spend years studying when Tim would earn enough for them to be comfortable. Hazel did hear her parents arguing about her final decision not to go to college. Her mother believed she should continue studying but her father said, "What was the point as she would only get married and have a family?"

Such were things in the early 1970s.

Unfortunately, Hazel had not factored into her decision that the extra years of study might have given her free spirit a chance to expand and mature.

CHAPTER 10
1971 ◇ The World of Work

What to do instead? Ray suggested she look for a job as a model maker or he could ask if there was a vacancy at the British Museum. Hazel knew the museum well. Her father's office was only around the corner and, as he had designed many of the new glass display cases, he was well-known there. He had sometimes taken Hazel with him to work on a Saturday morning. When she was younger she would sit at a desk and draw but as she got older he trusted the staff at the museum to keep an eye on her as she explored and absorbed all the exhibits. Ray reported that they needed an assistant in the restoration department. Simultaneously a vacancy for an assistant model maker with a design company in Shepherd's Bush was advertised. Hazel applied and was interviewed for both jobs.

The design company was housed in one of the few remaining exhibition buildings from the Franco-British Exhibition of 1908 (later called White City). She was interviewed by the model maker, Mr Munday, as he took her on a tour of the building. The vast upper floor with its glass roof was totally empty apart from a small fork lift. Here, she was told, the company made and housed props for the BBC, which was just down the road in another building from the exhibition. The emptiness suggested that they weren't too busy at the moment but the bright openness of such an enormous area tweaked cords in Hazel's imagination. The company was not large, with four designers and himself. He explained that apart from the props, the majority of the models were smaller and they used a variety of materials – plastics, acrylics and wood – and the job would involve some local travel to pick up supplies.

The museum's restoration department, in contrast, was a rather dark, enclosed area with only the few current projects lit up. Hazel would have been happy to accept either of these jobs. She received a letter first from the museum saying that all prospective employees had to pass a vetting process and that they would advise her as soon as this was completed. In the meantime, she received a job offer from the design company saying they would like her to start immediately. While Ray assured her that there was no reason she would not pass the museum's vetting process, Hazel made the decision to become an assistant model maker and travel five days a week by train and underground to Shepherd's Bush.

If her father was going to the office, she enjoyed travelling up with him in his car and he would drop her at Holborn, allowing her to complete the journey via the underground. It was great at the end of a busy day to look forward to relaxing on the drive home in her father's company. His driving was not gentle, though, and he displayed the fast reactions of a trained pilot as he shot around the London back streets and slow drivers. Her mother hated his fast driving. Hazel loved it. Ray wanted to enter rally driving with Hazel as a map reader. It was Hazel rather than his wife that Ray would insist read the map for him whenever they were travelling somewhere new. However, to their joint disappointment, she would start to feel queasy if she had to follow a map for any length of time. It was the same with reading a book in a car. So rally driving was not to be.

Hazel loved her job. Brian Munday was an easy man to work for and would take her out in his Morris Traveller to introduce her to suppliers or to transport models. Making them under his instruction was not difficult and only once did she slice the very tip of her finger off with a Stanley knife. A plaster from the workshop's first aid box, deftly applied by Brian, meant that the piece of finger actually reattached itself quite quickly. Keith, the youngest designer, occasionally took her to the BBC for lunch or for walks in Shepherd's Bush Park. He was twenty-six, tall, slim and dark-haired with a beard. Hazel was a little disturbed that, as time went on, she would not have minded if he had kissed her. He was single and gave the impression that a past break-up had hurt deeply, although he spoke very little of his private life. He appeared to enjoy her company and listened patiently as she wittered on about life in general, but he respected the difference in their ages.

As Hazel neared her eighteenth birthday Tim suggested they try camping together. Unsure of how her parents would feel about this, they discussed getting engaged. The decision not to go to college and university had been taken on the understanding that Hazel thought marriage, homemaking and children were ultimately more important than a career. Tim was reliable and caring with enough income to ensure that, while far from being rich, they would have enough to live on without any major financial worries. She loved him and never doubted the strength of his love for her. Getting engaged felt like a natural step.

Tim nervously approached Ray one evening to ask formally for Hazel's hand in marriage. Her parents did have some reservations, to do with the hope they had of her finding someone from a family socially higher than that of an off-licence manager, but they did not voice this to the young couple. Ray had joined Tim a couple of times for a pleasant few hours fishing off the pier and as he was now so often at their house the two men were slowly building an alliance. To Tim's relief Ray reassured him they would be happy to have him as a son-in-law but because of his daughter's age requested that they wait a year before getting married.

Hazel was delighted when they visited a small secondhand jeweller in the heart of Leigh-on-Sea and chose a small diamond solitaire ring set in a fine band of eighteen-carat gold. Burlington was stamped inside the band alongside the hallmarks. Small but so beautiful as it glinted and sparkled. Tim paid a deposit and they left it to be sized down for her slim finger.

Back then, eighteenth birthdays were not celebrated. It was twenty-one that marked one's entry into the adult world. Hazel's eighteenth fell on a Thursday, a normal working day unfortunately, but Tim came around once she had returned from work and in front of her parents he produced the little box. Tears rolled from her eyes as she lifted the lid to see her own dear little diamond shining up at her and she gently lifted the ring from its velvet bed. She passed it to Tim and asked him to slide it on to her finger. Such a perfect fit. More tears as she hugged her fiancé. Her parents were smiling as they congratulated them. She called to her brothers to show off her ring. Even Michael had slowly come to terms with his sister's boyfriend. Tim then took Hazel to a local restaurant for a quiet celebratory meal. They were very happy.

Tim had passed his driving test the previous year and bought a 1952 blue-grey VW beetle with a split rear screen. Hazel loved the deep throaty roar from its rear-mounted engine as Tim turned on the ignition. He was a gentle driver in contrast to her father and she was looking forward to filling it full of borrowed camping equipment for their first holiday together. Why a campsite in Canterbury was decided upon for their first long weekend away together, Hazel has no idea. And, surprisingly, the details of this break together are also forgotten. It may have been wet. However, they enjoyed it enough to buy their own igloo tent afterwards. It had a six-foot square groundsheet stitched to a blue dome of canvas that was attached to two rubber tubes that crossed at the top. As the tubes were inflated using a foot pump the igloo just rose. They chose it because it was easily erected in any weather once the groundsheet was firmly pegged down and, with the rest of the pegs in at the correct angle, it could withstand strong winds and rain. Which was what they might encounter camping wild on the edge of Portland! It had to be tested. They booked two weeks off in June to travel down to Dorset.

Back at work, another designer, Ramsey, who was thirty-one, had no respect for the difference in age to Hazel, or the fact that she was newly engaged. When Brian was out or on holiday he began to venture down from the design studios to the basement workshop to find Hazel. Initially he would come down just for a chat. Then he asked her if she liked Indian curries as the restaurant down the road was very acceptable.

"Why not?" agreed Hazel.

Apart from secretary Shirley, who was very efficient at her job but preferred not to mix with anyone, she was the only female in the firm and she felt at home in the company of men. 'So why not just roll with it?' she thought. Ramsey showed Hazel photographs of his two children and his wife, who was an extremely attractive lady with dark, curly hair and an enviable figure ("thirty-eight, twenty-four, thirty-eight," Ramsey informed her). After taking her out for a few lunchtime curries they returned one afternoon to be told by Shirley that Brian would be out for the rest of the day. Ramsey followed Hazel down to the workshop. As soon as the door closed behind them he enclosed her in his arms and kissed her. Passion took over her clear thinking and her body said, 'Yes, yes I want it all!' Still standing, Ramsey pressed her against the wall of the workshop. Hardly the most romantic way for sex. But, hey, it worked in films! Afterwards guilt gripped her. She voiced this while he was still holding her, explaining that she really did not want to hurt his wife or Tim, in any way. If it was to continue they must never know. He assured her it would remain a secret and admitted to another affair many years previously that had not been found out.

Fortunately, no one ever came into the workshop when Brian was out and they discovered secluded spots in Holland Park and other no longer remembered places. Hazel mentally slotted this into yet another life experience. After all, regardless of how Ramsey wished to live his life, she was not yet married. She argued with herself that once married she could remain faithful with no regrets for not having first played the field.

Six months later Ramsey's wife took the children away for a weekend to her mother's and he asked Hazel to spend the time at his home. She was pleased to be considered this important but slightly scared to comply in case his wife found out. Ramsey was insistent that this would not happen. Hazel told Tim and her parents she had to attend a weekend conference and caught the train to West Ham where Ramsey met her and took her, by bus, to his house. It was terraced, no larger than her own but stylishly decorated with a minimalistic Art Deco atmosphere. Her greatest surprise was the large mirror on the ceiling above the bed. She was not naive enough to believe Ramsey when he said his wife had lost all interest in sex after the birth of their children but she was not bothered by whether or not it was true. He filled in some sexual knowledge Tim had yet to learn. Hazel had no wish to hurt Tim but time with Ramsey continued to feel a planet away from home and her life with him.

During the early 1970s, England had entered a recession and model-making orders had been shrinking to the point of virtual extinction. Hazel was occupied helping out in the studio by tracing drawings. The cost of her rail fair was increasing, as was the time Ray spent visiting outside London and was unable to give her a lift. She had not had a salary increase since she'd started work. The company director explained that while they were happy with her work they could not afford to increase her pay. She was spending three hours a day travelling and was beginning to feel it was no longer worth it.

A barmaid vacancy came up for the small student bar at lunchtimes in the basement of a pub close to Southend Technical College. Tim was not too happy about it but Hazel assured him it would give her time to look for something more suitable. They had made friends with the young manager of the Peterboat pub in Old Leigh and his wife, as they sometimes enjoyed an evening meal there. They were soon invited to stay beyond closing time. Hazel's parents never went to a pub but she felt at ease among the lively company.

She attended an interview at the Southend pub for the student bar and later that day the manager rang and offered her the job. She handed her notice in to the design company and left a month later, saying goodbye to Ramsey and, more sadly, to Keith. He had known of her affair and while he had not actively voiced disapproval she knew it had altered his view of her. Married Ramsey was not an adventure she was proud of either.

Serving drinks to the lively bunch of students that poured into the basement bar at lunchtimes was challenging initially. Tim's father had taught her how to mentally add up set amounts with speed when she'd worked in his off-licence so she soon picked up the pace. But ensuring the till was spot on and not a few pence over or under at the end of the day seemed impossible to achieve. She was told that overall, weekly, it seemed to balance out, so Sue the under-manager didn't make much of an issue out of it. The manager and his wife were a pleasant enough couple to work for and Hazel got on reasonably well with Sue as she helped her behind the upstairs bar in the morning. The upstairs clientele were mainly old retired men who came in for some company. Tim offered the opinion that they also enjoyed ogling her and he soon asked, "Wasn't it time she found another job?"

She was regularly checking both the London and local papers but had seen nothing. During her second week at the pub, a guy that Hazel instantly recognised as Richie Warwick, who had been in Tim's class at school, came down into the basement bar. She'd watched him at the Leigh Regatta, the previous summer, climb the greasy pole with amazing agility right to the top. A feat rarely achieved by anyone. Although his hair was thinning, he had a stunningly tanned torso! He knew Hazel was Tim's girlfriend and they chatted a little as she served him. He returned the following week and asked what time she finished and was she doing anything. Tim just happened to be working the afternoon/evening shift so she said she had nothing planned.

"There's a great pub in Maldon I'd like to show you," he said.

After impatiently waiting for Sue to till up, Hazel left to find Richie just outside with his car parked over the road. Maldon was on the list of local towns that her father liked to take the family to for a Sunday walk. It was an attractive hilltop town overlooking the Blackwater estuary, just up the coast from Southend, with a history dating back to the Saxon period. At the base of the hill was Hythe, originally a separate village but for over a thousand years it had been the port for the town. Thames barges were always moored along its quay. Richie parked near the quay outside the Jolly Sailor, a traditional seventeenth-century pub. To pass the time before the pub opened they walked up the hill into the town. Conversation was easy and his perfect Queen's English reminded her of Danique and her elocution lessons. Hazel mentioned how impressed she had been to see him shimmy up the greasy pole with such skill. He chuckled and explained that he had worked for a couple of years on one of the last operating Thames Barges. Now he was a journalist for the Daily Star and ran a part-time diving school up in Leicestershire.

They slowly meandered about the quaint high street. Richie was a born storyteller and well suited to journalism, although the Daily Star was a newspaper that her parents might not endorse – not that she had ever read it. Time disappeared before he remarked that the pub would be open in five minutes so they made their way back down to the quay. Hazel used the phone just inside the door to ring home and say she would be late for dinner. They sat on a long pew under a window and she listened, absorbed as Richie related many interesting stories. He had published a book about his time on the barge, which had been reasonably successful and he said he'd give her a copy. She gathered that his parents were quite well off, although he implied that he didn't get on with them very well. There had also been rumours about the wild parties he threw, where he would drunkenly smash up stuff in his flat, including the cooker on one occasion. She saw nothing of this in him and began to look forward to his company.

A couple of weeks later she enjoyed his brilliant body. He didn't use a deodorant, although it was only in close contact that she noticed and it did not dampen his physical appeal. One evening, when Tim was working, Richie dropped her home a little later than normal, only to find her front door was bolted from the inside. Had her parents known she was lying when she said she was out with female friends? Luckily, they accessed the back of the house via the shared alley and found an open toilet window with a strong metal downpipe within reaching distance. Richie shimmied up much faster than he had the greasy pole and slowly squeezed his way in at the toilet window. Quietly, without disturbing anyone, he found his way down to the front door to let Hazel in. Nothing was mentioned in the morning. Many years later when Hazel asked her mother why she had been locked out, Edwina explained that Ray had presumed she was home and so had unwittingly followed his normal bedtime routine and bolted the front door.

Hazel did feel guilty about this fun behind Tim's back. But she was a free spirit and needed to be convinced that marriage was the right decision and that he was the right person.

Then Hazel and Tim had a great holiday together on Portland. They had driven right across the island to The Pulpit Inn, the last pub before Portland Bill lighthouse on the tip. Facing the pub was a track that trundled south over a field to the rocky coast. There are a lot of wooden cabins there now, on land purchased by the owners of the Lobster Pot Café. Back then this café was little more than a shed and the area was deserted. A perfect spot to erect their igloo tent on a grassy ledge surrounded by rocks and the sea. Inside the tent they had a blow-up double mattress with joined-up sleeping bags. They had bought a canvas windbreak so they could cook outside when it was dry as there was very little space inside. It was certainly cosy at night when Tim brought in his Tilley lantern as they returned from a night spent fishing on the rocks. The lantern also supplied enough light for Hazel to read by when she got bored of watching her rod. They definitely faced the elements on the edge there.

During a storm one night, Hazel woke to find the tent had collapsed on top of them. They had forgotten to regularly check the air pressure in the tubes. The rain was torrential and they could hardly stand up in the wind, let alone fit the foot pump or stand up to stamp on it. So they spent the rest of an uncomfortable night in the Beetle until dawn brought quieter weather and they were able to re-pressurise the tubes.

The outdoor freedom suited Hazel and she was quite happy to boil a kettle of water to have a good wash inside the tent before sitting outside to eat a breakfast of fried eggs and bacon with buttered toast. They used the toilet in the pub when necessary and enjoyed a drink there in the evening when they weren't fishing or if it was raining. They agreed to have at least one holiday a year on Portland.

Once home they began to discuss their wedding. Hazel wanted to make her own wedding dress and said it would be lovely if they could have a honeymoon somewhere hot. They contacted the vicar of St Clement's Church. It was Tim's closest C of E church and Hazel had been baptised there. It was a beautiful church, with its own bells, in the heart of Leigh-on-Sea, Hazel's dream for her wedding. A date was set – 28 October 1972. Hazel would be nineteen, Tim twenty-one. Her parents were paying for the wedding so Tim's parents wanted to pay for the honeymoon. They chose Majorca for two weeks. Magaluf was unspoilt then, with just one four-star hotel, which looked amazing in the brochures. The wedding breakfast was booked at Oscar's Diner, which sat on a corner of Leigh Hill overlooking the estuary. Oscar himself was a very welcoming, tall, slim, dark man with an enormous black, curling moustache.

It could be quite cold at the end of October so Hazel went to Richardson's fabric shop that sat right opposite the church and purchased some warm, white, brushed nylon to line the fine, white lace she'd chosen for the top layer. The lace, also nylon, had a slight silver thread running through it. This caused it to shimmer in the light. She'd settled on a pattern with a tight-fitting and fairly low-cut bodice, with leg-of-mutton sleeves that puffed out from the shoulder and fitted tightly to the wrist. From just under the bust hung a tight-ish fitting layer. A second, lightly gathered layer, hung from below her hips and it was finished by a third lightly gathered layer. The lace was quite heavy and so it all draped elegantly down her slim body. Platform shoes were fashionable then and a white leather pair gave Hazel an extra half inch of height. This would mean she would only be a little under her husband-to-be's short stature of five feet six inches.

Sue, the pub under-manager, was also getting married, but in just a few weeks and was going to be moving away. They advertised for a new under-manager. A young man (almost a boy, thought Hazel) with plenty of curly blond hair, quite short (only a touch taller than Tim) came for a trial period and was accepted. With a little more height Hazel would have said Andy was stunningly handsome. His startling blue eyes didn't laugh much though, and she found his arrogant personality irritating. However, after eating lunch with him a few times, she began to understand his character better. His mother had died when he was quite young and his father had attempted to bring up him and his older sister alone, until he had met and married Andy's stepmother. Unfortunately, the children did not get on with her so drifted away from their father, but had remained close to each other.

Tim was now constantly pressing her to get a full-time job. They were saving for a deposit on a house and once they were married there would be a mortgage to pay. His salary might cover all the bills but holidays and extras would be her responsibility. She continued to scan all the papers but had still seen nothing suitable. She had visited a local model maker and taken a model of Ruth and Lionel's house, built with the addition of a proposed extension that doubled its size. Ray had drawn up the plans, so Hazel was able to make a scale model in cardboard with clear plastic for the many windows. She had painted on all the red brickwork, white window frames and added the guttering. Ruth and Lionel were delighted with it. The model maker told her that, unfortunately, they had no vacancies.

Hazel did see an article in the local paper about an archaeological dig at nearby Rayleigh Mount. A masonry and timber castle had once existed there and was mentioned in the Domesday Survey of 1086. Only the earthwork of its large motte-and-bailey now remained. A windmill was built in 1809 on the outer bailey. This was to be refurbished and was being considered as a museum. Interesting finds from the dig would be exhibited there. Anyone interested could just turn up, suitably shod and clothed for any weather, with their own packed lunch. Hazel's O-level history teacher had inspired her imagination with lively, well-illustrated descriptions of everyday life in the past. The thought of finding and handling anything from local past times seemed interesting.

She invited Tim, but as the weather was predicted to be dry and the tides good that weekend, he decided to go fishing instead. She caught the bus. At least twenty adults of various ages gathered around a white tent. Inside on trestle tables were trays of the few finds to date: tiny pieces of pottery, nails, metal clasps that had once supported jewellery, the odd small dark coin and so on. After a brief demonstration of how to gently scrape away the earth Hazel was assigned to a trench with two ladies who regularly attended digs across the country. The edge of a stone wall had been uncovered and she began to slowly dust away the earth.

By lunchtime she had only found stones. Most people seemed to be there with a friend or had at least made friends during the dig and sat in small groups on the grass while they ate lunch. Hazel was happy to sit by herself. A lone male, a few years older than her, with long fair hair came and asked if she would like some company.

"Yes, that's fine," she replied.

He sat quietly beside her and for once she was lost for conversation. As they were called to resume the dig he mentioned his name was Steve and asked her if she would like to go to a café afterwards. She agreed. They finished at five-thirty and handed in their tools. Hazel had found one very small piece of brown pottery. Steve's work had not proved any more fruitful. They wandered into Rayleigh High Street and found a café. Steve explained he lived in Romford, some distance away by train, and that he had studied history at Leeds University. At the moment he was enjoying attending archaeological digs around the country and that at some point he would probably go into teaching. Hazel felt his general and historical knowledge far surpassed hers but he seemed interested to hear about her previous job and they both concluded that working for the British Museum would have been a great opportunity. Unfortunately, there were no vacancies at the moment and anyway she thought that they would now most likely take in university graduates. She was sure her father had been instrumental in the original offer. She talked about Tim and the wedding. She was also keeping an eye on the time knowing Tim would ring her as soon as he got home to find out about her day. She began to worry. He would probably tell her off if she was not at home and he knew that the dig finished at five-thirty. Hazel said she had better go and that she looked forward to meeting up the following day.

Hazel's mother told her Tim had rung several times to find out if she was home, so it was with apprehension that she rang him back. He was cross, particularly when she honestly told him she'd had a coffee in the café with an interesting young chap called Steve. Tim drove round and picked her up. They had an argument in the car and he told her he didn't want her to go tomorrow. She finally appeased him by saying she wouldn't go on the dig, as long as Tim didn't go fishing, then they could do something together. He agreed.

But inside, she felt a small worm of discontent begin to wriggle. Tim was the reason she hadn't gone to university and she was now beginning to question that decision. Was she seriously cut out to be a subservient wife (as was still half expected)? What, though, would she do with freedom? She knew that, ultimately, she was a homemaker and wanted to be a mother and who better to support that wish than Tim? She'd read that if you were really 'in love' you knew it one hundred per cent. How big was her doubt? She felt she was searching for something unknown.

The unrest continued to grow over the following month; to be married and faithful, with no regrets, for the rest of her life. A tall order. In the end Hazel discussed this unrest with Tim and told him the only solution was for her to take a break from their relationship. After explaining the depth of her feelings for him, she suggested they should not cancel the wedding yet, but spend a month apart. Seeing his hurt made her assure him that she would, no doubt, miss him so much that they would get back together and so follow through with the wedding. She was not so certain in her heart, though. She took off her ring but he told her to keep it until that time and with both of them in tears they broke up. It was a Wednesday.

On Friday she went down to the pub. Richie was there. After Hazel explained the agreed time apart from Tim, he asked if she would like to spend the weekend at his diving school. He had no lessons booked but said he had a caravan up there and could show her around the disused quarry where he rented a large shed for all the diving equipment – and he could even give her a lesson.

Anything to distract her mind she told him. Not wishing to upset her parents or to allow the details to reach Tim, Hazel told her parents that Danique had invited her to spend the weekend with friends just outside Leicester so they thought no more of it. They also knew she needed time to work out her future and were not up at five on Saturday morning to see Richie collect her.

It was very dark by the time they reached the quarry. Miles away from street lights and civilisation Hazel could see nothing beyond the headlights of the car as it quietly rolled down a narrow lane. Richie pulled up next to a caravan and she stepped out of the car. Total eerie silence. A soft, black blanket enfolded the air. She stood and slowly swept her eyes around a full 360 degrees, then up to the moon and stars. A strange experience, almost as though becoming one with space, they felt so close. A gentle shimmering below the moon highlighted some water and as her eyes adjusted they drew in the expanse of a lake. Dark cliffs rose steeply behind it.

Richie unlocked the caravan, disappeared inside, flicked a switch and light filled the doorway. After a minute or so his shadow reappeared. He asked if she would like a beer and apologised for having no other alcohol, she accepted then lifted her bag from the back seat and went to investigate the caravan interior. It smelt a little musty but was clean, with a standard layout. Richie had a large torch in his hand and said he would show her where the toilet was. Outside, the strong beam picked out a large shed by the water's edge. A small lean-to on the side housed a basic portaloo. Back inside the caravan he put on a Rolling Stones cassette and they settled into the corner seating that was already made up as a bed. Hazel was tired and only half listened to his tales of diving. Seeing her dozing, he suggested they go to bed. She could use the sink to clean her teeth and have a wash if she wanted while he disappeared to the toilet. As she stood at the sink she was aware that, as with that weekend at Ramsey's house, she was unable to find that comfy, familiar, relaxed sense that she had around Tim. If they passed some noisy wind they would merely giggle. Not so now, although perhaps it would have closed the distance somewhat. As she snuggled into the crook of his waiting arm, she was again aware of his strong natural body odour and his attractive, tanned features. His balding head at such a young age felt wrong. She loved his company, his vibrant stories and cared about him and, if Tim hadn't been a comparison, she may have grown to love him. Then she stopped thinking, and rolled into his body to enjoy slow, languid sex.

In the morning, after pleasuring each other's bodies again, Richie asked if she was happy with scrambled eggs on toast for breakfast. Certainly. As they ate he offered to fit her up for a dive. Never having considered doing this before she was a little apprehensive and explained that it was the water temperature that bothered her the most. In cold water she shivered to the point that her lips turned blue and numbness set in. When she tickled the edge of the lake with her fingers, it felt cold. Richie suggested that a dry suit might be best, as a wet suit relied on the wearer's body temperature to keep them warm, which might not happen in her case.

They wandered over to the shed and he sorted out a black rubber dry suit that wasn't too big and waited as she pulled it on, under his instruction, over some thermals. The flippers felt awkward and the single air cylinder he strapped to her back, heavy. He fitted the mouthpiece between her teeth and turned on the cylinder. She practised breathing for a few minutes. Then put on goggles. He offered to row her out into the lake to experience the easy option of falling backward into the water but she declined.

"Please, can I just wade in from the edge?"

Apprehension was really building now. He pulled on a wet suit to join her in the shallows. However, just walking the couple of yards with flippers was an interesting challenge. Attempting to wade with them almost impossible. He held her hand for support. The coldness of the water took her breath away. Fighting against the water she struggled to reach thigh depth. Richie told her to lie back and he would float her out just a little further. She complied. When she signalled her readiness, he let go. Total disorientation took over. Why could she not turn herself over? Why, when normally she was able to swim reasonably strongly, was she not even able to face forward or put her feet downwards? As she sank, she couldn't tell which way was up and which was down. Fear made her flounder even more. Finally, her flippers engaged with the silty ground and she pushed her head out and stood up. Fortunately, she was still in shallow water. Pulling off her goggles and taking out the mouthpiece, she breathed deeply.

"I'm really sorry but I just can't do this."

"That's fine, don't worry," reassured Richie. "Diving's not for everyone."

He took her arm and gently helped her back on to firm land.

"This evening I'll row you across the lake to give you a more relaxing experience."

Once they had washed and dressed Richie drove to a little country pub for lunch and she came to accept that there were limitations to her sense of adventure.

That evening, after a takeaway fish and chip supper, Richie told Hazel to wrap up warm as a chill breeze was blowing over the lake. Just beyond the shed was a small wooden rowing boat moored to a stump. He drew it partly on to the shore and told her to hop in and take the centre of the seat in the stern as he steadied it. Now she understood why he had remained in shorts with bare feet. Pushing it gently he jumped in, took the bow seat and lifted the oars into the rowlocks. He cut the water expertly. There was a slight breeze but it did no more than gently ripple the surface. Now she was able to melt into the moment. The quietness highlighted the slop of the oars, the strong rhythmic pull as they moved towards the middle of lake.

Once there Richie stopped. The soft rocking of the boat was soporific. It was romantic but Hazel's emotions were blocked by the fact that he was not ready to settle down and she was not ready to want to with him. Gazing at the crescent moon her imagination brought up the childhood nursery rhymes 'Hey diddle diddle the cat and the fiddle' and 'The owl and the pussy cat'. A few peaceful minutes passed with neither of them speaking. Richie then picked up the oars and slowly rowed back.

It had been an interesting and enjoyable weekend but, on Monday morning while working in the upstairs bar, Harry Nilsson's 'Without You' filled the air. It was number one in the charts and his heart-wringing words 'Can't live if living is without you', tore at Hazel's heart. It was playing everywhere. Shopping malls, individual shops, restaurants, cafés. Even going out for a mid-week drink with Richie was marred by the deep emotion it churned up inside as it swirled around them.

She missed Tim. How long before this awful rawness faded? She looked deeply into the whole of her life. Her father loved her unconditionally. Was this what she was subconsciously searching for? If so, the search could only end in failure. She knew compromises had to be made for a successful relationship. The articles she read in *Cosmopolitan* every month had taught her that much. She'd read about all sorts of things, from feminism to how to allow your husband to believe he had the leading role in the relationship, which only served to confuse her more. She liked and thought she understood men and didn't really class herself as a feminist, but that need to exist as an equal was strong. She didn't want to define herself as someone's wife, but she longed to use her design skills to make a beautiful home, her love of nature to create a calming space in a garden. Ultimately though, her deepest need was to be a mother, to grow and nurture new human life. To give her children love and guidance towards a happy and confident life. But how could she marry and remain independent? Her mother did fight for an equal say in her marriage but that may have been the source of her parents' arguments and discontent. Tim's mother appeared to cheerfully go along with her husband's wishes and they were very happy.

But, more and more the words of "Without You" (originally by Badfinger) were taking over her mind (listen to Nilsson's version on YouTube).

A fear began to grow that Tim may already be looking for someone else. That after a month he might decide he didn't want her back. Then there'd be a lifetime spent searching for someone to replace him. She knew so little of love.

After only twelve days Hazel rang Tim and told him she couldn't bear to be without him. They hugged, made love, and she put on her ring once more to cover the little white circle of untanned skin.

CHAPTER 11
1972 ◇ A Quandary

Tim and Hazel put down a deposit, using Tim's savings, on a small, three-bedroom, semi-detached house just across the Leigh Road from where Hazel's family used to have their flat. It was at the top of the road, only two houses from the Broadway. The building society granted them a mortgage, with a small retainer on the understanding that the damp on the ground floor was remedied and the rotten window frames replaced. Ray and Edwina knew a good builder who did the job. Hazel had decided that it would be best to knock down the wall between the lounge and dining room at the same time, to open up the space and leave the wall, with the two fireplaces, running the whole length in bare brickwork that could be sealed and painted white. The lower 1.5 yards of all the downstairs walls had been replastered following the damp treatment. Most of their spare time was spent repointing the brickwork and DIY jobs in preparation for the final painting. The young couple had a disagreement about the colour for the lounge-diner. Hazel wanted all-white walls, a brown ceiling and, as per Ray's suggestion, a hard-wearing brown-flecked cord carpet. Tim argued that white walls reminded him of hospitals – although the only time he'd spent in them was visiting elderly relatives. As Hazel was going to be doing the majority of the ordering and painting, she had her way.

Edwina was undertaking the majority of the wedding preparations with Hazel's input on invitations, hymns for the order of service and so on. Hazel was very pleased with her completed wedding dress. But something still niggled deep inside her psyche. She was nineteen. Wasn't she simply too young to contemplate marriage? But she felt older and thought that however old she was she might always face this dilemma. A lifetime with just one man, how could you ever be certain he was the perfect match? Of all the men she'd known Tim was still streaks ahead.

She wasn't too nervous about the actual wedding ceremony. After all, one just repeated the vicar's words and they had a practice session booked for the week before – just ten days away. But, a lifetime of Tim? She was unable to pinpoint the cause of this niggle. Apart from marrying someone really rich and travelling the world, what would be missing? Not that she thought much of rich men; she would need to maintain a high level of attractiveness and probably couldn't trust them not to have affairs. This was mostly gut instinct as she had no idea if it was actually true. She'd rather not find out, though.

Relaxing over lunch with Andy, at work on Friday, she began to talk about her wedding and attempted to explain her trepidation. All too soon lunch was over.

"Let me show you my flat after work and we can talk this out some more. You shouldn't be getting married if you have doubts," Andy concluded.

She did need to bounce her thoughts off someone. She'd last seen Carol at her marriage a year ago, when Carol was only seventeen. Hazel had kept her promise and asked Danique to be her bridesmaid, which may not have been the wisest decision, especially as they had not actually spent any time together since they'd left school. But Danique assured her she was over Tim and was happy to be Hazel's maid of honour. She'd chosen not to have a flotilla of bridesmaids, one would do. However, she felt neither of these friends would be able to offer an unbiased view on her future plans. She replied yes to Andy's offer.

His flat was only minutes from the pub. It was clean and tidy with minimal furniture since he spent very little time in it and had been offered rooms at the pub, but preferred to have his own space. He had three hours before he needed to return to work. He made them both coffee and they picked up the lunchtime conversation as they relaxed on the sofa. Hazel agreed that because of her doubts about spending the rest of her life with Tim, she should call it off. But all the invites had now been accepted. Her brothers had new suits and shoes. Everything was set and everyone was full of anticipation. Andy offered a solution. He was spending a few days with his sister in Lancashire. She had a very large house with a lot of bedrooms and would be happy to have Hazel stay for as long as it took to get her head sorted out. She could ring her parents from there to cancel the wedding if she decided that was best. Hazel asked Andy to confirm this with his sister first.

"Of course. She's at work now but I'll ring first thing this evening. I know she'll say yes though."

Hazel finished her coffee and sank deep into the sofa. That was the answer. To run away. Andy was travelling up by train on Monday evening, his day off, and said he would meet her in the downstairs bar at seven o'clock. His blue eyes were shining. He was offering her a lifeline. She asked if he was expecting anything in return. He replied that it was not a good idea for her to be involved with anyone while she made this decision, so no they would be going as platonic friends. She touched his hand in appreciation, felt his warmth, breathed in his aftershave. He looked beautiful. A true Adonis.

"I really would like to thank you, though. I'm so relieved by this way out. Just once may I thank you?" Hazel moved closer and gently wrapped her arms around his neck and drew his lips to hers. Their kiss instantly ignited passion and he didn't object when she took his hand and led him to the bedroom. Sweet, relieved, sex. But they both agreed afterwards that it was to be a one-off. For now, anyway.

That weekend she took out all her savings, which didn't amount to much. She gathered up the minimum of clothing, a little make-up, a toilet bag and her passport. She was not likely to need it, but felt it was a good idea to have it with her. She and Tim went round to friends for one of their regular drink and be merry Saturday evenings – and no one would have known that Hazel had anything on her mind other than her wedding.

She finished at the pub after lunch and went home as usual. She mentioned to her mum that she was meeting a friend and eating out that evening. She spent the afternoon in her bedroom, thinking. She should not have gone back to Tim after their break-up. Could she blame that song? It had contributed. At least she felt certain that running away was now her only option. She was not strong enough to face Tim, her parents, Tim's parents, to say she was calling everything off and wasting a honeymoon holiday. She was taking the coward's way out. She watched the time. It went slowly. At ten past six she picked up her bag and coat. She normally didn't bother with a handbag and just had a small purse and the front door key, so leaving the house with this bag might illicit unwanted curiosity. She had to slip out unseen. She opened her bedroom door and listened. Silence. As quietly as possible she went downstairs and out of the front door. It was stressful to walk down the road, waiting for someone to call after her, but as she turned the corner and made her way to the bus stop she breathed more easily.

Hazel arrived at the pub just before seven and went down to the student bar. The manager was behind the bar. She would rather he didn't see her and mingled with the crowd, most of whom were strange faces. At this time of day, it was a different clientele. Seven o'clock, no sign of Andy; five past seven; ten past seven. Where was he? She was getting anxious. She made her way back towards the stairs to catch him as soon as he appeared.

OH GOD, NO. Her father was coming down the stairs and he had seen her. She froze. There was nowhere to go. Her heart pounded as she waited for him to reach to her.

"Please come home," he said.

"Look, I'm sorry but I can't come home and go through with this wedding." She felt tears welling up.

"It's probably just nerves, please come home so we can talk. If you want to cancel it, we can, but please let's talk about it. Try and sort this out."

"No." She was adamant, "I can't go home. I need a break. I'm sorry, but you'll just have to cancel everything. I'll come home when it is."

"Please, please, the car is just outside. Please, come and just sit in the car, we can talk there," her father pleaded.

"But why, when there's nothing to say."

"Please, just for me. I need to understand why you are going."

She found the hurt in her father's eyes unbearable.

"Okay, we'll talk in the car. Only for a few minutes though."

Ray gently guided his daughter up the stairs and out to his car. Hazel asked what had prompted him to come and find her.

"Michael saw you leaving with a bag. He thought it was unusual."

The car was across the road. They waited for the traffic to clear. Hazel thought, 'What had happened to Andy? I could run now. But where to?' Her father's close presence deterred her and she followed him to the passenger door, which he opened for her. Once she was seated he ran around to take the driving seat. Too fast, he turned the ignition and the car leapt forward. Hazel swung open the door but her father leant over her, still with his foot on the accelerator, grabbed the handle and swiftly shut it. He didn't stop until they reached home.

Hazel remained glued to the passenger seat. Unable to accept that the father she adored and trusted had lied in order to kidnap her home.

"How could you do that?" she asked, "I trusted you."

"We just need to make sure you are not making a mistake. Please come inside."

There was little else Hazel could do. She lifted her bag and herself out of the car with a heavy heart. Her mother was sitting at the dining-room table, waiting for them. Her father took a seat and asked her to sit too. She obeyed reluctantly.

Her mother began, "Daddy thinks you might be suffering from nerves but regardless of whether or not that is the case we need to really consider exactly what you are doing. We can cancel the wedding, even at this late stage, if that is really what you want. But I suggest you go to your bedroom now, have a good night's sleep and in the morning have a serious think."

"I'm not nervous about the ceremony and I had done all the thinking necessary. It was cowardly to run away but it's what I needed to do."

"Where were you going?" Edwina asked.

Hazel explained Andy's offer.

"But he was late, otherwise I'd have gone."

"Well, you're here now," her father added. "So go to bed and see how you feel in the morning. Tim is understandably very upset and would appreciate a call first thing, either way."

He stood up to conclude the discussion.

Feeling deeply miserable Hazel went up to her bedroom. Why had Andy been late? Back at home all the familiar feelings rose up around

Tim, the wedding, all the guests waiting to enjoy their day, all the money they had spent on wedding gifts. Not to mention their house. How could it be cancelled now?

She imagined her life with Tim and it wasn't that bad. That niggle, was it caused by the thought of a long lifetime together? She did love him and many couples managed to remain happy, didn't they? You talk, you work things out. Marriage has to encompass some compromise, but Tim would always be there for her, always love her. She did believe that. It was unlikely they would have to worry too much over money. What had she to run away from really? Divorce was becoming more acceptable now, so marriage no longer had to mean an entire lifetime.

The emotional stress had worn her out and she slept surprisingly well. Before breakfast she rang Tim to apologise for worrying him and explained she wasn't sure anything in life could be guaranteed but she was happy to become his wife. She buried her doubts and concentrated on the positives of a glorious wedding and a life together.

Hazel worked a weeks' notice at the pub and left. Andy was very apologetic about his lateness that fateful evening. He had turned up only minutes after Hazel and her father had left.

The wedding was glorious. The sun shone. Tim and Hazel both spoke their words clearly, although she could hear the blood pounding in her ears. They kissed as expected, with eagerness now the solemn part was over. And the bells rang out from St Clement's. The wedding breakfast at Oscar's was perfect. Tim's best man, Graham, and Ray gave great, but short, speeches. One blip was Danique. She didn't smile all day and had insisted, as they were dressing prior to the wedding, that Hazel pay for her dress. Danique had originally agreed to pay for it as she had bought it to wear on other occasions too. Hazel didn't allow it to get to her and quietly wrote a cheque.

With a new home to decorate and furnish the couple could not afford a party in the evening, just as they had not engaged in hen or stag nights. They had booked to spend the night of the wedding at a hotel near the airport and were flying out early in the morning. As the wedding breakfast wound down the Beetle appeared outside Oscar's with 'Just Married' sprayed across the back windscreen and tin cans trailing off the rear bumper. After all the smiles, hugs and goodbyes, they clattered off. They arrived at the hotel to find that Hazel had forgotten her passport! But her father came to the rescue and dropped it at the reception later. Hazel loved her father again.

The clocks went back an hour that night, much to their amusement. An extra hour in bed on their wedding night! They settled themselves into a very comfy bed and watched *The Last Goon Show of All*, with Spike Milligan, Peter Sellers and Harry Secombe. They laughed so much they cried and agreed it was a perfect end to their perfect day.

The honeymoon in Majorca met their expectations, although the weather was a little unsettled. They sunbathed, swam, walked, visited caves and various places of interest. The food at the hotel was exceptional and they both looked forward to the menu each evening. Hazel did wander off on her own for a few hours while Tim slept on the beach. She told her husband she wanted to explore around the next cove. It was unspoilt and deserted, she paddled lazily, watching small fish darting around the rocks. Then she sank down in the shallow warm water. An octopus surprised her as it slowly curled out of hiding. She watched fascinated as it stretched its tentacles, grew to about two feet long and moved with grace among the rocks. Time stood still. Reluctantly Hazel thought she should make her way back. Tim listened with interest as she described her encounter with a real octopus.

After the honeymoon and the drive back from the airport, Tim parked outside their house. They had been very traditional and had not lived together prior to the wedding. They had bought a three-piece suite, a pine dining table with six matching chairs and a double bed that Hazel had made up with new linen before the wedding. As Tim carried his wife over the threshold they were welcomed by the warmth from the storage heaters that had been switched on and were overwhelmed to discover that the lounge-diner had been freshly painted and the new carpet fitted. But most glorious was a pale cream, marble fireplace set with an 'all night burner', to allow them to warm the space with a real coal- or wood-burning fire. The fireplace was a present from Ray, made for him by one of his works suppliers. The decorating had been a joint effort by both fathers.

The couple were keen to show their appreciation so invited both sets of parents to Sunday dinner the following weekend. Tim had regularly prepared the dinner on Sundays for his parents, while they had an afternoon nap, and since he'd known Hazel she had often helped. This practice meant the meal was perfect. The parents got on well together and all was a success.

CHAPTER 12
1974 ◇ Married Life

While Hazel's marriage was built on fate and a song, the freedom of living in her own home was wonderful. The couple had decided not to buy or rent a TV yet. Colour ones were expensive and the picture quality was not good. As Tim's parents were working in the shop every evening, Tim and Hazel could snuggle up on his parent's sofa upstairs and watch their black and white television uninterrupted. When Tim was working evenings she would often walk to her parents' house and join them watching comedies and dramas – also in black and white.

They did not have a washing machine but the launderette was only a block away, close enough for Hazel to go home while the machine did its thing then back to collect the finished load and hang it out to dry on a line strung down the garden.

The garden was not large and had simple borders down each side that they tended together. They made friends with their next-door neighbours over the chicken-wire fencing.

Tom and Emmy were an elderly couple who had moved down from the East End of London and during the warmer months regularly sat out in their garden drinking tea. On seeing Tim and Hazel, Emmy would shuffle off to make them a very acceptable fresh brew to share. Tom had been a master builder and explained with pride that Emmy had been a beautiful professional dancer when younger. After watching her perform on a London stage Tom had gone backstage and asked to meet her. Emmy was twelve years older but Tom stated that had made no difference to them and he'd never looked at anyone else. They had a daughter and grandchildren who lived up north and visited occasionally.

Tim helped with the cooking, depending on his shifts, but washing, ironing and housework fell to Hazel, particularly as she still had no job and was having to regularly sign on at the Job Centre. Unfortunately, she discovered that she hated housework, probably not helped by the fact that she was untidy. It took almost as long to tidy as it did to dust and vacuum. 'If I could find a job that paid well enough I'd employ a cleaner,' she thought. They had discussed having a family but Tim had made it clear he did not want to be a father until he had been married for at least five years. As they were so young she agreed it made sense.

Then they were involved in an accident. When their friends left the Peterboat and took over a pub in Great Wakering they asked Tim and Hazel if they would help behind the bar on Saturdays, at least when Tim was home and able to drive there. The pub car park was situated at the end of a blind bend and, as they were pulling out at the end of one such evening, a large truck, travelling too fast, piled head on into the Beetle.

Hazel felt the massive impact and watched in terror as the car spun round in a complete circle. She then lost consciousness. As she came round she saw blood covering Tim's face. He answered as she called his name and they staggered back to the pub where she fainted. The driver of the truck was unhurt. The police arrived and breathalysed both drivers. Tim, sensibly, had only had a couple of pints during the whole evening and was just inside the limit. The other driver was over the limit. An ambulance then took Tim and Hazel to hospital. She had caught her nose on a handle that sat across the dashboard to assist getting in and out of the vehicle, it was broken and she had a slight concussion. Tim had glass removed from his face and some stitches. They got a taxi home. The old Beetle was a write-off. They did get some compensation, eventually, from the farm that owned the truck. In the meantime Colin, their mechanic, found them a newer Beetle.

Not long after Hazel saw that the Royal Bank of Scotland were advertising for a clerk to work in their stock department in Lombard Street, London. She applied. It was an easy commute and might lead to a reasonable salary. Mustering her confidence, she did well at the interview and was offered the post.

Hazel found the basic filing boring and her butterfly mind made it difficult to be accurate. She seemed to make more mistakes than the other girls. Fortunately, the head of her department, Geoff, a slightly overweight, dark-haired man with a round face, appeared to appreciate that she was annoyed by her mistakes and was trying hard to improve. Geoff seemed to have a close and affectionate relationship with his very attractive second-in-command, Bernice. They spent their lunch breaks together either in the canteen or out. No one could say for sure how deep their relationship was.

Those were the days before sexual harassment at work was considered an offence and the odd lurid remark from a male colleague was simply considered part of working life. At least it was by Hazel, which was just as well because the office letch found her attractive, particularly as she had no problem countering his remarks reasonably intelligently. If words failed her she simply gave him a withering look. Once, while they were in the queue for the photocopier she felt his hand deliberately brush her bottom. She turned round slowly to face him squarely.

"I can't stop you looking at my bum but this body belongs to me and only I choose who touches it. Do you understand?"

As half a dozen people in the queue also heard this, he meekly replied that he did. He didn't touch her again. After she had ignored him entirely for a couple of weeks she was happy to continue with the banter he aimed at her.

The majority of the filing clerks were female and at lunchtime they congregated at several tables in the canteen. They were happy for Hazel to join them but as the weeks went by she found their conversation, mainly about men or clothes, to be almost as boring as the filing. She made the decision to sit at an empty table occasionally and just read her book as she ate. One day she noticed a group of three younger guys looking at her and one smiled. Her normal reaction to a smile was to return it. Two of them made their way over to her table.

"You look lonely sitting all by yourself. Do you mind if we join you?" one asked.

"No. By all means. I'm not lonely, though. It's just that sometimes I find female groups a little boring and my book is good," said Hazel.

They sat down opposite her. The tallest introduced himself as Neil and his companion as Dale. Hazel was courteous and, to ensure they had no undue ideas, went on to say she was recently married. They assured her they both had girlfriends and settled into general conversation. Their interests were more diverse than the girls' and she wasn't too put out by not being able to continue with her book. The following day she grabbed a sandwich and decided to stretch her legs outside and explore the shops. She wanted to vary her breaks. Neil and Dale did join her a couple more times when they found her at a table by herself, which she found quite acceptable. Then only Neil came to sit with her but conversation remained light. Next to the canteen was a bar that was subsidised by one of the bank's largest clients, Guinness. As Neil finished his lunch, he said, as it was Friday he was having a drink at the bar and asked if she would join him. She thought he was pleasant and honest and felt there was no need to say no. It became a Friday lunchtime norm for them to have lunch together followed by a drink.

As the winter months passed and spring brought glimpses of warm sunshine Neil suggested walking along the embankment and stopping at a moored floating bar for a change. Anything to break up her boring job. Neil was several grades above her and told Hazel he was saving to buy a house and marry. He added that he intended waiting a while as his girlfriend was still young. When she told him about all the concerns she had had about her marriage he confessed that his girlfriend's age and immaturity compared to Hazel's apparently mature head did bother him a little. He was in no rush, though, and hoped time would mature her a little. While he had initially paid for the drinks, Hazel then insisted that she pay every alternate time.

Married life, with Hazel's strong character refusing to be gentle or subservient, was unlikely to be easy but it wasn't helped by an affliction known to many women. Thrush. She had developed it before they were married. If you are ignorant of its problems please check on the internet. It's sufficient here to explain that it made sex uncomfortable at best, painful at worst. Fortunately, it was treatable – with pessaries for Hazel and a cream for Tim – but the problem was that it hardly cleared before the next bout began. He regularly pressed her for sex but she was beginning to lose interest. They'd been married for just over a year when, on yet another visit to Dr Quinn with the problem, he mentioned that the contraceptive pill seemed to exacerbate thrush. She was aware of the options if she came off the pill. While dealing once more with cream and pessaries she told Tim of Dr Quinn's comment and said, "Condoms are a nuisance for me as well as for you, but I've heard stories of women being damaged by coils so I don't want to risk the chance of that, not until we've had a couple of children, anyway. But I would like to see if coming off the pill for a while will stop me from having this so regularly. So I guess it has to be condoms."

After being used to spontaneous lovemaking, Hazel was the one whose desire dropped the most with the hassle of fitting a condom. During the first week after coming off the pill she felt it particularly.

"Oh please, can we not bother this time," she said as his kisses and gentle stroking were arousing her, and he broke off to fumble in the bedside cabinet for a condom.

"But I don't want you to get pregnant," was his reply.

She rushed to reassure him.

"They say that it can often take three months before you can conceive after coming off the pill. I only stopped four days ago and I've not started a period yet so I'm sure we'll be fine."

With no more discussion they continued to Tim's climax, which never took long – another problem for Hazel! As they lay quietly afterwards a strange certainty swept through her, 'I'm going to be pregnant from this.' She was unable to understand why she should be so sure, but it was the only time Tim allowed unprotected sex.

Eight weeks later and still with no sign of a period she told a worried Tim that she had an appointment with the doctor. In the bath she had noticed the area around her nipples was darkening and her breasts felt heavier.

Tim sat in the waiting room while the doctor examined her.

"Yes, congratulations are in order, you are pregnant," Dr Quinn announced.

"How far am I?" asked an incredulous Hazel. Regardless of Tim's reluctance to be a father, she knew she would have been disappointed if her doctor had said she was not pregnant.

"I think about eight weeks," he replied.

She'd been right then. 'What a weird person I am,' she thought. As she walked into the waiting room her eyes met Tim's, she smiled as he stood and she took his arm.

"I am pregnant," she told him as they stepped out into the fresh evening air.

Tim was silent for a moment. After taking a deep breath he replied, "Oh wow, I can make babies!"

"You're not unhappy then?"

"Perhaps I'm not."

In the reality of the following day, however, Tim mulled over this life-changing information. He was working the afternoon and evening shifts and Hazel was in bed, but not asleep, when he arrived home. He quickly got ready for bed and slid in next to his wife but remained sitting and looked down into her eyes.

"We did agree that we wouldn't have children until we'd been married for at least five years, didn't we?" he said.

"Yes we did but …"

He interrupted, "Look, we are young and there are lots of things I want to do with just you before we complicate things with a child."

"So, what are you saying?" she asked, stunned by the implication.

"We've got years and years ahead together. We don't have to have a baby now."

"You're not suggesting an abortion, surely?"

"Yes."

Hazel's heart clenched.

"Seriously. You can't ask me to have that. Financially we are comfortable and I'm healthy. I can't believe my doctor would allow it and anyway, occasionally, something goes wrong and I could end up never being able to have a baby. So no, I won't have an abortion."

Hazel turned away from Tim. Keeping her eyes open she stared across the room and into the future. She saw herself with a baby and no one would take it away from her. Tim had to accept that. Fortunately, he recognised that her decision not to have an abortion was non-negotiable and no more was said about it.

Her pregnancy proceeded without a problem, apart from some queasiness for the first three months, especially if her stomach was empty. Eating an apple, pear, banana or nuts in between meals helped.

The pregnancy book she'd borrowed from the library advised that a mother-to-be need put on no more than one and a half stone when pregnant. As she wished to ensure both the health of her baby and the return of her strength and figure, she sensibly followed the healthy diet they suggested. Tim's mum mentioned that a small bottle of stout a day was recommended when pregnant. When Edwina confirmed this, Hazel began to drink a small bottle of Guinness on some days. She was also given an iron supplement by her doctor.

Hazel was spending most of her work lunchtimes in Neil's company, going out for a drink, to the occasional art exhibition or simply meandering along the embankment. They would chat about anything and everything, just enjoying their break from work. Hazel had told him of her pregnancy, of Tim's request and her answer. They both accepted that their friendship would end when she left the bank to become a mother, although, as she said, when she came up to London occasionally for shopping it would be great to meet up for a drink. Neil maintained that he would marry his girlfriend in a few years' time and, while they were saddened that a platonic friendship had to end, it felt natural.

Travelling up to London in the heat of summer was not a lot of fun for a pregnant Hazel and she was relieved to be leaving the bank a month before her due date. At a get-together at the bar with everyone in the bank at lunchtime on her final day, she drank seven Bacardis with lemonade (drinking alcohol while pregnant did not appear to be that much of an issue in those days!). As a person was not expected to work the afternoon of their last day, Neil thought he should walk her to the station. He caught his train from Liverpool Street station so they didn't normally see each other at the end of the day. She was grateful for his company this final day, not because she felt unsteady, which she surprisingly didn't, but because she wanted to tell him she would miss him. As they neared Fenchurch Street station Neil slowed and stopped.

"You'll be fine from here and I don't like goodbyes." They turned to face one another.

"Can I kiss you, just this once, because I am going to miss you?" asked Hazel.

Neil smiled and bent down to bring their lips together as their arms went around each other. Hazel's not sure who opened their mouth first. It didn't matter. It was confirmation of feelings they had been keeping in check, but that respect had made their friendship all the more important. Too soon Neil pulled away. Life has to move on, she thought with a touch of sadness as she walked alone into the station. She turned once to watch Neil as he walked away.

The baby was due at the end of September which gave her the chance to spend the warm days relaxing and reading on the beach, dipping in and out of the water to keep cool. She had made herself a stretchy maternity bikini to allow for expansion. On cooler days she decorated the little third bedroom as a nursery and knitted a tiny cardigan out of soft, pure-white wool and a matching pair of little white socks to add to her baby wardrobe. Edwina had also knitted blue and yellow cardigans, as a blue cardigan could be worn over a pretty little dress if it was a girl.

To maintain some financial independence, as Tim was rather tight when it came to dispensing money, Hazel bought a commercial sewing machine and the delivery men set it up in the second bedroom. She took on some repetitive piecework and had to spend a good few hours to earn the minimum amount that the company required but at least she was able to decide when to fit it in. She also attended all the antenatal classes and practised her relaxation breathing.

Before Hazel left work, Tim had been worrying about his wife being alone while he was working nights, particularly now there was a baby to think about, and had discussed getting a dog. Hazel said she didn't want a long-haired one, she didn't relish vacuuming up dog hairs all the time. At least they had the lean-to conservatory with its mixed fleck carpet tiles that would be a great disguise for dog hair. It was a perfect place for a dog to have his bed with instant access to the garden during the day and no mud brought directly into the house. And she didn't want a small yappy thing, which narrowed the selection to a short-haired guard dog and brought up the obvious choice of a Doberman. Reading as much as she could from books in the library, Hazel gleaned that Dobermans had a very acceptable nature, if brought up with good training in a family setting.

A litter was advertised in the local paper. They went straight to the kennels to have a look and were shown a document with the puppies' very impressive ancestry. Both parents were prize-winning dogs. They had a choice of seven puppies. Hazel's experience of dogs and cats in general had led her to feel that males had a more reliable temperament. There were three males. The largest immediately showed an interest in the couple, wagging his newly docked tail. He had large, soft, silky black ears framing his dark tan, broad face with large eyes. She'd read that one should avoid narrow pointy faces and ensure a strong straight back. This puppy certainly had that, together with a deep barrel of a chest and enormous black paws. He was going to be big. He was happy, gentle and playful as they both stroked and fussed him. Tim handed over £650 and received the pedigree documentation. Hazel had brought an old blanket that her mother had given her and wrapped the puppy in it. She settled him on her lap in the Beetle and Tim drove home. She quietly chatted as she stroked the puppy to reassure him and build trust.

Once home she set him down in the kitchen and showed him bowls of food and water, then led him into the conservatory where she laid the blanket in an open cardboard box with a cut out front section so he could get in and out. He warily sniffed about. The kennel had said that the puppies had already been toilet trained by their mother but Hazel had laid out a large plant tray filled with pet litter just inside the conservatory door because at night he would be shut in. Once he seemed at home in those two rooms they opened the conservatory door and he sniffed and bounded his way around the garden with his little stump wagging while they drank tea on the loungers.

In trying to think of a name Hazel imagined him as a fully-grown dog. His healthy black coat was gleaming in the bright sunlight. He would be magnificent, definitely a great show dog with his pedigree. But they decided that he was to be a family dog, not for showing. Hazel thought a short strong name would suit him, one that would work well when training him.

"How about King?" she asked.

Tim agreed. That night she tucked a hot-water bottle under the puppy's blanket, shut the conservatory door and lifted him to his bed. She gave him a stroke, kissed his silky head and said, "Bed now, King."

They heard nothing all night. Tim went down early the next morning to let the puppy out to relieve himself. No puddles in the conservatory.

When Hazel was walking to school she would regularly meet the vet who had opened a new practice at the bottom of her parents' road. James Downes was a friendly, fatherly, middle-aged man with curling, speckled white and dark-brown hair. After giving King a full check over and administering a set of vaccinations, he recommended dog-training lessons in Ashingdon, a fifteen-minute drive away.

It was agreed that, as Hazel was to be the one at home with him all the time, she should be the one to train with him. Tim drove them to their first lesson. Slightly apprehensive about how their puppy would react to a hall full of other dogs she kept his lead short and pulled him close as they went in. He was clearly interested in the ten or so other dogs there and, apart from a Rottweiler pup, looked the youngest. As the evening progressed she felt confident in the intelligence of her animal. He did listen to her most of the time and Hazel followed instructions and gave short firm commands. By the end of the lesson she thought Tim looked pleased with the pair of them.

They decided that a chalet on Portland, with a proper bed, might be more comfortable than camping for a week at the beginning of September. Hazel's lively lump was getting larger and didn't seem too keen on letting her sleep much. The vet offered a gentle sedative for King for the long drive down. The car was packed up, King was given his pill and laid on his blanket in the back. As usual, they left about five in the morning to drive through the centre of London before the rush hour. Just as they came through Stratford a loud banging noise erupted from the Beetle's engine and it died. With little traffic about Tim managed to push it to the kerbside and went to find a phone box to ring the AA. He returned to the car. They had no option but to wait to be picked up. What a disappointment. The AA declared that the big end had gone. Tim and Hazel, with King stretched over their laps, endured a rather uncomfortable journey home in the pick-up truck. Once home they sadly emptied the car and Tim rang Colin, their mechanic, to ask if he could collect and fix it. The next call was to the chalet park. They were told there was a vacancy the following week, if they could get there. After inspecting the Beetle, Colin advised that he could fit a reconditioned engine but it was unlikely to be ready in a week.

Hazel and Tim always rang their parents whenever they went away, to let them know they had arrived safely. This time they rang with the disappointing news. Ray's reaction was to say that if the Beetle wasn't ready by the end of the week he would drive them down to Portland, stay overnight if that was okay, and return at the end of the week, stay again overnight then bring them home the following morning. The couple agreed, deeply grateful. And that's how it went.

Ray just managed to squeeze an old camp bed and sleeping blanket in with a, once more, dozy King and bags and boxes of food and drink into his Morris 1100. He fitted a roof rack for their cases. They arrived at the chalet without event. Ray spent a pleasant afternoon seeing the island with them, followed by a fish and chip supper, before making up his camp bed in the lounge. He said he slept well and after Hazel cooked them all an egg and bacon breakfast, he took his leave. They spent the week relaxing, fishing, reading, wandering about the island, drinking in the pub and throwing balls for King, who was excited by all the freedom. Tim found King frustrating as he came to Hazel's call, eventually, but generally ignored the master of the house!

As promised, Ray arrived on Friday afternoon and they drove to a pub for a meal, followed by another night on the camp bed before he drove them home after breakfast. The arrangement had worked well and he assured the couple he had really enjoyed his short breaks with them and understood why they loved Portland.

The final two weeks before the baby was due really dragged. The day arrived but was totally uneventful. Edwina had advised her daughter that due dates were only a guide.

Another week went by. A check at the clinic found no reason for alarm or interference. Six days later Tim left early for a morning shift and while Hazel was washing-up the breakfast things a strong sensation pulled her abdominal muscles. It wasn't actually painful and she continued at the sink. Six minutes later another strong pull. She finished drying up and after another two of what she conceded had to be mild contractions, she rang her mother. Edwina told her it was likely to be many hours yet before she needed to go to hospital and that going out for a walk was a good idea.

King needed his morning walk so Hazel took him for a slow stroll down to the old town and back. As she meandered through Leigh and watched everyday life continuing normally, she didn't feel normal. Life was about to change. She was not too scared but felt a weird detachment from the goings-on around her. As her mother had reassured her, her body was designed to bring this life into the world. She'd been doing squatting exercises that she'd read might help open her pelvis and she was determined to remain relaxed and allow things to go on unhindered. Soon this tiny kicking body inside her would be in her arms. Her hope was for a boy but, of course, a healthy baby of either sex would be loved and nurtured.

Tim was home by half two that afternoon, relieved but anxious now the birth was imminent. He had initially been reluctant to please Hazel and be present to support her through the birth but now it seemed like the proper thing to do. He'd felt the baby growing inside her and, while being a father still frightened him, this had to be seen through. The afternoon disappeared but by six the contractions were stronger and coming every three minutes. Tim gathered the packed bag that had lain, ignored for so many weeks, up in the nursery. After shutting King into the conservatory, he bundled the bag and his wife into the Beetle.

"Go slowly," begged Hazel, hugging her neat lump as they made their way to Rochford maternity unit.

After an initial examination she was given an enema, shown a toilet and told a nurse would run her a bath as soon as the enema had done its work. The toilet business over, she was left alone to relax in the warm bath water as the contractions passed through her, each one like a wave that grew, then crashed and receded. The water was just beginning to cool when the nurse returned with a towel and robe. After a further examination by a midwife, she declared that Hazel's uterus was overactive and that it would be hours yet before the birth.

"I'll give you some pethidine so you can have a sleep," she said.

These were the experts. Hazel wasn't going to argue. Once the injection had been administered she asked if her husband could come in. The midwife replied she'd call him. Hazel attempted to get as comfy as possible on the couch in the middle of an otherwise almost empty room. She could hear a woman screaming. She did her best to relax and breathe slowly through each contraction until she felt the pethidine work through her system. She felt dozy as Tim entered the room. He came and held her hand but the contractions were getting closer and within minutes she felt a need to push. She told Tim. He pressed the alert button. The midwife returned and another examination revealed that she was indeed ready to push. A nurse arrived and began preparing things on a worktop just out of Hazel's sight. After encouragement from the midwife she pushed on the next contraction and heard a high-pitched roar leave her mouth.

"If you close your mouth your pushing will be more effective," the midwife retorted. "And I can see the head."

Hazel attempted to comply. The midwife mentioned she was giving her a numbing injection so that a small cut could be made to her peritoneum to allow the baby to exit smoothly. Caught up in the strength of the contractions she was not aware of the injection or the cut and with only a few more pushes her baby slithered out. There was no sound as the midwife lifted a rather blue-grey baby upside down by its feet and blew into its face. The baby gave a cry and turned pink.

"You have a baby boy," the midwife announced.

Amazement washed through Hazel as he was weighed (6 lb 10 oz), wiped and laid in her arms. She and Tim beamed at each other. The baby flickered his eyes open a little then fell asleep. It was just before midnight. Tim said he'd go and ring their parents with the news and the nurse took the baby to clean him up properly. A young doctor brought in a pair of leg stirrups and delicately told Hazel he was going to give her a couple of stitches. Nothing could upset her now so she turned her thoughts to her baby and relaxed to let the doctor stitch her up.

After he had left Hazel gently lifted herself off the couch. She needed a wee. She found herself facing a mirror. Her face was flushed with both the warmth of the room and the effort she'd put in. She stared into her own eyes. 'I'm really a mother now,' she proudly thought. 'And it had been virtually painless.' No doubt the pethidine had helped. She found a toilet and returned to find the nurse rather astounded that she'd left the room.

"When can I have my baby?" asked Hazel.

The nurse replied that she and her baby would be taken down to the maternity ward now. They were reunited fifteen minutes later. Wonderment as Hazel cradled him and checked his tiny toes and held his tiny fingers. He was rather wrinkled, which she was told was due to his late delivery, but was otherwise perfect. They both slept. When she awoke the nurse asked if she was breastfeeding and, as the baby was stirring, whether she would like to have a go at getting him to latch on. The nurse lifted him out of the clear cot beside her bed. The baby snuffled about her nipple and Hazel attempted to push it into his mouth. How much should go into that tiny mouth? She didn't want to choke him! She knew that the colostrum produced before the real milk came in was very rich in immune-boosting antibodies and was a great start for the new life. She was not sure exactly how successful that first breastfeeding attempt was but a few drops of creamy liquid had oozed out into the tiny mouth as she squeezed the area around the nipple.

Tim arrived with an enormous bunch of flowers. He'd met another new father out in the corridor who'd said he hadn't brought anything for his wife.

"Were you there for the birth?" asked Tim.

"No," was the reply.

Tim suggested to Hazel that this was significant as he was so glad that he'd been present and had been overwhelmed to witness exactly what she had achieved. Both sets of parents appeared later, bringing much love and congratulations. After the doctor had checked mother and baby Tim was allowed to take his wife and son home that afternoon as Hazel had elected for only a twenty-four-hour stay. There were no baby seat regulations then. Hazel had decided the safest way to transport the tiny bundle was well wrapped up and tightly tucked on his side into his carrycot, which was then tightly fitted into the seat belt on the back seat. Hazel strapped herself in next to it. She was hardly able to take her eyes off the peacefully sleeping babe, his black baby hair sticking out around his little face.

King was eager to greet his mistress. She made a big fuss of him. As Tim laid the carrycot down in the lounge they allowed the dog to gently sniff the tiny newcomer. Not too bothered he bounded off when he heard Tim filling his food bowl.

The following morning Hazel woke early, worried that they had not been disturbed by the baby, still asleep in his carrycot at the foot of their bed (perhaps pethidine persisted in a baby). Tim slept as she gently lifted the tiny bundle and brought him back to bed. She stroked his little cheek. He opened his eyes, nuzzled towards her finger and begun to gently suck. She tucked him up to her breast. After a few failed attempts to get her nipple far enough into his mouth he fell asleep again. She knew the midwife would be there soon to help so relaxed and told herself to be patient, the baby was not too bothered at the moment so go with it. She had read that a baby not wanting to suckle at first is not unusual. Tim woke, made breakfast and brought it up to bed. The midwife arrived shortly after they had finished. Tim disappeared downstairs and Hazel and the midwife managed to get the baby to latch on and suckle a little. She was reassured that they were both fine, that persevering with breastfeeding would be rewarded and that it would help her figure to regain its old shape – something Hazel was determined to do.

A little later, while still relaxing in bed, she was surprised but delighted to have a visit from Arthur. He hugged his niece and said he needed to check she was alright. She happily reassured him. In fact, the euphoria she had felt as she saw herself in the mirror just after the birth, persisted.

Days later there was no sign of the so-called baby blues in Hazel. Having been taught by Edwina to be a mother to John, she felt a confidence rarely felt by new mothers. The baby may have felt that confidence, although he may simply have had a genetic tendency to contentment. He did get fidgety and apparently annoyed if he was cuddled too tightly or for any length of time, but he had no problems being cuddled by anyone for a short time. These contented characteristics lasted and he never showed a sign of the 'terrible twos'. This may be due to the fact that Hazel chatted continuously about the whys and wherefores of everything and had no problem distracting him if he appeared to get cross or annoyed.

With the help of Dr Spock's *Baby and Childcare* book and Edwina, who called in often during the first few weeks to help with housework and ironing, Hazel grappled with motherhood. She had made the decision that, as she was a light sleeper and would not sleep well if she was having to listen to all the baby's little noises through the night, at half past six each evening, after feeding and bathing, she would swaddle him up on his side in his carrycot and put him in the little nursery room. She drew the heavy curtains and left him, even closing the door to ensure nothing woke him. Hazel had fitted a little spy viewer in the door so she could check if he was awake or not. He then did not wake until about eleven.

Within a week he was sleeping until midnight. Breastfeeding remained difficult and tedious. While the sucking sensation itself was not unpleasant, and she was comforted by imagining all the life strengthening goodness he was drawing from her, the baby had to be continuously encouraged not to fall asleep. Feeds lasted a good half an hour on each breast. The night feed was the most arduous. When he was only two weeks old, after discussing it with both her mother and the health visitor, Hazel bought a tin of formula milk. Edwina gave her the small and large glass feeding bottles she had kept ever since John's birth and advised that it assisted the baby to draw the milk at an acceptable speed if she heated a needle over a flame and inserted it into the hole of the rubber teat, to enlarge it a little. Advice given to Edwina by her first midwife. It was only at the midnight feed that she offered this, after the baby had spent a short while on each breast. He slept through to six o'clock that first night, at only two weeks old! Hazel knew this was unusual, especially when she heard other mothers at the clinic having so many problems with crying babies who hardly slept at night. She felt truly blessed to have such a contented baby.

He was still without a name when Tim and Hazel dropped him off in his carrycot to Audrey and Ron one evening and went to the cinema. They watched *The Dove*. A true story of sixteen-year-old Robin Lee Graham's lone sail around the world. The actor had a strong resemblance to Tim and as the love story unfolded and the film ended Hazel turned to her husband and suggested they call their son Robin or even Robbie. Finally, a name for their baby.

With Tim back at work after a two-week holiday, Hazel's life revolved around Robbie. She had bought a boiler that ran on gas and was fitted in the kitchen to boil the nappies clean. Wooden tongs were used to stir the nappies while they boiled and then to lift them into a spin dryer, buckets of water were poured into the spinner to rinse the nappies and the hand-washed baby clothes. The spun-dried washing was hung on the line. This had to be done every other day and was boringly time consuming.

Robbie needed feeding every four hours and he still took almost an hour each time as he kept dropping off to sleep. Then changing his nappy, then he'd poo, so changing him again. Getting his wriggling body into a weeny coat, with hat and mittens, ready to take King out for a walk. Putting Robbie's carrycot into its pram frame. Turning round to lift baby into pram just as he vomited most of his last feed over both of them. Telling King, "No, no walk yet." By the time she'd changed both herself and Robbie he wanted feeding again, then changing. Late lunch again and King still hadn't been walked. With Robbie peacefully sleeping she could have done some sewing, but King needed a walk. Coat, hat and mittens on, Robbie waking then wailing, only consoled by another feed and a change. Eventually, all out for a walk.

Exhausted, Hazel returned home. A cup of tea and a half-hour doze. Most of the evening spent sewing. Each day she woke with a plan for that day and a hope that she would settle into a reliable routine. It never happened. But she loved Robbie so much, couldn't imagine a life without him now. She talked to him as a small companion, explaining all she was doing. She lifted him out of his pram when they were out, showed him and explained nature as it evolved around them. Watched and listened to the power of the sea on a rough day. Sat among the trees in the woods watching clouds scudding through the dancing canopy. And the baby listened and copied his mother's smiles and laughs and gurgled in response to her words, all at less than four weeks old. He would lie happily awake in his pram in the garden, watching the waving branches of the apple tree that leant over from next door, with King asleep by its wheels. Hazel pinned a little round smiling gonk by a thin elastic string from the upturned hood for him to watch on windy days. She observed them from the kitchen window as she washed up. Few mothers with babies worked in those days. How can today's mother miss five days a week of their tiny offspring's life? Inconceivable to Hazel, how would a tiny new life feel, suddenly bereft of his mother, among strangers all day? What exactly was the effect of stress hormones on such a wee body? Did it lower the immune system, perhaps even making it more susceptible to allergies?

Ray and Edwina had Robbie overnight about once a week. Ray, who was still always up first, would lift his grandson from his carry/ camping cot to feed and change him as soon he woke up. He remarked that it wasn't until Robbie was at least six months old that he actually heard him cry.

CHAPTER 13
1976 ◇ Infidelity

The Beetle sat outside the house unused for most of the time Tim was at work, as a work colleague on the same shifts passed through Leigh and picked him up and dropped him off. It became obvious that Hazel should learn to drive. Ray said he was happy to take her down to Two Tree Island and give her some basic clutch control lessons. Helpfully there was a disused building, half sunk into the ground, with a driveway ascending from it. Once Hazel had mastered driving slowly on to and around the island Ray drove the car to this building, did a three-point turn at the bottom of the drive so the car was facing up towards the road and taught her to slowly lift and dip the clutch and edge her way up in a controlled manner. When she was able to do this and had memorised the Highway Code, Ray said she was ready for lessons with a registered driving school.

BMC offered a reliable, well-known service so Hazel booked them for a time when Tim was at home. The instructor pulled up outside the house. Hazel sat in the passenger seat as he went through all the checks she must make before turning the key. They swapped places and she started up the engine and deftly pulled into the road after checking her wing mirror and indicating. Less than a hundred yards down the road a car was coming up towards them. Hazel slowed to a stop as instructed. The road was narrow, cars were parked on either side but with spaces for the oncoming car to pull into. But the driver didn't. He continued to drive towards them. Hazel sat still for a few seconds. Then her instructor got out of the car, shut his door and walked up to the now stationary car. The driver of this car also stepped out. She was unable to hear their altercation but within seconds the instructor threw a punch and the two of them were then rolling, locked together in the road between the two cars. A pedestrian walking up the road shouted at them and the fight broke up. The pair returned to their cars. Hazel waited as the other car then reversed down the road into the nearest parking space. Her lesson then continued as if nothing had happened.

At the end the instructor praised her driving and said that she only needed another five lessons before taking her test. Once home she rang the driving school and, after explaining what had happened, she requested a different instructor. This second instructor was pleasant and patient. She had some interim driving sessions with Ray, but only around Two Tree Island as his company car was not insured for a learner. She practised three-point turns and parking neatly alongside the kerb.

Her test was on 22 December and she was overjoyed to be told that she had passed.

"Thank you so much, this is the very best Christmas present."

Hazel was so excited and overcome with gratitude that as he handed her the certificate she gave him a quick peck on the cheek and jumped out of the car. No more messing about getting baby, bag and buggy on and off buses. Even though the new, blue-striped, Maclaren buggy she'd purchased folded down swiftly with two simple movements.

There was a small respite in her repetitive life. She had met Mrs Gardiner (the Scots lady who had given Edwina their cat Panda) in the Broadway and was invited back for a cup of tea. She dropped King back home as they lived only a couple of roads apart, since taking him to a house full of cats would not be the best idea (even though he had been taught to ignore all furry beings).

Mrs Gardiner told Hazel about her cottage in Kent and said she would be happy to let her and Tim stay there for a week or so. Two weeks after Christmas it would be empty and if they could take down the Christmas decorations, dust and run the vacuum cleaner around, she would let them stay for free. She explained that the only heating was from an open fire in the lounge that smoked if too much wood was used, and a very old Aga in the small kitchen that they would need to light as soon as they arrived to give them hot water. Then, if they built it up it would burn all night for a warm kitchen in the morning.

They took up this offer on a bitterly cold, frosty, early morning in January. In a heavily laden Beetle, they found, as per Mrs Gardiner's instructions, an opening to a narrow lane about 500 yards past

Ashford town and trundled about a quarter of a mile down this lane to the cottage.

The only other building nearby was the thatched cottage belonging to Mrs Gardiner's son-in-law, Jim Dale. They were told he and his family would be there but would appreciate not being disturbed.

Hazel remembered with embarrassment the one time she had met Jim. She was only seven when Edwina had taken her and Michael to visit the famous singer, who was acting in the 'Carry On' films and was staying for a few days with Mrs Gardiner. On being led into the lounge Hazel saw the silhouette of a male figure outlined against the window. This man didn't look anywhere near as handsome as Jim Dale looked on television, which confused Hazel, but having concluded that make-up artists may 'do him up' for TV, she approached him and exclaimed, "I could squeeze you so hard until all your juices run out!"

The surprise on his face registered with Hazel just as she heard voices in the hall. She turned to see Jim enter the lounge with her mother and felt an awful shrinking embarrassment flush through her body. She kept her mouth shut after that. This man was exactly as she had seen him on the television. Disappointingly, he and his friend didn't stay long. She always regretted missing the chance to give Jim Dale a squeeze! She doubted he would remember her.

As expected of all quaint country cottages, the porch over the green front door was covered with a rambling rose – at present a woody skeleton awaiting spring. The door opened into a dark, wooden-floored hallway. Almost directly in front, was the door that led into the cosy lounge with a large open fireplace. A bench seat covered in cushions was built into the alcove next to it. A smaller door in the hall opened on a narrow wooden stairway that led to the wonky upstairs landing, two bedrooms and a small bathroom with a very low sloping ceiling. The lounge was permeated with the smell of smoke but they were careful to start the fire small (once it was burning strongly it could be built up slowly without too much smoke). The Aga welcomed them each morning as promised and, apart from having to boil the nappies in a large pan every other day, it was a wonderful holiday. King had the freedom to run around till he almost dropped. Hazel explored the surrounding meadows and pastureland and found gatherings of large horse mushrooms (*Agaricus arvensis*). After breathing in their recognisable scent she checked them in her little mushroom and toadstool book and they made a wonderful addition to their egg and bacon breakfast. No sightings of Jim Dale though. The smoke had ceased curling out of his chimney only two days after they'd arrived so they surmised he'd left. To make sure, they quietly crept around the cottage and peered in at the windows. Neat, tidy and empty.

Tim left Hazel, Robbie and King a couple of times to go fishing at Deal and returned each time with good-sized pollack, codling and whiting. Cooked in the Aga, wrapped in foil with some wild fennel and parsley, they tasted even better than good restaurant fodder. They decided this should be another yearly holiday.

With both sets of parents regularly having Robbie overnight, Hazel and Tim maintained their weekly drinking get-together with friends. One of them decided to throw a masked party. It was intriguing to attempt to guess other guests' names. As each person was recognised by someone they were allowed to remove their mask. Hazel wore a golden silk blouse over shiny dance leggings that slid into her black stiletto ankle boots. She and Tim danced together for a large part of the evening. Tim was recognised by a lady who told him they had been in the same class at junior school. In response he guessed who she was. Hazel watched as Lisa lifted her mask. If she was here then so was Simon. She searched the busy room. Although he was still masked, she instantly recognised his tall slim figure as he leant against the door frame, drink in hand. She pushed her way through the moving bodies to stand next to him.

"Simon."

He removed his mask and smiled, "Do I know you?"

Hazel explained that they had been in the same classes at Chalkwell junior school and detailed their high jump practice, their various teachers, her ponytail and her double-barrelled name. He said, no, he couldn't remember her. She removed her mask but he shook his head. He said he had no recollection of her. Hazel was astounded. She asked if he remembered an incident in the cloakroom.

His expression remained unchanged as he said, "No, that couldn't have been me."

He was still smiling at her. Did his expression say 'I refuse to discuss that' or had he completely blanked it out? She felt him enfolding her with his eyes though, willing her to stay. Hazel asked how he was doing. He replied that he had married Lisa several years ago and was now a maths and music teacher at a primary school about ten miles away. Hazel asked if he would dance with her? He replied he didn't dance. They continued to chat until Tim came up, grabbed Hazel's arm and pulled her back on the dance floor.

Hazel had hoped that Tim would grow out of his habit of being unable to stop drinking until they left whatever venue they were attending. If hiccups began before he got home and fell asleep then they would continue until he was sick. This had happened as long as she had known him. In his drunken state he became overly affectionate, constantly hugging and kissing her. Only once, before Robbie was born, had he been violent, when someone had laced his drink with neat alcohol at a works do.

He had staggered in after being given a lift home by a friend. Hazel met him in the hallway. He laughingly slurred that he had been ill several times in his friend's car. He had promised her not to get drunk and ill at this do. Clearly, he had broken this promise. She began to berate him, expecting him to go all soppy and ask for forgiveness in his usual way. But he lunged at her and put his hands around her neck. He lost his balance but not his grip as he swung her around and her head broke the stained-glass window in the front door. He immediately let go but then swung a fist at her, fortunately missing. She saw the car keys on the hall radiator, grabbed them and swung out of the door. Tim was stumbling close on her heels.

Hazel jumped into the driver's seat and frantically fumbled the key into the Beetle's ignition. Tim hammered on the window. Scared he would break it she, who at this point had only driven a go-cart, turned the key. She'd watched Tim's feet enough to have an idea of what to do. With adrenaline pumping through her system she pushed down the clutch, rammed the gear lever into first and kangarooed away from the kerb. She remained in first gear until the top of the road. She could see him in the mirror running up behind her. She pulled out slowly and turned left into the main road, thank goodness there was no traffic on it.

Finally she found second gear, which somehow got her all the way to the off-licence. She ran into the shop, sobbing. Tim's parents were both in the office. Nonsensical words tumbled out between her sobs. Ron sat her down and poured a brandy. She sipped. The heat slid down. The warmth slowly relaxed her. She described what had happened and said she was not going back to the house that night. They didn't argue and tucked her into Tim's old bed. In the morning Ron drove her home. Tim was already up and, with a raging hangover, was attempting to clean the bathroom where he'd obviously been very ill. He apologised to his father and Hazel, citing the neat alcohol as the cause. He was never violent again.

He was ill after the masked party but in the morning told Hazel that she had talked to Simon for more than ten minutes and that was not acceptable. So what if they had been at school together, that was no excuse to spend so long discussing it. It was alright for her to talk to his male friends but not to outsiders, he thought it was unnecessary. Hazel began to imagine an invisible cage growing around her, enclosing her with feeding, changing, washing, cleaning, dog walking, sewing; feeding, changing, washing, cleaning, dog walking, sewing; feeding, changing, washing, cleaning, dog walking, sewing …

Each week she walked to the library with Robbie in his pram and King on his lead. All the books she chose at this time involved romance. Thomas Hardy's dark, lonely atmospheres were favourites. Every spare moment she lost herself in their fantasy. She came to be repelled by Tim's sexual advances, although she attempted to hide it from him as well as she could. She was now back on the pill. A D&C (dilation and cauterisation) operation following Robbie's birth meant that thrush didn't occur as often as before, thankfully.

Edwina had disliked the idea of putting a baby in a playpen so had never had one and Hazel agreed. When Robbie was four months old she saw a baby bouncer in Mothercare and thought she would see what he thought of it, as he was so strong. It was wonderful. Strung up from a lounge doorway he could slowly swivel around 360 degrees and observe everything around him. It wasn't long before he discovered his little legs could jig him up and down.

When he was out of the baby bouncer Hazel always had to be aware of exactly where Robbie was and what he was doing. He was first intrigued by plug sockets at six months old, when he was able to slowly push himself around on his stomach. Hazel spent many times one week watching as he regularly made a beeline for one of the sockets sitting just above the skirting board. Each time his little hand was raised off the floor to touch one, Hazel, like training King, would have to pick him up, say "No" and put him back in the middle of the room with his toys. But the greatest problem came when Hazel needed to go to the toilet. A quick wee was fine but having him crawling around the toilet floor during anything longer didn't feel right. So she bought a plastic pot with a raised back support and perched him on it next to her. As he became accustomed to it Hazel began to make exaggerated noises of what she was actually doing. One day he obliged by doing a wee too. Hazel showed him the potty contents and praised him.

Robbie was eight months old when they camped on Portland that warm and sunny June. He had reached all the baby milestones early and was now using any large object to pull himself up on to his feet and was happily jabbering words. For safety, while they were relaxing by the tent, Hazel fitted him with a harness attached to a long piece of rope that was tied to a tent peg. He amused himself with a bowl of water, pots, pans, spoons, a duck and a boat. They kept his regular six-thirty bedtime, in his camping cot in the tent. It meant Tim and Hazel had to spend the evening outside the tent reading as Robbie refused to sleep if he could see his parents. They had tried taking him up to the pub or out for a walk in his pram in the evenings but his devouring curiosity for all that was going on around him meant he refused to sleep, then became tired and fractious, cried and was then unable to sleep. It wasn't worth it.

A diver who passed by most days on his way to check his lobster pots on a couple of occasions gave them a large live edible crab to cook. After boiling it, Tim knew how to crack its pincers and legs and prepare its meat. Crab meat fresh from the sea, like freshly caught fish, is a delicacy not many people experience. Hazel embraced it.

One evening, as Tim was fishing within earshot of the tent and King was contentedly asleep by his feet, Hazel took the opportunity to wander off by herself. She took the torch and followed the coast path past a collection of fishermen's shacks, past the Lobster Pot café, past Portland Bill lighthouse to the three-sided, tapering Trinity House obelisk. The twenty-two-foot tall obelisk was built in 1844 on a high plinth to warn ships of the low shelf of rock extending thirty yards into the sea off the coast of Portland Bill. It was made of Portland stone, had a pyramidal crown and was inscribed on its north face with TH 1844. Hazel felt tiny and insignificant as she stood all alone next to it and watched the waves crashing below her feet.

On the surface she was happy (as always, as long as the birds sang) and while Tim was working, she and Robbie still spent a lot of time with her parents and John (Michael was now married, rather against their parents' wishes, to a pretty little sixteen-year-old). She went on picnics and for days out with them, but inside she knew that she could not spend the rest of her life with Tim. He was possessive. She knew he'd loved Robbie from the moment of his birth but he had no interest in playing with him and regularly complained that Hazel's attention was always on her son and not her husband. She wanted another child but felt Tim shouldn't be the father. Marriage was a cage. Trapped, her spirit was suffocating. For how many years would she visit this place? For how many years would she ache to be free?

Home again the ache grew. She had introduced Robbie to the beach and held him while he splashed in delight at the water's edge. Tim joined them if he was not at work or fishing. He watched them play but rarely took part. He wasn't the one digging holes, building sandcastles or floating boats. He wouldn't be the one to teach Robbie, when he was older, to ride a bike or fly a kite or to identify the butterflies dancing with him while picking blackberries in the countryside; or how to fit the track and race cars with him on his Scalextric track; or to enjoy building large and complicated train tracks with three oo/ho gauge trains; or to buy and set up an electrical signalling system and landscaping it with long sweeping flyovers. It would always be his mother. Tim would take him fishing. He had warned Hazel he was not ready to be a father.

By the end of the summer Hazel could not hide her unhappiness and the couple were bickering a lot of the time. Usually after Tim had voiced an opinion that Hazel disagreed with. If she only learnt to hold her tongue. Hazel said they needed to see a marriage counsellor. Tim refused and said she was the one with the problem, he was quite happy. So Hazel went alone. She admitted to herself that all she really needed was advice on how to disentangle herself from their marriage. She didn't receive such help.

The counsellor was a thin small man, probably in his early sixties, with a pointed goatee. Hazel made the mistake of saying that one of the reasons her marriage was failing was that she no longer enjoyed sex with her husband. The counsellor took up this point and suggested she was frigid and must learn to relax. Should Hazel have requested a female counsellor when he suggested she needed to return the following week? She couldn't be bothered. Wrongly or rightly she concluded marriage guidance wouldn't help her with advice on divorce. She didn't tell Tim the counsellor's conclusion as she was sure it wasn't true but she did explain to her husband that he needed to spend more time on sex and foreplay, particularly finger manipulation to ensure she had an orgasm. Something that hadn't occurred to him and probably not to many men at that time. So, their lovemaking changed. Hazel kept her eyes closed and concentrated on the sensations his finger managed to arouse until her climax. It took a while but Tim was patient.

A month later he announced he had accepted a job on an oil platform in the North Sea and would be away two weeks out of every four. This would give her the freedom she craved. It shocked her, though, that he hadn't discussed it with her first but she wasn't unhappy with his decision. After working out his month's notice at Shell Haven, Tim kissed Hazel and Robbie goodbye and left with his holdall to walk to the station. A train to London, underground to Heathrow and flight to Aberdeen, then a helicopter to the platform. There for two weeks.

Sony had just brought out a twelve-inch colour TV. The white cube looked very modern and the picture was brilliant. Tim agreed it would be a good time to buy one. On her first evening alone, when Robbie was asleep, Hazel switched on the TV and welcomed the peace she felt. She enjoyed her first two weeks alone. Her parents had Robbie on Friday night so she went down to the Crooked Billet in Old Leigh. No one she knew was there but, sitting in the window seat with a Bacardi and lemonade and watching groups of happy people laughing as they wended their way to other pubs, was somehow comforting. She had no real worries now, a marriage with two weeks to please herself and Robbie felt almost 'doable'. For now.

The downside was walking King twice every day, although it was easier as Robbie got older. They often walked through Leigh in the morning, meeting at least one person she knew for a quick chat. There were no supermarkets so they made regular stops at the butcher, the baker and the greengrocer. King would sit patiently outside next to Robbie in his pushchair; his patience rewarded with a run in the library gardens or down to the seafront. Otherwise it was a run around the park, where only the peacocks were left of the animals Hazel had known as a child. But there was plenty to interest Robbie in the baby playground.

The butcher regularly gave Hazel a large beef bone for King to chew. When she was either in the garden or watching from the kitchen sink as she did the washing or washing-up, she put Robbie and his toys out there too. While she would not have let dog and baby out of her sight she knew King felt protective of the small human. On several occasions she had to lift Robbie away from the bone with a stern "No", as King was happy to let him to join in the chewing!

There was one memorable walk with King when Tim was home babysitting on the evening of 27 July 1976. It was a warm but windy evening and as darkness descended she saw an enormous fire blazing out at sea. She stared in disbelief, as did thousands of holidaymakers on beaches on both sides of the estuary. The end of the pier was a ball of fire. Firemen were fighting the blaze from tugs in the sea as well as from the pier itself but were hampered by the low tide. Additional water was distributed from crop-spraying aircraft. But to little avail. A momentary sense of desolation. No more happy times with walks to the café at the end for lunch, or an ice-cream break before catching the train back, or the excited anticipation of boarding the steamers. By morning all that was left was a smoking skeleton of warped metal girders where the pier head had once been. Fortunately, there was no loss of life.

Not long after though there was real sadness when Grandpa Dorrit died of pancreatic cancer. Hazel attended the funeral with Tim and her family. Ron and Audrey were more than happy to have their grandson for the day.

By the age of eleven months Robbie's early sitting on the potty paid off as he now had a complete understanding of what it was for and was totally dry and clean during the day, and sometimes at night. He had also taken his first steps a week before his first birthday. Fortunately, the smallest size packs of white pants that Mothercare sold just about stayed up once his trousers were in place. Hazel marvelled at how different he looked against other toddlers with fat, nappy-clad bottoms.

In early spring they were going for a week's camping on a farm in Wales for a change. So Hazel thought it was best not to get him used to no nappy at night until after then as books warned that changes of any kind may upset their training. Disposable nappies were now appearing in the shops so Hazel bought a pack to use on holiday. On their first evening there, Hazel put Robbie down to sleep in his travel cot secured in a new disposable nappy, and went to join Tim in the Beetle to read. After half an hour Hazel quietly unzipped the tent and peeked in to check if he was asleep yet. Not only was he sitting up, wide awake, but around the tent was a blizzard of tiny, white, cotton wool pieces extracted from the, now removed, nappy. Hazel slipped back to the car and asked Tim to take a look. Neither made any sort of exclamation but Hazel lifted Robbie up and said to him that she had better put some pants on or he would get a cold bottom, while Tim gathered up the 'snow'. Robbie never wore any type of nappy again and, as far as Hazel remembers, there were rarely any accidents.

Tim had not allowed fatherhood to curtail his regular fishing trips and Hazel did not resent it. It meant even more time for herself and Robbie. But either set of parents would happily have Robbie overnight and the following day, so occasionally she could rise at five in the morning to accompany Tim on a drive down to Deal in Kent. They had a full English breakfast in a café catering specifically for fisherman and bait diggers. Then boarded an open fishing boat with a small cabin, with just a captain as crew, and chugged out through its diesel fumes to fish for cod and mackerel when in season, and sea bass when they were shoaling on warm balmy days. Hazel found it difficult to understand how Tim could do this as he always ended up puking overboard at least twice. It was the fumes he said. They weren't pleasant but did not affect her strong stomach or she would not have gone. She did really enjoy the skill of waiting for a bite then grabbing and swiftly yanking the rod up or allowing it to run for a bit before gently reeling it in, depending on the type of fish.

Tim also asked Hazel if she would come with him for a day's fishing on board a trawler. She's not sure where they picked up the boat from but she remembers the sight and the overpowering fishy smell of the hold that had just been emptied. It was a windy, rough day. 'This will bob like a cork,' she thought. 'I wonder how long before Tim's ill today!' And bob like a cork on the heaving sea, it did. All day. Hazel and the crew were the only ones not ill. Once again she was grateful for Ray telling his children, during a rough crossing to Margate, that they should look out of the window and keep their eyes on the horizon if they felt queasy. She certainly needed to stand on deck and use his advice that day. Between being sick Tim did haul in a good-sized cod and the couple caught some codling, whiting and pollack, which meant plenty for the freezer. Hazel was happy for the one experience but didn't need to endure a ship full of ill people again! Whether Tim set foot on a trawler again, she can't remember.

During Tim's two-week absences Hazel would occasionally take a midday stroll down to the Old Town with King and Robbie and sit outside the Billet with a drink. As spring arrived she was able to drop Robbie at one of his grandparents' houses and sit outside the pub in the early evening, with just King. The handsome and well-behaved dog drew admiring comments. On one such evening Richie was relaxing alone outside when Hazel approached. He fussed and admired King and Hazel asked if she could buy him a drink. After falling into easy conversation, as if they had not had a break, he mentioned that he was going to a friend's house for a party the following weekend and she was welcome to go too. The house had once been two and was owned by his friend Ivan's architect father.

"In the bathroom they have two sinks with gold taps and a bidet. You should come and see it."

At this point the reader might wonder why Hazel was not going out for a drink with friends rather than alone. The friends they regularly drank with were originally Tim's friends and she would be a singleton to their partnerships. If they had insisted she may have taken up the offer sometimes. But they didn't.

Another reason was that Hazel had not changed from those early school days when she had no driving desire to have a regular friend. She always felt her life was full, with not enough time as it was to do the things she wished to do, such as creative crafts, drawing, painting pictures and so on. She never felt lonely as a full-time mother with a house that always needed some sort of decorating or DIY work doing; a garden to enjoy pottering in when the weather was fair; a lively dog who had to be exercised; always bumping into someone in the Broadway who wanted to chat and admire Robbie and King; her parents that she loved to pop round to; parents-in-law who lived at the far end of the Broadway and loved to give her a welcome cup of tea. It was only a wish to get away from everything occasionally to 'just be' and observe the world – a strong characteristic that had never faded.

A further reason was that she still felt more at home in male company. Apart from Carol, who was in exactly the same busy position, with a baby and a husband away in Abu Dhabi for a month at a time. She was still living in Benfleet, not far from her parents for company, and they did chat on the phone occasionally and visited each other's houses a couple of times, with their spouses.

It was because Hazel had to fly out of her cage sometimes, to remain sane, that she agreed to go with Richie the following weekend.

Ivan's parent's house did indeed live up to Richie's description. The party itself was low key, with a variety of people attending. Richie introduced her to a tall, blond, handsome Viking named Robin. He was very tanned and wearing a check shirt and she immediately imagined him as an Australian lumberjack. Hazel surmised he was quite a bit older than her and momentarily thought, 'I'm married. What a shame!' as she thought him wonderfully attractive.

She had every intention of walking home after the party. Richie, with affectionate determination, told her he had his own small room there and, while it only had a single bed, please would she stay the night with him. He assured her that Tim would never find out.

Her intention had always been to be faithful but her body longed to lie in Richie's arms as she was no longer gaining any pleasure from being within Tim's. In fact, she had woken one morning in suffocating fear as she felt locked down. A sleeping Tim had simply had his arm around her and had involuntarily tightened it on feeling her move.

That night she gave in to infidelity and left early the following morning to let King out of the conservatory and collect Robbie from her parents.

Hazel is unable to say how many times she met up with Richie. It was not often. It was not a full-blown affair. She cared enough about Tim's feelings to not want to hurt him. If that made any difference! And it did end.

Hazel had left Robbie with Edwina for the day to travel up to London to fit in some shopping around meeting up with Neil at twelve-thirty for lunch and with Richie for a drink at two.

There was plenty to catch up on with Neil as he was preparing for his wedding. Time slipped pleasantly by over lunch and a drink on the floating bar. It was two-twenty when Hazel checked her watch. With a rushed goodbye to Neil she hurried to the Bank tube station where she'd arranged to meet Richie.

At two thirty-five, surprisingly, Richie was still waiting. Hazel ran up and breathlessly poured out apologies, honestly saying she had met her old colleague for lunch and not realised the time. Richie stared silently at her for a moment.

"That's it," he said finally, "It's the end. There's just no point anymore."

And he strode off leaving Hazel feeling guilty and sad. She'd always thought nothing deeper would happen but he'd been a refuge for her restless spirit and she had cared about him.

CHAPTER 14
1979 ◇ Tragedy

At three Robbie was a lively, happy, intelligent little boy who, as his mother had chatted constantly to him from birth, likewise chatted all the time, to everyone. Even to himself when playing alone. He loved being around adults as well as his little contemporaries. As he was an only child, Hazel felt that he would enjoy and benefit from attending a nursery school. Playschools were emerging in 1977 but nursery schools were more of a precursor to full school and, in fun ways, introduced a basic understanding of maths, science and reading. Robbie went for the mornings and loved it.

Because Hazel was determined that Robbie would not encounter her problems with reading as a child, she regularly let him choose his own books from the library and, with him snuggled up on her lap, she would point to each word as she read. His only apparent failing, if it could described as that, was that he was a constant fidget. It explained perhaps why, even as a baby, he only wanted to be cuddled for a short while. He was always happier if he was lifted into an upright position, allowing him to observe all that was going on. And, while he loved looking at the books with his mum and listening to the nursery rhymes and stories, he would not stop fidgeting. Hazel concluded she should not expect concentration at such a young age.

She bought a pack of basic word cards and placed them around the house. For words such as train and cat, Hazel would find Robbie's corresponding toy and King very patiently put up with the dog card tied to his collar. Robbie loved the game but was not able to recognise the words once they were disconnected from their object. Hazel presumed that, perhaps, as he was a boy, he was not yet ready for this process and she eased back on her expectations. She was just pleased that he enjoyed nursery school.

Robbie was at nursery, so did not witness the strange event that turned King from a happy, obedient, affectionate and reliable family dog to one that had an issue around unknown small children. Although King did not change around his family and people he knew.

Hazel was walking, with King off the lead, along the seafront path between Chalkwell and Leigh stations past a bridge that swept over the railway track from the path by the 'wild' swimming pool. She had never liked it as there were unseen rocks scattered below the muddy water and much preferred to walk out to the Ray if the tide was out. King now reliably reacted to 'King, come' and 'King, heel' (at least, if she was commanding him rather than Tim!) and to the whistle she carried when she had no wish to strain her voice, such as when a train might be nearby. It was a pleasant, sunny, autumn morning. Hazel was enjoying the peace when King disappeared behind a tall wall around the bridge's lower steps and a terrifying unearthly scream rent the air. She felt the hairs on the back of her neck rise at the sound and rushed towards it to find a middle-aged woman with a young Down's syndrome boy. King, who had not even barked, was doing his usual 'happy to see you' bouncy dance at least a yard away.

"It's absolutely fine," the mother said, as soon as she saw Hazel's distress. "It's only that he doesn't like dogs. Your dog did not go close to him."

She was very relieved as she called King to heel. She did not remonstrate with him, as he had done nothing wrong, but did fit his lead immediately. After being assured again by the mother that no harm had been done, Hazel left them to continue their walk along the path. She walked King up and over the bridge and home. She tried to explain the awful ghostly scream that the little boy had emitted as she told Tim what had happened. She didn't dwell on it but never forgot the sound.

Two days later Tim, Hazel, Robbie and King were visiting Ron and Audrey. They were all in the office with the door to the shop open. King was curled up, bored, resting in front of the gas fire while they happily chatted over a cup of tea. As the bell tinkled over the door King leapt to his feet growling and rushed into the shop barking. Ron was the first to react. Not fast enough, unfortunately, as King grabbed the arm of a little girl who immediately began to cry. Tim also rushed into the shop fast on his father's heels. Hazel turned to block Robbie to ensure his natural curiosity didn't lead him to run into the shop after them. Audrey also went into the shop to check what had happened. She returned to inform Hazel that one of the dog's fangs had made a small break in the skin but had not drawn blood.

After a discussion with Ron the girl's father said he would not be making a complaint as long as the dog was kept muzzled in future. Everyone was shocked. Hazel walked to the pet shop in a daze and asked for a muzzle for a Doberman.

The dog accepted the muzzle but Hazel's sense of trust in him was shattered. Two days after the incident with the little girl, Hazel was walking him in the park and let him off the lead for a run in his muzzle. Within minutes he saw a small boy with his mother. Yards away from the boy she heard King growl, called him to heel and put him back on his lead. Deeply upset she now knew she'd lost her beloved, trusted dog. She collected Robbie from nursery and returned home intensely disturbed. After detailing this event to Tim, she left King in the conservatory with the run of the garden for the rest of the day. After Robbie was in bed she sat down with Tim and explained that, for Robbie's safety, she felt in her heart that the only sensible thing would be to have King 'put to sleep'. She felt a deep hole open up in front of her, one without her magnificent dog. But she would never forgive herself if Robbie, or any child, was harmed by him. She got an appointment with James Downes, the vet, in the morning. After explaining fully all that had happened the vet said that, yes, occasionally this happened with dogs and then suggested that she consider sending him away to be used as a stud dog. He had such a great pedigree.

Hazel returned home. King had grown up as a family dog. How could she make him understand why she was sending him away? And to what? A life in a kennel? For the first time she broke down in tears. Tim put his arms around her. He said it was her decision, he would support either option.

Hazel rang the vet the following morning. She told him that, as she could not bear the thought of him locked in a kennel, the best choice was for the vet to give him a lethal injection. King was fond of the vet so after dropping Robbie at nursery she walked him down to the surgery. With tears streaming down her face she gave her dog a long hug, then handed his lead to the vet and left, unable to watch him die.

Hazel was certain that James Downes would have honoured her request to put King down but as she didn't witness it and didn't want his dead body to bury, she would wonder, whenever she saw another Doberman, whether he might have put him to stud because of his superb pedigree and as he cared about the dog too. But it was almost forty years before she saw a dog as beautiful as King.

She never had another dog.

CHAPTER 15
1978 ◇ Losing Robbie

Edwina surprised Ray by passing her driving test first time. Much to his chagrin as he'd failed on his first attempt. It coincided with the Beetle needing some welding work done to pass its MOT. Edwina suggested she pay for the welding and then buy the car from Tim. Feeling it was time to have a newer vehicle anyway, Tim asked Colin the mechanic and he mentioned a VW 1600 Fastback he knew was up for sale. It was a sporty looking car in white, with a shape not unlike a Porsche, an automatic with a 'kick down' that gave excellent acceleration. Tim bought it and transferred the Beetle to Edwina. It was comforting to see their dear old car outside Hazel's family home while Edwina enjoyed the freedom it afforded her to visit friends or pop into Southend to shop. And Hazel felt proud to own and drive the Fastback.

Ray and Edwina had been to the Broads the previous year and asked Hazel and Tim if they wanted to join them aboard a narrow boat this year. To get away from Ray's snoring, Edwina chose to sleep with Robbie in the bow where two narrow beds lined the sides and touched at the bow's tip. Robbie thought it was a great idea and Ray was happy to take the lounge sofa as it allowed him to be first up in the morning and to make tea with biscuits for all. That left the double berth for Tim and Hazel.

With King now gone, Hazel felt a guilty relief that she no longer had to go out for a dog walk every day. On the Broads, she only needed to concentrate on Robbie. She ensured he had his life jacket on while he was on board, from as soon as he got up until he went to bed. She kept her eyes on him at all times, which wasn't difficult. Ever since his birth, Hazel felt she had an inbuilt antenna constantly tuned to his whereabouts. It was a dream holiday. Sunshine most days. Being rocked asleep by the lapping waves. Waking to the sound of ducks and a cup of tea and biscuit in bed, followed by a fried breakfast with

Hazel's favourite black pudding every morning. They moored by pubs in the evening and went for forays on foot to local museums, cafés and places of interest. Then they discovered Roy's on a long wharf right next to the river. It was a large, single-storey wooden building that sold everything one might need while on a Broads holiday.

After tying the boat to the wharf only seventy yards from Roy's, removing Robbie's life jacket and putting on his coat, they all left the boat to enter the shop. Once inside, they separated, heading for different sections. Hazel and Tim wanted to look at the clothing. Robbie, not interested in clothing, turned to go with his grandpa. Half an hour later, after various purchases, Hazel and Tim saw Ray and Edwina outside. But Robbie was not with them. Hazel had thought he was with his grandfather. Ray had thought Robbie was with his parents. Fear gripped her. An abyss opened up where Robbie should have been. She felt life shift and panic rise as they all split up and went back inside Roy's to search for him, calling his name.

Hazel's thoughts were filled with visions of someone grabbing hold of her son's hand and dragging him off. She doubted that he would go quietly with a stranger. With growing trepidation, she reached the far end of the shop, her eyes constantly scanning for a sight of his little blue check coat through the throng of moving bodies. Edwina was the last to return to the entrance. No Robbie. Pounding fear throbbed through her. Where was her son? She was filled with visions of him being gagged or having some substance pressed over his mouth to render him unconscious. He was still small enough for people to assume he had fallen asleep on someone's shoulder. Hazel's antenna had let her down badly. She would never trust it again. She attempted to lock into a kind of telepathy. She believed mothers would know if their child had been killed. All she felt was that he was alive somewhere.

Could he have returned to their boat? He was intelligent enough to know that was the safest place for him. As a group, they all moved to the edge of the wharf to see a large paddle steamer moored where their boat had been! Ray ran towards it. He returned to say their boat had been moved further down towards the end of the wharf. Hazel, with only her son in mind, ran to find it. There was Robbie, with his life jacket on, sitting on the padded seats in the open back of their boat. No words can explain the relief Hazel felt. She jumped down to

187

hug him and told him how clever he was to have found their boat and put his life jacket on. He appeared unfazed and said he had found their boat without a problem, a man tying up the steamer had pointed it out to him. He said he had intended to follow his grandfather through Roy's but had lost him in the crowd. The relief they all felt meant the holiday had not been spoilt and the many happy memories outweighed the brief panic.

Robbie had enjoyed nursery school for a year. He was now approaching four and Hazel considered that he might blossom even more at the private Ridley's Art and Drama school by Chalkwell Park, which was as close as his nursery, only a five-minute walk. He could attend full time for a year before he was due to begin regular school at five. She took him for a look around on the open day. He was impressed and pleased to settle into their early year's class that September.

With Tim away every alternate two weeks and Robbie at full-time school, Hazel felt a need to work again. Tim was against this as he believed he alone should provide for his family. But she needed a say in how she spent some money and she craved interaction with other people. It was one more thing for them to argue about. Then, while Tim was away, she saw a job at Southend Technical College for a part-time technician in the art and design department. She immediately rang for an application form, filled it in as soon as she received it and sent it back. Within a couple of days she received a phone call inviting her to an interview.

At the interview she learnt the technician was responsible for repairing all the wooden equipment used in the department, such as easels, donkeys (a bench with a prop to support a painting), weaving looms and so on. The printing presses would also need regular maintenance. It required only twenty hours a week and they were happy for her to only work mornings. The job was perfect as the college holidays were the same, or even longer, than Robbie's school holidays. They felt that her experience as a model maker meant she was their preferred candidate and offered her the job on the spot. She could start the following week.

During her first month at college Hazel made friends with Dean, the photography tutor. He was tall and skinny, quite a bean pole! Even his bearded face was long and thin, reminding her of the actor Donald

Sutherland. They got chatting in the college canteen queue. She mentioned a couple of pictures that she needed to frame. He said that he was driving to the framer that morning if she would like to come.

Slowly, this friendship became the lifeline she needed to save her from the creeping misery of her marriage. Over the months Hazel poured out her heart to him regarding her feelings for Tim. She felt such guilt because, apart from being himself, she felt Tim had done nothing to deserve the hurt he and Robbie would suffer if she left him. Her feelings were confused as, towards the end of Tim's two weeks away, she looked forward to his homecoming. Then, within days, his strutting around, attempting to lay down the law, together with his continued criticism of everything Robbie did, bored into her and she couldn't wait for him to leave again.

Coincidentally, Dean mentioned that The Crooked Billet in Old Leigh was becoming his favourite Friday night watering hole. She'd not seen him there before. So, when Tim was away, Hazel started to join the noisy, lively, Friday night clientele more regularly.

Dean was also a member of the Westcliff Leisure Centre, which was built on the foundations of the old Southend swimming pool on the seafront. The members-only facility was built on three levels. A small, gloriously warm swimming pool with showers and changing cubicles in the basement, along with a large snooker room with three or four full-size tables. The middle floor housed the squash courts, a dance floor and a bar. A circular stairway with a wrought-iron handrail led from the dance floor to the top level with a second bar and restaurant and access to an open deck next to a casino area. The casino had a separate entrance and Hazel only entered once, just to have a quick look. It was as you'd expect, she thought, with thick, plush, red and gold carpet dotted with roulette tables.

Hazel had requested a tour of the leisure centre not long after it had opened. With a pool to take Robbie to in the winter and a reasonably priced restaurant overlooking the estuary to enjoy in the summer, a family membership was worthwhile. It also meant guaranteed free parking on the seafront. As their weekend drinking friends were members and regularly played squash together, Tim accepted the idea without too much argument and Hazel signed up. They bought squash rackets and occasionally paired up with friends to play singles same-sex games, as they had no desire to play each other. This membership allowed Hazel to follow Dean in their separate cars to the leisure centre after The Crooked Billet's closing time, to continue drinking and dancing – as was common in the days before drink/driving laws.

Did sex feature within this friendship? After college one day, they enjoyed a pub lunch together then Dean invited her back for coffee to a flat he shared with a fellow photographer. In the pub Hazel had begun to experience an ache, a strong desire to be enveloped in Dean's arms, to banish thoughts of her hollow marriage for just a few moments. As they walked into the empty flat, she turned to Dean. He removed her jacket, threw it over the sofa and tenderly put his arms around her. Their first tentative kisses ignited her passion but Dean withdrew his lips and whispered, "There's no rush, we have the rest of our lives."

He unwrapped himself from her to put the kettle on. Slightly confused, Hazel slowly digested this and decided it was a comforting thought. Yes, from this point anything could happen, but it felt he was implying that, regardless, their friendship would always continue. Acutely aware of her emotional difficulties Dean was careful not to complicate matters further. Her need to be cuddled did lead to occasional sex but she was aware that, as a photographer, he met many beautiful women. He had a close friendship (platonic, he assured her!) with a dancer from Pan's People, a troupe that featured regularly on the popular *Top of the Pops* on TV. He did not ask to photograph her and she accepted that, since she was a married woman, he did not feel a serious affair was appropriate. But within a year she cared for him with a depth that didn't appear to be reciprocated. She explained her feelings to him one evening, in her lounge, concluding that it was an extra complication she wasn't able to cope with. He didn't question her decision to break completely. As she heard the front door close behind him she slid off the sofa, where they'd sat together, to the floor. There she remained for a couple of hours, crying out the misery of loss.

Robbie's end of term report came home together with his hand-drawn Christmas card. The first entry on his report was for 'Command and Understanding of the English language', which had 'Excellent' next to it. However, apart from 'Good' next to physical education, the rest of his report was average to poor. Mystified, Hazel went to discuss this at the parents' evening.

Robbie's teacher said Hazel should not worry too much at this stage as it appeared to be his concentration that was lacking. His fidgeting had not settled, which Hazel knew was a problem. It wasn't until the end of his second term when he brought home his next report that she did begin to worry. Still excellent at understanding and speaking English, but very poor marks for written English. His teacher was also concerned. He was becoming disruptive, she said, and he appeared to have trouble holding a pencil. He was left-handed, like his father, and Hazel had watched Robbie drawing pictures at home and had not attempted to correct his wish to hold a crayon or pencil in his left hand. She was perplexed as she had not felt he had a problem with actually holding the crayons or a pencil. He seemed to struggle with copying his name mainly because of his fidgeting and lack of concentration.

As Hazel walked home, she attempted to imagine Robbie's world as he saw it but his being disruptive seriously concerned her. He was a lively boy, constantly on the go, with very little sense of fear and she was frustrated when she felt that he did not absorb the importance of certain things she told him. Perhaps too much information from her had caused him to turn off. She wondered whether disruptiveness implied a need for more attention. She certainly believed that she gave him enough, but what about attention from his father? Tim was away for two weeks in every four. He would tell his son, as he left him to go away for another two weeks, that he was the man of the house now and must look after his mother. Then, when at home, he criticised him for every little thing, from his shoelaces not being tied properly to his hair not being brushed. While he sometimes brought toys home, he never actually played with his son. Hazel argued with Tim about his constant criticism, but made sure that they never argued in front of their son. She also considered the fact that she sometimes smacked him, perhaps too much (smacking with an open hand, across the bottom or the leg, was then considered an acceptable form of punishment). She told herself it was mainly done for his own safety, after telling him at least three times not to do something. The problem was either he failed to absorb the severity of what she was explaining or, as seemed to be the case, he forgot it ten minutes later. Hazel felt that a short sharp smack was the only way to press the message home.

Edwina, who was babysitting, respected Robbie's six-thirty bed time and so he was asleep when Hazel got home. This gave her a chance to discuss Robbie's problems with her mother but Edwina had no answers. Hazel discussed it again with her husband a couple of days after he had returned from the oil platform. Unfortunately, like his son, Tim also appeared unable to absorb the importance of the information his wife was imparting. As far as he was concerned he was in the right. Hazel tried to counteract her husband's criticisms by ensuring she praised Robbie for every small achievement. She would try not to smack him as much, particularly when his bedroom was untidy. However, Robbie throwing his clothes over toys he could not be bothered to put away was a safety issue! Quite a few of his toys were metal. That was her excuse anyway. The truth was his untidiness did frustrate his mother at times. But she loved him so very deeply, deeper even than her love for her father, and the worry that something might be causing a problem for her son ached inside her.

Chalkwell Hall Junior School was their catchment-area school, where she and her brothers had gone. But it had a poor teaching reputation with less than a forty per cent chance of passing the eleven-plus, whereas West Leigh Junior School near Belfairs had the best reputation in all of Leigh. In light of Robbie's problems, Hazel began looking at selling their house and buying a property within West Leigh's catchment. She discussed with Tim the maximum he thought they could stretch to. As usual he gave a modest amount. Because of the school and because it was close to the expensive Marine and Highlands estates, housing in this area was valued more highly than elsewhere in Leigh.

Scanning the local papers while Tim was away, Hazel saw a long rectangular bungalow on a large corner plot. It was surrounded by tall leafy hedging and was only about 200 yards from the woods. Hazel knew she should view it. It was above Tim's budget but they might accept a lower offer.

Too impatient to wait for her husband to return home, Hazel booked to view it alone while Robbie was at school.

The bungalow and garden felt secluded behind the tall hedging. The front door could just be seen down a short path. There was a good-sized, south-facing lounge made very light by the large French doors set within full-length glass panels that overlooked the rear garden. Two heavily laden pear trees stood just outside, either side of the lounge, framing the wide view. From a spacious kitchen an open pine stairway rose up to a large, long attic room with a dormer window overlooking the rear garden. Its sloping ceiling was boarded and painted white and the floor had good solid wooden floorboards. It was a wonderfully uplifting space, perfect for Robbie's train set. Hazel was immediately in love with it all. The estate agent confirmed that the chimney would allow for an open fire in the lounge.

Already able to picture their furniture in place, Hazel knew she would put in an offer as soon as she got home. The vendors refused her first offer. She waited for Tim's phone call the following evening and enthused to him about the bungalow, explaining that it really was everything they wanted and was only yards from Belfairs woods. Tim grudgingly agreed the amount Hazel suggested for her next offer, which was accepted.

Hazel was so excited about their new home. She had to ring the solicitors a couple of times to urge them to speed up the purchase, but everything seemed to be moving successfully. The young couple buying their house had been granted a mortgage. The vendors of Tim and Hazel's bungalow were cash buyers of the property they wanted. Her excitement fired her imagination, which meant she was finding it difficult to quiet her racing mind at bedtime. This created a vicious circle as lack of sleep sped up her brain activity during the day, making sleep at night almost impossible. After three nights of no sleep she could contain her excitement no longer and rang Edwina to ask if she would like to see the bungalow. The vendors were happy to allow Hazel to visit again. She collected her mother in the Fastback after finishing work at lunchtime and enthused about it all as she drove.

At one point her mother said, "Hazel, you have just driven through a red light!"

'Oh no,' thought Hazel, 'it would be so awful for Robbie if we ended up in heaven instead of in our new home.' She slowed down and realised that she must concentrate on her driving when she was suffering from insomnia. It was the first time that she felt her sleeplessness was affecting her negatively. Edwina was suitably impressed with the bungalow.

Collecting up boxes when her father-in-law managed an off-licence was easy and Hazel began packing up everything not in use. They decided to hire a van and move themselves. One of Tim's fishing friends offered to help on that Saturday, fortunately while Tim was home. They dropped Robbie with Edwina and Ray then collected the van. Tim drove it home with Hazel following. They'd dismantled the beds and had slept on mattresses. They actually managed, with methodical manoeuvring, to get everything in, so needed only one run. Hazel quickly ran the vacuum cleaner over the floors, stowed it in the car and whispered, 'Goodbye house', before closing its door for good.

The bungalow was on the corner of Bonchurch Avenue, so the family simply called it Bonchurch. Moving in went smoothly. It was a long, tiring day but not as bad as Hazel had expected. After collecting Robbie she picked up fish and chips. They slept on mattresses again for their first night and the following morning began the laborious task of unpacking.

They loved their new home and Hazel's spirits were greatly lifted. She felt a mental freedom within the bright space and wide garden, even when Tim was home. She dug out a large, kidney-shaped hole at the bottom end of the garden, in direct view of the French doors, and laid in a pond liner. She used the displaced soil to build a rockery around the back and cemented paving slabs around the front. After filling the pond with water and allowing it to stand for a couple of days for the chlorine to dissipate she took Robbie to the aquatic department of a large garden centre. They bought oxygenating plants and a waterlily, and chose some fish (six golden Orff, seven brightly coloured barbed carp and one ghost carp, so named for its golden skeletal markings on a tawny background). They left the fish in their bags to float on the pond to reach the water temperature and put the pond plants in baskets, which they lowered to the bottom. A couple of hours later, Hazel gently cut the bags open and, as Robbie watched, she tilted them to allow the fish to swim into their new residence. With the rockery planted up it added a meditative peace. Again with Robbie, she gathered some toad and frogspawn from the ponds in Chalkwell Park and they watched the hatched tadpoles grow tiny legs and hop out on to the lawn. Hazel didn't mow the grass for a few weeks, by which point the pond was now occupied by some fully-grown frogs.

Hazel had intentionally spent a little more on the fish to ensure they were large enough to resist the clutches of frogs and toads, which she'd read could strangle young fish. The fish, in turn, produced enough fry to create a natural cycle.

Although on the surface Hazel was happy, the bickering within her marriage did not abate. But she was Tim's wife and had signed up to a lifetime of love and support. All those years ago her parents had said she could cancel the wedding. She'd had a choice. As Tim had told her, on a couple of occasions when they discussed how unhappy she was, "You've made your bed and now you have to lie in it."

But even Tim's kisses were beginning to revolt Hazel. A marriage without sex, as far as she was concerned, could only exist if both were happy with it. Why should either or both of them have to find sex outside their marriage? So she continued to consent. She would often awake at night, regardless of whether Tim was home asleep next to her or not, and get up to make a milky drink. In tears she'd sit in the lounge or stand at the French doors with the curtains open, staring at the stars. Robbie's happiness was everything to her, they loved their home. How would they all exist if she split them up?

However, life was not all doom and gloom! While Tim was not thrilled about spending money on holidays abroad, Hazel managed to persuade him to spend ten days in Lanzarote. She had pushed her worries aside as they travelled up to Fire Mountain on a camel, explored lava tunnels and generally relaxed in the warmth. Robbie's ability to make friends anywhere was also proven here when he engaged with a little German girl at the swimming pool a few times, even though neither understood a word the other said.

They now enjoyed regular camping holidays in Cornwall rather than Portland but, as Tim regularly travelled up to Scotland and back, Hazel had the idea of taking the camping equipment and meeting Tim in Aberdeen. To break their travel to Scotland, Hazel and Robbie camped just outside the walls of the city of York and spent five days visiting the Jorvik Viking Centre, the Motor Museum, York Minster, the Shambles (a fascinating narrow street of houses, some dating back to the fourteenth century) and exploring the city from sections of the wall.

After picking up Tim from Aberdeen airport they travelled through Edinburgh and went on to camp at the foot of Ben Nevis. The weather turned and torrential rain during their first night meant the nearby river rose to within six inches of their tent! Not wanting to risk being flooded out, they moved to a campsite in Glencoe. The weather refused to brighten and after a few damp days, followed by a very wet day in Oban, they concluded that Scotland was set to be wet for a while. This left them with the only option of travelling south. More heavy clouds dispersing their rain over the Lake District urged them to continue to Wales. It wasn't until they reached Tenby that they finally glimpsed the sun, only for it to disappear again once they'd set up the tent. But regardless of the weather they all managed to enjoy the holiday.

Hazel was still going down to The Crooked Billet occasionally. While she was able to avoid Dean at work, it was inevitable she would meet him there. Hazel missed his company desperately and for a while his smile and friendly chit-chat at the pub were enough. But one evening he asked if she was coming to the leisure centre at pub closing time. Once there, with a little alcohol, every muscle felt loose and fired up by the beat of the music. Dean was on the dance floor with a cluster of friends. Hazel knew she couldn't compare to his professional dancer friend but she didn't care, so joined them. With each new tune Hazel moved closer to Dean. They locked eyes and he touched her hand then held her arms gently as they moved together. She stretched up towards to his ear.

"Please come home with me tonight," she shouted over the music.

He gave the slightest nod. Hours later, as he slept next to her, she knew that without Dean's occasional company, life looked bleak. His friendship, his warm body, comforted her. They never spoke of love.

Dean invited her to accompany him on a college field trip with his students. Hazel had bought a manual Pentax K1000 SLR camera and had been lucky enough to come across a professional tripod in a secondhand shop. It was worth £80 new and was in excellent condition so was a bargain at £25. Having read most of the up-to-date books on SLR photography in the library, Hazel stupidly said that while Dean had demonstrated his excellent teaching abilities to his students, she had learnt little that she hadn't already known. He didn't invite her again! But their friendship deepened and although Hazel didn't see him as often as she would have liked, he assured her he was at the end of the phone day or night if she needed to chat.

Meanwhile Robbie, smartly attired in a yellow and brown West Leigh school blazer with matching tie, had begun his first year at the school that was now just up the road. He appeared to be happy enough and, as usual, had no problem making friends. He was still struggling with reading and writing, despite the help Hazel gave him at home. His teacher said his behaviour was acceptable, with no hint of the disruptive nature he had shown at Ridley's and his maths in his two infant years was average.

During their second term all children were given a health check by a local GP. Robbie returned home with a letter explaining that a slight heart murmur had been noticed during the examination. During Tim's medical, prior to taking his job offshore, a slight heart murmur had also been noted but was not considered to be of any real consequence. As medicals for offshore work were quite stringent neither Hazel nor Tim felt any real concern regarding Robbie's slight murmur.

Robbie had always been comfortable with Dr Quinn. Following his retirement, he was replaced by Dr Quashi, an Indian with a very strong accent that even Hazel found difficult to decipher. Looking back Hazel wondered whether Robbie had found this a little frightening, causing his heart to pound and exaggerate the problem. After listening to his heart Dr Quashi asked whether Robbie had been a 'blue baby'. A little confused by this question Hazel replied that he had looked grey when he was born, until his first cry, when he immediately turned pink so, no, she did not think he'd been a blue baby.

"Can he run around in the playground without getting breathless?" was the next question, to which Hazel said he was able to do all exercise without getting breathless. Unimpressed by these answers, the doctor said he was going to request an appointment at Great Ormond Street hospital as the heart murmur appeared severe. He told Hazel to take her son home, keep him well wrapped up and not allow him to do anything strenuous. While she knew that his heart murmur should be checked out, she believed that it was no worse than his father's. Great Ormond Street Hospital, as a renowned children's hospital, treated Robbie with a gentle kindness that put him completely at ease. The doctor, with cheerful banter about making him bionic, carefully fitted wired pads to his chest. Once the results were checked, Hazel and Robbie were called.

"I don't understand why Robbie was referred here," began the consultant, "as his heart murmur is only slight and nothing at all to worry about."

Hazel said she had no idea why as she had also felt it was not significant. She said she was just glad her GP was wrong. It was the first time she had ever questioned a doctor's judgement.

When Robbie started in the junior section of West Leigh school, Hazel was shocked to discover that he had been placed in the remedial class. Apart from explaining to her son that this would allow him to have more help with his reading and writing and then checking with him that he liked his new class, which he did, she made no fuss. Within two weeks, though, she had a phone call from his teacher asking her to come to the school for a chat. Mrs Woodford began by saying she was mystified as to why he was having such a problem with his reading and writing, as he was clearly an intelligent boy. Hazel, unable to enlighten her, detailed his year at Ridley's and described what she had done with reading cards and so on. But that she had decided not to push him when he appeared to have such difficulty.

About a month later Edwina mentioned to Hazel that she had watched the actor Susan Hampshire on TV, describing her problems with dyslexia. Could Robbie have dyslexia? Mrs Woodford agreed that this might be his problem. Hazel rang the Dyslexia Institute in Chelmsford and was told her son needed to be assessed by a psychologist first before they could admit him for help. They recommended one in Bury St Edmunds. Hazel made an appointment for a date when Tim was home. It was quite a distance by car and they might as well make a day of it. Robbie was given what looked like IQ questions and the psychologist talked to him to put him at ease. He asked him to work through the questions at his own pace and not to worry if there were some he could not answer. With plenty of fidgeting Robbie answered all the questions. The psychologist thanked him and disappeared to work out the results. He returned to say that Robbie's IQ of 124 was above average (average is 90–110) and therefore he should be able to gain entrance to a university but that his reading age was six months behind his actual age. He said the discrepancy between his IQ and his reading age suggested there was a problem but because Robbie had not displayed all the characteristics of dyslexia the psychologist felt it would be unhelpful to label him as dyslexic. However, he agreed that the Dyslexia Institute could provide some help with their preference for phonetic reading and writing. He gave them a letter to pass on to the Institute.

It was fortunate that Tim's salary was comfortable enough to allow Robbie to attend the Institute two afternoons a week. Mrs Woodford was very happy with the outcome and by the end of that first term he was able to return to a mainstream class. Hazel agreed with his new teacher, Miss George, that they would work together to give Robbie every possible help and encouragement. They told him that if he had worked hard for a whole week Hazel could buy him a treat, which varied depending on Robbie's wish. Sometimes a toy car, sometimes a book or a visit to the pictures. This bribery appeared to work and most weeks Miss George felt he was, at least, trying.

On a visit to a garden centre with a pet section Hazel and Robbie were intrigued to see a large enclosure full of tortoises. She was sure a ban on their import had been in place for months. They might not get another chance to buy one of the world's longest-living land animals. As they observed this gathering of at least fifty, one tortoise stood out as being the most active. It had a tiny chip on the surface of its shell but Hazel concluded that it was the healthiest, as it was the only one vigorously stomping about and chomping on piles of cabbage leaves. She bought him for £8.50. They were given a box to transport him home in and made a good-sized run out of some spare floor boards lying around in their shed. Hazel used some odd bricks to build two walls out from the run and sawed down a wider piece of wood for a roof. Robbie gave him a bowl of water and some cabbage, lettuce and cucumber. They'd watched him eat these at the garden centre. They tried other recommended foods but these remained his favourites.

To help build up his non-academic skills, Hazel thought it would be useful to enrol Robbie in a local Cub troop, which was the first step to becoming a Sea Scout. This he thoroughly enjoyed, particularly going away on camp – just as Hazel had.

CHAPTER 16
1982 ◊ Hazel's Greatest Loss

By the end of 1981 Hazel was seriously concerned by Tim's constant criticism of Robbie, worried that it might undo all the confidence she and his teacher were instilling in him. Hazel's mother later told her that Ray had exclaimed to his wife on several occasions, "Why can't he leave the boy alone?"

On 1 January 1982 Hazel decided it was time to make a New Year's resolution. Something she'd never previously seen any point in. But what Hazel was planning required a strength that had to be found; to leave her husband, to wrench her son from a life he was secure in, to embark on an unknown path.

Hazel had been checking the list of local jobs in both the free papers and the *Echo* each week for a full-time job. An advert from a hi-fi company caught her eye. They required someone able to solder and who could learn to build turntables and tonearms using precision components. She put together a CV and called round to Edwina's to type it up. The company rang her a week later and asked if she would attend an interview.

Hazel was nervous as she drove towards Southend. It was only a few minutes' walk from the high street. She allowed plenty of time to give herself a pep talk, knowing that it was best she appear relaxed and reasonably knowledgeable.

She was interested to see what looked like a modernised old mill building with the number of the property cut out of thick board and painted in light green on the bare brick wall above the door, 119. Hazel had an impression of good design even before she rang the bell. An attractive, red-haired young lady opened the door and Hazel followed her up a steep flight of stairs. The inside of the building matched the bare brick outside. All doors and door frames were painted in the same, easy-on-the-eye, light green. Hazel followed the woman through a small office and into a large room, which also had bare dark brick walls that felt a little oppressive with only one window at the end. Four turntables were mounted along one wall. Two large speakers stood in front of the window. Either side of the door were shelves stacked with record albums. Two small, low, light-green sofas and a couple of green canvas armchairs occupied by two men completed the room.

They stayed seated and introduced themselves as Rouse and Trevor. Even seated, Rouse was long and slender, with a prominent beak nose and dark penetrating eyes. Trevor had a balding head atop a round face with a mixed gingery, salt and pepper beard. His thick-rimmed glasses gave the illusion of very large blue eyes. Both men watched Hazel as she settled into a sofa. She willed herself not to be intimidated, but it was difficult. She described the work she had undertaken as a model maker and detailed the various materials she'd used. She also told them how she had worked on a model of a seed silo for a court case, which had to demonstrate how a weakness had caused it to collapse.

"So you understand stresses and strains?" asked Rouse.

"There is the equation for force, which off the top of my head I'm not sure of, but I can check it," Hazel declared. She also mentioned that, as a child, she had loved listening to music with her father and that they had discussed the merits of the fine sound produced on his new stereo system.

Trevor talked about pay and holidays and then the interview was concluded. Hazel left with the feeling that she had made a positive impression but thought there would surely be someone better qualified for the job. Two days later, she received a phone call asking if she would be able to come in for a two-day trial. Her trial was successful.

After some argument, Tim capitulated to her decision to take a full-time job. Hazel was not ready to tell him that this could signal the end of their marriage.

When chatting with other mums, someone had mentioned that a retired teacher was looking for a little child minding. Hazel rang her and asked if she would like to drop round and meet her son. Mrs Silk seemed more like a friendly aunt than a school teacher. Robbie and

Hazel warmed to her immediately, especially when she said she would help Robbie with his homework.

Robbie had completed two years at the Dyslexic Institute. After phonetic training his reading age was now three months behind his actual age, which was still below the level predicted by his IQ. However the Institute felt there was nothing further they could offer. The only advice they could give was to continue with any extra help his school could provide. It was one less expense and it solved the problem of travelling to Chelmsford twice a week.

Full-time work was pleasant enough and Robbie was happy to walk home alone from school with Mrs Silk waiting for him. Edwina was able to keep him occupied during the parts of the school holidays that Tim and Hazel couldn't cover and Hazel ensured her four weeks' paid holiday leave were spread around Easter, summer and half term holidays. The hi-fi company closed between Christmas and New Year, as long as all the orders were completed. They always were.

Edwina had been close to her father but was even closer to her mother and felt her loss in 1980 terribly, also from pancreatic cancer. Her entrenched English 'stiff upper lip' had held her together.

Then in October 1981 an even larger cloud loomed over all of their lives. It appeared when Hazel, Tim and Robbie were holidaying at Mrs Gardiner's cottage.

Hazel learnt of it through a phone call from Edwina: "Hazel, you need to brace yourself for some bad news about your dad."

Ray had developed a cough a few months ago after doing some decorating at home. He thought it had been triggered by plaster dust but when it refused to clear up Edwina insisted he saw the doctor.

"He's had some X-rays taken of his chest and they show shadows on his lungs. They say the cancer is too far advanced to operate."

Hazel was stunned. Her mind exploded, shattering her world. She attempted to grab some of the flying pieces. Her father had always been there for her. She loved him to bits and, next to Robbie, he had always been the most important person in her life. The thought of him dying was unbearable.

It occurred to Hazel then that, while she'd been able to imagine her mother in old age, she'd never been able to picture her father as an old man. Now it seemed she knew why. He was only fifty-nine.

"We're coming home," Hazel replied.

The company Ray worked for had decided to move to Wimbledon. Not wishing to increase his travelling time, he was now working for a shopfitter in Shoebury. Swapping the tedious daily commute for a leisurely drive along the seafront made up for a drop in salary. On hearing of his illness, the company assured him he could take off as much time as he needed.

Ray started chemotherapy. Ice packs were applied to his head to prevent hair loss so, outwardly, he was unchanged. He managed to work around his chemo but was grouchy, especially as he'd also stopped smoking. Once his nicotine cravings subsided, he became more buoyant and decided to make the most of life. He'd not been told that his cancer was terminal, but Hazel suspected that he must know. They never discussed it.

John had married a local lady in 1980 and Michael and his wife now had two young daughters. They both owned houses in Leigh. The whole family were determined to ensure Ray's life was filled with family days out, picnics, laughter and happiness.

Ray's illness meant the plan that Hazel had begun to formulate for ending her marriage had to remain a secret as her parents had more than enough to cope with. Although her resolution to end it that year was unchanged and she told only Dean.

For most of this time Ray had remained reasonably fit, but after a second bout of chemotherapy he did lose his hair. He bought a wig that he was very pleased with. He told Hazel that, after leaving a meeting with an architect the previous, very windy, day his wig had blown off, rolled up like a little animal and tumbled down the road. He'd raced after it, with cars all around him screeching to a stop. It had suffered no damage and was put safely back on his head. They had a good giggle.

One of Hazel's last memories of her father was of a hot day in August when the tide was out and he felt strong enough to walk out from Chalkwell beach to the watery Ray with Edwina, Hazel and Robbie. Ray even dived under Robbie as he bobbed about on his lilo.

Another memory was after Hazel had been given a complimentary turntable, six months after starting her job. Through their dealers she purchased a secondhand amplifier and speakers, which gave her the opportunity to invite her dad round to listen to her new LPs. The last time they enjoyed this together was on a warm sunny day. Robbie was at Tim's parents. The French doors were open. Her father had bought her an album called *Reflections* for her birthday, which included the theme from *Brideshead Revisited*, 'Cavatina' from *The Deer Hunter* and 'Don't Cry for me Argentina'. She had just purchased the sequel to this album, *Imaginations*, and a Jon and Vangelis album, *Private Collection*. They sat on the steps outside the French doors and listened, saying very little, lulled by the beauty of the music and the heat of the sun.

Then Hazel came across a two-bedroom cottage up for sale in Leigh, not far from Bonchurch; an opportunity she could not allow to pass. After negotiating a mortgage with a building society, she prepared to tell Tim that she was leaving him. When he had rejected her plea for a divorce all those years ago, after she had returned from the marriage guidance session, she had regularly discussed her unhappiness with him. It surely couldn't come as a surprise. After Robbie was in bed, she asked Tim to sit down with her. Calmly she told him of the house she was about to purchase, with the intention that she and Robbie move in on the completion date if it all proceeded well. But it was reliant on him selling Bonchurch or finding the money to buy her out.

Having read up on divorce in the library she told Tim that, as there were no affairs on either side, it was technically a breakdown of their marriage, which meant that they ought to be able to get a divorce in two years, without expensive court proceedings. She reiterated that their marriage felt like a cage to her, plus that she could no longer accept him in a sexual way. He seemed to agree that a marriage without sex was certainly not what he wanted. But it was a heart-wrenching time. He appeared to weather it far better than she had expected. She worried that he might be in denial. She felt a deep guilt at splitting their family and cried when she was alone.

Dean had nothing to do with her leaving so Hazel thought it best to continue with the pretence that it was only a platonic friendship, as she had assured Tim. It seemed pointless to add further hurt by mentioning that, regretfully, she had not always been faithful.

They put off telling Robbie initially, doing their best to put on a brave face in front of their son.

It was two weeks later, while Tim was away, that Hazel received divorce papers, citing her unacceptable behaviour as cause for divorce. There was no mention of any affair, merely that she had not supported him in any way during the last few years. Reading the petition, she had to believe it was a fabrication. She had always supported him and had continued to care about him. Even when he was away they had exchanged regular phone calls. She had continued to have sex with him, even when it became abhorrent to her. To say she hadn't supported him had to be a lie. She was devastated by its untruth. But should she be so hurt? Was it not a small detail compared to all she had done behind his back?

Tim remortgaged the existing home and passed half of its value to Hazel. Once contracts were exchanged, they sat down with Robbie and explained that his mother no longer loved his father. They assured him that their love for him was unchanged and that he was not in any way to blame. While his main home would be with his mother, he would still have his old home and was welcome whenever his father was there. Hazel, finally, told her mother that her marriage was over. But added that the good news was she had managed to buy a dear little cottage in the heart of Leigh. They also agreed that there was no point in upsetting her father with any of this news.

Tim was distressed by his wife and son leaving, but maintained a jovial facade in front of them. Even on the day they appeared in court to give details of Robbie's care and maintenance, they were able to walk together and share a laugh. Tim set up a standing order for regular monthly maintenance payments.

Moving into her own dear little cottage, situated right in the heart of Leigh but still close to Robbie's school, was an amazing relief to Hazel. In all the years that she had been considering her suffocating marriage she had not dreamt that she would be able to afford to buy a house. It was semi-detached with its own sideway and a small drive. She loved that the front door retained its original stained-glass window from 1890 and that the front lounge had an open fireplace and bay window. The wall between the lounge and dining area had been removed, as they had done with their first home. A small kitchen with bright-red floor tiles ran off from one corner of the dining end. A glass door in the other corner led on to a small, glass-covered, paved patio. A good-sized lawn on two levels with a little step linking them stretched down to a large old shed at the bottom. It felt perfect.

Robbie appeared to take the move in his stride. He was, after all, used to his dad being away two weeks out of every four. And Mrs Silk was there in his new home to greet him every day after school.

During the first two weekends and the evenings following her move Hazel was so busy decorating and sewing that, in her excitement, she had almost forgotten that she should say nothing to her father about the divorce. But the cancer had begun to consume him. X-rays found more tumours, including one at the base of his skull, and he'd had to spend a few days in hospital. At the end of her first weekend in the new house she popped in to see him when he was back home and began to say she'd just ripped out the old gas fire, when her mother coughed and gave her a glare. Her father immediately questioned her. Hazel recovered and said that the mock-coal, gas fire that they had fitted in Bonchurch wasn't efficient enough so she'd bought a cast-iron basket to burn real logs in. Phew. She had come so close to upsetting him with the truth. It had been such a frantic few days.

Over the next week she painted the lounge walls white and had a pale Berber carpet laid, striped with tones of pastel greys and beiges. She covered a sofa bed her mother had given her with a Habitat pastel, modernist, floral print and bought yellow material, with a white wavy line through it, to make curtains across the back door and matching cushions for the sofa. She fitted shelves into the empty fireplace in the dining end for her turntable and amplifier and ran the speakers into the alcoves at the other end, facing the sofa. Next to these sat two Habitat director's chairs in natural canvas. She matched this material with Roman blinds in the bay window. She'd bought an oval, cast-iron, fire basket called a cob for the open fireplace. Her grandmother's oak table and four chairs in the dining area completed the room. It was now cosy and stylish. But she was exhausted.

As Ray was now too weak to attempt the stairs, Edwina had made up the sofa bed in the dining room. Robbie was staying with Tim on the second weekend following their move, so Hazel visited alone on Sunday. Lying wrapped up on the sofa he was still smiling and optimistic, but his breathing was becoming more laboured, even as she chatted to him. He agreed with Edwina that it might be best to go back into hospital that evening. Hazel had to leave to collect Robbie. She hugged and kissed her father and said she'd visit him in hospital after work on Monday. As she reached the dining-room door, she stopped and glanced back at Ray. He smiled at his daughter. She returned to his side and took his hand.

"I love you," she said.

"I love you too," was his reply. They hugged again and Hazel left.

At seven o'clock the following morning the phone rang. It was Edwina. Ray had been diagnosed with pneumonia and had died at ten past two that morning.

"Why did you not let me know how serious he was? I wanted to be with him."

"He didn't want anyone there. He even sent me away. I really think he didn't want anyone to see him at the end," said Edwina.

Weak with anguish Hazel could not argue. Too pointless. Her dear, dear dad had left her life. Without her by his side.

"Are you okay? Do you want me to come round?" Hazel asked.

"No, I'm all right. Your brothers are here."

Lost, Hazel put down the phone. Emptiness overwhelmed her. She stood, unable to move or think. Then she began to imagine how her father would feel if he could see her now. Upset by her suffering most likely. Her father had loved Robbie very much too. She had to find strength for her son. She must get him up for school as usual and wrap her head around telling him this evening.

As she was getting his breakfast ready, she slid into their natural weekday routine and even managed a little breakfast herself. She then decided she could not bear the thought of the empty day stretching ahead of her, so she might as well go into work. She told the office of her father's death but explained that as her mother didn't need her, she would rather work to keep her mind occupied and that she would probably only take one day off for the funeral.

She told Robbie of his grandfather's death after Mrs Silk had gone home. They cried and hugged each other.

She rang Edwina who told her that John was staying the night and she would be fine. Once she had tucked Robbie into bed, Hazel went downstairs and stood in the lounge. Desolation enveloped her. She couldn't face the empty nothingness of night. She walked to the phone and dialled Dean's number. She told him her father had died.

"Do you want me to come round?"

"Please. I can't take this emptiness alone."

Within an hour, he was there. She asked if he would just hold her. She couldn't cry. After attempting to sleep together on the sofa, a chill encouraged them to retire to her bed. And yes, losing herself in their lovemaking helped. She got through the night and Dean left before Robbie woke up.

Hazel worked through the days mechanically. She hardly spoke to anyone in the factory all week, allowing work to swallow her and fill a little of the emptiness. A week after Ray's death, Hazel began to accept that he would not wish her grief to swamp her life.

Somehow a weekend passed and, on Monday evening, she was tired from work and Robbie was in bed. As it was still not cold enough for a fire, she lit a candle in the fireplace to radiate a relaxing light. The candle made shadows dance around the room.

She'd spent a large part of her day in the newly fitted tonearm department learning how to adjust bearings to a perfect tolerance. Another lady had been employed, after Hazel, to assist in building their innovative tonearm. They had been joined by Pete from the turntable department. Details of the tricky bearing adjustment still filled her mind as she settled to listen to some music.

She closed her eyes to allow the sounds to wash over her. After a few minutes, her eyes drifted open. She saw her father sitting on the director's chair, only feet away, right in front of her. He was smiling gently. Knowing her father's expressions so well, she felt he was conveying a message. Letting her know he was okay, he was happy. She mustn't grieve.

He looked solid, human, real. She got up and went towards him, certain she could touch him. Halfway across the space between them, he dissolved. She felt no shock, no surprise, only peace and the knowledge that their love would not die. As she sat back on the sofa the lyrics, 'peace will come', soaked into her awareness.

Hazel listened until the music fell silent, the needle caught in the centre of the record. One song had taken up the whole side of an album. Why had her father appeared among those haunting words?

She got up and lifted the record from the deck, it was 'Horizon' by Jon and Vangelis, from their *Private Collection* album. A memory rose up. This was one of the final albums that she and her father had listened to. Reading through the words, Hazel was moved to the depths of her grief, filled with awe that he had appeared while such a song was playing (the complete lyrics by Jon Anderson can be found online). It only confirmed her belief regarding the brain's power. Because of her close bond with her father a subconscious picture of him and all his expressions and movements had to be entrenched in her brain. The fact that they had recently listened to that track together had to be the trigger for her vision.

It was his spirit she had seen, but not a separate physical spirit as some believed. For her, it was the spirit of her father that lived within her, and always would. Within the depths of her own brain. It would take scientific proof to change that belief. She clung to the happy, comforting memories of his spirit within, which eased her anguish.

On the day of the funeral, Hazel met her brothers at their mum's house to be conveyed by a black car behind the funeral hearse. She had declined her mother's invite to visit her father's body. The memory of her father in life would always burn brightly. She had no wish to tarnish it with a picture of his empty shell. In her imagination, the body being transported in front of her was no different to that of her father sleeping. While travelling to the crematorium, she felt his invisible presence watching over her, trying to quell her misery. And it was for him that she held her emotions together through the service by watching water tumbling into a pool of gliding, weaving goldfish positioned directly outside the window. She couldn't upset his presence by breaking down. She couldn't cry.

But in the days, months and years that followed she sobbed for the empty space in her life. Usually only when alone. When no one was around to disturb her memories.

CHAPTER 17
1983 ◊ Moving On

Within the one year Hazel had lost her father and ended her marriage. But her divorce gave Hazel the freedom and strength to cope with the loss of her father. Living in her own little cottage, positioned very close to Leigh Old Town and the lively Broadway, lifted a great weight from her. She had not recognised the true cost of all the worry about the marriage until she was finally free. And that freedom felt exhilarating.

Hazel asked Colin, the mechanic, if he could find her a reliable Beetle. Within a week he'd found a dark orange one with lowish mileage and she bought it with a small loan. To save on petrol, though, she rode to work most days on Rosemary's fold-up bike – which Edwina had passed on to her, keeping her father's on which she felt more comfortable.

Hazel also decided to get a kitten for Robbie. He was an affectionate, little black and white thing that captivated Robbie when it began standing up on its haunches to spar with him. They thought Boxer would be a great name.

Ray had left some money to each of his children. With her portion Hazel bought a set of four white garden chairs that fitted around a matching metre-wide round table. It looked like wrought iron but was actually lightweight aluminium. Her father had loved sitting outside with her at Bonchurch. She imagined that, if he'd lived, sitting at this table in her new garden would have helped him get over the shock of her failed marriage.

Wherever she placed this set – under cover on the patio or on the grass in the sun – the large rotten workshop across the end of the garden spoilt the view. Hazel asked Michael and John if they would help her pull it down and burn it. She would then buy a small shed and place it unobtrusively on a new base near the bottom of the garden, behind an apple tree.

She chose a Sunday when the forecast was for dry and sunny weather to allow her to offer a barbecue at the end of their hard work on her new black cast-iron barbecue. Michael and John and their wives were now vegetarians. So separate tinfoil trays allowed Hazel and Robbie to have chicken drumsticks and meat burgers while the others had their alternative sausages and burgers. All served with salad and jacket potatoes.

Michael brought his two daughters. Olivia, Hazel's goddaughter, was the eldest and five years younger than Robbie. Ella was seven years younger. They had spent a lot of time together at family get-togethers, including a week with Hazel and Robbie at Mrs Gardiner's house.

Earlier that summer Hazel had taken the three cousins to Bekonscot Model Village in Beaconsfield. The trip had been memorable for two reasons. First was the atmospheric depiction of village life in miniature, even with a tiny cricket match. The steam trains chugging around were an added fascination. They had a wonderful day, topped by a picnic lunch and ice creams.

The second came on the way home, after Hazel pulled into a garage to fill the Beetle up with petrol. Robbie needed to go to the toilet, the girls stayed in the car with Radio One playing. Hazel moved up the queue of people and finally paid, then thought she would pop into the toilet too. She jumped back in the car, pulled away and got lost in the music on the radio, so it was a while before she noticed it was rather quiet in the back. It was unusual not to hear Robbie's constant chatter. She looked in the mirror. She could see Olivia in the middle and Ella on her left.

"Where's Robbie?" Hazel asked.

"He's still at the petrol station," replied Olivia.

A terrible fear shot through Hazel, she pulled over and stopped, forgetting to indicate, causing the driver behind to hoot in annoyance. They must have been driving for at least fifteen minutes. As soon as there was a break in the traffic she did a U-turn. Her heart was pounding and the heavy traffic was frustratingly slow. How could she have forgotten her son? What would he do when he found them gone?

How did he feel? Hazel tried not to panic, praying he'd be alright. At last she could see the petrol station and as they approached she could see Robbie sitting on the wall. 'Oh, thank heaven.' She jumped out and hugged him.

"I'm so, so sorry. I'd presumed, as I took so long, that you must have been back in the car. How could I have been so stupid?"

"It's alright, Mum," said Robbie. "I knew you'd come back."

The repetitive production work Hazel continued to undertake five days a week was incredibly boring, but the hi-fi company had its perks. Prior to every Christmas, Rouse and Trevor reviewed each employee's work over the year and then had a private meeting to discuss their merits and failings and to award a bonus. While her speed at repetitive work was not the best, her understanding and ability to tighten bearings to an accurate torque and generally build to a high standard was appreciated. Her first bonus was £500, which was brilliant timing just before Christmas. Together with the monthly maintenance payment from Tim it meant that, as long as she was very sensible, her income was just sufficient.

Tim had been happy for Hazel to take the camping equipment, with the option that he could borrow it. This meant they could always have cheap UK holidays. Hazel had often taken Robbie camping by herself, during his summer holidays, to Wales, Devon and Dorset. But this year, to get away from all of last year's traumas, Hazel felt like a change. Jersey was an easy destination from Southend airport and there were affordable, well-equipped tents on quality campsites. She asked Edwina if she would like to come – particularly as her father, during the final weeks of his illness, had asked Hazel to look after her mother. Edwina didn't fancy camping but found a hotel close to the campsite. Hazel booked a hire car for the week and, with a coastline that was so like Cornwall and plenty to interest all three of them, they had a wonderful holiday. Despite Ray's absence.

The following month Edwina suggested they visit Lieselotte, who had also been devastated by Ray's death. At the funeral she had cried, "You don't imagine your son dying before you."

Ray used to call in each week to the little terraced house she'd bought after Alf died to do the odd DIY job or to have a chat. She had now moved into a managed complex for the elderly in Maidenhead to be near Arthur but she did miss Edwina. Hazel drove up with Edwina and Robbie. Lieselotte was still very fit and proudly showed off her maisonette's brightly coloured front garden, planted full of geraniums, begonias and rich blue lobelia. The four of them spent a pleasant few hours walking along the Thames to Ray Mill Island, stopping briefly for a café lunch.

Dean, apart from being a tutor and professional photographer, also arranged events for charity, including an annual ball. This year he suggested Hazel should go. He had recently begun a relationship with an attractive lady he'd been asked to photograph and he told Hazel that for the first time he was 'in love'.

"That would mean going by myself, though," replied Hazel.

"That's not a problem. There's a lady gardener friend of mine going that I'd like you to meet. You have a lot in common."

Most years, Hazel had gone with Tim to off-licence managers' balls at the London Ritz. She enjoyed an excuse to dress up. She'd seen a sexy, very clingy dress advertised in the *Daily Telegraph* that would work for Dean's ball. With a single shoulder strap the dress was split down one side, tethered with a set of buttons running down to the thigh, allowing glimpses of flesh and one leg. It came in red or black. She drove up to try it on in the shop in East London. The red one felt too garish, almost to the point of tacky. But as she paraded in front of a mirror wearing the black version, she spied a pair of long, black, slinky gloves that stretched almost to her armpits; buttoned full length, they were the perfect complement. She had a pair of black stilettos and bought sparkling 'bling' earrings and a black ribbon necklace.

Hazel spent the whole afternoon before the ball bathing, washing her hair, twisting it into large rollers. She then pampered her tanned body with glossy lotion. Once dry, she unleashed her hair into tumbling locks and spent some time playing with styles. She decided to pin it up, with some curls allowed freedom to bubble on top, with wisps feathering her neck and face. Finally, with make-up as natural as she could manage, she dressed, added the jewellery and stilettos and viewed herself in her long mirror. She could not outshine Dean's beautiful lady, but she was confident this friend would not go unnoticed.

The venue was the Hollywood Restaurant in Benfleet. Hazel parked her car and entered shyly, searching for Dean. He had put on weight during the last few years but, as tall as he was, he stood out handsomely in his black tie. Self-consciously, she made her way through the large room. He smiled as he saw her and said he would introduce her to various people. The first was his girlfriend, Claire. Having seen photographs Hazel was surprised that Claire had not felt the need to dress up. She was attractive but, to Hazel's eyes, not stunning. Dean had told her about Claire's background and her impression was of a troubled lady who had left a tempestuous relationship to be with Dean but who was unsure about what she was searching for.

Dean had arranged the seating so that Hazel was placed next to his gardening friend, Maggi, who flashed a smile at her. As the meal progressed their conversation turned to plants and gardens. Maggi mentioned that she looked after a few friends' gardens professionally. She also introduced her partner, Morris, who chatted with those around him, almost ignoring Maggi. Hazel had found a lifelong, female friend. It came as no surprise to her when, a couple of weeks later, Maggi told her that Morris had left her and moved away.

Hazel continued to go to The Crooked Billet about once a fortnight on a Friday, regardless of whether Dean might be there. She'd got to know enough of the regulars to have various people to chat to. She didn't see Richie again but his 'lumberjack' friend, Robin, began to make an almost weekly appearance. But, strangely, once in close proximity, she did not feel physically drawn to him. As he was an intelligent, very attractive man, this remained a mystery to her.

One Friday Robin was accompanied by another of his friends, Simon Ash. This was an unexpected, very pleasant surprise for Hazel! Her first love, only supplanted by Tim. After tentative questioning, he again denied remembering their encounter in the school cloakroom or indeed remembering her as a child at all. He said he did remember Tim pulling her away from their conversation at the fancy dress party, though. Simon began to accompany Robin more often on Friday evenings, allowing Hazel to delve gently into his life with safe questions about his work and children. Once she was confident that he was enjoying her company, she asked how his marriage was. Adding that, of course, it had obviously been more successful than hers. He looked at her as he said, "We lead separate lives." He then dropped his eyes from Hazel's penetrating gaze.

In the seconds that followed, so many thoughts and emotions swept through her. Finally, they rested on the fact that he was still married with two children. Having broken her own marriage, there was no way she could be instrumental in breaking up another's. Then she felt anger well up inside her at the lost years because she had known in her heart all those years ago how it would be for him. She was at a loss, now, how to react. She was torn. Part of her wanted to suggest a walk that would end with her kissing him. But, even presuming she could cajole him into that, she would never be happy with an affair and was unable to overcome her anger. She squeezed his arm and said, "Sorry, but I've got to go."

If they had continued to meet at the pub, could Hazel have resisted falling for him again? Fortunately, or maybe unfortunately, events intervened and another path opened.

At work, Hazel heard rumours of Trevor's divorce, apparently caused by his wife's discovery of his affair with Chrissy, the pretty little red-haired secretary. The secretary, however, must have decided that Trevor wasn't for her, as she'd resigned and left. Hazel was still spending the largest amount of her time in the tonearm department, which had grown to five or six workers, but the whole company exuded a warm, friendly atmosphere where she continued to feel at home. Rouse tended to appear only if there was a problem with parts, to advise the departments on solutions. As factory manager, Trevor was there every day. His strong character pervaded the building. It appeared to Hazel that most workers in the factory regarded him with a mixture of fear and respect. Hazel only understood their fear through stories she'd heard of him losing his temper and, on one occasion, he had apparently punched a hole in a door. He frequently appeared on the top floor, generally in bouncy good humour, to check everyone was working. On one such visit, he mentioned to the department that he was offering, to all employees and partners, free tickets to a concert at the Royal Festival Hall, on the South Bank, London. One or two were interested. He fixed Hazel with his large blue eyes, made larger by his thick-rimmed glasses.

"Might you be interested, Hazel?' he asked.

"I don't have anyone to go with," she replied, not happy at the prospect of being alone among all the couples.

"But I'll be going alone. You're welcome to join me."

"Oh." She hesitated, "I'll think about it."

She asked for Pete's thoughts on her accompanying one of her bosses to a concert. As they were both single, he couldn't see a problem. The following day, she sought out Trevor to ask if his offer was still on.

"Of, course."

He arranged to pick her up from her house. Hazel couldn't help but admit that seeing his red Ferrari parked outside her home gave her a warped sense that, perhaps, money could buy a certain amount of happiness! Trevor did not have the looks to sweep ladies off their feet but a red Ferrari just might do the trick.

Not long after she'd learnt from another employee of Trevor's affair with Chrissy, Hazel had seen the two conversing together in the car park. Her thought then had been, 'As a very attractive lady, what exactly does she see in him?' She concluded that, apart from money, he was probably good in bed. Since Chrissy was a gregarious, flirtatious and tactile lady Hazel felt that she could probably get any man she wanted. Now, though, her thoughts did not go beyond looking forward to a ride in his car and the concert. Both exceeded expectations.

About nine or ten of them ate together at the Festival Hall after the concert. Rouse and his wife then left for home and Trevor asked if anyone would like a short stroll along the embankment to complete the evening. It was dry and comparatively warm so they all joined him. As they meandered along in couples, Hazel and Trevor chatted. She walked close beside him and became aware of an emerging attraction – it was a great end to an excellent evening.

Trevor dropped Hazel at her house and it felt appropriate to offer him coffee as a thank you for a grand evening. Their conversation continued easily and he was impressed with Hazel's modern interior decor. With their coffees drunk he rose to leave. Hazel followed him to the lounge door where he stopped and turned.

Two single people. An attraction. No reason not to kiss.

They did. Pleasant and long. Then Trevor left.

A couple of days later, he met her on the stairs and asked if he could take her out for a meal the following Saturday evening. Hazel agreed to it.

She'd not wanted to rush into another relationship, but it had been almost eighteen months since her move. It felt time to be wined and dined by a man with a red Ferrari and a large house in Thorpe Bay! Her ultimate need, after ensuring Robbie's happiness, was to have some fun (after all she'd been only fifteen when she'd tied herself up emotionally, missing out on the life she would have enjoyed at university). She also wanted a man who was not only prepared to be a good father to Robbie, but who also wanted his own child. Hazel desperately wanted another but knew this might be a challenge. She was thirty-one. Theoretically, she had a few years to search.

Trevor had an intelligence beyond any she had found so far. He was able to instantly add, subtract and multiply large numbers. He managed the company finances and had been instrumental in paving the way for foreign dealerships, enabling the company to sell all over the world. Hazel was impressed. Within a short time she also decided he was, by far, the best lover she'd known. He appeared to gain the most pleasure from simply pleasuring her. All she had to do was lie back and enjoy, allowing her to let go of the belief that she always needed to please a man. It took a few years for her to realise that actually this was a form of power for him.

Leaving all past intimacies behind, Hazel knew that, from now on, she would stay totally faithful to any future partnership. She wasn't proud of her infidelities to Tim and, while she may never marry again, she would not spread her affections around. She felt a need to be monogamous, for her own self-worth.

She'd been seeing Trevor for less than a month when he asked her to join him on a holiday he'd booked in Jersey. Not a tent this time but a five-star hotel. On the second day, as they sat in bed first thing, drinking tea, Trevor asked her about past boyfriends. As honesty was Hazel's best policy, she told him. Mostly everything. Trevor began to cry. Hazel was stunned. Had honesty been wrong? She stared at the opposite wall as, between sobs, he said that her story was so similar to Chrissy's. And she had broken up his marriage and then dumped him. He had been certain Hazel was different. Speechless, Hazel couldn't argue. Her first inclination was to get dressed and leave. But as she sat, frozen, pictures of Jersey floated through her mind drawing her to conclude that unless he asked her to go, she may as well enjoy her time here, then think about leaving him once they were home. That did feel calculating. But otherwise it would mean spending money on a flight home. As his sobbing subsided, she asked him if he wanted her to go.

"No," he replied. "I'll try to work through it."

By the end of that day, it was as if it hadn't happened and, as they flew home, Hazel attempted to bury the incident. He made her feel good and for now that was enough.

Two months later Hazel went down with flu. As Tim was home, Robbie went to stay with him for a couple of days. Hazel huddled up with a hot-water bottle in bed and Edwina called with soup, lamb casserole and a bottle of Lucozade.

Her back had been feeling stiff for a few days prior to this, probably because she spent a lot of time sitting at work and was now indulging in regular sex after a long break. It hadn't been a problem until, on the second night of her fever, as she edged her aching body out of bed to go to the toilet, she suddenly coughed. A searing pain split through her. Gathering herself, she managed an excruciating trip to relieve herself, then eased her shivering body back into bed. But the pain from whatever had happened, on top of the flu, was almost unbearable. She'd taken paracetamol only two hours previously so, in desperation, she returned to the bathroom cabinet and placed two dissolving aspirin in water. Half an hour later there was only slight relief. She continued to alternate between paracetamol and aspirin through the night and hardly slept. The next day, exhausted, she slept intermittently until Edwina called in the afternoon. After they discussed a possible slipped disc Edwina suggested her daughter had a warm bath. Following a hot soak with more paracetamol Hazel felt able go downstairs but, unable to ease the pain, she returned to bed half an hour later.

Hazel had informed work she had flu that first day and Trevor rang back that evening to check if there was anything he could do.

"No," answered Hazel. "I'll let you know if there is."

He phoned again on the fourth evening and suggested she see a physiotherapist once she'd recovered from the flu. He insisted that he would pay and Hazel was grateful that the physio was able to see her on the day she rang for an appointment. They diagnosed a prolapsed disc. It felt marginally better after the first treatment and the physio told her she should return again later that week. By the fifth week of treatment, though, the pain had only improved slightly. As well as pain in her back and right down the sciatic nerve of her right leg, her right foot was partially numb. Then the physiotherapist went away on holiday and a locum made the decision to perform traction. Hazel could barely remember the procedure but knew that she was in more pain as she left the surgery than when she'd entered.

Hazel had managed to return to work two weeks after the flu had begun, even though the constant pain wore her out. Following traction, she found she was unable to stand or even sit for more than a couple of hours before the pain overwhelmed her and she had to lie down. She had no option then but to stay at home. Her GP prescribed strong anti-inflammatories. They afforded little respite. Robbie diligently followed Hazel's instructions after school and at the weekends, helping where he could. Edwina and Trevor helped with the shopping, and she just about survived! Trevor suggested he pay for her to see a consultant at the local private hospital. From his experience he knew that, following a private consultation, she could be fast tracked to the NHS for any necessary treatment. Although the hi-fi company were still paying her, they wouldn't indefinitely. So she agreed with Trevor's suggestion.

After an X-ray confirmed the prolapsed disc, the orthopaedic consultant said that he would be able to perform a manipulation on her spine with a cortisone injection under anaesthetic. An appointment was made for a couple of weeks later at the local general hospital. She was able to return to work the day after this operation but her painful back still felt strangely twisted. Back on the anti-inflammatories, she was driving home at the end of each day with a constant nagging pain dragging her down. Driving along the main road at rush hour was always very slow. Hazel usually cut through quieter roads, which involved crossing Chalkwell Avenue. It went down quite steeply from Chalkwell Park to the seafront. One day, as she drew up, the view up the hill was obscured by cars parked closely on either side. Tired and anxious to be home she pulled out to cross the Avenue. A young male driver was speeding down the hill. He crashed headlong into the side of the Beetle. Apart from jarring her back, Hazel and the young driver were unscathed. The Beetle was a write-off. After a phone call, Trevor took her home. She was so upset. He told her not to worry, he'd sort something. Painfully and very reluctantly she left early for work the following morning and caught the bus.

By now, Robbie was completely accepting of Trevor's relationship with his mother. Sadly, his father was drinking more and, as no definite arrangements were in place, the time between phone calls inviting his son to stay got longer and longer. Robbie began to say he wasn't at all bothered if he didn't see him. He explained that when he did go to his house, his father would just take him to stay the night at his grandparents' while he went out drinking. Unfortunately, Hazel didn't consider that he might be hurt by his father's easy dismissal of him.

One afternoon, she had a phone call from Robbie asking her to collect him from his father's house as his Tim was drunk. He'd taken his son out on a lunchtime binge. With hindsight, if she had taken the time to sit and really discuss the problem with Tim's parents a better solution may have been worked out. But Robbie was happy to spend time in Trevor's house, which was not far from Ron and Audrey – who had moved out of the Leigh off-licence and bought a house of their own in Great Wakering.

Having always been so active, Hazel's continuing back pain was making her depressed. She looked at her garden with sadness. Robbie, or sometimes Trevor, cut the grass for her, but there was so much more she wished to do to it. Feeling crippled made her dependent on Trevor. As well as paying for private physios and consultants, he bought her jewellery and stylish clothes. And he loved her body, taking great care to protect her back. Following her crash, he bought her a bright-red XR3. When she said she couldn't accept it, he said she could pay him back one day and not to bother about that now. He was reluctant, though, to consider marriage again – or children.

On this point, Hazel had begun to question (only to herself) whether his sperm was sterile. Often after sex she would have a wee, mainly to ensure that any semen left within her didn't trickle out later into her knickers! The normal reaction of semen, as it came into contact with water, was to froth up. But Trevor's sank immediately and remained at the bottom of the pan as a white blob. Her conclusion was that it was dead.

Considering that Hazel was essentially searching for a husband to father a second child she is still not sure why she continued with the relationship, given her suspicions. Especially as Trevor made her emotions swing like a pendulum. But she felt she understood him and thought she loved him. Or was it more to do with the pleasurable, wonderful fulfilling sex and his money? Certainly, Trevor's moods were not predictable. After spending a couple of happy days together, something unexpected and trivial would suddenly turn him and he could become almost abusive if he felt she had done something wrong.

Another issue was his aversion to family get-togethers. He was happy to visit Edwina or join Hazel and Robbie for Sunday dinner at her house occasionally, but at birthday celebrations and gatherings he insisted they left early. Or he would find an excuse not to go at all. This did not endear him to her brothers, although they did not voice this to her.

However, Trevor did treat Robbie with a welcome maturity not seen in his own father. If he hadn't Hazel would not have hesitated to end the relationship with her boss.

After a follow-up visit to the hospital, the orthopaedic consultant agreed to try a further manipulation, again under anaesthetic. Unfortunately, she was still feeling euphoric after the operation when a nurse told her she could get dressed. Not thinking, she bent down to put on her shoe and immediately felt something snap in her back. 'Oh shit, that was so stupid. I think I've just undone whatever the consultant has attempted to correct.'

Mortified, she sat still in a chair until Edwina came to take her home. She went to rest, stretched out flat, in bed. The following day, after carefully driving to work, her back still didn't feel completely straight, although the sciatica was less. The toes and ball of her right foot still felt numb.

Amid all these swirling issues Hazel received some welcome news regarding Robbie's dyslexia. During his final year at West Leigh school, Edwina's attention was caught by a mention on the news that forty per cent of dyslexic children had a problem that meant their eyes did not scan in unison. A unit had been set up in the Royal Berkshire Hospital as the discovery had brought about a solution. Hazel immediately rang the hospital and booked an appointment for Robbie.

It was a long drive to the hospital in Reading to meet the head of the unit, Mrs Fisher. After filling in a questionnaire on Robbie's problems she gently placed a pair of glasses on his nose. She explained that LED diodes were incorporated within the glasses that would pick up exactly what each eye was doing as Robbie attempted to read. Then, she took Robbie's hand and, after asking Hazel to wait where she was, led him off down a corridor. He returned, alone, in about fifteen minutes and they waited for the results. Mrs Fisher returned a little later with a sheet of paper that showed two, separate, compressed zigzag lines. One each for the left and right eyes. Below they had been superimposed. Normally the readout from both eyes should be identical. Mrs Fisher said that in the six months the unit had been operational Robbie's eyes were the most 'out of sync' of all the ones she had recorded. She was impressed that his reading age was now only three months behind his actual age of ten years and seven months.

She assured them that he would be completely cured using the eye exercises she had devised and that, once corrected, they would not become unstable again. Amazed, Hazel concentrated on Mrs Fisher's instructions. She showed them four cards she was giving them to take home. The first showed the top half of a clown, which was matched to his bottom half on the second card. Mrs Fisher explained that they could train Robbie's eyes to pull the two cards together to form a complete clown. The third card was a car. Robbie's eyes should line this up and drive it into the garage pictured on the fourth card. Hazel was fascinated.

To do the exercises, Robbie needed to hold and stare at a biro pen or a pencil about ten inches in front of his face while Hazel held the two clown pictures side by side about ten inches behind the pen. While still attempting to concentrate on the pen, he had to make his eyes draw the two pictures together and hold for a few seconds. Mrs Fisher asked Robbie to take her pen while she held the cards, then asked him to follow the instructions she'd just given them. Within a minute or so Robbie exclaimed that, yes, the two cards had now merged together and he could see one complete clown.

"Do exactly the same with the other two cards once or twice a day," said Mrs Fisher. "It is important to do this regularly and I'll make an appointment for you to return in two months to retest your eyes."

Robbie was happy to do the exercises once or twice a day as instructed. It took no more than three weeks before he was instantly able to pull the pictures together. They continued most days until his return appointment. This time the printouts showed his eyes to be working in complete unison. Mrs Fisher confirmed that the problem was now cured.

Meanwhile, Hazel's back had not improved and she returned to the orthopaedic surgeon and asked if any more could be done. She was unable to garden for long, even on her knees, or to do the gentlest of exercise without having to take anti-inflammatories. He said they could do a myelogram, which involved injecting dye into the spine and an X-ray to identify the damaged disc. Then they would perform an operation to remove the disc and fuse the two vertebrae together. Hazel wasn't keen on having this procedure, particularly as she'd heard that this caused undue pressure on the discs either side of the fused vertebrae. However, she couldn't imagine continuing as she was. She couldn't allow depression to set in so the myelogram was booked.

It was not a pleasant procedure. At one point, she felt her head might burst! The results highlighted the damaged disc and the operation was booked for three weeks' time.

A couple of days later she was in Southend looking for a present for Trevor's birthday when she came upon the *Which?*® *Guide to Back Problems*. She went straight home after purchasing it and read it from cover to cover over the following two days. It explained exactly what a prolapsed disc was, using enlightening diagrams. It listed regular swimming as one of the solutions, advised against breast stroke and suggested Hazel's preferred back crawl was the best. And it showed daily exercises in diagrams at the back of the book.

Realising she now had a choice, she began swimming three times a week in her lunch break and worked through the exercises each day. With three days to go before her operation, she rang the hospital to cancel. Hazel asked the receptionist to mention the book to her surgeon and to explain it was really helping. She dropped to swimming twice a week and continued each morning with four or five specific exercises that she thought worked best for her. After a month she was confident enough to carefully begin gardening again, always remembering to bend correctly.

She also began yoga to build flexibility. Now in her mid-sixties, Hazel still does the same exercises from the book most mornings. They only take six minutes. She swims, does yoga, hikes and mountain bikes! And her back has remained strong.

Robbie failed the eleven-plus by only a small margin, so they needed to consider his other options. The only senior and non-grammar school in Leigh was Belfairs. But the boys' and girls' schools had combined to form a mixed comprehensive and reports about its standard were not good. Now that Robbie's eye scanning had been corrected, Hazel felt he required the best teaching to help build his confidence, but Tim would not consider paying for private education. The two senior schools in nearby Benfleet were not particularly good either.

Hazel read a report in the paper on Thorpe Bay High School, situated the other side of Southend. It had been a failing school but had been renamed and the excellent new headmaster was bringing about a prodigious change. Hazel and Robbie visited Thorpe Bay High School and two others around the outskirts of Southend that were considered to be acceptable state schools. The entrance to Thorpe Bay school was through a large glass conservatory hung with plants. Walking around the light and airy building and talking to the maths, English and science teachers, Robbie agreed with his mother that this was definitely his preferred school. That left Hazel with two choices. The first was to sell her dear cottage in Leigh and buy one in nearby Shoebury. The second was to keep her Leigh cottage for the time being but move in with Trevor for a trial period. Trevor agreed that the second option was the best idea.

The move involved no more than packing up their clothes and all of Robbie's belongings and dismantling the sturdy Habitat bed that Hazel had bought her son after moving out of Bonchurch. Fitted over its own combined desk and shelving, it was perfect for quiet study in his own bedroom.

The tortoise was tucked into a box and Boxer into a cat basket.

Having already spent a lot of time at Trevor's home, the pair had a good idea of what to expect. Absolutely no crumbs were to be dropped anywhere, which meant always using a tray if they were eating in the lounge. Tidiness was essential. Robbie was not allowed to do the washing-up in case he broke something and, when Hazel did it, she must only use a washing-up brush. Cloths must only be used to wash down kitchen surfaces, not plates! She was told off for using a cloth even when a brush did not appear to remove all of the grease.

Hazel naturally resisted subservience, so was rather regularly told off. She received another regular scolding for pairing up washed and dried socks, by rolling the open end of one pair over its twin. Trevor said this caused the elastic to stretch and he actually lost his temper when she continued to do it.

It was Hazel's memory that caused the most problems. As well as losing things within the house, she would regularly come in from the garden and forget to immediately lock the back door. When Trevor returned one day to an empty house to find the back door unlocked, he waited for her return, incensed. With a reddened face and clenched fists, he spat out that it was unacceptable. He was totally unable to understand that she seriously did try to remember, to the degree that it really upset her too. She asked if he could offer any ideas on how she might remember. His angry reply was that it was her problem and she should not to make it his.

Living with Trevor wasn't all bad. There was fun: expensive meals out; ten days in the US; a week staying with the hi-fi company's French dealer, which had included a delightful visit to Monet's garden and house in Giverny. It was enough for Hazel to want to persevere. In some ways she saw Trevor as a lion cub who became frightened by not being in control.

Trevor's house was a large, three-bedroom, detached property built by the locally known architect Goldsworthy. There were whole roads of his well-built houses and bungalows. Trevor's property was particularly attractive as it faced a large green. Hazel was not happy with the interior, though. The walls of both the lounge and hall were painted a dark beige with a deep-green nylon carpet. The lounge ran the depth of the property, but was not that wide. The fireplace was in the centre of the long wall and left little choice but to place the seating opposite it, which made the room feel even narrower. There was also a corner cut out at the garden end to allow the room above to overhang a paved corner of the garden. There were no French doors, or indeed any way of accessing this small paved area apart from via the back door in the kitchen. Together with the dark walls and carpet and old black leather seating and two very large black speakers, Hazel found it oppressive. Trevor agreed to modernise it but refused to use Hazel's favourite pure-white emulsion paint to lighten the walls or even the recently introduced white with a hint of colour. The lightest Trevor would contemplate was magnolia. At least he intended to do most of the painting. He also agreed to buy and lay a light-beige Berber carpet, not unlike the one Hazel had fitted in her cottage and at Bonchurch. The finishing touch was a new, pearl coloured, chenille fabric, three-piece suite.

Before these changes were undertaken Trevor bought a pine table and matching single bench (to allow it to sit against a wall) for the large kitchen. As Robbie tended to be messy with food, he was expected to eat in the kitchen. There was a dining room but Trevor preferred to eat meals in front of the TV and he would not allow Robbie to sit on the new suite. Hazel was very unhappy with this and told Trevor that, if that was the case, she would join her son and always eat in the kitchen. She would definitely not have him eat alone. She then bought a bean bag for Robbie to use in the lounge when watching the television.

Trevor bought a small television for the kitchen, allowing them to watch as they ate. He also suggested that Hazel set up her hi-fi system in the spare room. With his leather armchairs in there, she would have her own little space. Robbie's bedroom was quite large and Trevor stuck up cork tiles over one wall to allow Robbie to put up posters.

Robbie had settled in well at his new school and moved confidently into Sea Scouts. His mother drove him to meetings in Leigh Old Town during the week. On Saturdays he would sometimes cycle to help with the renovation of an old building recently bought by the Scouts called the Cole Hole in the old Town. And he assured his mother he was happy living with Trevor.

It was years later that Robbie admitted to her that, occasionally, when he was alone in the house he would strip naked – "Just so I could wipe my bum all over the sofa!" – adding that he made sure his bottom was clean first.

He also told her of another incident when she and Trevor were out. He had been doing his homework with the required fountain pen when he heard the phone ring. He'd tucked the pen behind his ear and run down the stairs. On replacing the receiver at the end of the call he realised that there were ink splatters all over the wall, from where he was standing by the phone, all the way upstairs and into his bedroom. After trying to clean it off with all the different types of cleaner he could find, he resorted to toothpaste. Thankfully, it had worked.

For a couple of years, they were all content with the arrangement. Hazel would check regularly on her house in Leigh but baulked at renting it out or selling it. Trevor was still resisting the idea of marriage and Hazel was becoming more convinced that he would be unable to father children. But he had allowed the garden to become her area. She had dug out and built a pond similar to the one at Bonchurch but had surrounded this one with gravel and Japanese-style planting. She'd put up a small plastic greenhouse in the corner to grow tomatoes and next to it was a small patch of bare earth where she grew strawberries and a few veg. She loved the garden, as did Boxer and the tortoise. Robbie enjoyed it too, particularly as on occasional warm, dry summer nights Trevor allowed him to put a camp bed under the paved overhang. Cuddling Boxer and wrapped in his sleeping bag it was his space for freedom with the stars.

Hazel had bought a book on suggestions for improving one's memory and potential. Basically, it described the 'mindfulness' that is now very accepted. Hazel read the book and set her mind on remaining in the present. For three weeks she kept drawing her attention back to exactly what she was doing in an attempt to block her naturally wandering thoughts. In this way she remembered to lock the back door. Towards the end of those few weeks she began to notice that this rigid mental training was causing her to lose something she considered vital. By blocking her free thought, she was freezing her imagination. Those rampant pathways in her mind were closing. She sat in her own little room listening to music and considered this realisation.

Rouse had baffled all the hi-fi employees by giving everyone a copy of Richard Bach's book *Jonathan Livingston Seagull*. It seemed that Hazel was the only one who understood that Rouse was trying to show that we should all follow our individual strengths, just as Jonathan had. She could see Jonathan's strong need to achieve his own desires reflected in her own character. Ultimately, Jonathan had only found happiness doing the thing he really loved, flying to exhilarating heights not normally allowed among seagulls. By stretching himself to do untried manoeuvres and figure-of-eight dives he had unbound himself. She was so impressed by the story that she had given the book to Robbie to read. He'd also enjoyed it and understood its meaning.

The story made Hazel think. Was altering her brain to please someone else's wishes the path she should tread? She had left Tim in an effort to discover freedom. What exactly was she doing to her mind now? To her imagination? To her free spirit? Without these, she would be bound. Caged. Again. She made the decision to put the mindfulness training book away. Trevor would have to take her as she was or not at all. She accepted that she was living in his house and would still try to follow the obvious rules of locking doors and so on. But she would not alter her mind for him.

One breakfast time, while Robbie was away camping with the Scouts, Boxer didn't come in to Hazel's call. As she was driving to work she saw his body lying under some shrubs by the side of the busy road that edged some fields, not far from the bottom of their garden. She knew, even before she reached him, that he was dead. She gently lifted his still, slightly warm body and placed it carefully on the front seat. She felt his chest to double check that there was no movement. Then his neck. No pulse. There was no obvious trauma that she could see. She drove straight back home unable to absorb that he was definitely dead.

Trevor never left for work before nine-thirty so he was still there. Distraught, she lifted Boxer out of the car and asked Trevor if he was certain the cat was dead. Trevor took him out of Hazel's arms. He declared that, yes, unfortunately, he was dead.

"What do I do with him?" Hazel asked, too upset to think clearly.

"I'll bury him in the garden. Don't worry, leave him with me. You go to work."

She got on with her day and went to work, but she couldn't help but dwell on having to tell her son of his cat's death when he returned from camp. It tore at her heart, as surely as it would at his. When she returned home at the end of the day Trevor led her into the garden. Down by the far fence was a small mound. He had fashioned a little wooden cross with BOXER etched on it. With tears falling, Hazel leant into her partner's arms and thanked him.

Telling Robbie was one of the hardest things she'd ever done, next to ending her marriage, and her heart bled. Without tears, Robbie said he would cycle down to the station and catch a train into Leigh to see his best friend Drake and talk to him about it. Hugging him, Hazel said she thought that was a good idea, as long as he cycled carefully and was home in time for dinner.

All three missed the affectionate cat's vocal and warm presence. Hazel was actually surprised at how deeply she felt this loss. So much so that she was unable to face the prospect of having another cat.

Hazel decided to put her dear little Leigh cottage on the market. Travelling each week to check it and keep the garden in a passable order was becoming tedious. But she was worried that if her relationship with Trevor became untenable she would not have a ready bolt hole, given the rising house prices. Trevor agreed that property was still her best investment.

She found a house in Shoebury. It was larger than the Leigh cottage and built later, in the 1930s. Shoebury was not an area that Hazel would have ever thought to choose over Leigh-on-Sea, but this house was positioned on the south end, close to the seafront and a large park. It was owned by a fireman who, in his spare time, had added Tudor-style beams to the interior and to the external fascia. All the walls between the beams were painted white and, although leadlight had been stuck, in Tudor fashion, over all the windows, the atmosphere within the house was bright.

A large open brick fireplace sat between leadlight wall cabinets. On the left side, under the cabinet, was some open shelving, including wide shelving for a TV and hi-fi. On the other side was an aquarium, complete with an aerating unit that sent up streams of bubbles through lush green, swaying aquatic plants among which meandered large, fancy, long-tailed goldfish, calmly enjoying their home. In the largest bedroom the fireman had built a four-poster bed that he said would stay in the house, along with all the fish.

The garden, with a very large garage at the bottom, was even more interesting. The driveway down the side was shared and the large garage doors facing the house were accessed by sliding aside tall fence panels that had been fitted into substantial rollers. On the first viewing Hazel asked if she could try to open them. It was easy.

However, most of the garden was filled by a raised, 6,000 gallon fish pond with a large glass panel facing the house, allowing the fish to be viewed underwater. The fireman explained that it was six-foot deep with a shallower end that was filled with gravel to act as a natural filter. If the gravel and fish were removed, the pond could be used as a swimming pool. The rest of the garden was paved and had a raised area that was in the sun all day.

Everything was in good condition. There was even a dishwasher in the open-plan kitchen-diner and an enamelled wood-burning stove in the fireplace that would also remain. Just outside the split stable door that opened from the kitchen was a double outhouse containing a large boiler, a washing machine and tumble dryer in one half and a well-designed toilet with an electric hand dryer in the other – so one didn't need to contend with spiders on towels; apparently, a common problem in outside loos!

Hazel was impressed and asked for a second viewing. Robbie was equally impressed and Hazel mentioned that the garage would be perfect to build a large model railway track in. The survey she ordered highlighted no problems.

Her cottage in Leigh sold quickly. She negotiated a slightly higher mortgage and was soon the owner of a mock-Tudor house in Shoebury. She hired a Luton van and, with Trevor's and Robbie's help, moved everything left in the Leigh cottage to the Shoebury house. Still very much in love with Trevor she remained living with him. Easier, though, to keep an eye on her house now that it was much closer.

Having to push herself all day to concentrate on repetitive production procedures at work was causing Hazel problems. Once, just before she moved in with Trevor, she was cycling alongside a stream of stationary vehicles waiting for the traffic lights to change. She was tired and her mind numb from hours of repetitive work. The lights changed and traffic began moving forward. A large lorry in the queue was a little slow to pull forward. Hazel thought nothing of it. Too late, she realised he was allowing a car to cross from the opposite lane to enter the side road on Hazel's left. The car hit her front wheel. Hazel's instant thought, as the bike was whipped away from under her, was to go soft, a natural instinct for her. She rolled over the bonnet of the car and fell into the road. A couple of pedestrians reached her before the driver of the car had overcome his shock. They peered down asking anxiously whether she was alright. She carefully stood up. Unhurt.

"I'm actually fine," she said. "Not sure about my bike though."

She walked over to retrieve it and, very gingerly, sat on it and rode a few yards. The front tyre was wobbling slightly but not enough to catch on the brakes.

"I can ride it home, fortunately," she assured the now emerged, pale driver and the concerned pedestrians.

She knew it was due to the mind-numbing tiredness that she experienced every day as she left work. It was not safe to ride a bike in that state and so she only used her XR3 to get to work.

There were days when she arrived back at Trevor's in tears, due to the immense strain of having to push through the tedium. Trevor had no answer, apart from suggesting she search for another job.

Hazel had found that Daniel, at work, was very approachable. He was responsible for quality control of all parts and for repairing the faulty tonearms and turntables returned from dealers. And he worked on whatever research and development projects Rouse set him. This meant he often felt stressed by his workload. As she was passing his bench one day, Hazel asked if it would make sense for her to take over the repair work.

In her early days with the company, before production was fully underway on the tonearm, she had worked in the turntable department and had found building turntables was more laborious than building tonearms. The banter between Melvin, the department supervisor, and the couple of elderly ladies who worked under him, offered the only light relief. But she was able to build turntables unsupervised, as she could the tonearms that were fitted to them. With a little advice from Dan she was certain she could resolve faulty returned parts. Daniel was relieved at this suggestion. He also believed she was very capable and had it approved by Trevor and Rouse.

At most, the repair work occupied only a couple of hours of her time but it was a welcome break from repetitive production work. It meant she regularly flitted between the turntable and tonearm departments. Hazel's optimism had never outwardly dimmed and her singing along and whistling to the radio as she worked in each department was like a signature. Now she was also happy inside. A pay rise and a £1,000 bonus that Christmas were also much appreciated.

CHAPTER 18
1985 ◇ Quality Control

Not long after, Trevor began having serious arguments with Rouse regarding various aspects of managing the company. They were unable to reach an agreement on many things. And Rouse was probably correct in telling Trevor he was a manic depressive. After much soul-searching and discussion with many people, Trevor made the decision to resign and sell his shares to Rouse's wife.

When it became known that Trevor was leaving, his secretary Laura asked him if he thought she would be able to take over his job as factory and finance manager. Trevor confided to Hazel that he did not think she was particularly capable of doing either job but, at Laura's request, he spent a whole evening after work discussing with her the possibility of her taking over. He convinced her she would be able to do the job well enough.

Within months of Trevor leaving, both Daniel and Melvin left. The company's bright and experienced salesman, Shaun, then departed to become a ski instructor. A young, very attractive lady was employed to take his place. While she had a small understanding of the hi-fi industry she had no knowledge of how the products worked or how problems with them might be resolved. However, the immediate concern was the quality control of parts. Hazel offered to take this on. Daniel had shown her how to measure components accurately with a Vernier gauge and reading the engineering drawings, with all sizes and tolerances, was virtually second nature to Hazel, who had grown up watching her father's skills as a draughtsman. She bought a book that explained the importance and principles of good quality control.

Hazel had been aware of problems between Dan and Kevin, the engineer, regarding quality control, but not the detail. As Hazel had always got on well with Kevin she naively believed it would run more smoothly for her. She was given a company car, an Escort Estate. Hazel's XR3 had been an immense thrill, but she was now glad that she could return it to Trevor, knowing she would be unable to pay back the value without a loan.

Hazel also took over the final research and development work on a single-piece cartridge encapsulating a diamond-tipped stylus. Fitted to the tonearm, this completed the turntable unit. Hazel then built, alone, the first 1,000 cartridges, which were well received, with brilliant reviews. She then helped set up a new department for cartridge production. Once the green benches were fitted in the white-walled, windowless, ground-floor room, she coached Jeffrey, who had worked as Pete's second in the tonearm department, to build and test cartridges. He was soon proficient and able to supervise a small team with minimal advice from Hazel. She had also worked out the correct torque for fitting the cartridge firmly to the tonearm and the details meant Kevin could produce a neat little torque wrench to help fit the cartridges perfectly, without any danger of crushing the plastic body.

New speakers were also ready to go into production. Rouse had handed Hazel various resistors and capacitors and asked her to work out which she would need for the correct frequency output for the base driver units. She researched the required equation in Southend library, during her lunch break. After confidently telling Rouse her conclusion, she soldered the correct resistor and capacitor in place on the jig Kevin had put together. Hazel then sound-tested each large base drive unit to eliminate any that made the slightest rattle. All considered, it was a busy time. Hazel often worked beyond five o'clock. With Trevor at home for Robbie, cooking dinner, this was not a problem.

Within a few months Hazel felt that there was a slow, insidious drop in the number of parts waiting for her to check. Kevin, who was free to run his own timetable, insisted on collecting certain parts from suppliers. He would leave the boxed parts under a couple of benches in the engineering room, ready for Hazel to check. Increasingly the spaces remained empty and the percentage of parts falling outside the tolerance began to rise slowly. Kevin assured her that he would bring this to the supplier's notice. With no improvement, it was clear to Hazel that she must work directly with these suppliers to find a solution. Friction arose when Hazel realised that Kevin, because of the close bond he had with these companies, was not going to allow her to interfere. He ensured that he returned the rejects himself and collected the replacements. Increasingly, Hazel chased Kevin for parts she needed to check and increasingly she was unable to find either them or Kevin. She would ask Laura when he might be picking them up. Production would come to a standstill if she was not able to check them. But Laura either had no idea or gave her inaccurate details. On several occasions, Hazel returned in the morning to discover Kevin had already checked in the parts, claiming they were necessary for production. By then, this was true.

It was as Hazel left after work one day that she noticed Kevin's car parked outside. Among the many boxes stacked in his car was a box marked with the name of the suppliers of the stainless-steel bearing housing. Hazel had been waiting for days for Kevin to collect them. Production of the tonearms could not be completed without them. First thing the following morning she searched the few boxes awaiting her. Nothing from the bearing housing suppliers. She questioned Kevin, and he again explained that, yes, he had checked them last night as they were desperately waiting on them for production. Hazel was now seriously worried by this continued undermining. She was about to ask for a meeting to discuss it all with Rouse when Kevin took a two-week holiday.

Problems were occurring in production. The fit of the bearings in the stainless-steel housings had become unacceptably variable. Hazel checked the stainless-steel housings Kevin had passed to production. Many were not within tolerance. Going through the complete stock, Hazel packed up all that were out of tolerance and paid a visit to the company supplying them. She took with her a tube of bearings and demonstrated why it was essential to ensure a snug fit with components. If tolerances were not adhered to this was impossible. Hazel was reassured by her reception. They told her no one had explained this importance in detail to them.

Two days after Kevin returned from holiday Hazel was called to a meeting in the listening room. Rouse and Laura were seated and looking very grave. After asking Hazel to take a seat, they told her that they were not happy with the way quality control was working out.

Stunned, she listened as Laura explained that she was clearly too busy on other projects to check all the parts as they came into the factory.

Then it dawned on Hazel just how much Kevin had not been putting out for testing. It seemed Laura had accepted whatever Kevin told her. Hazel had known that a female interfering within the tight, male-dominated, engineering fraternity might be difficult, she now wondered whether her inexperience and lack of confidence might, in part, be to blame. But this meeting was unexpected.

Her mind rapidly scrolled through all the times she had been aware of Kevin holding back parts to check himself, early in the morning or after she had gone home. Of her frustration at Kevin not allowing her direct contact with some suppliers. In particular those producing the stainless-steel components from where most of the problems were stemming. How could she stand up to someone with Kevin's expertise? Was this why there had been tension between Daniel and Kevin? The company would manage without her but losing Kevin would be more difficult. He was an absolute wizard when it came to making jigs for production.

Hazel couldn't think of anything positive to offer that would not incriminate Kevin and she was sure that that would only lead to further unpleasantness, even if she was able to convince Rouse of what had gone on. The meeting concluded with Laura explaining that quality control would be given to Kevin and she would lose the company car. She was also told to spend all her spare time helping with cartridge production and they required her to fill in a time sheet, every day, to show exactly how she was spending her time.

Desperately upset Hazel immediately went to sort out all the repairs for the day. At least they were pleased with *that* part of her job. And she filled in her time sheet: timed all her calls from dealers who required her advice; timed the repairs; timed how long it took to explain to department supervisors how anomalies were showing up in sold products, because of part intolerances, and what they should look out for. Then time taken discussing this with Kevin. Any spare time she had was then spent in and logged to the cartridge department, as asked. But that evening, after much heart-searching, she decided that she must speak to Rouse alone. Unsure of what this might achieve, she felt she needed to say something in her defence.

He made time for her the following day. Hazel did not mention that Kevin had deliberately kept parts from her, but did explain that he had insisted he alone dealt with certain suppliers. But Rouse believed that if the right person was doing the right job, one that was suited to them, problems would be sorted. In her case it had not happened. She had not been strong enough to overrule Kevin. Rouse stood firm on the decision, saying it was down to Laura and each individual to sort out their own problems. At least Hazel felt that she'd now tried all tacks. There was no alternative but to accept that she had lost quality control. Even though she thought that, with the correct support from Kevin, she would have been able to make a difference. The company's loss, she told herself.

Trevor was finding it hard to accept that Hazel wanted to continue working for the company, meaning that Hazel hadn't felt as though she could discuss work with him. He regularly told her she was overconfident and her belief that she was able to do a job in which she had not succeeded would confirm it for him. Hazel thought now that perhaps he was right. But he had also commented that he thought her parents had been wrong to allow her to be the person she was. With that she couldn't agree. It seemed he thought she should have been made to question herself more often. Had he simply wanted her to have more insecurities? Like himself? Hazel was never sure. However, she did have to explain why she had lost the company car. Trevor had sold his Ferrari and kept the XR3 so he initially took her to work and collected her. Until he decided to buy a new Renault Clio – they had just produced a sporty turbo version that he fancied.

Hazel submitted worksheets for only two days. They clearly showed that a lot of her time involved sorting out problems with whole units or parts, both within the company and with dealerships. And the amount she achieved while doing cartridge production was very acceptable. No one could argue that she was not worth her salary. What was most irritating, though, was Kevin. As soon as he heard she was no longer involved with quality control, he began imitating her constant whistling and smiling, certainly whenever she was within earshot. As mature as a child, thought Hazel!

The whole episode made Hazel think about starting her own business. What were her loves, her passions? Interior design? Or gardening with garden design? Most of all, she loved being out of doors, which swayed her thoughts towards garden design and maintenance. Her back was strong enough now, with her continued few minutes exercise each morning. She did discuss it with Trevor. He was enthusiastic and helped her work out a liveable hourly rate. It was viable. And she needed a vehicle now anyway. To this end, Trevor mentioned that he had looked around a Dacia car showroom in Leigh that sold basic, solidly built vehicles. Rather like a cross between a Land Rover and a jeep and relatively cheap. A trailer and a good professional lawnmower appeared to be the only necessary extra start-up costs. Hazel would be able to design and print off some leaflets herself. Starting one's own business would be a big step but Trevor's enthusiasm for her idea gave her confidence.

The following Saturday Trevor drove Hazel into Leigh to look at 4x4 Dacia Dusters. They were rather square, enclosed and definitely jeep-like, with no frills. But they all came with a tow bar and a good, plain, tall interior that would be great for transporting tools and plants. On the forecourt stood a blue one that, although it was three years old, had a low mileage and a reasonable price tag. A salesman approached and asked if they needed any help, to which Trevor replied, "We'd like to take this one out for a test drive."

"Certainly, sir, come inside and we'll go through some details."

For a salesman he seemed a genuinely pleasant guy and not too pushy. Once all Hazel's details had been taken, she jumped into the driver's seat. Trevor sat in the back and listened as the salesman went through all the controls.

"You may find the clutch and gears heavier than you're used to," he warned.

Hazel fired up the engine, depressed the throttle a little and thought, 'Yes, this feels very different from an XR3!!' The throaty roar may have been similar but as Hazel pushed down on the heavy clutch and forced it into first gear then gently lifted the clutch, the weighty, jeep-like van didn't move much. 'Oh well, I need something strong and solid,' she conceded.

They went on a little jaunt down to the A127 to check out a bit of speed, which it did eventually achieve but the poor engine was incredibly loud. Still, for the price it did seem to be her best choice. Its MOT was due, it needed a full service and Trevor noticed that one of the brake lights wasn't working. He haggled and said that they would only buy it if the MOT and full service were included in the price. This was finally agreed upon so Trevor handed over a deposit on the understanding that they would return next weekend and collect it once the work had been done. This would give Hazel time to transfer the money into her bank, most of which was her last generous bonus from work.

That Sunday evening Hazel began to feel unwell. She'd not been sleeping very well, caused by a combination of the excitement of buying the 4x4 Dacia, her move into self-employment, some late evenings at work and the constant rollercoaster of her relationship with Trevor – which, as he still was not working, had got worse.

They'd had another argument about the back door not being locked. Hazel knew it was an important issue and berated herself each time it happened. This time she had written 'Back Door' on a sheet of paper, left it on the kitchen table, then blindly walked past the table with her mind on other things. She had been relaxing upstairs, listening to music, when Trevor burst in, raging that, yet again, the back door was unlocked. She couldn't help but be angry at her own stupidity, at the hopelessness of not remembering something so vital, knowing it would cause distress. She began shouting back at him that they must work together to sort this out as, clearly, she was incapable. Trevor's temper couldn't handle her retaliation. He picked her up and held her over the stairwell and threatened to drop her if she said any more. Shock and disbelief set her heart hammering. Could he hold her without his hands slipping, even accidentally?

"I'll stop. Please don't drop me," she pleaded.

He lifted her back over the ledge and stood her on her feet. As the shock receded and Hazel walked away her mind churned. She could never allow that to happen again. But how?

Another argument ensued when Trevor stormed out of the kitchen saying Robbie had drunk all the milk. Hazel reminded him that if he had increased the order with the milkman, as she had suggested, it wouldn't have happened. He ignored her comment and said it was

Robbie's selfishness that was the problem. She felt this was yet another issue that wouldn't be resolved and she lost her temper, throwing the keys she was holding against a wall, which took out a lump of plaster. Strangely, Trevor's anger evaporated. But Hazel didn't feel good, this was the first time in her life that she'd ever remembered feeling such sheer, uncontrollable anger. With all this stress her immune system was taking a battering, and the aching and shivering she felt that evening had all the hallmarks of flu.

Trevor cooked dinner but after only a few mouthfuls Hazel filled a hot-water bottle, took a couple of paracetamols, undressed and slid into bed. She ached and sweated all night, despite taking further paracetamol. Trevor slept soundly.

In the morning she asked him to ring work to let them know she had the flu. Trevor brought her a cup of tea in bed but she couldn't manage any breakfast. She took some more paracetamol and drifted in and out of a sweaty sleep, all the time aware of how deeply every part of her body ached. Monday passed slowly and Hazel only got up to go to the toilet. She just managed some toast that Trevor brought up for lunch.

Robbie put his head around the door when he got in from school to say, "Hi, I've got some maths homework to do," and disappeared.

She managed to swallow some soup about six. At his bed time, Robbie popped in quickly to blow her a kiss and say, "Night, night. Hope you feel better in the morning."

But Hazel didn't at all and was in for another day in bed trying to sleep and forget about the incessant aching everywhere. She did try to eat some egg for lunch and a little steamed fish with mash in the evening. But she ached so much all over that she thought dying may not be so bad if it meant oblivion. The only consoling thought was that, on the few occasions she'd had flu before, she remembered feeling a little improvement on the third day.

So, roll on Wednesday …

CHAPTER 19
1986 ◊ Hazel's Illness

'Oh no, what's this?' Hazel thought as her mind rose to consciousness the following morning. She was struggling to breathe. It felt as though a heavy weight was pressing down on her chest. She could hear her breath rattling painfully as she attempted to draw it in and out against this invisible pressure. It reminded her of the sound of her father's breathing when pneumonia surfaced on the last day of his life.

As Trevor awoke she said, "It's really hard to breathe. I think I might have pneumonia. Can you ring for a doctor?"

Trevor got up and wrapped a dressing gown around himself. "Yes. I'll try about eight to see if someone's at the surgery? If not, I'll call next door to see if Clive's in."

Their next-door neighbour was also their GP.

A little later Robbie looked around the door to say, "Bye, see you after school," and blew a kiss.

Half an hour later the phone rang. Trevor called up the stairs, "It's your brother, John. Can you take it up there?"

The phone was on the dressing table, only a few feet from the bed. Hazel struggled to get herself off the edge of the bed, leant over and picked up the phone.

"Hello, Hazel," John's voice always sounded so happy and bouncy, "I ..."

The rest got lost as Hazel started to cough. She couldn't speak. Trevor came into the bedroom. Hazel held the phone up for him to take and managed to choke out, "I can't talk."

Trevor took the phone and explained that Hazel wasn't well and she would ring back when she felt a little better.

To Hazel he said, "Clive said he'll call in after surgery this morning. Would you like any breakfast?"

"No, thank you," Hazel managed and slid back into bed to wait.

Hours passed before Clive arrived. Hazel had drifted in and out of sleep, willing the time away. Then she heard the doorbell and Clive's voice. She struggled to sit up as he stepped into the room.

"Ah, what do we have here then? Let's just have a listen to your breathing. Can you lift your top at the back?"

Hazel fumbled with her pyjama top until Clive decided to help her and she felt the chill of his hands on her burning back. Then the cold stethoscope.

"Oh, so lovely and cold," she said.

It sounded like a joke but that brief touch of cold really had felt wonderful as he moved the stethoscope to listen to her chest.

"Does it hurt when you breathe?" he asked.

"Yes," replied Hazel.

But what she should have added was that it was more than just pain; more of a problem was the totally exhausting effort and strength needed just to get her lungs to expand, to draw in each breath. She was simply too weak and ill to consider that this might be important information.

"It's bronchitis," he declared.

Hazel didn't question his diagnosis. Why, oh why, did she not say she thought it was pneumonia? She believed she was in capable hands.

"I'll give you a prescription for some antibiotics," he said as he scribbled on his pad, smiled, said goodbye and left.

Trevor let him out and returned with some diluted orange juice and said he'd go out straight away to pick up the prescription. Hazel melted back down into bed and was thankful that she would soon have some antibiotics. She had never had bronchitis before but was sure that it was not as serious as pneumonia and berated herself for having believed she was really ill. As she lay there, she thought about her new car and that she'd said she would collect it on Saturday. She thought that by Friday the antibiotics should be working their magic and she'd be up to going into Southend to transfer money from the building society into her bank. The only thing that filled her waking mind as she lay in bed feeling so awful was the thought of starting a new life with her own business. That and how rotten every part of her body felt.

Trevor returned with the tablets she should take every four hours, and a bottle of Lucozade. Her mum had given it to her as a child when she was ill and its wonderful, crisp, sweet flavour always woke her taste buds. She also managed to eat a little. She had the radio on to soothe her and tried to keep an eye on the clock so she'd know when to take her next pills. But she realised that her brain was unable to add four hours to the time she'd taken her first pills. It worried her that so simple a calculation seemed beyond her. Trevor assured her he would bring her pills every four hours. By the end of the day she still felt far too ill to get up, so another day went past. At some point, when it was dark, Trevor woke her with water and more pills to take. The following afternoon Hazel wrapped her dressing gown around herself and ventured downstairs on very weak legs to greet Robbie when he came home from school. She curled up on the sofa and they watched TV together until Trevor called Robbie into the kitchen for his dinner.

"It's okay, Mum, you stay here. I'll be fine to eat by myself."

For once, she was able to forgive Trevor for making her son eat in the kitchen because she seriously didn't know how she would have managed without her volatile partner.

Friday morning arrived. Hazel knew she'd have to get up at some point to drive into Southend. She'd have to walk down the high street to the building society to withdraw all her savings and go back up to the bank. She still felt so weak that the task seemed impossible, but the thought of her blue Dacia Duster with a lawnmower bobbing behind in its trailer was the only cohesive thought that had filled her mind for four days.

Trevor brought her two Weetabix with a covering of milk and sugar and Hazel was able to eat most of it. She put the tray down on the floor when she'd finished and fell asleep for a while. At about eleven o'clock, she roused herself for a bath, which helped to return a little normality to her life. Feeling refreshed, she dressed slowly and went downstairs.

She ate a little of the beans on toast Trevor had cooked for lunch. She was still a long way from her usual appetite.

"Are you okay to drive into Southend?" Trevor asked.

He wanted to watch some tennis on the television. Hazel nodded. She watched with him for a bit until she lifted herself weakly off the sofa, then went back up to the bedroom to put on a little mascara and some colour on her very pale cheeks. She stared at herself in the mirror and imagined a new period of her life opening up. Her excitement fuelled her weakened body. She gathered up her handbag, building society book and coat and left.

Her heart both warmed and saddened a little as she saw the red XR3 sitting on the drive. It was a bit grubby. She had put off washing it because she knew that as soon as she brought the Duster home, Trevor would sell it. She slid in, still feeling incredibly frail and shaky and drove slowly into Southend. After finally parking the car, she stepped out and felt awful. How was she going to get all the way down the high street then up again to the bank? 'Oh, come on Hazel, do stop being a weak wimp. It's only bronchitis. Just put your mind to it, one foot in front of the other.' And so, somehow, after resting in both the building society and the bank, she managed to make it back to the car with her money transferred.

She fell into the car with relief. Feeling like death, she sat for a while before driving carefully home. Once in the front door, she threw her coat on the arm of the sofa, sank down and fell asleep. She was woken by Robbie with a cup of tea. As she sat sipping it, listening to her son's lively chatter, she felt so happy. Tomorrow she would be the proud owner of a Dacia Duster 4x4. It would take her and Robbie anywhere they wanted to go.

It's lucky that we cannot see into the future.

Tim called that evening to pick up Robbie for a night at his Gran and Granddad's. He said that he'd drop him back about five-thirty the next afternoon because he knew his son was excited and wanted to see this off-road 4x4! That night, it was excitement rather than illness that kept Hazel awake, so when morning came she felt both ill and exhausted. After helping Trevor with the washing and shopping, Hazel lay down on the bed to rest.

Trevor woke her at three-thirty with a cup of tea. "You've not had any lunch. Would you like me to get you something before we go into Leigh?"

Hazel sat up. She felt rather nauseous and the thought of food didn't help. She shook her head.

"Just tea is fine."

She felt strange and disorientated, but the sweet tea brought her thoughts to her new car, the start of her new life. She gathered herself up, made sure her cheque book was in her handbag, went downstairs, put on her coat and followed Trevor out to his Renault. She relaxed into the seat, closed her eyes and let her mind wander to a new world, with her Duster full of gardening tools and the new lawnmower bouncing along in the trailer. Then her mind drifted to the exciting trails she and Robbie would be able to explore off road. Yes, she felt ill, but she was fired up by the thrills that her imagination was bringing to life. The traffic on Saturday was heavy as usual, especially through Southend, so Hazel had over half an hour to chill out and drift off into pleasant daydreams. When they finally arrived at the garage, Hazel was already living with her Duster and couldn't contemplate not taking it home. The manager led them into a small, dark, cramped office with only two chairs – Trevor had to stand.

"Unfortunately, because my colleague's been away on holiday, I've not been able to complete the service on the vehicle yet, but it does have its MOT so if you would like to bring it back next weekend, I can get that completed then," the manager began.

Everything sounded muddled. Was her hearing going? She thought Trevor said something to her about not being able to take it home yet. Then he mentioned the rear light.

"I'm sure that would have been replaced for the MOT," replied the manager.

Trevor went to leave.

"Come on, Hazel. We'll come back once everything's been completed."

Hazel felt dazed and confused, she had her cheque book all ready. It sounded as though it had a MOT. Surely it wasn't that much of a problem to bring it back in a week to complete the service. She followed Trevor out of the office on to the forecourt.

"I want to take it home now, Trevor," Hazel pleaded.

He turned and looked at her and, without saying anything, walked back to the manager and asked if he could check to see if the rear light was working. The manager brought out the key and they walked over to the car that she already felt was hers. Trevor turned on the lights and walked to the rear. Hazel watched with a strange detachment.

"The bulb hasn't been replaced. How could this have passed a MOT?" said Trevor, clearly quite angry.

"I'm very sorry," replied the manager, passing the MOT certificate to Trevor as authentication. "They did rush it through. But I can replace it now."

Hazel was feeling so ill and confused that, as they returned to the office with Trevor ranting on about how they should leave and not return until all was completed, she was only able to focus on writing out the cheque.

"I'm taking it now. I'll bring it back next week," she said to Trevor.

He said something about it being her decision and strode off. Hazel asked the manager to confirm the date and price, before he went to replace the bulb. She had to really concentrate to complete the cheque. A task that would normally take seconds seemed to stretch to long minutes as she fumbled to write it out. Finally, Hazel was relieved to see the manager back and all the paperwork completed and she was handed the keys.

'Wow,' Hazel thought as she walked towards her car. 'My 4x4. At last. What fun.'

The adrenaline must have kicked in as she pulled herself up into the driver's seat. The manager went over all the controls.

"Don't forget it will feel heavier than what you've been used to, so go gently to begin with," and he closed the door.

Silence. All alone. 'Concentrate. Okay, turn the key.' The engine growled. 'Great. Down with the clutch. Gosh, that's even harder than I remember. Where's my strength?'

She forced it down. The black round knob on the gear lever was cold and Hazel used all her strength to move it into first.

'How weak I've become. It must get easier.'

She checked the mirror. It was dark, the street lamps were lit and there was very little traffic. She lifted the clutch slowly. The 4x4 moved sluggishly forward. Then, with great difficulty, she pushed the gearstick into second as she pulled out round a parked car. More pressure on the accelerator and she could feel a little more power.

'Oh, this is going to be fine,' Hazel thought as she fell into the flow of the road with an instinct born of years of driving.

It still felt very heavy and gear changes were challenging. As she drove past her mother's road, Hazel thought she'd stop briefly to show off the ungainly thing. She was so happy. She knew her business would work. This was the beginning.

Ruth and Lionel were at her mother's, about to enjoy a fish and chip supper, and they all popped out to have a look. Her mother remarked later that she had looked very flushed! Hazel realised she hadn't eaten in ages and so left for home. The drive was laborious and she continued to struggle with the gears. Finally, she pulled into the drive, feeling very unsteady as she climbed down and made straight for the kitchen. She registered Robbie's smiling face sitting at the table and something cooking under the grill. When Trevor walked towards her, she could see his mouth moving but could hear no sound and suddenly felt very sick.

"I've got to lie down," she said.

As she staggered up the stairs, her stomach began to heave. She just made it to the toilet before she began to retch. But nothing came up. Only a little spittle. It had been so long since she'd eaten there was nothing there. She pulled herself up off her knees, stumbled into the bedroom and collapsed on the bed. The waves of nausea seemed to subside as she lay flat on her back and began to relax. Then Hazel heard a sudden strange bursting POP at the base of her head. Freezing water poured upward over her brain then blackness …

Unconsciousness or death?

Slowly … consciousness. Hazel feels herself rushing through a white endless tunnel of cloud.

'This must be me dying.'

She feels no fear, just an acceptance and a wonder at what she might find. Minutes seem to pass and still she's in this white tunnel. Then, thankfully, a dark pinhole appears. It gets larger and larger and Hazel sees that it's the end of the whiteness and she moves into dark blueness.

It is all so silent. Stars are shining in their millions, everywhere, going on forever.

'This is space. How can I be breathing? I have no space suit.' Hazel looks down. She has no body, so needs no oxygen.

'I am dead then. Is this what happens?'

Her mind is totally and utterly alone, floating weightlessly, slowly, further and further into space. Then she knows she's not alone. She can see nothing except the vastness of space, but a gentle power moves her around, although she feels no touch. Just below her is Earth. We all know what it looks like from space, we've seen it in books ever since childhood and, yes, it is a cloud-covered, blue sphere and now it's about the size of a football, turning so very slowly as Hazel watches, in awe.

Then fear begins to permeate.

All the horror, all the pain, all the suffering that she knows from paintings, from the newspapers and TV, from all that she has stored in her memory of every awful thing, begins to seep through her being. It is so unbearable, so uncontrollably painful, the total agony of it all makes her long for death, but she's no longer alive, so death cannot bring relief.

Hazel is seeing all of hell, there on Earth. It feels like a lifetime of everything terrifying: purgatory. She is being torn apart by pain.

'Hell, this is where I've been sent. This agonising torment is Hell. Is this what I have to suffer for eternity? No, no. Surely I haven't caused enough pain to warrant this? Please, please, I cannot deserve this.'

Her mind frantically rummages through her life, searching for the hurt she may have caused. To Tim? To Ramsey's wife? Who else?

Then, she senses rather than hears, a voice. Its silent power belongs within the invisible matter wrapped all around her. She feels it let her know that it's sending her back. It has shown her Earth and all the suffering on it and it can do no more to help, not by itself. People have been returned before. But there are so many people now and all the religions that have evolved to bring comfort, compassion and love – not only within each separate religion or tribe but to all in need – are such a very, very long way from working.

Hazel realises the unimaginable. This presence has to be God and, alone now, it is powerless. It is not able to work without vessels within which to manifest itself. Every single human alive on that small floating ball in front of her could be God's vessel or, more simply, a vessel for good matter. She feels goodness at the very heart of this presence. But now it is watching helplessly. With utter relief, she believes it is sending her back. It had let her know it needs her help.

The next thing she knew, she was up in the corner of her bedroom, gazing down on her unconscious body. She sank back into her body, but was paralysed. She could only open her eyes and, as she did so, a pulsing, flashing light revolved around and around the room. It was behind and in front of her eyes. She tried to blink but it would not stop. She lay there completely helpless for what felt like hours, so sick all the while, and terrified that if a doctor wasn't called she might properly and finally die!

Then, out of the corner of her eye, she saw the door move. Trevor poked his head around, but Hazel was still paralysed. After their argument he probably thought she was ignoring him. How little he knew her. He disappeared. Time passed by with no hope of a doctor. The terrible pulsing, beating light remained, constant and unrelenting.

Then slowly, very slowly, Hazel's legs began to feel the softness of the bed, she felt herself move them. Her arms and body had feeling and movement again. She gently slid out of bed. The curtains were still open. She walked slowly, unsteadily, to look out. Inside her head, and in the room, the pulsing remained, but outside all looked normal and quiet. Hazel thought it must be late.

She suddenly needed fresh air; she felt she was suffocating. Inside the room it all seemed confusing, her brain was badly misfiring, she couldn't hear or speak, but her mind wanted to be outside, near normality. Outside was cool air and below her was the flat roof of the garage. If she could jump out of the window she wouldn't break much and if she hit her head it might actually stun it back out of this terrifying fault.

She fumbled with the window catch but it seemed locked. She was becoming frantic. Why did Trevor never leave them unlocked? She had to get out.

Her sixteen-inch TV was sitting on the chest of drawers near the window. It was heavy but portable, with a handle on top. She might be able to smash the window with it. She slid one hand under the handle, the other under its base. She lifted it just as she felt movement behind. Trevor grabbed the television but Hazel hung on. She still couldn't hear or speak but her strength was suddenly formidable. She pulled it from his grasp but he wrestled it back again. They fought viciously. Trevor was frightened by her abnormal strength.

Finally, he replaced the TV and got her on the bed and, with all his might, sat astride her. Hazel gradually relaxed, her terror abating a little. Would he call a doctor? Did he know that she couldn't speak? He stroked her hair, her face, felt her calm down. He gently rolled off the bed and left the room. Then she heard his voice. Was he on the phone? She could hear again, but the pulsing light had not changed, which was blurring everything. She desperately hoped Trevor was ringing for a doctor. But time just stretched on endlessly. She thought she glimpsed her mother briefly, but perhaps that was just a dream. Still no doctor.

The house then sounded very quiet. What was happening? This awful, constant, flashing light was still boring into her eyes, like nothing she'd ever known and she was trying again to fight a rising panic. Nothing was going to happen. She was going to be left to die.

She got off the bed. She knew it was pointless to find the stairs. She knew that Trevor would not allow her out of the house but she had to have fresh air. She tried the window again. Locked. There had to be a key. She frantically searched the drawers. Nothing.

Then there was Trevor again, trying to pin her arms down, trying to force her on to the bed, but Hazel so did not want to die. She had to get him to call a doctor. She simply couldn't understand why he wouldn't. The thought then came to her that if she bit him he might, just might, think she had rabies or something. She knew it was a long shot. But without speech she felt she had no choice.

He had his arms around her shoulders and was pulling her towards the bed. He sat on the edge of the bed and as he attempted to roll her on to it she bit into his arm as hard as she could. He whipped his arm away and Hazel collapsed on the bed. She was spent; there was nothing more to do.

Trevor disappeared and, minutes later, Robbie came in. He sat on the edge of the bed and took her hand and gently stroked it. Hazel would not do anything to alarm him further. She knew he must have heard the fighting and would be scared. She thought she heard Trevor talking. This time, surely, he was calling for a doctor. Robbie left. Hazel curled up on the bed and waited, but the pulsing, flashing light, if anything, seemed to worsen,

At last, there was a doctor. Hazel felt hands roll her on to her front and felt an injection in a buttock, then another. Did she get up then, did she fight? She doesn't remember because, apparently, she was given two more. She heard the doctor say he thought she'd be alright now and he'd arrange for a doctor to visit in the morning. Relief began to wash through Hazel, the flashing seemed to be receding.

But Trevor started arguing, "No, no, she needs the hospital, something's not right."

Hazel drifted into sleep, then suddenly she awoke.

Men in white coats. Fear gripped her again. Now what?

She was bundled downstairs. Her eyes still couldn't clear the flashing lights but the pulsing was less. Out of the front door. Cold air at last. Her brain felt as though a severe alcoholic-like haze was clearing. She breathed deeply.

There on the road stood an ambulance. Wonderful! Then it struck Hazel that it looked rather old. She was led towards it by the two white coats, one on either side of her. As one of them leant forward to open the back doors Hazel saw there was nothing inside but two wooden benches, one down each side – it wasn't an ambulance for the physically sick. She still couldn't speak and knew that she had no choice but to get in.

During the drive, Hazel attempted to understand the misfiring of her brain. It had to be due to some kind of damage. Something was causing some synapses not to fire or pass on a signal. Whatever the problem was, whatever had paralysed her and initiated the out-of-body experience, it didn't seem to be affecting her rational thinking now. But why was her speech not returning? Something still wasn't working correctly.

Through the rear windows she watched the road rolling away and knew that they had travelled out through Southend. So, she wasn't being taken to Southend General Hospital. This was not looking good. They wound on through the countryside. Then she recognised the road into Rochford.

'Oh, Rochford Hospital then,' thought Hazel, and yes into the gates it rolled. This was hopeful. The ambulance followed a lane that led past the main building, familiar to Hazel because Robbie had been born there, but still they continued driving. They went past sheds and older buildings, until the ambulance stopped outside an old red-brick building. A white coat helped her out and led her to a wooden door with an old mesh glass window. Looking around, it felt as though time had shifted. Everything was old fashioned.

Confused, she thought, 'Now I've travelled back in time! Does that mean Robbie's not been born?' She immediately felt loss and grief for her son. 'Just what has happened to me?'

Before Hazel could dwell on this, a short corridor opened into a long, large room bathed in a subdued light. A wooden counter stood above a plain, bare, wooden floor. Hazel was ushered into a chair where she sat and waited.

There was no one about although she could discern distant voices. She thought she was beginning to feel slightly better and knew she had not slipped back in time. But the waiting continued and then there it was again, a flashing light, misfiring in her brain. The cold air had clearly helped but now her recovery seemed to be going backward.

A young woman brought her a glass of water. Hazel sipped some. She appeared to be wearing a nurse's uniform and had a reassuring smile. She gently touched Hazel's elbow and indicated she should follow her.

There was seating to be manoeuvred around. Hazel took a shortcut and ended up in front of the nurse just as they were passing a fully decorated Christmas tree. Suddenly it struck Hazel that there were lights decorating it. Electricity. If she threw water at the tree then grabbed and twisted a light, she might get a shock. Anything to stop this flashing fault in her brain.

She had to be quick.

She swung towards the tree. Threw the water. Unfortunately, the nurse was now level with the tree and was caught in the drenching.

'Poor girl, I didn't want to upset her,' thought Hazel, seeing her wet uniform.

She had no recollection of what happened next.

CHAPTER 20
1986 ◇ Terror

Slowly, Hazel awoke, aware she was lying in a bed. All that had happened came flooding back. Her mouth felt very dry but she made a few guttural ah and oh sounds to test her voice.

"Yes!"

Thank God she could speak again. She hardly dared open her eyes but, as she did, her worst fear manifested itself. She was in a large, dingy dormitory with a row of empty beds along each wall, separated by small bedside cabinets. None of the high-tech equipment you'd find in a hospital for the physically sick.

Total and utter terror.

'Please, dear Lord, I've seen hell, now I'm incarcerated.'

Hazel and Tim had seen the film *One Flew over the Cuckoo's Nest* starring Jack Nicholson as Randle McMurphy. The film demonstrates how easy it is to incarcerate someone in a secure psychiatric unit and establishes that McMurphy is not, in fact, crazy, but that he is trying to manipulate a system to his advantage. His belief that the psychiatric hospital would be more comfortable than the Pendleton Work Farm, where he was serving a six-month sentence, was his downfall. McMurphy discovered the power of Nurse Ratchet, who sent him for electroshock treatments and kept him committed. He was finally lobotomised and then suffocated by an inmate.

Hazel's behaviour the previous day had been enough to warrant a straitjacket to begin with! So the fear that gripped her now surpassed all that she'd just suffered. How was she ever going to convince them that whatever had happened was due to a physical illness? She'd been shown hell, now this was a living nightmare.

Hazel had been stripped of her clothes and was wearing a cotton wrap-over gown. She shakily struggled out of bed and stumbled to a set of double doors at one end of the room and noticed as she got closer that they opened on to a balcony. Only they didn't. They were locked. Her heart was hammering as she ran to the other end of the room, certain that she would find that locked too. Such relief as she heaved one open and slid into a dark landing with a grey concrete stairway going down on one side. Just as she was about to start down them a nurse turned the corner at the bottom and looked up at her.

"You're awake. I was just bringing you a drink."

Hazel froze and waited for her to ascend.

"How are you feeling?"

"I should be in an ordinary hospital, if anywhere. I've had some sort of virus that caused a seizure and I still have some antibiotic pills I need to take. I feel very weak and my chest is very tight. I should not be here."

The nurse saw Hazel's fear.

"You're not locked in. This is an open unit and you're free to walk out at any time, but if you wait until nine you can ring home. I have some orange juice and these pills will help make you feel a little better."

Hazel looked at the sealed plastic pot with a picture of an orange on top. That looked safe to drink, but looking at the pills Hazel asked, "Are they antibiotics?"

"No," the nurse replied, "they will just help relax you."

Hazel was defiant, "I don't need those."

"That's fine, I won't force you. Breakfast has finished but I can probably find you a sandwich if you like."

Hazel answered that she was very hungry and anything would do.

"You'll find some clean clothes in your cabinet. Come downstairs when you're dressed."

In the cabinet were the clothes she had arrived in plus some clean jeans, clean underwear, a fresh T-shirt and a jumper that must have travelled with her, courtesy of Trevor! There was her toilet bag. She put her clothes on and went down the concrete stairs, cautiously, aware of how weak her legs were. The stairs opened on to the lounge that she remembered from the previous evening and there, against the back wall, was the Christmas tree. The counter was also still there. Behind this was a pleasant-looking man, probably in his late thirties, dressed in dark cords and an open-necked shirt with a badge that said Roger clipped to the pocket.

Hazel walked over and leant on the counter for a little support. "The nurse said she would get me a sandwich, and is there any chance of a cup of tea?"

He said she would find all she needed in the dining room and pointed to the left of the stairs. Hazel found a stack of clean plastic cups, tea bags, a jug of milk, a pot of sugar and a hot-water machine. Making herself a cup of tea comforted her with a tiny sense of normality and she carried it back into the lounge. A television, up on a bracket, was showing the news. She sat in an armchair and looked around at all the others: roughly ten men and women, most with blank faces, wandering aimlessly; one man was pulling his hair frantically as he plodded around the seating; another shuffled, staring at his feet; a woman was asking where her baby was; another rocked and moaned in an armchair. Dreadful wailing suddenly drenched the air. On and on it went. Someone out of view.

The nurse finally found Hazel and handed over a cheese sandwich. "You can ring your family when you've eaten that. The phone's in the office behind the counter."

Hazel ate as quickly as she could and returned to the counter.

"Roger, may I use the phone?"

Who should she ring? She chose Trevor.

Even to her own ears, Hazel sounded desperate.

"Please, I need to get out of here. Can you come and pick me up? I don't have any money with me or I'd get a taxi."

She heard Trevor hesitate.

"Just wait, Hazel. Robbie, your mum and I are going to come and visit after lunch. We can have a chat then."

That wasn't the reassurance Hazel needed.

"Can you bring my coat and some money?"

"Yes, of course. We'll see you later."

Hazel put down the receiver and stared at the dirty beige wall in front of her. There was no reality. Nothing she could hold on to. What had happened to her life? A life that, regardless of whatever struggles she'd encountered, she had always loved so much. Her dear father was gone; she had managed to get through that. Whatever would he have made of this?

She wandered back into the lounge, sat down and did her best to shut out all the wailing and poor people around her and forced her mind to concentrate on daytime TV trivia.

The sandwich was beginning to revive her a little and she decided to find out whether she truly could 'walk out at any time'.

It would be cold outside and she still felt physically very weak, but she had to try. Opposite the counter was a door through which she could see a second one leading directly outdoors. She pushed open the first and let it shut behind her before opening the second, obviously designed to keep the draughts out, not people in.

Her spirits lifted a little as here was a small garden surrounded by tall sections of wooden trellis. An archway, covered by a climbing rose that was still in its winter sleep, heralded an entrance. Hazel breathed deeply, but then coughed and worried that the cold air might not be good for her fragile lungs. She wouldn't be long though. She slowly walked around, recognising familiar shrubs and various perennial plants, even a grey curry plant. She leant down and gently squeezed a branch tip – 'Ah yes, simply curry!' She sat down on a wooden bench with lavender bushes on both sides. She could see what looked like the back of the main hospital. So, this was like an outbuilding.

The winter chill was seeping into her so Hazel reluctantly got up and gingerly returned to the two doors and entered what she really hoped was her very temporary home.

Mealtimes were not memorable, other than for a smell of school dinners. But at some point on that first day a pill trolley appeared, manned by a nurse, and everyone wordlessly formed a queue. Someone told Hazel she needed to as well, so she obediently complied and watched as those in front of her dutifully took what was given to them. The nurse asked Hazel her name, searched the list and handed her a plastic cup of water and two pills.

Hazel asked, "Are they antibiotics?"

"No, they are simply relaxants," the nurse replied.

"I really don't need these," said Hazel, very worried about the effect they might have.

"Just try them this once. They're not going to hurt you and you'll find they do make you feel better," she urged.

Hazel swallowed the pills.

She remembered seeing a shelf of books in the dining room so wandered in to find one, to help pass the time. She chose a story set in Cornwall – at least that felt familiar – then returned to the lounge where she found an unoccupied sofa from where she could see visitors entering. As she read, she became aware of a fogginess seeping through her, a dullness to her perceptions.

She shouldn't have taken those pills.

Physically, she was still feeling very weak and her breathing remained more laboured than normal. She had felt up to fighting it before taking the pills, but now exhaustion was just pulling her down. She wasn't going to accept any more!

She looked up and there was Robbie across the room with Trevor and her mum. Her heart wrenched at the anxiety on her son's face as he scanned the occupants, looking for her. Hazel was already used to the screaming and wailing, but to watch Robbie absorb all this around him as he searched for his mother made Hazel angry. It was one thing for her to have to suffer because of a mistake, but to see the effect it was having so clearly etched on his twelve-year-old face was unforgivable. She tried to stand on legs that no longer felt part of her and she waved to catch his attention. As they walked over, her son was all that mattered. She folded her arms around him.

"Please don't worry, this is all a terrible mistake. The seizure or whatever was caused by the virus I had. But I'm okay now, just a bit weak and it won't happen again. I'm so sorry that you've had to see me in here. But I'm coming home."

She noticed Trevor had her coat and a large bottle of lemonade. Oh, so welcome, she was so thirsty. She poured some into her plastic cup, gulped it down and filled it twice more. Then swallowed one of the last few antibiotics from the packet that Trevor handed her. A little clarity dawned through the drug enforced haze as the liquid hydrated her.

"Can we go now? This place is really not helping me," she asked him.

"The doctor wants to see you later this afternoon, so it's best to see what he has to say," was his answer.

From a physical point of view Hazel thought this might be sensible.

"So, can I go home afterwards?"

"I really do think it might be best to stay another night, until you at least feel a little stronger."

She certainly didn't have the strength to argue with him. She hugged Robbie again. Her mother said he had spent the night with her and he might stay with her for another day. It really wouldn't matter if he missed a day or so of school.

"That's good. Being with Grandma is always fun, and I'll soon be my normal self again."

"Just do try and stay calm though," warned Trevor.

This disturbed Hazel far more than anything that was going on around her. He seemed to be implying that she had caused whatever had happened. Or perhaps he was simply scared. She let it pass.

They stayed for about an hour before saying their goodbyes and giving her a hug. They promised to return the next day. Trevor had left her coat and purse and her final antibiotic pill.

She went to the counter and asked if she could have a large glass for her lemonade. When one appeared she swigged down two glassfuls. They made a difference to the dullness in her brain and her exhaustion was lifted a little. She put on her coat and told Roger at the counter that she needed some fresh air.

"The doctor would like to see you in half an hour," he told her.

Hazel remembered seeing her watch in her cabinet. She slowly went up the stairs to get it and came down again, aware all the time of her weakened body. She pushed through the doors and went and sat down on the bench in the garden, allowing the peace of the little retreat to wash over her. She kept an eye on her watch. Wrapped in her coat, the winter sun felt cheerful and Hazel happily allowed this wave of pleasantness to push aside the awfulness inside.

After twenty minutes she went back in to wait by the counter. Finally, a nurse announced the doctor would see her.

An Asian doctor sat behind a large wooden desk, writing. The nurse sat and directed Hazel to do the same. Minutes seemed to pass before he lifted his head to look at her. Hazel had had more than enough time to read the narrow plaque sitting on the front of the desk and digest the fact that he was, of course, a psychiatrist.

He stared at her, saying nothing. 'I won't be drawn into this sort of game,' thought Hazel, so she stared back. Eventually he sat back in his large leather chair and asked with a palpable arrogance, "How do you feel, now?"

"I've had some sort of virus, that must have been the cause of whatever happened. I still feel weak and my chest is very tight. I really should have been taken into a proper hospital, not here at all."

He continued to stare at her and said very deliberately, "You do know you have a family history of mental problems."

Dread hit Hazel. Her thoughts rapidly trawled through all she knew about her family.

"No, no. You must have me mixed up with someone else. The only thing I can think of is that there was some mystery surrounding my paternal grandmother's death, but her brother who saw her last said her eyes were bulging, so we assumed it was probably a tumour. We also think her younger brother may have been epileptic, but that's not a mental health issue is it? Is that what you are talking about? I'm still certain my illness was caused by the virus I had."

His gaze didn't waver.

"I'm going to advise you stay for observation. Now you can go," and he waved her away.

Hazel followed the nurse out. She felt livid. She did not know of any doctor that had ever shown such unbelievable arrogance. Surely, as a psychiatrist, he could have shown a flicker of care.

She went into the dining room, made herself a cup of tea and carried it into the lounge. Her book, lemonade and glass were still all reassuringly on the coffee table where she'd left them. 'Here for observation!' she thought. Well, she could do no more than act normally and drinking lemonade, water and tea was certainly helping to unfuzz her brain. She had read various articles about what was 'normal', and she knew that, rather like Randle McMurphy in the film, she could not easily be 'one of the sheep'. Her parents had encouraged her and her brothers to speak their minds and not, in her mother's words, 'hide their light under a bush'. But she understood that this assertiveness was not always welcome and she considered that perhaps some people were intimidated by her. She would attempt to humble herself. Not difficult now she felt so lost.

A little while later a nurse came to take her over to the main hospital to have her chest X-rayed. So, Mr. Psychiatrist had listened! But she'd finished her course of antibiotics now so would there be much to see? Hazel rather doubted it. The brief visit to the main hospital was a welcome respite from the psychiatric unit and was over all too soon.

After breakfast the following morning Hazel noticed a door with BATH written on it. The room was empty and a clean towel was folded up on a chair, so she filled the bath and was pleased to find the water hot enough for a deep soak. She attempted to empty her mind of all that had happened.

As the water cooled she gathered her concentration to dry herself and dress, still feeling weak. Then she became aware that the air in the room had changed and the temperature had dropped. Yes, she was warm from her bath, but the steamy humidity had vanished and Hazel felt consumed again by a presence. Not only all around the room but within her very being. It felt reassuring, comforting. As before, she neither heard nor saw anything material, but she felt she was being pressed with knowledge. An incredible, telepathic message filled her; she would have another child and this child would be special. It would be able to help. Then the presence was gone. The bathroom was warm and steamy again.

With a strange sense of calm Hazel left the bathroom and went to sit on her bed. She allowed this further inexplicable occurrence to flow around her mind. Did that mean she would get pregnant? When? Was she pregnant now? How was this child going to help?

'But I'm in a psychiatric ward! This is not something I could ever discuss. It merely adds to the credence of being here. Oh well, if I am or I do fall pregnant, I certainly won't be able to say I'm a virgin! I just need to get out of here.'

She was now desperate for a sense of normality. She grabbed her coat and purse, left the building and made her way out of the grounds.

Since knowing Trevor she had become familiar with Rochford's streets. He regularly visited the butcher to buy meat and at Christmas they enjoyed soaking up the atmosphere around the town square. She bought a newspaper, queued in the bakery to buy a pastry and made her way over the main road to the park surrounding the Rochford reservoir. Apart from a couple of dog walkers, the park was empty.

Hazel chose a seat closest to the water, ate her pastry and scanned the first few pages of her paper. She considered catching a bus to her mum's, but her home was with Robbie at Trevor's. It felt essential to pick up life from there, but the intense weakness of her body and finding herself in a psychiatric ward had disconnected her from the normal world she knew and life was now flowing through what felt like a parallel universe. She obviously had been very ill but didn't doubt her strength would eventually return. Buying a paper from the town square each morning, to read by the lake, helped to ground her mind.

Trevor arrived the following morning with Hazel's mother and Robbie. Then he disappeared.

Hazel stood and waved so her mum could see her across the lounge. She hugged Robbie as he came up. She said she hoped he was alright and not worrying too much about his mum. Hazel knew, though, that seeing his normally strong, confident mother in this place would not be forgotten.

"Where's Trevor gone?" Hazel asked her mother.

"To find out how they think you are, I suspect."

"Mum, what is this about a family history of mental problems? I had to see the psychiatrist yesterday and it sounded as though he was mixing me up with someone else."

Her mother paused, "It was here in this actual unit where Dorothy, your dad's mother died."

Hazel was shocked.

"You knew this but never said. Why not? You told me that you thought it was a brain tumour because Great-Uncle Chris said her eyes were bulging. I know you said that she tried to throw Aunt Bess out of the window because she thought the house was on fire, but that could have been a result of a brain tumour couldn't it? But she died here, actually in this building?"

"According to your father, who was told by Lieselotte, yes. As you know, your grandfather destroyed all her records so we don't actually know what was stated as the cause of death. But I thought I should tell the doctors."

"Oh Mum, how awful. But she hadn't had anything like it before, had she?"

"No, we don't think so, but apparently she hadn't been physically well for a while."

'Oh,' thought Hazel, 'this puts things in a new light.'

Why had her mother felt it necessary to tell the doctors about something so steeped in mystery? She'd placed her daughter right into their hands. There really was no one she could trust.

She knew her father was twelve when his mother died, although he wasn't told of her death until months afterwards. She looked at Robbie. He was also twelve.

When Trevor finally reappeared, Hazel told him about the physio appointment she had scheduled for that afternoon and said she hoped she'd be able to go home afterwards.

"Look, Hazel, I need to be sure that you can remain calm. They can't be certain that if you get excited it won't happen again. I'd like you to stay for a few more days just to see how you are."

Hazel stared at Trevor. What exactly did he think had caused her strange outburst?

"But whatever I had must have been caused by that virus, and I'm not going to be able to recover here. It's difficult to feel normal when I'm surrounded by screaming, moaning people who are clearly very unhappy. I need to come home."

"And I have to feel that it's safe for you to do so. I'm going to take Robbie home now. He has school tomorrow. You're happy with that aren't you, Robbie?"

Robbie nodded and looked at his mum for reassurance.

"You don't seem to be giving me a choice."

Hazel had her arm around Robbie and she gave him a little squeeze.

"Okay, but please, only another day at the very most."

"Perhaps," said Trevor.

Hazel hugged and kissed Robbie and wished him a good day at school. It was so hard to watch him walk out.

Hazel felt so utterly alone. The solid reality of her life had vanished, her usual strength and confidence had been completely wiped away by things she couldn't understand. She couldn't help but feel sad about the grandmother she had never known. Who knows what it was like for her all those years ago to die in this place of torment?

It did occur to Hazel that if she had still been with Tim, she wouldn't have ended up in here. She didn't blame Trevor though. Under the circumstances, he believed he was doing what was best.

A nurse arrived to escort Hazel to the physiotherapist over in the main hospital. He was a balding man in his late fifties. The nurse didn't enter with her.

"I'm going to attempt to loosen up that congestion in your chest. If you could remove your top but keep your bra on and lay on your front on the couch."

Hazel complied.

"I'll unclip your bra now, if you are alright with that."

"No problem," consented Hazel.

He began by massaging her shoulders, neck and back. Hazel was good at relaxing at will so gave herself up to these competent hands. Once he'd loosened her muscles he began light karate-type chops all across the top of her back. They got a little heavier. He then pulled her shoulders back a few times then returned to the chopping. Some more massaging, more chopping, more pulling. He then clipped up her bra and asked Hazel to sit up.

"How does that feel, now?" he asked.

"Yes, that has helped. My breathing does feel easier."

"Good. Now, if you can stand, I'll look at your posture."

Hazel slid off the couch.

"I know I can slouch a bit," she said.

"Yes, your back does have an S shape. Do your emotions go up and down a lot? Do you have a tendency to get very excited?"

Hazel considered this sudden change of tack.

"No, my emotions don't go up and down abnormally. I've always had a naturally bouncy character and an optimistic outlook and, yes, with things like Christmas and holidays and other pleasant happenings, I can get quite excited, but definitely not unusually so. And I've never been depressed, in spite of having been divorced, and my father, who meant the world to me, dying a few years ago. I am confident enough to believe I can find a way to sort most problems out somehow."

"Improving your posture may help you to breathe deeper and stay calmer," the physio persisted.

"I'm sure my posture needs improving. But I've been ill and that's what caused whatever it was to happen to me. I don't have a problem with staying calm when necessary," Hazel countered.

"Let's lift your head, then."

The physio placed his hand under her chin and lifted, gently.

"Relax your shoulders backward."

He continued to lift her head up and backward.

"This may feel as though you are leaning backward, but try walking with your head in that position."

As Hazel walked slowly forward she agreed that, yes, it felt strange. She walked over to a full-length mirror and saw that this was an improvement.

"Try and consciously maintain that at all times and it should eventually become a habit."

Hazel said she would as she put her top back on.

"Can you find your way back?"

"Unfortunately, I can, thank you," Hazel replied.

Hazel passed the rest of the day immersed in her book, surfacing only to watch the odd thing on the TV. She finished her lemonade and drank plenty of water and cups of tea. She ended the day with a short laze in the bath and took sleeping pills. Knowing sleep was vital to her recovery she had accepted these pills each night.

The following day, after breakfast, she dressed and, after making her way to the newsagent and once again relaxing by the lake with the newspaper, she decided to spend some time in the library, looking for another book and reading magazines. Anything to put off going back to the unit.

Trevor called in after lunch with another bottle of lemonade and some grapes. Hazel pleaded with him to take her home.

"Look, how about coming home for a few hours tomorrow to see how you feel?"

"I really won't begin to feel better until I'm home permanently," replied Hazel, petulantly.

But Trevor was adamant. At least there was a glimmer of hope for a few hours' reprieve. If he hadn't offered something, Hazel thought she'd have taken a bus to her mother's. She had no strength to stand up to Trevor. Still, at least she had a new novel from the library.

After Trevor left, Hazel made a cup of tea and got comfy in the corner of the sofa. She looked up at Roger behind the counter. She'd noticed from her first day here that he seemed to watch her closely. She didn't have a problem with that. Hazel caught his eye and gave him a weak smile. She hoped he would conclude that she didn't need to be here.

The following day, time dragged by while she waited for Trevor to appear. Finally, he arrived after lunch. She had already gathered up all her belongings and followed him out to the car park.

"How are you feeling now?" Trevor asked, as she strapped herself into the passenger seat.

"I do still feel quite weak. I just need to be able to relax at home among normal surroundings. Please don't say I have to come back again."

"I'll bring you back before Robbie gets home. I think it'll upset him to see you, only to have you go back again. If you seem fine, I'll pick you up tomorrow for a little longer."

There on the driveway sat her blue 4x4. Hazel remembered how ill she had felt when she had ventured into Southend to transfer her money and then when she had collected the car. It could all have waited another week couldn't it?

Her few hours at home passed pleasantly enough, but the thought of returning to the psychiatric unit made it seem somehow surreal. She wished she could stay, but Trevor was insistent and Hazel was unable to argue.

The following morning she again went out for a paper and sat on the same bench by the lake. The sun shone and Hazel felt some warmth on her face. She stayed for quite a while, digesting the news. Life and war were going on as usual. How long before life was 'as usual' for her? Somehow, thoughts of her new car and her own business had no place in this present.

It was all a very strange and inexplicable experience. Was there a point to it? While she thought she should take the message imparted during her 'out-of-body experience' and the message that she would have another baby seriously, it was hardly something she could mention to anyone, not after ending up in a psychiatric ward! She came to the decision that it would have to remain her own private story.

The only part she would feel comfortable talking about was the white tunnel. This was a documented phenomenon. It's now known that, when people experience this, it's because their organs are going into shutdown. It's usually resuscitation that retrieves them. But no one had resuscitated her.

Was it a miracle that had returned her to life? If she fell pregnant … Well she would have to wait and see.

Trevor collected Hazel and all her belongings again after lunch. As they were strapping themselves into the car, he said, "We need to do a shop; we're low on everything. If you're up to that?"

"Yes, fine."

How wonderfully, boringly normal!

"There's the Christmas party on in your ward tonight. I've told them you'll go back for that and one more night. I just need to be sure you're not going to get excited."

"Oh no. You must be joking. I can't go back, not again, not for a Christmas party. Please!"

She didn't belong there, she couldn't fit in, most certainly not for a party. And she clamped her jaws tight at Trevor's continued reference to getting excited. There was no point having a go at him now. But why could he not believe that it was connected to the virus she'd had? She would have to talk to him when they got home.

Asda was quite quiet. Trevor had his list so Hazel trailed around with the trolley, glad to have something to lean on. Her strength wasn't really up to this domesticity yet. Finally, they got through the checkout and Trevor loaded the bags into the car. Back home, Hazel attempted to help him stow the shopping into the relevant cupboards, but her energy deserted her.

"I've got to sit down," she said and wandered into the lounge.

Trevor made some tea and carried in a tray with two full mugs and two pastries. He laid it on the coffee table and sat next to Hazel. She wrapped her hands around the mug, feeling the hot, sweet tea relax her, and slowly enjoyed the sweet stickiness of the cake. She licked her fingers, took a tissue from the box on the coffee table and wiped them. She took Trevor's hand.

"Trevor, please, you must know that whatever it was that happened was because I was ill, physically ill that is. It's just not going to happen again. You probably didn't know that when I laid down on the bed I heard a pop-like noise at the back of my head, near the top of my neck, and it suddenly felt like freezing water was pouring up over my brain. It paralysed me completely. I don't know how to describe it, but it felt as though the synapses in my brain, or whatever controls my body, weren't working properly, but my actual thoughts didn't seem affected. And there was this constant flashing, pulsing light. I did see you come into the bedroom, out of the corner of my eye, but I couldn't move or make any noise. It seemed like I was lying there for hours. I was frightened that I might die if you didn't call a doctor. When I was finally able to move I felt desperate for some fresh air but the window was locked and I wanted the awful flashing to stop. In the end, because I still couldn't speak, I thought that if I bit you, you would have to call a doctor. I thought perhaps you might think I had rabies! I was just desperate, after all that time, for you to get a doctor. I didn't know what else to do and, yes, I was very frightened. I couldn't let myself die without a fight!"

Trevor smiled weakly and showed her the little teeth marks on his arm, "It did rather hurt."

Hazel hugged him, "I'm so sorry. I really didn't want to hurt you."

She listened as Trevor explained that, no, he hadn't realised she was paralysed and that, after fighting her to release the television, he knew she would stay calm for Robbie so he brought him in to give him time to ring her mother. Ruth and Lionel were still with her and so had driven her over. They had also stayed for a little while. Lionel apparently thought it may have had something to do with fumes from the Duster or that there was perhaps some noxious chemical on the steering wheel! But because Trevor had thought it was just a severe panic attack he had delayed calling a doctor, worried that they might only offer a psychiatric solution.

"But in the end that's exactly what you did allow, even though I heard the locum doctor say he thought I would be alright."

"Have you looked at the seat of your white cords?" asked Trevor.

"No," replied Hazel.

She'd thrown them in the dirty linen basket yesterday. Trevor went upstairs to retrieve them. He handed them to Hazel and she saw four round circles of dilute blood stains against the whiteness. One about three inches in diameter the other three a little smaller.

"The doctor said two of those should have knocked out a fully-grown man, but he had to give you two more before you calmed down."

"I did feel those," remembered Hazel.

"But it still took three men to manoeuvre you down the stairs."

Hazel only remembered two men on either side as the fresh air hit her when she walked outside.

"I've had a chat with Clive," continued Trevor, "and he agreed that it was probably a panic attack. Anyway, by then I was worn out.

Your strength was phenomenal, I wouldn't have been able to restrain you any longer. And the doctor said they wouldn't have accepted you at the General Hospital in such an agitated state at that time of night. So, there was no other option."

"Really?" said Hazel weakly. There seemed no solid ground to stand on, even though she was certain it hadn't been a panic attack.

"Now you're going to take me back, just so I can enjoy a Christmas party there?"

"I told them that I would. They're expecting you. But I'll pick you up in the morning."

"When are you taking me back?"

"The party starts at seven so I'll get you back for about six-thirty."

Trevor checked his watch and tucked his arm around her.

"We've got about an hour before Robbie gets home. Would you like to go upstairs for a cuddle?"

Perhaps Hazel could change his mind with a little lovemaking. She clung to him for some sense of sanity. It wasn't enough to change his mind though.

Afterwards, she showered, lathered up some shampoo and rinsed it out. That felt good. She would rather have spent time resting in a bath but, more importantly, she wanted to spend as much time with Robbie as possible before she went back. She pulled conditioner through her hair, left it in while she washed the rest of her body. She didn't allow herself to contemplate the evening ahead.

Once dry, Hazel studied her wardrobe. She took out her favourite black skirt and a sparkly top, pulled on a pair of black tights and found her black stiletto ankle boots. Well, that's what she might wear for an evening out, so that's how she tried to view it. Robbie was obviously happy to see her home, but she had to tell him that she couldn't stay. She had to go back for the Christmas party.

"That's the very last thing that I want to do, but Trevor has promised I can come home permanently tomorrow, and we can start to think about our own Christmas, and digging up a tree. I do still feel quite weak so perhaps we can persuade Trevor to help us at the weekend. But you must believe that whatever happened was tied to the flu virus I had. I probably should have rested more. I know it won't happen again, so *please* don't worry. I'll be back to your normal tough mum in no time at all."

She kept him company in the kitchen while he did his homework. Then they watched some television together until, all too soon, it was time to leave. She hugged and kissed him.

"I love you so much. Can't wait till tomorrow. I know you'll be good. See you then."

Trevor dropped her off, with her bag, outside the garden.

"I'll be back around ten tomorrow morning. Enjoy your party," he said as they parted with a kiss.

'Enjoy the party! That's not going to happen. I suppose I do have a choice; I could wander into the town.' She had seen one of the patients walking up the steps of the pub one morning, so there was no reason for her not to do that. But it would be a long evening and she didn't feel up to having to parry with single men! She also thought that nobody could stop her taking her book into a quiet corner or even to bed if she wanted. So, she took a deep breath and walked through the garden.

As Hazel stepped through the doors, she saw a disco being set up along one wall and Roger behind the desk. She ventured up to him.

"I'm sorry, but I've only returned because my partner wanted me to, so is there anything useful I can do?"

Roger looked at her in a clinically appraising way. Hazel instinctively felt she could trust him.

"I think they would appreciate a hand in the kitchen; there's a lot of sandwiches to be made."

After stowing her belongings once more in her cabinet, Hazel wandered down to the kitchen and, indeed, there were two nurses who had only just started buttering bread. Hazel approached the older lady.

"Roger said you could do with a hand."

"Oh, lovely. Yes, there's white and brown bread here. A tub of egg mayonnaise, ham, hard cheese, pineapple, cocktail sticks, some soft cheese triangles. There's also small sausages and sausage rolls that need to go on plates, and pizza that needs cutting up. I'll leave you both to it then."

Hazel shot a look at the younger nurse as the older one disappeared and smiled.

"Just us then!"

There did appear to be a lot to do, so Hazel got stuck in. First, buttering a load of white bread and putting in various fillings. Cutting the pile into triangles and laying them neatly on plates. Then the same with the brown bread. The younger nurse took out the plates as she and Hazel finished them. Hazel did clock that there were a few times when she didn't return for a long time, far longer than it would have taken to simply put the plates on the table. But, hey, she had offered and why shouldn't the nurse have time to relax a little, perhaps with patients or staff, at a Christmas party?

More than an hour and a half went by and she would rather be doing this than standing around listening to the music that was drifting in from the lounge. She certainly wasn't up to dancing. In fact, her legs were aching now, and she was already tired. It had been a busy day and all Hazel wanted to do was take her book up to bed. But she thought she'd try to show a little willing, so she left the kitchen to sit in an armchair facing the disco and attempted to keep her eyes open.

There were around eight of the regular patients, but the numbers were swollen by about six or seven plain-clothed helpers. A couple of patients were dancing with a helper. The majority of the other patients looked much as they usually did, disconnected from what was going on around them.

Roger was out from behind the counter talking to a helper. Hazel lifted her weary body and walked over to him. He looked at her as she approached.

"I'm sorry, but it's been a long day and I'm very tired, so I'm going to read in bed for a bit."

He nodded in agreement.

Once in bed, she only managed to read a few pages before her eyes drooped.

She awoke early but had slept soundly without sleeping pills. After breakfast, she had a quick wash, got dressed and for the last time gathered up her belongings. She would get Trevor to stop off on the way to buy a paper, so she settled down on the sofa to watch the news and carry on with her book. She did, however, take some time to reflect on the four whole days she had spent here.

It had been an enlightening experience to say the least, and one that surely would not happen again. Hazel's conclusion was that it had been a mistake to lie down when she'd felt that overwhelming nausea and dizziness. Maybe she wouldn't have heard that pop if she had remained propped up. She remembered seeing Trevor's lips moving when she had walked into the kitchen after returning with the Duster, but she had felt so very ill that she'd not really processed the fact that she had gone deaf, nor had it frightened her, she had just wanted to lie down. And not for one minute did she believe that it was caused by her getting excited.

That pop and the sensation of freezing water pouring over her brain seemed to suggest a momentary loss of oxygen or blood or some pressure suddenly pinching a nerve. How could she understand that? She wasn't a doctor. But both the psychiatrist and Trevor seemed to want her to believe that it could occur again. No, she hadn't been excited, she'd actually felt too physically ill by then, and that alone convinced her that it was definitely not a panic attack!

It did worry her now, though, that it was what Trevor and the psychiatrist believed. So, God forbid, if it did happen again would a doctor feel compelled to pronounce it a panic attack once more? Hazel decided that, if she suffered from anything flu-like again, she would treat it with the greatest respect and rest until she felt properly recovered. She could not allow it to happen again.

Ten o'clock … five past … ten past … ten-fifteen … ten-twenty.

Relief washed through Hazel when she saw Trevor's familiar balding, bearded face. There was no one behind the counter as they exited through the doors, past that little haven of a garden.

Goodbye to all that had been so terrible.

Home to Robbie and her life.

CHAPTER 21

1986 ◇ Recovery

Hazel's physical strength was very slow to return. She ate normally, healthily, and drank plenty of water in an effort to build up her strength. On the Saturday, two days after leaving the unit, she proudly drove Trevor and Robbie in her blue 4x4 to a Christmas tree farm nestled along the side of the A127 in Leigh. They parked outside a Portakabin and with two spades and forks, a pair of loppers for the roots and a sheet of plastic, they wandered around the woodland of growing Christmas trees.

For a good few years now, Hazel and Robbie had enjoyed this personal Christmassy sense of achievement at being able to choose and dig up their own tree. The woodland only contained traditional Picea Christmas trees that were grown in a natural way. Tall trees towered over smaller ones, with all sizes in between. Some were compact, some were slender, some were wide so, while it did take time, it was possible to find the perfect tree. Finally, after deliberating between two trees that were a good distance apart, down wiggling paths designed to get you lost, Robbie and Hazel agreed on one. Hazel and Trevor dug a large circle around it, Hazel lopped off a couple of thick roots and stood back as Trevor completed digging under the roots and easing it all loose. Hazel then helped him lift it on to the plastic. The three of them wove it through the wood to pay at the Portakabin. They then loaded it into the Duster after putting down one of the rear seats. It was satisfying but hard work and she knew that this year she would not have managed it with just Robbie.

Apart from her lack of physical strength, there were two other anomalies Hazel had noticed. One was with her vision. It happened most noticeably when she was standing by the kitchen window, washing-up or preparing food on the worktop. If she lifted her eyes to look out on the garden, she would feel momentarily dizzy. It wasn't bad enough to make her feel as though she might fall over. It was simply noticeable.

The second was to do with her thinking! There was no difference in the type of thoughts she had. It was more that there was a discernible stiltedness in the flow of her thoughts. As though each thinking cog, which usually connected so smoothly, had a minuscule hesitation as it linked into place.

Towards the end of the following week, Trevor suggested that Hazel return to work on Monday for a week of half days, to see how she felt. She had a good idea about how she would feel. With so much still to do before Christmas she would feel incredibly tired. But, yes, fully engaging in normal life again probably was the best option.

She had to make various trips into town to go Christmas shopping. She did it all with as much planned calmness as she could muster to ensure she did not overtire herself. Before she left one day, Trevor reminded her to order a fresh turkey from the Rochford butcher, his preferred butcher for fresh meat.

She thought she'd managed well with all the pressure of Christmas preparations and working; until Christmas Eve when, at 6.00 pm, with a helpless dismay, she realised she'd totally forgotten to collect the turkey. She rang the butchers only to receive a message saying they were now shut. A rushed trip to the local supermarket proved fruitless. There were no turkeys left and only a couple of chickens. She bought the largest.

Edwina arrived the following morning expecting the traditional turkey that she so loved. She couldn't believe Hazel had forgotten to get the turkey.

"I'm really sorry, Mum but less than a month ago I was very ill and it's been so hectic since. At least I bought everyone's presents and I've made mince pies! Did you remember the holly for the Christmas pud?"

She had, of course.

Hazel made an appointment to see Clive the following week. She needed to know if he had any answers for her but he had not yet received a report from the unit.

Hazel explained the strange pop she'd heard at the base of her skull when she had lain down and the subsequent sensation of freezing water pouring over the surface of her brain. She added that this appeared to have precipitated the seizure and an out-of-body experience, and she described the white tunnel.

"Oh, these problems are usually half mental, half physical," he explained flippantly. "That was just a panic attack."

Hazel was certain that explanation was not what her old family doctor, who had known her since the day she was born, would have offered. Such a shame he had retired.

She also explained the slight dizziness that she was experiencing.

"That's also due to anxiety," was his reply.

"I'm sorry but I can't believe it was a panic attack. I felt physically very ill. And I've never suffered from anxiety. However, my mother told the psychiatrist that my paternal grandmother died in that unit. That was a shock. My family had been under the impression that she might have had a brain tumour, due to my great-uncle reporting that her eyes were bulging," said Hazel.

Clive considered, "That sounds like encephalitis."

Following Hazel's quizzical look, he explained. "It's inflammation of the brain, usually the frontal lobes, which causes the eyes to be pushed out."

"Do you think I could have had the beginnings of that? I was confused after you visited me and found it impossible to work out the simple maths of when to take the pills. I relied on Trevor to dispense them at the correct time."

"It is possible you had encephalitis. To be certain, you would have to have had a lumber puncture and that carries a risk of infection and, as you appeared to be improving, it wasn't worth that risk."

"So I had to end up in a psychiatric ward!"

Clive shrugged his shoulders.

"At that time of night, there was no option, because of the state you were in. But I do appreciate that to someone without a psychiatric problem it could be very frightening."

"I would like to know when you receive the report from the unit. I did have a chest X-ray and was told there was some congestion in my lungs and I was given physio to help with that."

"Of course."

Hazel left. As she drove home, her mind kept returning to her poor grandmother. It had been terrifying enough for Hazel. But back in the days before antibiotics, how aware was she of where she was? How excruciatingly frightened might she have been? Encephalitis though. That was not a mental problem. If only my grandfather had known that. While they may not have been able to save her, at least my grandfather would not have been so traumatised and dreadfully worried that his children would find out that madness was in their family. He had destroyed all her records. It must have been an agonising time for him as well.

Even in these modern times, Hazel had come too close to death. At least now she was certain that mental illness did not run in the family, and finally, yes, it explained what had killed her grandmother.

Hazel decided she would get a copy of Dorothy's death certificate. She wanted to know exactly what the official disclosure was that her grandfather had destroyed. Just what incorrect belief had he carried for the rest of his life? Somehow, being able to say that it was most likely encephalitis would grant her some much-needed closure.

A copy of the death certificate arrived about a week after Hazel had applied for it. There, under Cause of Death, was 'Acute Mania'. In 1935 that was a stigma and her grandfather would not have wished to burden his children with that worry. So now it all made sense.

A few weeks later she asked the doctor's surgery whether there was a report from the psychiatric unit, but was told that they had lost her records! So that was that. She would probably never know exactly what they thought had caused her seizure.

A couple of weeks after Christmas, Hazel read that calcium can help to repair damaged nerves. She wondered whether this might help her slightly stilted thinking. Within days, the calcium tablets she bought cleared the anomaly completely. She continued taking them for three weeks and the fault never returned, which she felt confirmed that nerve damage had affected her brain.

Six months after her illness Hazel come across a newspaper article about a woman suffering from encephalitis who'd thrown herself off a train and died.

Four years later a new doctor arrived at the surgery and her records came to light.

CHAPTER 22
1987 ◊ The Hurricane

The hurricane that swept across Essex, East Anglia and The Fens in the early hours of the morning of 16 October 1987 will remain forever in the memories of those who felt and witnessed its ferocity. Hazel believes it brought back long-submerged memories for Trevor.

Trevor and his older brother Sidney had lived just over the road from Hockley Woods, an ancient woodland covering 250 acres, consisting mainly of oak, sweet chestnut, hornbeam and birch. Sidney was thirteen when Trevor was born and, as his mother thought he was a sensible boy, she had no qualms about letting Sidney take baby Trevor out in his pram for a walk. The roads were quiet then so Sidney would often take Trevor over into the woods.

Sidney probably didn't realise how terrified Trevor was when Sidney ran off to play with his friends: birds shrieking unexpectedly as they swooped across the canopy; twigs cracking as someone walked by, unseen behind the pram's hood; and, occasionally, the head of a stranger poking an ugly, gruesome face at Trevor to try and make him smile. Amid this growing fear was the constant rustling of the wind through the leaves. As the wind became stronger, the noise became louder and Trevor howled his heart out in intense fear. So small and utterly powerless. Did his brother not hear him?

Home was also unsafe, with a brother ready to torment him at every opportunity. Added to which was a mother who would punish her sons if she felt they had misbehaved by completely ignoring the offending child. Sometimes the punishment would last for days on end. Sidney, being older, was usually more successful at blaming his brother for the wrongdoing.

Trevor's childhood awoke in him a severe need to control all aspects of his life. He was fortunate to have a great mathematical brain, but never pursued it by going to university because there would have been too many unknown bodies constantly interacting in uncontrollable ways and that would have been too daunting. A couple of years at the local college studying accountancy was less pressurised – and he did end up as a partner in a small hi-fi manufacturing company, which was where Hazel ended up when looking for a way out of her marriage.

So, perhaps it was not surprising that as the wind grew on that fateful night it triggered an unbearable subconscious fear.

Trevor and Hazel listened to Michael Fish's legendary weather forecast: "It has been suggested that a hurricane may be on its way, however I can definitely say that there will be no hurricane tonight."

Oh, those famous words. Hazel forced herself to stay awake until Trevor felt ready for bed at about 11.30pm. She sensed he was not relaxed when the wind, which had been strong for the last few hours, continued to build. But they both slept, at least initially.

It was still very dark outside when Hazel was woken by the sound of the wind rattling the roof tiles. Then the crashing of a metal dustbin as it bounced down the road roused Trevor with a start.

"This sounds bad," Hazel said. "I'm not going to get back to sleep so I'll get up and make a drink. How about you?"

"You're right," agreed Trevor. "It doesn't sound good. I'm getting up too."

Hazel wrapped her dressing gown around herself and opened the bedroom curtains. In the light of the street lamps Hazel could see branches and the odd bag flying down the road. But what most caught her eye was the flexing of the glass in the window frame. Confident the glass could withstand such an onslaught she turned and went downstairs. Trevor was in the kitchen, putting the kettle on to boil, so Hazel walked into the lounge and turned the radio on. Trevor brought in two mugs of tea and put them on the coffee table. Hazel had opened the curtains a little and stood mesmerised by the howling wind that was bending the trees on the little green.

"Would you believe this glass is really moving? We're so lucky to be here in this well-built Goldsworthy home. They're saying on Essex Radio that we should sit or stand under a door frame but I'm sure this house will withstand …"

She was cut short as Trevor rushed over to her and grabbed her neck with both hands. He tightened them.

"Shut up, will you, I can't stand to hear any more. Just shut up."

He shook her hard.

"Stop, stop, you're really hurting me," Hazel just managed to choke out.

Trevor dropped his hands and staggered backward in tears. He turned and left the room.

Hazel's heart was thumping. She knew he could be volatile and thought about the story of when he had punched his fist through a door in frustration at work. This was not the first time he'd taken her shoulders and shaken her, in spite of her reminding him of her prolapsed disc. But attempting to strangle her! That she would not allow again.

She sat down on the sofa to calm herself, then went upstairs to gently open Robbie's door to see if he was awake. The sound of his slow breathing was a relief in contrast to the battering sounds outside. So great to be a deep sleeper. She closed the door again and walked along to her bedroom. Trevor was lying face down on the bed. She was so shocked by his fear that she walked away and went back downstairs to watch the dawn break and listen to Radio Essex until Robbie awoke. The devastation that the hurricane brought is well documented, but Hazel's memories are blurred into a mix of emotions about Trevor and a relationship she now knew she must end.

Robbie brought some balance once he was up, especially as the radio reported that his school was closed. Tim rang from offshore as Robbie and Hazel were eating breakfast and asked if his son could go and check on his flat in Leigh. The flat sat right on the top of the cliffs with just the railway line below between it and the sea – on the hurricane's front line. Robbie set out on his BMX with strict instructions from Hazel to be vigilant around weakened trees and roofs with loose slates, as the wind was still quite strong. He cycled down the dual carriageway to the seafront. The middle of this dual carriageway had once had a tramline running down it, then, after the track was demolished, trees had been planted. Many of these trees were now quite large. Or had been. The sight of them in full autumnal colours, lying on their sides with huge roots exposed was mortifying.

Down on the seafront, boats in various states of damage were dotted along the beach and several had been lifted over the sea wall and smashed on to the road. Travel by anything other than foot or mountain bike was impossible. Robbie cycled on down Southend seafront, past damaged amusement arcades and the crippled funfair that would take a while to be made safe again. On past the Westcliff cliffs with so many flattened trees. Past the famous arched cafés. What tattered awnings were still left, flapped frantically.

He continued into Leigh and up through the devastated Belton Hills to his dad's flat. He couldn't see Tim's classic silver Jaguar that should have been parked on the front drive. All that was visible was an enormous pile of jumbled tiles that had crashed down, not only from his father's roof but also from both neighbours' roofs. On closer inspection, Robbie could just make out glints of silver paintwork – bad news for Tim.

Hazel went out with her camera and walked down into Shoebury to check on her house in West Road. Fortunately, she could only see a couple of slipped roof tiles. Inside, she put the kettle on and sat down to ponder her present situation and her future.

Living with Trevor's volatile nature had never been easy. But now she understood. He was a damaged lion whose ferocious roar had developed merely to hide his fears. They were never far away, as last night had demonstrated. Regardless of how much he cared for both Hazel and Robbie, she knew this was not what she wanted for the rest of her life. She still felt a strong need for another child. But she couldn't have one with Trevor. As she sat at peace on her own sofa, in her own house, her next move was obvious. The only thing she needed to consider was timing.

To build her gardening knowledge, Hazel enrolled on a twenty-week crash course for the General Certificate in Horticulture at a local college. She thoroughly enjoyed the course and usually got top marks for her homework. Not so difficult when all the answers were in the notes she'd taken off her Dictaphone – bought when she discovered how quickly their tutor whipped through the lessons! Then, with the exam only two weeks away, she contracted flu yet again. It was spring and, although the weather was warming, the virus was still doing the rounds.

She took two weeks off, determined to fully recover. It did mean that she was able to relax in the sunshine during her last week and revise seriously. But then, when she came to sit the exam, she was ridiculously nervous. Considering how chilled she'd been for her school exams, this came as a shock. As she sat waiting to be allowed to turn over the paper in front of her, she began to shake.

"You may begin now," the invigilator called and as Hazel turned over the paper and scanned the first few questions her mind met a brick wall.

She attempted to relax and focus. Gradually she managed to retrieve some facts relating to the questions. Then the exam paper asked for a certain plan. Under the question was a large space. She drew the necessary plan there. It was only when she received her 'Failed' result that she remembered that she had, so stupidly, drawn the plan on the question paper and not on the answer sheet! She guessed that she had been so nervous because she worried her business might rely on her gaining her General Certificate of Horticulture. But she was unable to understand why her mind had struggled so badly. She concluded that it must have been partly due to being ill again. Her body and brain were drained. That was her excuse to herself.

Fortunately, it hadn't dimmed her dream and she designed and printed off a hundred leaflets advertising lawn cutting and weeding. She'd bought a heavy-duty professional lawnmower and Trevor had made a ramp to allow her to push it easily up into her trailer. All the tools and wheelbarrow were her own and she stowed them in the back of the Duster. She'd dropped the leaflets through doors along roads around Trevor's house. It was a service that people in Thorpe Bay would have no problem paying for.

Within a week she had five clients. Three of them women. During that first year she worked every Saturday to ensure they were all pleased with her work. None of them asked about any qualifications and Hazel had all the notes from her course to turn to if she was unsure of anything. The women in particular were very knowledgeable gardeners. It was their age that now dictated the need for some help. She learnt a tremendous amount from them all. Hazel's natural confidence bloomed and word of her abilities quickly spread. She'd also had magnetic signs printed for her jeep showing her business name, Garden Style and Care, and a clear phone number.

Hazel was working on the hi-fi company's first service manual, which she had suggested as their service manager. Producing the complete work, from drawings to text, was giving Hazel great satisfaction. She would not hand in her notice until it was finished and, in the meantime, she had to build up enough of her own clients to almost equal her present income. It meant she was working six days a week. But by the end of her first year, through word of mouth, her clientele had more than doubled. She completed all their autumn tidy-ups by Christmas, thankfully giving her weekend breaks until the beginning of March. Then she was working six and a half days. Even before the hurricane, she'd made the decision to continue living with Trevor until she was confident she could rely solely, not only on her business, but on her business acumen to ensure it continued to be successful. Having his excellent financial advice was reassuring and he helped her with the tax side by devising a spreadsheet to help her correctly log all her outgoings and income. He also knew a reliable accountant who ensured she paid no tax initially, managing to lose it all in the start-up costs of her vehicle, trailer and lawnmower.

While remaining with Trevor for a little longer did feel calculating, Hazel wanted to ensure that she left the hi-fi company on a high note in case her business or her back failed. If that happened, she hoped they would consider re-employing her. It meant she felt covered for all possible scenarios and that would give her the emotional strength to leave Trevor and stand on her own two feet once again.

CHAPTER 23
1989 ◇ A New Life

Pruning hedges, shrubs and fruit trees was now becoming a regular part of Hazel's part-time business and her love of climbing trees was put to good use. So it was disconcerting to find that, although the calcium pills had worked for her stilted thought processes, the slight dizziness she had experienced when altering her vision from close to distant was exacerbated if she was working up in a tree. On one particularly windy day she rested her ladder against a large laurel bush to prune it. The strong, thick laurel was not affected by the breeze but Hazel was aware that trees and other shrubs, around her, were swaying and this was making her feel slightly nauseous. She made an appointment to see Clive and explained that working from a ladder had to be part of her business and as such she thought the dizziness should be checked out.

Hazel was seen by a consultant in the ear, nose and throat department at Southend Hospital who asked if his registrar could sit in on the examination. Hazel agreed. She thought that, if anything, this might mean he would be thorough. A hearing test was given first. Then she was asked to lay down on a couch to have warm water gently poured into each ear. The consultant told Hazel to stare at a light fitting in the ceiling above her and not to move her gaze. All seemingly undertaken with efficiency. After a short wait she was called in to see the consultant and his registrar. The consultant told Hazel she had a hearing loss of twenty-five per cent in the upper frequencies and that her eye movements during the warm water treatment proved that her balance organs were overly sensitive. His conclusion was that this was most probably caused by a virus of some type.

"Yes. I certainly did have a virus, it may even have been pneumonia, and I did completely lose my hearing for a few hours."

The consultant said it was amazing how the brain was able to adapt to hearing loss, as Hazel had not really noticed it. He prescribed her low dose Stemetil tablets to help calm the dizziness. They did help and the dizziness gradually subsided. Hazel managed with the hearing loss, which was only noticeable in a busy pub.

At work, Shaun, the original sales manager, had returned from his time as a skiing instructor looking very tanned. He was now able to cover many of the phone calls from dealers with product issues, thus lightening her load and freeing her to be more involved in the research and development of new speakers, as well as all the normal repair work. She had completed the service manual and Shaun was the perfect person to check all her work before it went to print. Together they checked it again when it was returned from the printers. Hazel had tracked down a supplier of sturdy binders that exactly matched the green of the company's logo. The text and line drawings were in the same green. The manual was sent out free to all dealers. Everyone, including Rouse, was impressed. Hazel believed she had two choices.

Her business was now ready for her to work full time. But since she had been forced to relinquish quality control, work at the hi-fi company had become almost equally as satisfying. All their products, including their first new speakers, were continuing to get the best reviews. But CD players had entered the market. Rouse had befriended two engineers who could design the necessary circuit boards. However, he was unsure who to choose and was still uncertain about travelling down the digital route. Hazel considered getting together with Pete and Kevin to convince Rouse to take the plunge and make the decision to produce a CD player. But was this effort worth it for someone else's business? While she'd had a £3,000 bonus this Christmas, her monthly salary was no more than average, even taking into consideration the free lunches and refreshments. Whereas, with her own business, she would be master of her own destiny. Trevor and her clients had given her confidence that she could manage financially. In the end it wasn't too difficult a decision.

She handed in her notice in March 1989. Laura wrote her a shining reference, proof that she was aware of all Hazel had done for the company. As leaving presents, they gave her a purple turntable, knowing that it was her favourite colour, and a drawing board to plan her gardens on. Trevor paled when Hazel showed him her reference. He grudgingly admitted it was excellent. Whether he was put out because it showed Laura was doing a good job or because it showed Hazel had been far more involved in the company than he had realised, she didn't know. It was probably coincidental but, after hearing Hazel had handed in her notice, Rouse thought about selling the company. Fortunately, Pete and Kevin were able to convince him otherwise.

During the two years Hazel had worked part time to build up her business Trevor had assisted with heavy jobs, such as digging out large shrubs or small trees. In a large sloping garden that needed to be completely returfed, Robbie had proved very useful, first with some rotovating then with ferrying heavy, turf-laden wheelbarrows from the front of the house up to where she needed to lay it.

Now Hazel contacted the Job Centre to find a permanent assistant. They rang her back with details of Tony, a man in his forties who had a genetic problem that caused learning difficulties. They told her that while his appearance was similar to someone with Down's Syndrome, his had a different genetic fault. But for cutting the grass or digging holes for planting, they felt he would do admirably. Tony arrived at Trevor's house for an interview and he assured Hazel that he enjoyed cutting grass and digging holes. She said she would need him three days a week. This worked well for him and he was able to begin immediately.

Hazel worked alongside him initially, doing weeding, pruning or planting, just to check he was certain what to do. He was reliable and her clients were pleased with him. She was now able to complete all the regular maintenance required by her clients, within three days a week, leaving her time to do small garden design jobs as they came along. Hazel devoured as much knowledge as she needed from all the new garden design books in the library. With her creative imagination she concluded that her design skills were acceptable without a formal qualification. Hazel would occasionally mention she had undertaken a crash General Horticultural Certificate course, but she was never asked to prove she'd passed. Her clientele were always enthusiastic about her well-thought-out plans and passed on recommendations to friends, which made a garden design qualification feel superfluous.

Within a month of leaving the hi-fi company, Hazel informed Trevor that she and Robbie were moving into her own home in a couple of weeks. Initially he refused to believe that she would, until she ordered a small transit van to remove all their belongings. He did try to dissuade her, saying that, in spite of their differences, he loved her. She said she was happy for them to remain friends if he could deal with that, but their physical relationship was over. He agreed that they could remain friends and assisted her with the move, including helping her to dismantle Robbie's heavy Habitat bed and desk combination and finding a suitable box to transport the tortoise in. Once the van was emptied and Robbie's bed re-erected, he gave Hazel a quick hug and a kiss and told Robbie he was welcome to call round sometimes, then left.

However, he refused to accept that their physical relationship had ended and attempted on a couple of occasions to coerce Hazel into sex. But she refused. She told him she no longer loved him. The final time he frightened her when, as they were talking in her garden, he suddenly forced her into the outside toilet and began kissing her. Hazel used all her strength to push him off and shouted, "That's the end. I won't have a friend I can't trust. Get out of my house. Now!"

Realising he'd gone too far, he left. But he rang her constantly. Initially, Hazel answered to tell him she had nothing to say as they were finished but usually ended by having to put the phone down.

She was concerned to discover, shortly after her move, that her brilliant reference was not among all her paperwork, meaning she had no option but to ring Trevor. He said she would have to go around to pick up a few things she'd left, although he didn't think her reference was among them. He went on to say that he was getting help with his wind phobia. He also said he'd had his sperm checked out to see if Hazel had been correct in her diagnosis. She had been. After finally putting the phone down, she thought, 'Oh well, hopefully I'll never need the reference, because I'm not going to set foot in Trevor's house again.'

The fear she'd felt when he pushed her into her garden toilet had been a reminder of his unpredictability. If she did need the reference, the company would surely have retained a copy. But Trevor continued to ring. Hazel would have to ignore the phone or keep cutting him off. She had to threaten that she would get a court order. That worked.

Robbie knew his mother had made the right decision to move into their own home. As promised, they began to build a large model railway track in the garage, giving them both hours of fun. Hazel was able to slide open the fence after work and push her trailer into the garage without it taking up any space, so large was the area. She had also gathered a useful set of tools for all general work and she allowed Robbie to use these whenever he wanted. He had taken science together with all the compulsory GCSEs and his science teacher told Hazel at the end of his final term that it had been the right decision to send Robbie to their school. He was granted a place at college in Shoebury to study engineering. He surprised himself by tackling technical drawing with ease. When he came to do welding his tutor said he was almost as good as him and he'd been welding for twenty years. All great for building confidence.

Released from Trevor's tenacious grip Hazel felt a similar elation to that experienced when she'd left Tim. Life was good. She sung and whistled as she went about her clients' gardens. Using OS maps she and Robbie found quiet, off-road spots to picnic and she went each year to the Chelsea Flower Show. Then in 1990 she took Edwina to the first Hampton Court Garden Show. Hazel had soon discovered that her Dacia Duster had a fault. During a long run the temperature gauge would show that the engine was overheating and she would have to stop to allow it to cool. Neither the Dacia garage nor Colin the mechanic had been able to resolve the problem. It was a fantastically hot day for their drive to Hampton Court and Hazel watched the temperature gauge climb and had to pull over on to the motorway hard shoulder and stop. Because of the outside warmth it took almost an hour for the engine to cool. Very frustrating. The glorious day, though, made up for it and they enjoyed their picnic lunch dangling their bare feet in the waterway that ran alongside the show.

Hazel took masses of photos at all the garden shows she visited and began building an album of style ideas that she could show clients. She also supplied hanging baskets that she lovingly put together on the wall surrounding her pond. The fish, fascinated by her presence, gathered around the surface to watch.

As life had moved on so brilliantly, Hazel's grief over Boxer's death had receded and when she saw a tiny little black and white kitten in the pet shop up their road that looked remarkably similar to Boxer, she was unable to resist his imploring little face. There were popular adverts on the TV for the stout drink Guinness, one of her favourite tipples, and Robbie agreed that it would be cool to call him Guinness. Confident that she could teach the cat to be wary of roads, Hazel bought a collar and lead and, once he had had all his vaccinations, she let Guinness out of the front door with the lead attached. As he ventured on to the pavement and a car raced past, Hazel pulled on the lead saying 'no'. She repeated this a few times. Then she carried him back into the house, removed the lead, opened the back door and called him out to discover the back garden. She then fitted a cat flap in the back door. Periodically she would repeat the process of deterring him from the front of the house. It appeared to work. Whenever she came home and Guinness was out, she only ever saw him appear from the side way as he jumped over the low wall to wait on the doorstep for her. She never saw him cross the road. He had no intention, though, of making friends with the tortoise, as Boxer had, and totally ignored the reptile, who now had the run of the whole garden.

One morning Hazel was reminded that you can never stop worrying about your kids. She had just left home on the way to a client's garden when she remembered she'd not put the drill in the car and needed to fit a trellis that morning. She returned home and was horrified to find Robbie in the back garden, smoking. As he saw his mother, his face paled. He knew exactly what she thought of smoking. Having it kill her father was enough. There was nothing he could say as he stubbed it out in the ashtray he was holding. Shock had frozen Hazel. Then disappointment began to seep in with a feeling that she had failed. She found her voice and said they would talk about it that evening. She collected the drill from the garage and waited for him to leave for college before she left herself.

Hazel was unsure how to deal with it. Two things had made her presume he would not smoke. The first was that Tim's father had been a heavy smoker and his mother had also smoked two or three during the day to keep him company. As a young boy, after spending a weekend with them, Robbie would bring his bag of clothes home and complain that everything smelt of cigarettes. Hazel would take the opportunity to reiterate all the reasons one shouldn't smoke and Robbie had totally agreed. The second was that when Robbie was about ten he had come home from school to tell his mother that the parents of his best friend, Drake, had given their son a cigarette to smoke, with the intention of putting him off ever doing it. But Drake had said he rather enjoyed it. Hazel discussed this with Robbie and told him that she felt she should have a chat with his friend's parents. He didn't disagree. Drake had been Robbie's best friend since infant school and Hazel knew his parents reasonably well. After ringing to ask if it was convenient to drop round, she called in. Hazel attempted to be diplomatic and explained that she did not agree with their exposure to smoking tactic and that it appeared to have had the reverse effect. She argued that by allowing their son to try a cigarette they were actually condoning the act. Whereas it may have been more positive to stress all the awful effects on health and the monetary costs. After saying that they thought they were doing the best thing, Drake's parents did acknowledge that she might have a point. It wasn't an unsuccessful chat but, unfortunately, the harm had been done and both boys were smoking.

That evening Hazel stressed how upsetting it was to discover that her son smoked. Robbie apologised and said he completely understood his mum's feelings and promised he would try to stop. Hazel saw no sign of him smoking again, so eventually put it from her mind.

Dean was single, again. The tremulous affair with Claire had finally ended just before his fortieth birthday and she had returned to her old boyfriend. He had been deeply hurt but recovered to enjoy his birthday with friends, including Hazel, at a local seafront pub. He displayed real affection for Hazel, wrapping his arms around her and planting warm kisses on her face and lips throughout the evening, something he had never done in public before. He was also, as he told her, very pissed!

He had always held a special place in Hazel's heart but since her relationship with Trevor her feelings for him had altered. He meant as much to her as her brothers and to begin a relationship with him now he was on the rebound from someone he had loved so deeply, didn't feel right. She'd been free for him when she left Tim but this time she would only be second best. Time was called in the pub and his friends slowly left. She then explained her feelings to Dean and said that it was as a friend and brother that she would always love him. They kissed briefly and left the pub, each to their own home.

Southend Council had launched 'Southend in Bloom', a competition that all gardens in the region could enter. Hazel saw the advert in one of the free local papers, which added that if anyone was interested in helping this enterprise would they give the council's horticultural officer a ring. Thinking this might prove a useful PR exercise for her business she rang the number and was put through to the horticultural officer, Martin. He told her a meeting had been arranged for all Southend in Bloom committee members the following week and she would be very welcome to join them. He mentioned the names of some of the members, including Lynn Tait. This was Lynn from Guides and Rangers. A familiar name helped her make the decision to attend.

The early evening meeting was held at the Civic Centre in Southend and a tall, slim, well-spoken (and younger than her) Martin was waiting to show her to the correct room. Put at her ease by a quick chat with Lynn, Hazel joined everyone seated around a large table. The meeting was interesting, although Hazel was not sure how she might be of use. As they were leaving Martin asked whether she would like to go for a quick drink to talk further about Southend in Bloom. Now Robbie was old enough not to need a babysitter, she agreed. They spent a pleasant hour and a half in a nearby pub discussing gardens and their horticultural experiences in general. At the end Martin said he hoped Hazel would come to the next meeting.

A fortnight later she did. Again, Martin asked her to join him for a drink afterwards. They discussed more personal details this time. He was twenty-six and lived in Chalkwell Hall in Chalkwell Park and owned a white Toyota MR2. Hazel was now thirty-nine. He asked if he could take her out for a meal sometime. They exchanged phone numbers and Hazel said she would let him know.

Once home she asked Robbie's advice, explaining that Martin was thirteen years younger than she was and was asking her out! Should she go?

Robbie's reply was, "If he can make you happy, why not enjoy it!"

Four days later Hazel succumbed to the flu virus yet again. She wrapped up warm with a hot-water bottle and stayed at home. After a week she rang Martin to tell him and apologised for not getting back to him sooner. She said she would let him know when she was well again.

It was another couple of weeks before she rang to invite him to her fortieth birthday get-together.

Believing a new relationship might be looming Hazel made an appointment to see her GP to discuss going back on the pill. Clive was away on holiday so the appointment was with a new doctor. As required, he asked a list of questions, the final one being whether she had had any serious illnesses.

"Well, I did have something serious. Bad enough to cause me to have a seizure, during which I had an out-of-body experience. Then, when I came to, I was totally paralysed. Unfortunately, I ended up in the Rochford psychiatric ward and afterwards was told my records had been lost."

"Oh really? I'll see if I can track them down for you."

Hazel thanked him and left with her prescription.

Two weeks later she rang the surgery to be told that, yes, they had her records now from the psychiatric ward. She made an appointment to see Clive. He was standing, staring out of the window with his back to Hazel as she entered his surgery. He turned towards her, holding a letter, his face ashen.

Angrily, he asked, "Why do want to dig all this up now. What is your problem."

Hazel, completely taken aback, answered, "I was asked if I'd had any serious illnesses. What could I say? Also, although it's not relevant now, a couple of years ago I did consider training as a parole officer. I thought it might not go down well if they discovered I'd been in a psychiatric ward. It would be nice to know what conclusion was drawn."

He walked over to his desk and signed at Hazel to sit. He laid the letter down and immediately covered the larger part of it with both his hands (almost a year later patients were given the legal right to see their records).

"They found no psychiatric reasons for your admittance."

Relief flooded Hazel.

"No panic attack, then! Any mention of pneumonia?"

"It was most likely pneumonia," he said, then angrily rushed on. "But serious bronchitis is no different from mild pneumonia."

Clive was clearly very upset and with hindsight Hazel wished she had made it clear that in no way did she blame him for the mistake. She only wanted to know the truth. Overpowered by the relief that she would not have a psychiatric problem on her records, her view of his suffering was clouded.

"So, what caused the seizure?"

"Probably encephalitis. As we had discussed. And it doesn't mean it might not happen again."

Finally, there was an answer and Hazel could let it rest. It seemed that Clive had deliberately either not asked the unit for Hazel's records or had withheld them. Both felt disturbing but highlighted how distressed he must have been by his mistake. It brought to mind the time that, following a visit to a conference in the US, Clive had approached Trevor, asking for his advice on how to insure himself against litigation. Trevor had to tell him he didn't think that type of insurance was available in the UK. For Hazel, the whole episode of her illness had added to the tension of her life with Trevor and had stretched her confidence to almost breaking point – although she had not admitted it to anyone. Now, once again, she felt firmly planted on a solid planet.

She had decided to celebrate her fortieth birthday in a popular bar in Leigh and was pleasantly surprised by the number of friends and acquaintances who turned up. Her brothers and wives were also there by the time Martin joined them. Hazel introduced him to everyone and, considering he was in the midst of strangers, he appeared cheerfully relaxed.

Hazel had only been drunk enough to be sick twice in her life, but she'd never reached the point of not knowing what she was doing.

Both times were as a teenager when she was out with Tim. The first time it had been on cider, down in the Old Town. She was very aware of how awful she felt and was quite ill walking home. The second time was on ginger wine at a party. Having the room spin round when she got home and not finding relief by throwing up was so unpleasant she vowed never to put herself through it again. Watching Tim drink until he was ill was disgusting enough.

On this occasion Hazel paced her drinking and was no more than merry. She thought how life truly does begin at forty. With a handsome, intelligent, young guy, smiling across at her often as he chatted to her friends and family, then moving to spend the final hour by her side, made anything feel possible. At closing time she asked Martin home. The details are lost in a swirl of emotions He later admitted he was surprised when she asked him to sleep with her that night. He normally took things a little slower. Hazel had been encouraged when he told her that his only long-term, serious girlfriend had been similar in age to Hazel. It was maturity that drew him, he explained. Younger girls berated him for not being dominating enough.

A non-dominating male. Wow, this was new to Hazel. The following weekend, while the two were taking a stroll around the beautiful and familiar Chalkwell Park, Martin said that, as she was forty, he knew she would not change, so was more than pleased to just relax and accept her as she was and do with her all the things that she wished them to do. That was what would make him happy.

Then he took her into the basement of Chalkwell Hall to show her the chalk well. In the dank, dark basement Hazel could just make out the large round wooden cover with a central handle, sitting over a raised brick circle. Martin lifted it to reveal only blackness. Hazel found a small stone and dropped it down the well. She guessed it travelled a good distance before she heard a splop. Hazel was fascinated as she'd had no idea that such a well existed or that this was how the park had got its name. Then Martin took her up to his flat on the first floor, which he had been sharing with a friend, who also worked for the council, as a landscaper. Jock had recently moved into his girlfriend's house. He was the same age as Martin and they'd been at Writtle College together and, strangely, his girlfriend was the same age as Hazel. Martin said that he would love to have her stay the night with him, but he warned her that the peacocks would wake them at dawn. Hazel had taken her first steps in this very park and had many memories of times with her brothers and parents, of relaxing with baby Robbie in his pram, of King, and of roller skating around all its many paths with an older Robbie. It was as though she had come home. She stayed the following night. The peacocks did wake her but she slid into Martin's arms. They made slow love then drifted back to sleep.

A couple of weeks later Martin asked whether she would like to spend a long weekend with him in Cornwall. His parents had recently retired there, taking his sister. She was two years younger than Martin but had suffered from anorexia since her late teens. They only had a two-bedroom bungalow so were unable to put them up, but would book a nearby guest house for them in a week's time. Martin then took Hazel out to an Indian restaurant to celebrate his twenty-seventh birthday and wove an enchanting picture of what she could expect from her Cornish visit.

Robbie had no problem looking after himself for a few days. His mind was very much on the Land Rover his parents had bought him for his eighteenth birthday. He had spent a great five days with his best friend Drake, his mother and Edwina at Center Parcs in Suffolk. He'd been presented with a surprise cake and candles as everyone sang for him in the restaurant. Then he'd come home to find his father waiting outside their house with a Land Rover. It had belonged to Robin, Hazel's lumberjack friend that she now used for all the large tree work her clients needed. The Land Rover was his original works vehicle and had been sitting, mainly unused, on the piece of ground he rented for his logs and trailers. He was pleased to sell it to Hazel quite cheaply. Robbie was now having driving lessons and had joined the local Land Rover club.

The instructions for the guest house took them, in Martin's MR2, to an imposing twentieth-century house that stood, all alone, on the edge of a cliff. From their bedroom window the colours danced across the waves, changing almost hourly and the sunset that evening was mesmerising, as they stood looking out, wrapped in each other's arms after an enticing meal downstairs. All incredibly romantic. The next day Martin took Hazel to meet his family. Their bungalow was at the top of the hill that led down into the picturesque village of Coverack.

Martin's father, Nathan, had taken early retirement from his job as a forensic scientist for the Metropolitan Police at Scotland Yard. A type of arthritis had begun to affect his joints and his GP told him that he needed a rest from his daily walk up the Leigh hills to their family home. Hazel had walked past it on numerous occasions since it was right outside Robbie's old school, Westleigh, where Martin's mother, Kathy, had taught the juniors when Robbie had been in the infants.

His parents instantly warmed to Hazel and it was mutual. His sister, Sue, was also friendly, if a little shy. Stunning views over the bay from their lounge and kitchen and Nathan's love of gardening, combined with Hazel's business all made easy, interesting subjects for conversation. They went for morning coffee at Lizard Point and Martin showed Hazel the dark red and green serpentine rock. His A-level geology meant he easily impressed her with his knowledge. They walked down to the village in the afternoon and introduced Hazel to Roskilly's organic ice cream and all the fascinating, quaint gift shops and art galleries, then bought fish and chips and ate it sitting by the harbour.

The following day Martin took Hazel to Kynance Cove to show her its rich, dark serpentine rock features and caves that produced a breathtaking contrast to the fine white sand. After the steep, stepped walk down the cliffs Martin was disappointed to find it was almost high tide. The sand was completely submerged but the power of the sea as the waves crashed against the glistening, stunning serpentine made the area truly beautiful, even though the day had turned drizzly and grey. Martin apologised for choosing the wrong day and time to bring her.

"Oh, gosh," replied Hazel. "It doesn't matter. It's still amazing."

Martin took both her hands and again apologised, this time for not being able to get down on one knee because of the rocks and said, "I hope this won't frighten you away … but … will you marry me?"

Hazel, momentarily overwhelmed, stared at him. Then she found her voice, "We've only known each other for a few weeks! But, yes, I have fallen in love with you, because it's all been so perfect."

She paused.

"Look, give me a month. I'll definitely give you an answer then."

Not too fazed, he agreed that was an acceptable suggestion.

During the following week Hazel discussed his proposal with Robbie. He congratulated her and said he was genuinely pleased for her. Edwina had also met him a few times and was delighted that her daughter had found someone who clearly adored her. Hazel also reminded her mother of the elderly couple Hazel used to live next door to. Emmie had been twelve years older than Tom and they were the happiest couple she had ever known. If it had worked for them, why not for her?

The following weekend she was sitting with Martin in the rose garden at Chalkwell Park. The warm sunshine soaked the air with scent. They were discussing the future, if they married. Martin knew she wanted another child and said that while he would love to be a father, if it didn't happen, it was more important to him to have Hazel as his wife, beside him for the rest of his life. This sincerity clinched it for Hazel. Why wait? She was certain now, a few more weeks would not change her mind.

"I've spent this whole week imagining us married. And now, yes, I'm sure it's what I want too."

She was, indeed, one hundred per cent certain this time.

Martin had told her about regular migraines he had inherited from his mother. But he was able to control them with over-the-counter painkillers and did not have to retreat into a darkened room. In fact, being outdoors in the fresh air really helped. Hazel only recognised them by his pale, drawn face. Martin knew that cheese, chocolate and alcohol were triggers but refused to exclude them entirely from his diet. It seemed to Hazel that the migraines could not be that severe or he would have cut them out.

It was hard to believe she'd finally found someone so perfect for her. She was almost afraid that the bubble of happiness would evaporate. But then Martin suggested that it made sense to begin trying for a baby as soon as possible, and that they should organise the wedding now. His parents were both very religious. In fact, his father had been disowned by his staunchly Roman Catholic parents for marrying a Protestant lady and turning to her faith. The family had gone to church together every Sunday. Martin had only given up joining them since they had moved to Cornwall. He preferred that they marry in a church, if possible.

Fortunately, the United Reform Church over the road from Chalkwell Park had a newly ordained female vicar who said over the phone that she would consider marrying a divorced lady if she believed the couple were sincere in their feelings.

They made an appointment to see her. After a brief chat, she was surprised to discover that they'd known each other less than two months. Then she was speechless as she wrote down their dates of birth. She looked from one to the other, then back again.

"Are these dates correct?" she finally asked, shaking her head, unable to believe the age gap. "You seem so right for each other," she conceded, then, "I'll be happy to marry you. Congratulations!"

They explained that they wanted to try for a baby so, because of Hazel's age, could the wedding be as soon as possible? It was fixed for three weeks' time.

Unbelievably they managed to arrange everything smoothly and at very little cost. Robbie said he would be proud to give his mother away. Hazel made her dress from ivory slubb silk and chose a pattern that was long and tightly fitting, falling in ruffles at the back to what was described as a flowing fish tail. She stitched lengths of drop pearls around the low neckline and the top of the short sleeves, which were thickly layered to match the fish tail. She bought a long ivory veil, held in place by a headband on which she sewed more pearls, leaving space to fit in some large white daisies. The large daisies were also included in her bouquet with white lilies and yellow roses. They decided to have the reception at Chalkwell Hall. The food was a gift from the couple who ran the council canteen. All the flowers, including the bouquet, buttonholes and arrangements in the hall and church were given to the couple by the council's greenhouses manager.

Martin's father had a new white Ford Granada. After fitting a white ribbon around its bonnet, he collected Hazel and Robbie from their house and transported them along the seafront to the church. Martin had chosen his best friend Olly, who he had also met at Writtle College, to be his best man. They had spent two months travelling around the Far East and New Zealand, spending a lot of the time in a small tent together, so there was not much they didn't know about each other. Hazel liked and got on well with all Martin's friends. Michael's two beautiful daughters, Olivia and Ella were bridesmaids, and wore deep emerald dresses their mother had bought. As the wedding car drew up outside the church Hazel just caught sight of Martin and Olly disappearing inside. The bridesmaids were waiting with Edwina by the entrance. After pausing by the car for the photographer Robbie guided Hazel to them.

"Where's your bouquet?" Edwina asked her daughter.

Oh horror, her hands were empty! Her calmness was broken by sudden panic.

"I must have left it at home."

"Oh Hazel! Too late to worry now."

And her mother disappeared into the church as the music announcing the bride's entrance began. Hazel's mind whirled, what on earth could she do? It would take at least three-quarters of an hour to get home and back. Probably more on a Saturday. With her bridesmaids ready behind her, she hesitated.

"Do you have the front door keys, Robbie?"

He retrieved them from his pocket. Looking down the church, Hazel could see Maggie standing right next to the aisle.

"Can you pass them to Maggie as we walk past, Robbie and I'll quickly ask her if she can drive home and pick up my flowers. I might just have them in time for the photos."

And that is exactly what happened. Maggie, poor thing, missed the whole service. She'd had to stop to put petrol in her car but made it back just as they were signing the register. Hazel was so grateful to her friend. Everything else on that warm, gloriously sunny day, made up for it. They only had to walk across the road from the church and into the park.

Hazel felt amazing happiness as, clutching Martin's arm and her bouquet, they walked slowly with their families and friends through the beautiful and wonderfully familiar park; as they posed for the photographer among flower beds so brilliantly planned by her husband; as they gathered in a building that was so majestic in her memories to eat a buffet of gorgeously prepared food and to drink sparkling champagne also given by the council. They'd bought the rest of the wine on a quick trip to Calais the previous weekend. They'd managed to compile a gift list and had received some truly useful presents, including a dishwasher from Edwina, Ruth and Lionel jointly – Hazel disliked wasting time washing-up! Martin's grandmother gave them a cheque for £250.

It was an amazing day, but where did they go that evening? Did they remain in Martin's flat for one final night? The only thing that stands out is that, alone, she viewed herself in a long mirror as she removed the sexy white lingerie she had carefully chosen. Martin was so drunk by then that he just wanted to sleep.

Two days later they flew to the Greek island of Skiathos for a week, chosen because it was still unspoilt by tourism. Warm sunshine greeted them but Hazel was not impressed to find two separate, single, metal-framed beds in the basic room they had booked in the self-catering complex. She pushed them together. But the first night they broke one. In the morning Hazel explained to the reception that it was their honeymoon so they would prefer a replacement double bed.

It was a lazy week and Hazel had to quell her natural impatience waiting ages for food in cafés and restaurants and accept the relaxed Mediterranean pace of life. They took a boat trip for the day to visit Kastro, to walk among the ruins of the fortified, fourteenth-century former capital. The boat then took them on to Lalaria beach. It was surrounded by steep grey and white cliffs and was only approachable by boat. The grey and white pebbles of the beach, polished by the sea, shone glaringly and the bleached submerged marble rocks along the shore turned the water a rich turquoise. At one end of the beach was a huge rock archway. No one told them the story that that those who swim through the arch will get younger – because Hazel would have swum through; not because she believed the myth but just for a laugh. The rest of the time was spent discovering quiet sandy coves, mostly on foot. In one bay Martin scooped up a wrinkled grey sea cucumber and gave it to Hazel to feel. She imagined old men's willies might look like that but it felt like jelly. The week disappeared all too quickly and they wished they'd booked two weeks.

Martin moved everything out of Chalkwell Hall into Hazel's home – now legally his too, of course. Martin's one wish, other than to be a father, was to have his own plant nursery, which would be a perfect complement to Hazel's business. They immediately put their house on the market with the intention of finding one with a large garden suitable for a plant nursery. Plenty of people viewed the mock-Tudor semi with its 6,000 gallon fish pond. But no one made an acceptable offer.

The Dacia Duster was becoming more unreliable and, frustratingly for Hazel, it was not possible to take her mother or Robbie and his girlfriend out for the day. Knowing this was getting his wife down Martin agreed they should look to replace the 4x4. A colleague at work was selling, very cheaply, an old Renault Fuego that happened to have had a tow-ball fitted, so Martin bought it. The sale of the Duster for parts only just equalled the price. For a while the Fuego was great.

They bought a tent with two separate double sleeping areas sectioned off from the kitchen and lounge area with the money Martin's grandmother had given them and drove down to Cornwall for a week at Easter. The Trellowarren Estate offered camping and was only a few minutes' drive from Martin's parents. It rained a lot and living in wellingtons meant they had to line the lounge and cooking part of the tent with newspaper to soak up the mud they trampled in. But they enjoyed it.

Martin had not been to an orchestral concert before so Hazel bought tickets for Beethoven's Ninth Symphony at the London Barbican. They drove up and parked in the Barbican car park and enjoyed a meal followed by a wonderful concert. On arriving back at the car Martin noticed a puddle just in front of the bonnet, it was obvious the radiator was leaking. The council had supplied all their outdoor staff with the latest, still large, mobile phones. Glad he had it in the car, he rang the AA. They said they would be there in about half an hour. The mechanic plugged the radiator and assured the couple that it would get them home.

"Are you sure we shouldn't get some water to top it up with on the way?" asked Hazel, explaining they lived just this side of Southend. But the AA man said, "No, it'll be fine. Just get it sorted tomorrow."

They got as far as Basildon before the engine began making a knocking sound. Very reminiscent of when the big end went on the Beetle. Martin immediately slowed down and pulled over on to the side of the A13. As he did so the engine gave one final loud clonk and stopped. Fortunately, at this late hour there was very little traffic. He put on the hazard lights and asked Hazel to hop out while he pushed it on to the hard shoulder. Then rang the AA again. They said it might be up to an hour this time before they got to them. Forty minutes later an AA truck pulled up. After Hazel gave him the details of the radiator leak and the promise that it would get them home, the AA man, after a quick look under the bonnet, hoisted the Fuego up on the truck and drove them home.

Martin used a mechanic not far from the council offices and the following morning, after a call from Martin, he arrived with a trailer to collect the dead car. His verdict that afternoon was that it required a replacement, reconditioned engine.

"No surprise there then!" retorted Hazel.

After the mechanic had given them a price for fitting a reconditioned engine Hazel sat down and wrote a scathing letter to the AA. They agreed to pay for the engine and fitting. A cheque duly arrived for the full amount. At least they still had the MR2, as it took almost two weeks to fix the Fuego.

They had dispensed with any form of contraception once a date had been fixed for the wedding. Hazel felt confident a pregnancy would happen. It took six months of great fun. The mock-Tudor four-poster bed, left by the previous owner, squeaked if they were too rampant so they had to go gently if Robbie was home! Having bought a book on pregnancy, Hazel knew that miscarriages before twelve weeks happen much more frequently than is realised and accepted that it might occur, particularly at forty. Afraid to get excited the couple told no one when Hazel missed a period, only her GP, who confirmed the pregnancy and prescribed folic acid.

They were looking forward to a long weekend in Scotland for a winter break. It was a great value offer in the Daily Telegraph. They punctuated the long drive with an overnight stop halfway, at a Travelodge. The MR2 had just reached the snowcapped mountains after the tedious two-day drive when Hazel began to experience slight period pains. When they arrived at the hotel there were some blood spots on her knickers. The pregnancy book said this did happen sometimes, even in normal pregnancies. The pain was mild and only slight bleeding occurred so they enjoyed their few days without doing anything strenuous. Instinctively though, Hazel was worried. She did consider that it might signal a miscarriage. She held on to a tiny hope but tried to be practical.

As soon as they were home her doctor sent her, with Martin, to the hospital. A scan revealed no viable foetus and they said they would keep her in to do a 'scrape'. They did then tell their parents. It was very disappointing but Hazel and Martin refused to get upset. They knew that her age was stacked against a healthy pregnancy; no point in thinking otherwise. Five months later Hazel visited her GP for advice about trying for another pregnancy. He prescribed Clomid, a fertility pill to boost ovulation.

A month later she missed her period. Yet again, they kept it to themselves, but were overjoyed when at twelve weeks it was confirmed that her pregnancy was progressing normally. Hazel did feel slightly nauseous, as she had with Robbie. A healthy snack helped, as it had before. Because of her age she was advised to have a blood test for Down's Syndrome, which was returned with an inconclusive result. An amniocentesis was required to be certain. Hazel had read of the risks involved with this procedure but an elderly mother coping with a young adult with the syndrome was not a proposition she thought she could consider. What would happen when she got really old or even died before she should? There was a one in 400 chance of the procedure causing the foetus to abort. She thought back to her out-of-body experience and what she'd felt she was told in the psychiatric ward bathroom. Still believing it had all been concocted by her damaged brain, she now thought she should consider the possibility that it might have been a prophecy. 'In that case, if a child is meant to be, according to that prediction, it will be. And as I don't realistically think I could cope with a Down's Syndrome baby, I think I should at least know.'

Martin went with Hazel to the hospital but was asked to wait outside during the procedure. Hazel knew exactly what it would involve. She just managed to calm her apprehension as she laid out on the couch ready for the scan to locate the placenta and foetus. Hazel could not help but notice the large syringe with a very thick needle that the young male doctor was holding. As he pushed it against her abdomen, seconds seem to pass and the indentation that was forming, as the needle was not piercing her, was getting larger and deeper. Hazel glanced at the doctor's face. Was that puzzlement on his face that the needle was not puncturing her? Immediately Hazel thought of all the exercises she'd been doing for years now to strengthen her abdominal muscles, to support her back. Surely this doctor had encountered strong muscles here before? Suddenly POP, a sound like a slightly deflated balloon, quietly bursting. The monitor showing the scan was only just in Hazel's view. She had been able to make out her tiny baby. It hadn't been moving much before she was punctured and there was no sudden movement now. She's not sure she saw the needle. The doctor drew off some amniotic fluid and gently withdrew the needle. The baby was now slowly moving. So, still alive! Hazel then caught sight of a swirl of blood in the syringe as the doctor passed it to a nurse. The nurse questioned this as it was obviously not something she usually saw.

"It's only the mother's blood," was his quick response.

Hazel was not convinced that the needle had not caught her baby. The nurse told Hazel to join her husband and sit for a while to allow any shock to her body to pass. As she walked out to join Martin the sound of the pop kept replaying in her head. As she sat, she suddenly felt very dizzy. She told Martin she needed to put her head between her legs. The nurse checked on Hazel a little later and when she said she still felt dizzy the nurse disappeared, then arrived back with a cup of tea. Sipping the tea slowly helped and soon Hazel felt well enough to go home.

Fortunately, the result from the amniocentesis was negative for Down's Syndrome and her pregnancy proceeded well. A post-amniotic scan at twenty weeks revealed she was carrying a healthy little boy. There was no reason to presume that Hazel's instinctive thought that her baby had been pierced was true. But she remained certain that he would have a perfectly round birthmark somewhere on his small body.

They couldn't find a buyer for their house and came to the conclusion that the pond might be deterring people. Its solid concrete walls wouldn't be easy to demolish. They asked Martin's best man Olly if he could help. He came armed with his Kango drill but it made no impression. Then he returned with the heaviest Kango he could hire. It took Martin and Olly two days to break up the base and remove the walls, filling a skip. They left some of the rubble in the bottom of the hole to ensure drainage and ordered a load of topsoil, which Martin wheeled down the side and in through the opened fence while Hazel levelled the ground. She was meticulous, heeling it in (shuffle walking, using all one's weight on the heels), then raking it level, then heeling and raking again. They laid new turf then Hazel planted a small tree, one of her favourites, a *Gleditsia triacanthos* 'Sunburst', to add a glowing, light yellow character to the garden. They had a buyer for the house a month later.

Another recession was underway and many households were now suffering from negative equity – meaning houses were now valued at less than their mortgages. Hazel and Martin were lucky and they made a clear £20,000 profit from the sale. The building society were happy to grant the couple a mortgage of a maximum of three times Martin's salary. To allow for all the buying and moving costs Martin decided that £85,000 was the maximum they could afford.

A large garden suitable for a plant nursery was a prerequisite in their house hunting. Hazel very much wanted to move back into Leigh. But house prices there had always been well above those in Shoebury and it was usually only large houses that had large gardens. They did view one in Leigh; a detached Victorian property with a large L-shaped garden. It was beautifully decorated inside and had retained all its Victorian fireplaces and coving, which Hazel loved. Unfortunately, it was priced at £95,000 and the vendor would not accept an offer of less than £90,000.

Hazel pleaded with Martin.

"Is there nowhere that we could borrow that extra £5,000 from?"

But he was adamant that £85,000 was the maximum they could afford. Then details of a large detached house fell through their letter box. It had a sixty metres by twelve metres garden and was on the Hadleigh/Benfleet border. It was a modern house with an ugly frontage of painted, coloured, faux stonework and white-painted shiplap wood around an imposing dormer window on the first floor. Apart from the large neglected garden and the large rooms with very large windows, Hazel was not impressed. It was priced at £90,000 and had been on the market for a while, but the vendor had found a bungalow she was now desperate to move into and the estate agent said an offer of £85,000 would be acceptable. There was a reason this large property on a large piece of land was so cheap.

It was built in 1960 and the builder had lived in it while he built two semis of the same design next door. Three years later he sold it to an architectural designer who had added three separate extensions. One as an extra lounge facing the garden that he'd used for his billiard table. The second as an extension to the kitchen. And the third and largest was built out from the small third bedroom, which was now a dressing area with fitted wardrobes. Two steps down led to a new large fourth bedroom with a long dormer window. A large third bedroom was also added above the garage and was also accessed via the dressing area. All three extensions had flat roofs. Once these works were completed in 1970 the designer had bought a barn in Suffolk and moved to live nearby while he renovated it with the intention that his wife would join him once it was completed. But by then the designer had changed his mind. He no longer wanted his wife and began divorce proceedings. According to the neighbours, his wife, the present vendor, was distraught and very angry. She threw all his belongings into the front garden where, apparently, they stayed for a long time.

Finally divorced, she could not afford to maintain the property. The wooden shiplap and wooden window frames were rotting. The flat roofs were leaking. According to the estate agent, she had put it on the market at £164,000 and refused an offer of £141,000. Unable to realise another offer she got a loan to replace the flat roofs. Over a couple of years, as house prices in general dropped, she dropped her price to £90,000. Still no one made an offer.

The long garden meant Martin could hedge off the lower part to use as his nursery and Hazel could design the area nearest the house. While, hopefully, the flat roofs would not be a problem for a while, Hazel worried that the cost to maintain them against future leaks might prove expensive and the only thing inside she found attractive were Habitat cubes fitted to the front lounge wall. The rear lounge facing the garden had no outside access, just a single pane of glass, two metres wide, that reached the ceiling. The ceilings in this lounge and the third and fourth bedrooms were raw unsanded timber. Unusual, thought Hazel. The lounge ceiling had been given a dark-brown stain. To cover water stains she suspected. Just as unusual was a mezzanine area above the third bedroom. It was very bright due to the large windows that dropped right down from the raw, natural coloured, wood ceiling above the mezzanine to the floor of the bedroom below. Another large pane of glass was fitted on the second side of the mezzanine overlooking Hadleigh Country Park and the Thames Estuary, combined with the views over the Benfleet Downs from the larger windows this mezzanine was an exciting space. It was, altogether, a very modern, architect-designed house, but one that needed some extensive renovation.

The couple had already made the decision that as soon as Martin had a workable plant nursery he would join Hazel's business, with the intention of dropping regular garden maintenance and concentrating on designing and planting up new gardens. Offering seasonal maintenance only on those gardens, if required. They would place an ad in the local Yellow Pages to relaunch the business and were certain they could match Martin's present salary, at least. Using this idea, Martin convinced Hazel that if their offer of £85,000 was accepted they could slowly afford to renovate the house. He felt that as it was situated down a quiet cul-de-sac rather than in busy Leigh it would be perfect for his nursery and their business. Hazel capitulated and their offer was accepted.

CHAPTER 24
1994 ◊ A 'Special' Child

Once the contracts on the house were signed and exchanged Hazel passed over all her regular garden maintenance work to her current assistant Phil. Tony, her original assistant, after working with Hazel for three years, had found that his arthritis, which was part of his condition, was worse. He had worked for years as a clown collecting money for charities at weekends and thought he would expand on this line of work. Hazel was sad to see him go and put an advert in the local newsagent for a gardener's assistant.

A young guy, Paul, who answered, was very enthusiastic. He told Hazel he wished to learn as much as he could to help her with all the gardening work she undertook. Hazel, naively, didn't realise that this was so he could go off and start his own business after only six months.

Hazel then tried the Job Centre again and they sent Phil for an interview. He was young, slim but strong and was her best assistant, capable but content for Hazel to be boss. Now, after working with her for almost three years, she told him that he was quite able to take over all her maintenance work if he wanted to. All her clients had their own lawnmowers and tools so he'd be able to travel by bike. Her clients, although sad to see Hazel go, all accepted that Phil would take over.

The Renault Fuego, although cheap, turned out to be a poor buy. Robbie had already done some welding on it to get it through its MOT. Now the gears needed replacing. Even with the reconditioned engine they decided it was not worth continuing to spend money on it. They sold the engine and had the breakers take it away.

Martin agreed to sell the MR2 and bought a Toyota Hiace diesel van, in readiness for their new business. With three seats at the front it would take a baby seat. It was all they would need for a while.

Robbie was working for a local Shoebury engineering company as a welder and enjoying it. He'd had a couple of girlfriends (one at a time!) when, through a friend of a friend at the Land Rover club, he met a lady he felt serious about. She was nine years older than him, had been married and divorced, had a four-year-old daughter and lived in a pretty council house in a secluded cul-de-sac in Southend. What could Hazel say against this relationship? Nothing, of course. Her son was a mature eighteen-year-old and the age difference was less than that between her and Martin. So, when he told his mother that his girlfriend, Annie, had suggested he move in with her, he highlighted the one bone of contention Hazel had with her son by saying, "She's promised to get me out of bed in time for work!"

Robbie knew that Martin was not best pleased that his wife still had to worry about rousing her deeply sleeping, adult son, every morning. His alarm would clang away for ages before it was finally turned off, only for Robbie to fall instantly back to sleep. Hazel did worry that he was too young to settle down. But Robbie seemed certain it was worth trying and it solved the problem of him moving away from his job and girlfriend. He would be unable to afford the fuel for his old Land Rover travelling back and forth from their new house in Hadleigh.

Loving and marrying Martin, finding herself pregnant, having Robbie move out, totally changed Hazel's life. More than her situation though, her whole view of life had been altered. Her inner elation had risen to a level she had never considered possible. Yes, there was an emptiness without Robbie, but she consoled herself with the thought that she had successfully brought up her son to be a mature and useful adult, who could even cook and iron!

She still grieved for her father and was sad that he would never meet Martin. As an adult she questioned whether there was a heaven after death, but felt her father existed within her and her brothers, and his memory would always be with them. This elevated her happiness to a plateau that somehow felt above ordinary life. Life for her was as perfect as it could be, even though she was very conscious that they only just about earned an average income between them.

They'd hired a Luton van for the move and – even though they suffered the slight hiccup of the estate agent not having the key, meaning they had to dump the first lorry load on the front garden and leave Robbie to guard it, while crossing their fingers that it didn't rain – this euphoria continued.

Back in Shoebury for the second run, Hazel gathered the tortoise into a cardboard box and shoved an unwilling Guinness into a cat basket, while Martin loaded their last pieces of furniture. She couldn't stop the poor cat meowing all the way there. Martin followed in the van but stopped off at the estate agent to wait for the key. Hazel and Robbie, with an unhappy cat locked in his basket, waited on the front lawn of the new house for two hours before Martin finally arrived with the key.

That first night, they heard from their bed, even above the sound of the heavy rain from outside, a constant plip-plopping from somewhere in the house. On investigation they found that the ceilings in both kitchen and garden lounge were leaking. They frantically searched in boxes for buckets and saucepans to put underneath, wondering what they had let themselves in for. But these ordinary, down to earth, everyday problems had no impact on Hazel's inner brilliance. Considering her non-religious beliefs it was strange, but Hazel felt that she had truly found heaven here on Earth. All around her, on her beautiful planet. Within the bubble of her life. And for seven years this was exactly where she felt she existed. In Heaven on Earth. Weird really! Thinking about it now.

Someone had recommended a good builder to replace all the rotten window frames and shiplap and some rotting flooring around the large panes of glass in the garden lounge. As a seventies feature these single panes did not open, so there was no ventilation, causing condensation to pool on the floor. The downstairs toilet must also have been leaking for years, rotting the floor beneath it. Hazel rang the builder on their first day, after they'd emptied all the buckets and saucepans. He was concerned when he heard about the leaks and came round that afternoon. Fortunately, it was only the flashing between the wall and the new roofing felt that had lifted in the summer heat, which was easily repaired. He agreed to replace all the rotting wood and, to keep his costs to a minimum, he would just leave the wood primed so that Hazel and Martin could apply the top coats themselves. Martin knew he would be able to borrow a scaffold tower from work for the front of the house. The rear first floor could be reached from the flat roofs.

Hazel's first job, however, was the kitchen. It took her three days to scrub out all the kitchen cupboards. Thick layers of grease and grime surrounded cleaner circles where crockery must have sat. According to the neighbours, the lonely owner always ate out, not being bothered to cook for herself – and that included breakfast! So nothing in the kitchen had been used for years. The units were well-made German ones with dark wood doors and white worktops over a central dividing bar, so would last for a good few years yet. There was a built-in double electric oven with a separate gas hob, although only three of the four burners worked.

When they lifted smelly carpets, they found dried pools of what they thought was cat's wee. Then Hazel found tiny birth bracelets belonging to a pair of twins, so maybe it was toddler's wee!

Hazel used a whole reel of film during those first weeks: she got Martin to take photos of her six months pregnant, painting up the scaffolding tower (Martin knew better than to discourage her and, in fact, quickly discovered she was far more experienced than he at all DIY); photos of her painting the French doors the builder had put in to replace the single enormous pane of glass; photos of Martin digging out huge pampas grasses and clearing all the brambles that completely covered a brick shed and a greenhouse; and of Guinness and the tortoise exploring the large garden. The roll of film seemed to last well beyond the thirty-six photos she thought were available and when Hazel wound the film back and opened the camera she discovered that she had not loaded a film! Ah, pregnancy.

As well as her emotionally heightened state, Hazel bloomed physically. Even her blood pressure remained low. During the final trimester, though, her appetite diminished. But she forced herself to eat all the oily fish, fresh fruit and vegetables that the pregnancy books advised. There were no more scans. More than one was not advised then, as they were unsure of the effect they might have on the baby. But Hazel went for her regular checks at the clinic and was assured the baby was growing normally. She also went to antenatal dance classes. And took Martin to the standard antenatal classes, even though not much had changed since she'd been pregnant with Robbie.

All the major repairs to the house had been completed by the middle of December. The baby was due around the first or second of January. Hazel had chosen the bedroom at the back of the house, next to the bathroom, to be the nursery and decorated it pale yellow and pastel blue. Her childhood friend Carol had given her a cot she no longer needed and Hazel bought a new-looking Moses basket from a boot sale. Hazel padded some Winnie the Pooh material to make soft sides and a head bumper for the cot. She bought a Peter Rabbit musical mobile that she clipped to the side. Then stitched a matching quilt and made and hung matching curtains. The nursery had a lovely view over the garden towards the Benfleet Downs and had a spy glass already set into the door. Presumably it had been a nursery once before, possibly for the twins whose bracelets Hazel had found.

All the bedrooms were double rooms and theirs at the front of the house over the garage was the largest. Since she had a baby monitor Hazel wasn't worried that there was another bedroom in between theirs and the nursery. Hazel initially thought they would have the baby in their bedroom in the Moses basket, anyway. With everything complete, she was able to concentrate on Christmas decorations for their new home and, with Martin, went to find a suitable tree to dig up from the usual Christmas tree farm.

It had felt very strange not having Robbie move in with them but his relationship with his older girlfriend had proved successful and Hazel had the impression that Annie was a caring person who dearly loved her son. Even her daughter, Justine, who had initially come across as a rather angry little girl, was, with Robbie's influence, becoming an engaging child. Robbie had also bought a dog and built the close bond that he'd had with his cat Boxer. So, within Hazel's bubble, heaven continued.

As Robbie wanted to spend Christmas Day at home with his new family, Martin and Hazel were more than happy to have Edwina stay on Christmas Eve so she could enjoy an early Christmas morning with them and help with dinner. Edwina had sold the old Beetle when the body work begun to rust badly and it became too costly to keep on the road. It was easy to catch a bus from the bottom of her road, with a straight run along the London road to the top of Hazel's road, but not early on Christmas morning.

Their front lounge had a feature sloping chimney breast that separated the front lounge from the dining area. There had been an old gas fire set within it when they moved in, which Hazel had quickly removed. After fitting some heat-resistant, terracotta tiles as a hearth, she had installed her cast-iron, chestnut cob fire basket, she'd kept from her Leigh cottage. The tall chimney had a good draught, so they stocked the garage with plenty of logs to burn through the winter. There was also a large floor-standing boiler in a cupboard in the kitchen that efficiently supplied hot water and central heating and was a perfect place to hang washing to dry when it was too wet or cold outside.

During Christmas Eve and Christmas Day, the fire burnt brightly. A perfect setting for the perfectly cooked turkey that Edwina had paid for. And for the perfect, bought, brandy blazing Christmas pudding that Edwina had supplied the holly for.

As a Christmas present to themselves, Hazel and Martin bought a camcorder to record the birth of their baby and beyond.

In the early evening they all fitted into the van to spend the evening at Michael's house for fun and games, together with John and his wife. It was a tradition that Hazel had missed out on during her years with Trevor. Michael's son, David, was now six and his babyhood had sadly passed her by.

Hazel had read that the physicist, Stephen Hawking had said, after *A Brief History of Time* had been published, that he could not discount a God. If he could not, she shouldn't. So Hazel quietly prayed that night, once Martin had fallen asleep, just in case it made a difference, for a happy, healthy baby and concluded her prayer by giving thanks for all that she had.

On Boxing Day the good cheer continued when Robbie, Annie and Justine visited for a cold turkey dinner. With Edwina's help on Christmas Day and Martin's help on Boxing Day, Hazel had been able to relax and enjoy the celebrations.

On the evening of 27 December Hazel went to bed with back pain. By morning her contractions had begun. She suggested she and Martin go for their regular walk over to Hadleigh Country Park, where a path led directly through the Salvation Army fields to Hadleigh castle. It was not until late afternoon that the contractions started to come every three minutes. Martin took Hazel's bag and followed her out to the van.

Without help she hauled herself up into the passenger seat and relaxed through the contractions as Martin drove to the maternity unit, still at Rochford Hospital. At her last clinic check-up, the midwife had said the baby's position was good and she expected his weight to be about seven pounds. Similar to Robbie, thought Hazel. Thus, she expected the birth might only take a little longer than his, due to her age.

After she'd had an enema and a bath Martin joined her in the delivery room. The pain was far more powerful than she had experienced with Robbie and, as time went on, it began to wrack her body. She asked for some pethidine but was told labour was too advanced for that. She tried standing, bending over, leaning heavily on Martin and moaning loudly, until she was exhausted. She crawled on to the bed for another examination and was told she needed to start pushing. She hadn't clocked the hours passing and now desperately wanted it over. Pushing with what little strength she had left was ineffective. She heard the midwife say to a nurse that she was unable to feel which way the baby was facing. Then she heard her mention the doctor and a ventouse. She seriously did not want a suction cap used on her baby if she could help it. Babies she'd seen born by that method always had marks and scars on their face.

A doctor appeared briefly, but Hazel said she would try to push harder. The fear of a ventouse spurred her to gather every scrap of strength. Finally, the midwife said the baby's head was almost out. He'd been facing forward, a difficult way to traverse the birth canal. On the next push his head was free, and with a last hard push his body slithered out.

Momentarily, Hazel felt herself far above the bed looking down on her son. He'd only made a small cry and was already looking around with wide, dark eyes. He had a long sausage shaped head, covered in dark hair. It reminded Hazel of tightly bound babies' heads that she'd seen in museums.

Hazel heard the concern in Martin's voice as he asked, "Why is his head like that?"

The baby moved his head towards his father. Did the deep tone of his father's voice sound familiar? Had it resonated through her womb?

It was Hazel who reassured her husband that it was okay and would soon reshape itself. Instinctively, she was not worried.

"But how long will it take?" Martin asked.

Before Hazel could answer, the midwife asked Martin if he would like to cut the cord. Shaking, he did so. By then their son's head was almost normal in shape. The nurse wrapped up the baby and took him to be weighed.

"Five pounds, eight ounces," the nurse said. "But he is long."

Then she placed him into Hazel's arms. She murmured to her son but it was still his father's voice he turned to, not that Hazel minded. The nurse said that she could try to suckle her alert baby if she wanted. And this baby, within seconds, seemed to know what to do. Later she saw his Apgar score. After one minute it was nine. After five minutes he scored the maximum of ten. Really good. He was underweight but healthy. She probably hadn't eaten enough, or her ageing placenta had not functioned at a hundred per cent. Whatever. No one seemed bothered. The hospital worked out that his final height would be about six feet two inches. Two inches above his father. Martin went to phone the grandparents with the welcome news.

She was given some stitches but was too tired and blissful to care. After a short sleep Hazel had visits, first from Robbie, Annie and Justine. Brilliant to have them there to hug. Then her mother. Great to hug her also.

Martin registered the birth before he left to go home for a short rest. He had to admit that he was still so overwhelmed from watching the birth that he'd not written the full name they had both agreed on. Only the gentler sounding variation that they would have called him anyway. Hazel didn't mind. But for this story his name is Scott.

After a sandwich and a check-up by the doctor Hazel was ready to leave. Martin arrived with the baby seat fitted into the passenger seat of the van. The centre seat only had a lap belt so wasn't suitable. Hazel slid over the driver's seat into the middle and Martin proudly drove them home that afternoon.

Back in the comfort of her own home, Hazel cradled the tiny scrap, not wanting to put him down. Martin had lit the fire. Martin's best man, Olly, his girlfriend and her daughter, called in to congratulate them. Lovely to have some company on such a cold, grey day. It was dark when they left.

Martin was now exhausted as he'd not slept for forty-eight hours and after cooking a cottage pie he'd defrosted (Hazel had prepared casseroles, cottage and fish pies for the freezer during the previous weeks), he asked if it was okay for him to go to bed.

"Of, course," said Hazel.

The fire crackled in the silence of the house. The baby was awake. Gazing at him as he lay in her arms, Hazel wondered where the future would take him. 'Should I believe this baby is special?' Then argued with herself. 'But all babies are special. Beautiful in their uniqueness. Just why would this one be more so?'

He began to whimper. Hazel fed him a little, until he lost interest. He was wearing the weeny vest and Babygro that Martin had given to the nurse. Dressing a newborn was their perk. From the changing bag Hazel removed a mat and a first size disposable nappy.

As she gently pulled his legs free from the Babygro and removed the hardly damp nappy he began to cry in earnest, surprising Hazel. The lounge was warm and she was being very gentle. Surely there was no reason to cry. She could find no birthmark on his lower body. Once the dry nappy was in place, he quietened, so Hazel lifted his vest to check his upper body.

There it was. Just below his nipples. A perfectly round birthmark indisputably made by a hollow needle and looking almost like a third nipple. Not exactly in the centre, but slightly closer to his left nipple. She lifted him and carefully turned him over. In the corresponding place on his back was a tiny nick. Had the point of the needle just caught here? Gone right through him? What really shocked Hazel was how close it was to his heart. How had it missed? She had to concede that it was a miracle this baby was alive and healthy.

'Does this make a difference?' She thought. 'Should I take this as a sign that he is more than normally special? Will he help in some way with the suffering on Earth? If God is simply goodness, as I believe, then a whole lot of goodness worked to bring this child to us and all I can do is try to be the best mother I can.' Hazel very much believed that it was the parents' responsibility to ensure a child reached his or her full potential. Of course, school was important but among such numbers how could every teacher understand what was best for each child? Their local library had just installed computers so it was possible for parents to help their children even if they had little money, and libraries were full of books offering free advice.

As a more mature mother, she wondered, had she learnt lessons – about how not to shout or smack?

Thinking back over twenty years, memories surfaced of the accidents Robbie had had on his BMX bike. First, breaking three fingers while cycling down to the beach with Edwina. Then there were the two occasions he'd fallen from climbing frames in Chalkwell Park. Each time causing a massive swelling to his elbow – fortunately, X-rays showed no damage, only a bad bruise. Then, during their time in Thorpe Bay with Trevor, Robbie had been cycling along the very edge of the pavement, jumping over driveways. He misjudged one and his bike, with his weight still on top, came down on his lower leg. He'd split both his fibula and tibia right down to what the consultant called the growth plate above his ankle. That had been very worrying as it might have left him with a limp. The consultant assured Robbie that he would do all he could to ensure that didn't happen. He operated and fitted a long bar with bolts into his leg. The bolts were removed a few months later so natural growth wasn't impeded. And Robbie never limped. But surely you had to let children learn their own limitations? What heartaches would occur with this little one? Getting frustrated with them to the point of shouting and smacking them, as she had with Robbie, was now believed to be detrimental. Hazel was determined she would not subject Scott to that.

She could think no more and swaddled Scott in a soft warm baby blanket (she'd heard newborns found this comforting) and tucked him into the Moses basket. She carried him up into the bathroom while she cleaned her teeth and took off her clothes, so as not to disturb Martin. She gently placed the basket next to her side of the bed and slid in.

Immediately Scott began crying. Hazel, not wanting Martin to be disturbed, picked the baby up. He stopped crying. She sat in bed and rocked him, now desperately tired herself. He was still not asleep but Hazel, unable to stay awake, laid him back into the basket.

A wail let her know he was not pleased. Again, she lifted him into bed and loosened the blanket to make sure he wasn't too hot before gently rocking him again. Martin had briefly moaned then fallen back to sleep. Finally, Scott seemed to be asleep and Hazel slowly and carefully laid him back in the basket.

He was crying before she was even completely back into bed. 'This baby doesn't want to be parted from me,' presumed Hazel and picked him up again. He wasn't interested in feeding so she settled herself comfortably on her back and laid Scott on her chest. She hated the idea of sleeping in bed with a baby, particularly a newborn. But tiredness overcame her apprehension. She dozed lightly and fitfully, aware she must not move, and fed the baby when he cried. At four-thirty Scott was in a deep enough sleep to allow Hazel to put him into his basket. At last. She slept deeply.

Martin had a migraine the following day but didn't let it stop him from bringing breakfast up to Hazel in bed or doing the cooking that day. Hazel left Scott for a couple of short periods during the day in the nursery cot, in his Moses basket, and set off his musical mobile. Each time it was a while before he began to cry.

After his six o'clock evening feed, wash and change, she laid him, again in his Moses basket, in the cot. This time Hazel closed the curtains. She had lined them with blackout material so the room was now quite dark. She waited, silently, until the mobile had finished then wound it up again and quietly left the room and closed the door. Half an hour later, on the baby monitor, she heard him having a little moan. A few minutes later he began to cry. Hazel resisted the desire to rush to him immediately. Within a few minutes the crying subsided to an intermittent grizzle. Then, apart from the odd snuffling sound, the baby's breathing settled as he slept until just after eight. Hazel switched on a night light to feed and change him and again left the baby listening to the Peter Rabbit mobile. And from his bedtime at six forty-five until his six o'clock morning feed Scott remained in his darkened bedroom with the door closed. The monitor was always on to reassure Hazel that her baby was breathing! Yes, he had the odd short cry or grizzle but Hazel left him until he cried with a recognisably hungry gusto. Then she only switched on the dim night light, to allow the baby to learn the difference between night and day.

The midwife called to check on mother and baby. Hazel showed her Scott's birthmark and said there could be no doubt it had been caused by the amniocentesis needle. The midwife replied that they wouldn't accept liability for it. Hazel told her she had no intention of complaining, she had known the risks, she was just relieved that it hadn't caused any harm. Hazel also pointed it out to her GP when he called. He said nothing.

Three days later it snowed, just as Scott took on the jaundiced hue that she remembered with Robbie. Hazel rang the doctor's surgery and was told she should take him to the hospital. She fitted Scott into his car seat in the van and settled in next to him as Martin took the driver's seat. But the road surface under the snow had turned to ice and the van was unable to even turn out of the drive, let alone get up their quite steep road. Back in the house and another call to the doctor. She was told that a midwife lived at the top of their road and would try to get to them later that day. Scott was feeding normally so Hazel didn't worry, overly. The midwife arrived and concluded that, as long as Scott's colour didn't get any worse, he should be alright and she'd check him again the following day. By then his colour had improved. Thankfully.

A week after Scott's birth, Martin's parents and sister came to spend a couple of days with them to cuddle and acquaint themselves with their first grandson and nephew. Perhaps it was her maturity but Hazel doesn't remember having felt the frustration she'd felt with Robbie, of not finding a daily routine around all the baby's needs. Martin took two weeks off work after his son's birth and was around each evening and weekend to help with the baby. And he did help with everything, from feeding to changing and bathing. And he sat and talked to his son and danced some soft toys within the baby's view. Hazel had been right about him making a great dad.

This second motherhood only added to Hazel's general euphoria. Her dear little baby, her Martin, her garden design business, all on her imaginary, beautiful, green plateau that sat above all life as she had previously known it. This happiness continued to feel close to a heaven. She'd not suffered from baby blues with Robbie and she didn't with Scott. She thanked her hormones for being stable and began her back exercises, gently, within days of the birth. Her figure had returned to normal within weeks of Robbie's birth. She'd not been certain it would be as quick, now she was older, but she'd not put on any unnecessary weight with Scott. In under six weeks no one would have known she'd been pregnant, apart from her fuller breasts.

She was managing to feed Scott reasonably successfully. Her nipples weren't so sore that she had to wear nipple shields. She had attempted to use a manual breast pump to express milk, to enable Martin to share the night feeds. Her breasts, though, just didn't seem to want to give it up to the pump. With Scott wanting feeds every couple of hours, even through the night, it was exhausting. She wondered whether she was producing enough milk. But he was putting on weight fast and had reached the correct weight for his age within a few weeks. But, after four weeks of exhausting two-hourly feeds, Hazel decided to top up her own milk with powdered baby milk. There were adverts on TV for Aptamil that said it contained the same unique fatty acids found in breast milk that were vital, in particular, for brain development. She was sad that she would not be able to continue to feed him completely for another five months, as she had hoped. But every two hours? For her own sanity, if topping up with this milk was the best option, she'd give it a go. Scott still fed for the same length of time, until none of her natural milk was left, it seemed, before she gave him an ounce of Aptamil. Time then began to stretch between feeds. Within another month her own milk had dried up. By then neither Hazel nor Scott were bothered about it. Aptamil continued to be his only milk.

Whether it was instrumental in his brain development, who could say? Hazel had relaxed by listening to Mozart and Bach, particularly during the last three months of her pregnancy, as she had read research that suggested it made the baby's brain more active. Hazel tended to keep an open mind on all research and relied on her instinct as to whether there might be a grain of truth in the findings. She could see no harm in enjoying the music with her baby-to-be; or in giving him one milk over another. She only felt they were good options.

Another good option, she decided, was to introduce Scott to the warm water of the baby pool at the local swimming pool and to meet up with mothers from the antenatal classes at each other's houses. Scott showed an early fascination for the gurgling and cries of other babies.

He would watch, intrigued by their expressions and feel no need to join in with any crying. And he always had a ready smile for the mums.

By the time the meetings had gone down to once a month Hazel had made a particular friend of one mum. Rachael was intrigued to discover that she was only a couple of years older than Robbie but the age difference was never an issue. Rachael and baby Spencer lived with his father, Stefan, in a detached house, similar in size to Martin and Hazel's, on the other side of Hadleigh, near a small wood. Their garden, though, was much larger and boasted a small lake with a bridge. The friends would alternate weekly visits to each other's houses, with lunch included, to give the babies time for companionable toy and food sharing.

Throughout the winter of 1994/5 Martin spent most of his spare time preparing the lower half of their garden for his plant nursery. There was a long line of large old oak trees that stretched from the country park and right up between the large gardens of Hazel's road and the adjoining gardens of the houses in the nicknamed 'Millionaire's Row' of Benfleet Road (because that is what the enormous mansions were worth, even years ago). Their gardens were approximately the same length as Martin and Hazel's but about double the width. No one was overlooked and squirrels chased along from tree to tree. Martin built a line of compost bins either side of their oak tree. About midway down the north side of their garden, so it didn't block the light, was a large, graceful weeping willow. Hazel's tree guy, Robin, pruned it back to ensure it didn't swamp the garden. From the willow Martin planted out a row of yew trees across the garden as hedging, with a small gap for a path big enough for a wide wheelbarrow. Once the yews were large enough Hazel would train the two on either side of the path to form an arch. This hedge would hide the nursery from the house.

After getting official permission from the council to use the land as a private nursery Martin laid the whole of the lower area with permeable black landscaping sheet to stop weeds and, with Hazel's help, erected an eleven-metres long polytunnel. Again with Hazel's help, he extended the concrete area that the existing shed and greenhouse stood on, to make room for two more greenhouses that, fitted together, were seven metres long. This gave him plenty of covered space to grow hardy perennial plants that, under cover, would not need artificial heat.

Hazel had a large collection of plants in pots that she had lifted from her Leigh garden and then added to while living in Shoebury. The vendor of their present house, fortunately, had been willing to allow Hazel and Martin to move all these plants into the garden before their actual moving date. After making a rough plan of the garden area nearest the house Hazel dug out sweeping flower beds. Edwina had bought Hazel, when they were still in Bonchurch, a stunning white flowering *Magnolia stellata*. Hazel placed it at the centre of a circular bed and surrounded it with various coloured day lilies. She then split most of the perennial plants and gave half to Martin to split further for his nursery. The following year the ones she planted in the garden would have grown into large enough clumps for Martin to lift and divide many times. Thus, the garden area became the stock beds for Martin's nursery. It gave them a great excuse to travel to the renowned Beth Chatto garden in Suffolk to buy some unusual perennials. With the composted manure and blood, fish and bone that Hazel planted them in, they would soon clump up for Martin to split ready for sale and for Hazel to use in her plans.

Scott was only three months old when Martin returned from work with the news that a local MP had rung the council and asked if someone would like to design his new garden. Martin suggested he recommend that Hazel did the design, as it was not something the council could directly involve themselves with – if she was okay with that? At Martin's suggestion she hadn't worked, other than on the house, since their move. Now she felt the need for something more stimulating – and the bedroom under the mezzanine made a great office.

The MP agreed that Hazel design his large garden and he enthusiastically showed her around on her first visit. He loved his garden and wished he had more time to work on it. Hazel had a series of design questions and she measured up the space and used the camcorder to record its current state. Then, over cups of tea, they sat around a table with his wife so that Hazel could go through the photos in her ideas album. She asked them to point out the pictures that most highlighted the type of garden they were looking for. After ascertaining their budget, Hazel asked them to give her three weeks to come up with a plan, explaining that she would imagine living in their garden for a week or so before she began. Then she slowly built up a design around the photos they had liked and continued to live with the new design in her mind until she was satisfied. She then took an initial pencil drawing for their approval before commencing the final copy.

Now was the time to buy the latest computer. Professional garden design software was available but it was ridiculously expensive. Hazel found a reasonably priced CD in a garden centre that allowed photos to be layered with planting. She only used it a couple of times as her clients seemed to get a good idea from the combination of Hazel's plan and her verbal description as she walked her fingers around the plan for them. A complete list of the planting was included as a numbered key on the side. But Hazel just loved computers and one was necessary for the paperwork, which Martin took control of, much to Hazel's relief.

Whenever Hazel or Martin were outside, Scott was warmly wrapped up in his pram under the swaying branches of the willow, with the birds for company. Hazel did regularly walk him up to the shops or into the country park and they enjoyed walking in Belfairs woods with Martin and stopping for a coffee at the café. But, with their large house and garden, it wasn't necessary to go out daily, as it had been when Robbie was little. The supermarket was at the top of the road so it was quick to take the van up for a weekly shop. With disposable nappies, a washing machine, even a tumble dryer (for occasional use when the space above the boiler was full of drying baby stuff), domesticity was almost a breeze twenty years on. Hazel told herself that keeping the large house clean and the garden weed-free, on top of designing and planting gardens for others, would keep her fit.

Hazel was not able to resist a few hours on the beach on pleasant days when the afternoon tide was warmed as it rolled over the sun-baked mud up to the sandy beach. Occasionally, Robbie, Annie and Justine would meet them on Chalkwell beach for a picnic lunch. Having her two sons together was always wonderful. It still rocked Hazel's mothering instinct that the two brothers had twenty years between them. For eighteen years Robbie had been so closely tied to her life. Even when he was away at camp or with his father, he was in her head. Now she had to separate her maternal instincts into one for a mature adult, one for a baby. She still missed Robbie when he wasn't there.

Four months after Scott's birth, the planning and plant buying for the MP's garden was complete. During the following four weekends Martin, with Hazel's help, cleared all the large weedy areas and dug out the overgrown shrubs, which Hazel heaped into the van and took to a green waste plant in Shoebury. Then she laid out all the plants as per her plan and together they completed the planting. Edwina had Scott on those Saturdays and Hazel took him with them on Sundays. It all went smoothly and Martin and Hazel knew that working together was the perfect option. Scott would fit into their lives without requiring outside childcare. But they needed a second vehicle if they were to do this full time, to allow Hazel to leave early if Scott became fractious or if she needed to do some housework. Michael mentioned that his mechanic, who specialised in Toyotas, lived and worked near them in Hadleigh. He was the obvious choice to service their van and he found them a Toyota Tercel 4WD Estate.

Edwina came across an advert for a five-day break in a caravan in Suffolk in the spring and she offered to pay for them to have a much-needed respite. Hazel and Martin agreed to go if Edwina would come too. Hazel's relationship with her mother had been pretty good since Hazel had first married and moved out of the family home all those years ago and she and Robbie had enjoyed her company so much in Jersey. But living together in the confines of a caravan didn't work – even for those five days. Hazel was not the tidiest of people but her mother was worse. When Edwina offered to do the washing-up, Hazel would have to re-wash a large portion. Her father had always complained about that. Bags of shopping were just put down, anywhere, with no attempt to put the stuff away. And her mother talked in depth about how she disagreed with the way Michael's wife fed their children a poor vegetarian diet and didn't stick to regular bedtimes. When watching the television she would make unnecessary and often racist remarks. Constant little irritations. Edwina only offered to babysit once, when Hazel and Martin mentioned going for a walk along the coast. Hazel does blame herself, though, because she surely would have been pleased to babysit more if she had only asked. For the first time ever, Hazel was glad to return home from a holiday. Martin had not been unduly upset by his mother-in-law's company, and suggested it was more a clash of personalities. Hazel didn't disagree.

Six months after Scott was born, Hazel fell pregnant again. She and Martin had decided not to bother with contraception – just in case there was a chance of another baby – not expecting it to happen this quickly. She felt fit and fully recovered from Scott's birth but lost the pregnancy at ten weeks. She was disappointed, as much for Martin as for herself. She had the second child she had so desperately wanted but Martin had confided that he would like a daughter, if it was at all possible.

Following the miscarriage she was told that, apart from her age, there was no reason why she might not have another baby. Six months after the miscarriage she was pregnant again. Then, again, at ten weeks she miscarried. Realistically, thought Hazel, life cannot be perfect and up on her beautiful plateau all was still too good to feel real grief. Her GP actually suggested fertility treatment but she had accepted that another baby wasn't to be and Martin agreed that he didn't want the hassle of such treatment. Robbie had told his mother that he had never missed having a brother or sister. Hazel hoped Scott would feel the same.

They got a few more jobs through the council, including redesigning and planting a garden for the mayor. In between jobs, while Scott had his afternoon nap and during the evenings, Hazel managed to decorate the downstairs and build two sets of shelving from floor to ceiling. One set in the front lounge for all their books and the second in the dining area for the hi-fi and all their records. At last, she no longer had to stare at piles of books and records across the floor.

In January of the following year they put their business in the *Yellow Advertiser* and Martin handed in his notice. That year Hazel designed forty-one gardens and all but two of those clients wanted Martin and Hazel to implement the design themselves. Ruth and Lionel had a landscaper pave a large area around their house. The quality was impressive and they recommended him highly. Luke was a similar age to Martin and agreed to do all the hard landscaping that Hazel planned. She'd used two landscapers previously but it had always been difficult to ensure they met the design exactly as she had envisaged. She had no such problems with Luke.

On most dry Sundays, Hazel and Martin sold large numbers of Martin's plants at boot sales. Once their stall was set up Hazel wheeled

Scott around searching for good quality educational toys and books so there was always plenty to occupy him. It was an incredibly busy year. Word of their business had spread and they stopped advertising, apart from the board they displayed when selling plants.

While his parents worked hard, life for Scott was pretty idyllic as he always had at least one parent or grandmother 'on tap'. He was teething at two months but as long as soothing Bonjela gel was rubbed into his gums it was not a problem and, exactly like Robbie, he had six teeth at six months. He didn't crawl but shuffled on his bottom almost as soon as he could sit up and by one, again like Robbie, was walking and talking with a large vocabulary.

After his first Christmas, Hazel introduced him to the weekly local mother and toddler group. He faltered. The hall was full of shouting, shrieking, crying, small people, who were running and rushing around the many tables, attractively laid out with various pots of Play-Doh, building bricks, jigsaws and drawing and painting activities. More little people were scooting around on cars and tricycles, honking horns and ringing bells. Bewildered, Scott remained quietly by his mother's side.

Over many weeks Hazel gently coaxed him, never letting go of his hand unless he pulled it from her to spend time playing on the quieter tables, until, as long as Hazel was with him, he relaxed enough to spend time at all the activity tables. He always enjoyed the final part of the morning when the mothers all sat round in a large circle, with their toddlers on their laps, to sing and mime songs. He continued to avoid the slides, sit-on cars and tricycles. To boost his confidence Hazel bought a slide for their garden from a boot sale and built a sand pit just outside the French doors. He had his own sit-on car and was very outgoing in his own space with the toddlers he knew from Hazel's antenatal group. For a few weeks he needed Hazel to hold his hand and guide him up the steps of the ladder of his own slide before he would attempt it alone. Then, at mother and toddler group, he began to go down the slide providing no other children were near it, although often it wasn't until his mother went down the slide herself that he would follow. It took a full year of gentle encouragement and coaxing from his mother before he was as confident as the other toddlers.

Even as a very young tot, Scott had a habit of telling Martin what to do, such as not coming into the house with his shoes on, or which end of the sofa he should sit on; and he would tease and chase Guinness, then block the cat flap so the poor cat couldn't escape from the wretched toddler. Otherwise, though, he was unusually good and would only need to be told once not to do something. Towards bedtime, however, when he was getting tired, he would get silly, which was far from his normal character. He became overactive and did daft stuff, such as deliberately walking in a wonky way or dancing about as he went up the stairs. A bath, full of bath toys from boot sales, would calm him and Hazel, who would not leave a young child alone in the bath, loved joining in the play.

But not every night. She was too tired. On the evenings he didn't have a bath, he stood on a plastic toddler stool at the sink in the bathroom and Hazel would help him to wash his hands, feet, bottom and teeth. One evening he was refusing to stand still on the stool, insisting on dancing about, even though Hazel had repeatedly asked him to stop. She explained that if he slipped he would probably bash his jaw on the sink and it would be incredibly painful, especially as his teeth might split his lip. Hazel had never needed to smack Scott but she was at a loss as to what to do with her normally sensible son. By now Hazel was kneeling on the floor behind him, attempting to get him to hold a foot up long enough for her to wash it. She was failing and her patience had run out. She told him she would smack him if he didn't stop. He chose to ignore her. She slapped his leg. Scott immediately swung around and slapped his mother, hard, across the face. Harder than she had smacked him! Stunned, Hazel quietly stood up. Scott had stopped dancing. He had made his point. He then allowed Hazel to finish washing him. Hazel never attempted to smack him again. Her little son had taught her a lesson.

Interestingly, neither Robbie nor Scott showed any signs of the 'terrible twos'. Was this because their language was advanced enough for them to explain their frustrations? Or because they understood Hazel when she explained the consequences of their bad behaviour? She doesn't know the answer. It just didn't happen.

Cornwall became a regular, twice-yearly holiday to see Martin's family, usually around Easter and in September. They only went for a week each time as Martin was worried about watering his plants. He told Hazel that irrigation systems were unreliable. Fortunately, their next-door neighbour offered not only to drop in each day to feed Guinness and the tortoise but also to water the plants a couple of times. He was a fireman at the local Hadleigh fire station and assured them he would be pleased to help them out.

Martin's parents wanted to see as much of their grandson as possible and suggested Hazel, Martin and Scott camp in their back garden. To keep down the cost of the long drive Martin and Hazel took the van, as diesel was much cheaper than petrol then. It was always a welcome break and Scott was regularly amused by Kathy and Nathan with various games, which allowed Hazel and Martin to go for walks along the coast, to visit many of the beautiful gardens or to simply enjoy time together. Sue kept guinea pigs, an added fascination for the toddler. With the tent positioned right by the door to the lounge, the couple were able to relax in the evenings, watching films or videos while their son slept in his camp bed with the baby monitor on.

Martin's family would also visit them twice a year, although, as Sue's anorexia was going through a particularly bad time, they only spent the days with them, returning to a Travelodge after dinner.

They also visited for a few days around Scott's christening, which Hazel and Martin hadn't got around to organising until he was eighteen months old. Hazel had finally traced the vicar who had married them but was told that she didn't do christenings as she had a phobia of young children and babies. Fair enough, thought Hazel. Having been married in a United Reform Church, the one in Hadleigh seemed a good choice and the family attended their Christingle service just before Scott's first Christmas and were impressed by the friendly atmosphere.

They had argued about who should be godparents though. Hazel, contrary to what her mother thought, believed Michael and his wife were good parents. And when Robbie was little, although he wasn't christened, it was understood that if anything happened to either set of parents, the other would look after the orphans. Martin said that if they were Hazel's choice, for the other two godparents his choice would be Sue and his cousin Tom. Unfortunately, Sue's worsening anorexia meant she was in a very fragile state, both mentally and physically, and Hazel wasn't sure she would be well enough to attend the service. She also voiced her thoughts on whether she would make a reliable godparent. Hazel thought Robbie would be a better choice. But Martin wouldn't agree to having three people from Hazel's family and only one from his. He spoke to his parents, who confirmed that Sue really wanted to be a godmother and that they would ensure she was well enough to be present. It hurt Hazel that Robbie would not be a godparent but Martin won the argument by pointing out that being a brother meant he was closer than a godparent anyway.

Scott did understand that a church was where people went to pray and sing songs to God. Hazel believes he understood his mother when she explained she thought that God stood for all that was good in the world and that by having Scott baptised into a church, his mummy and daddy were promising to bring him up with an understanding of the difference between good and bad.

But what should an eighteen-month-old boy wear for his christening? Hazel saw a child's bow tie in Mothercare depicting differently coloured faces of boys from across the globe against a white background, with some wearing gaily coloured scarves or hats. They also sold Fair Isle cardigans with all the same colours, including a rich blue, and Hazel bought corduroy trousers in that blue. A white shirt completed his outfit.

Hazel held Scott in her arms throughout the short service. He listened quietly to all that was said. Hazel was so pleased they had waited for this christening. Scott would not remember it but at the time he seemed to be fully aware of what was happening. He certainly enjoyed the attention from the large party of friends and family who came back to his house afterwards.

Lieselotte's health was failing and she was now in a care home near Maidenhead, so had not been at the christening. Edwina had travelled by train to see her a couple of times, but Hazel had not seen her since she'd driven up for the day with Robbie and Edwina. After Hazel chatted on the phone to Arthur and told him how she had missed Lieselotte, he suggested they come and meet him at the home. He'd been working and had not made the christening either.

Hazel, Martin and Scott arrived a little earlier than expected and then received a call from Arthur saying he had been held up and would be late. Hazel was not prepared to find her bright and intelligent step-grandmother so very frail. She did recognise Hazel but was rather confused by Martin and Scott. They had taken a bag full of toys for Scott to play with but after a couple of hours he was getting bored. Hazel was at a loss on how to converse any further with Lieselotte, who'd worn hearing aids for years but was now not wearing any, which made it hard for Hazel to make herself understood and wore her out.

Arthur still didn't appear and Hazel couldn't get him on the phone. After hugging and kissing Lieselotte they left. Arthur rang them later that evening, unable to understand why they hadn't waited for him. He couldn't comprehend that a fractious toddler was no fun for anyone. In all, it was a strange and sad day. As a child Hazel had found Lieselotte's German accent bewildering but as an adult Hazel had loved her dearly and it was the first time she had been confronted with such frailty. Lieselotte died a couple of months later.

Robbie and Annie had mentioned a while back that they were thinking of getting married, but plans were put on hold when Annie found out she was pregnant. Unfortunately, she miscarried within the first few months. Hazel thought then that they might go ahead with their wedding plans. She still held the belief, albeit tentatively, that it was best to have a child within a marriage. But the disappointed couple decided to try again. Baby Tara delighted everybody when she was born on May Day 1997. Hazel was captivated. A grandmother at forty-four to a darling baby girl. Unfortunately, their business meant there was very little spare time to babysit her granddaughter but Robbie and Annie would regularly drop in with the baby. Scott, at two, was lovingly gentle with his niece, and proud when his mother explained he was very lucky to be an uncle at such a young age.

CHAPTER 25
1997 ◇ Spain and Nursery

Hazel's Uncle Jack had begun to feature in her life again. He'd divorced and remarried. Jenny, his new wife, was only a couple of years older than Hazel and had lost her mother when she was very young and been brought up in a children's home. Jenny warmed to Edwina and encouraged a closer link between her husband and sister-in-law. Jack, for years now, had made a living buying and doing up old properties. He had invited Edwina to visit them at a beautiful lock cottage he had recently restored in the Cotswolds. She was enthusiastic about her stay. This encouraged Hazel, Martin and Scott to also take up an invite when it came.

It was an enchanting week spent eating, drinking, relaxing, chatting and laughing as they watched the barges pass by. Jack explained that he and Jenny had almost completed building their 'castle' up in the mountains above Tossa de Mar in Spain. In the photos he showed them the imposing white, turreted and crenellated building that did, indeed, look like a castle. Jack needed some help with the sprawling garden and asked whether Hazel and Martin could spend a week there with them the following year to bring some order to the grounds and add some exotic planting. They agreed they would.

It was May when they loaded the van with some suitable planting. Not wishing to spend money on overnight stops, they squeezed in their double blow-up camping mattress and a lilo for Scott. With pillows and sleeping bags it would be comfortable enough for one night each way. A cooked chicken with cold potatoes, salad, egg sandwiches, plenty of crisps and biscuits, plus a gas burner to make fresh cups of tea or coffee, made them self-sufficient. The drive to Dover and the ferry over to Calais were uneventful, as was the drive around Paris to just beyond Clermont- Ferrand, where they pulled off into a small side road to spend the night.

It was unfortunate that Scott had a cold because this often affected his stomach and made him vomit, usually just once. He was fine until ten miles before they reached the castle. He had been saying for a few miles that his tummy hurt but Hazel was hoping they would arrive before the inevitable happened. They didn't and he was sick all down himself. Using a towel and loads of wet wipes Scott was cleaned up as much as possible and given a change of clothes, ready for an enthusiastic welcome from Jack and Jenny. As usual, this stomach evacuation heralded the end of the cold and left Scott fully recovered to enjoy his holiday.

Jenny had mentioned that friends would be staying at the same time and that they had a little boy who, although he was five and two years older than Scott, was smaller. That was irrelevant to the two boys who, once safely fitted with inflatable armbands, spent hours playing with water-pistols around the swimming pool or pushing small toy trucks through the undergrowth. All interspersed with games of hide and seek.

Jack had designed his castle with a basement and two, separate, ground-floor apartments to allow his children to stay at any time, with he and Jenny living on the first floor. Each apartment had two bedrooms, with a double bed in one and two singles in the other, so Scott had his own room.

As Hazel believed sleep was crucial to both her and, particularly, Martin with his migraines, they had never allowed Scott to sleep in their bed, apart from that very first night. He was content to sleep in this strange bedroom as long as Teddy was with him. Brown, furry and about thirty centimetres high he'd been bought by Kathy and Nathan when Scott was born.

During their third evening, while Martin and Hazel were upstairs enjoying drinks with Jack and Jenny, they were startled by a cacophony of dogs, barking all around them. Jack explained that most of the surrounding villas were holiday homes and that guard dogs were used in each property to protect them when they were empty. Unfortunately, if one dog was upset it set them all off. Hazel rushed downstairs knowing that Scott was frightened whenever a little dog opposite them at home barked, expecting him to have been woken by this horrendous noise. She quietly opened her son's bedroom door and tiptoed over to his bed to find him sound asleep. Amazing! She remained downstairs, with his bedroom door slightly ajar, checking him regularly until the barking subsided. He didn't stir.

However, he must have been subconsciously aware because the following night he refused to go to sleep. Martin read him his bedtime story and Scott uncharacteristically clung to him as he called Hazel in to kiss him goodnight. When they both went to leave his room he began to cry. Hazel lifted him out of bed and sat him on her lap. She asked whether he had had a nightmare the previous evening. Scott said he didn't remember having one and wasn't able to explain why he didn't want to be left alone. Hazel told him about the dogs barking last night and explained that perhaps this had permeated his brain. She went on to reassure him that he was completely safe here, from everything, including dogs, and that Mummy and Daddy would keep his door open and would not leave their bedroom next door until Scott was awake and up in the morning. But he would not be consoled. It was several hours and books later that, exhausted, he fell asleep. The following evening he was also reluctant to be left to sleep. Hazel firmly reassured him that they would stay downstairs and quietly watch TV next door, so he was totally safe. Eventually he did fall asleep by himself.

Martin and Hazel worked most of that week, only having the chance to relax in the evenings when they all (Scott included) retired to the roof of the 'castle' to enjoy a finely cooked barbecue with Jack as chef. On a couple of evenings they all went out to local restaurants.

They did have a delightful day with Jenny when she took them via train to Barcelona. They caught the hop-on, hop-off bus for a tour of the city. Scott, having carried Teddy to many places, knew exactly how tightly to hold his bear. Hazel was confident that her son would take care not to lose his dearest companion. Jenny, though, was worried; on the top of the open bus, on the Port Cable car, everywhere, she thought Teddy was bound to get dropped and lost. But Teddy remained firmly clamped in Scott's arms and, in spite of Jenny's concerns, survived Spain and is still around today.

Hazel was fascinated as the bus took them past the beautiful curved and undulating stonework of Gaudi's La Pedrera and was surprised that she'd not heard of the architect before. Then La Sagrada Familia came into view. The unique, bold, towering fantasy captured Hazel and she coaxed Martin to climb the 300 or more tightly curling steps inside one of the towers to peer down on miniature Jenny with tiny Scott resting in his pushchair.

They also had a trip to a local garden centre to supplement the plants they'd brought. The gardens, front and back, looked impressive. It had definitely been a working holiday and as they said their farewells Hazel and Martin wondered where the week had gone.

Martin and Hazel lived within the catchment area for Hadleigh Junior School. Reputedly a good school with an attached state nursery. Hazel received an offer of a place for Scott in the nursery, for the mornings, after Easter. He was three years and four months old. His understanding and speech, as with Robbie, stood out above his contemporaries and was often remarked upon by other mothers. He knew all the colours and numbers up to a hundred. Through the ABC song he had memorised at mother and toddler group, he could recognise the alphabet and was able to read basic words. His confidence around strange children had also matured. He now enjoyed all company and was looking forward to nursery.

Hazel, knowing how much she would miss her son, made the decision to bring Scott into bed with her on his first morning for a quiet fifteen minutes as Martin got up, so that Scott could read to her. Relaxed together, it became a precious time that would soon put Scott's reading age two years ahead.

Parents were allowed to come into the new class with their children and stay as long as they felt necessary to get their child settled. Once inside the classroom, Scott immediately left his mother to explore. Hazel stood for ten minutes watching her son confidently playing with the other children before she asked him if he was happy for her to go.

"Yes, go," he said, as he continued to play with spades and coloured moulds in a large tray of sand with a little girl.

Hazel planted a kiss on her son's cheek and left, relieved that her sensitive child was relaxed enough to let her go. When she collected him at the end of the day he told her he had made friends with a little boy named Water.

"Do you mean, as in water that comes out of a tap?" she asked.

"Yes, that's it," confirmed her son.

The following morning he said she didn't need to come into class with him. Each day he was able to relate to his parents details of at least two activities and Water's name was regularly mentioned. After a few weeks Hazel asked his teacher to clarify this strange name.

"Ah, that's Walter," his teacher told her.

Hazel tracked down Walter's mother in the playground and invited her, Walter and his baby brother round one afternoon. Walter and Scott amused each other with the large assortment of toys, accrued mainly from boot sales. The mums got on well with each other – female friends were now invaluable.

Hazel was aware that Scott had always soaked up everything that was going on around him. As they regularly had the television on for the news at breakfast and at six o'clock there was ample opportunity for him to watch world happenings unfold and he would discuss whatever caught his attention. As a toddler he was enchanted whenever Princess Diana was featured. He saw the starving and underprivileged children she visited and seemed to understand the charity work she was doing. He was as stunned as his parents the morning they learnt she had died. When he returned from nursery one day he reported that most of the other children had not even known who Princess Di was.

CHAPTER 26
1978 ◊ Trauma at Robbie's Wedding

Scott was just four when Robbie and Annie asked if he would be a pageboy at their wedding. Delighted by the idea of walking down the aisle with Tara and Justine as bridesmaids, the little boy said yes. No one could have predicted what would happen on the day.

It began poorly for Scott. He vomited up all his breakfast. Knowing how much her son had been looking forward to dressing up as a pageboy for his brother's wedding, Hazel didn't think it could be due to nerves. Scott assured his parents he wanted to go. Robbie had agreed to collect Scott that morning as he had to pick up Annie's mum. Apprehensively, Hazel kissed her sons goodbye. Robbie said not to worry, he would be well looked after.

Hazel and Martin picked up Edwina on the way to the United Reform Church in Southend. It was a glorious July day and the wedding service was perfect. Scott and Tara walked demurely behind Justine as she followed her mother and grandfather down the aisle. As they gathered after the service Annie mentioned that Scott had been sick once at their house and then actually in the wedding car on the way, but having had the forethought to provide him with a bag it hadn't been a problem.

The wedding reception was at The Freight House in Rochford. It sat on an imposing hill above the lake where Hazel used to take her newspaper to temporarily escape the horror of the psychiatric unit. That was all far from her mind on this day and, after the photographs were taken, she was relieved to notice that some colour had returned to Scott's cheeks and he was able to eat a little at the wedding breakfast. Following the speeches, most of the guests, including Hazel and Martin, moved to tables and chairs on a large patio area outside to enjoy the sunshine. Two-year-old Tara had fallen asleep on Annie's mum's lap. Scott was running around the outside tables with Justine and several other children.

Finally able to relax and take pleasure in the fact that the day had been successful, despite Scott being ill, Hazel didn't immediately notice that the children had all disappeared. Gentle adult chatter permeated her senses, causing her to realise the lack of noisy kids. There were people with children in the distance, down by the lake, but she instinctively knew her son would not go far from his parents without informing them. She rose from her seat and told Martin she was going inside to check on Scott. There were no children inside. Attempting to push down a rising panic she rushed back to Martin.

"He's not inside," she threw at him. Sensing her alarm, he stood up. He'd just seen Justine and some of the other children running up the hill. Hazel turned to follow his gaze. Scott was not with them.

"He can't be far," he tried to reassure her as they waited for Justine to come puffing past them. He asked her if she had seen Scott.

"No, he's not with us," she stated.

Martin said he would ask around outside, if Hazel would check the toilets and ask everyone inside. As Hazel ran through the hall and found Annie and Robbie, she attempted to keep the alarm from her voice, not wanting to upset their very special day. But they'd not seen him. Edwina was sitting with Annie's mum but they'd not seen him either. Hazel dashed to the toilets, panting, sure though that he wouldn't be there. In the ladies' toilets she called Scott's name to the closed cubicles. No one answered. Outside the men's toilets she asked a gentleman if he could check inside for a little boy, her heart battering wildly as she waited for his answer. Receiving the negative she expected, she ran back to Martin, her legs no longer belonging to her, as her mind desperately searched for a plausible answer to his disappearance. One that meant he was safe. She thought of none. Outside she found Martin, his face white.

"No one's seen him," he confirmed.

One last child was making his way up the hill. It was ginger-haired Joe, Justine's close friend. As he reached the top Martin asked if he had seen Scott. "Yes, he's down in the train tunnel."

"Please, we don't know where that is. Can you show us?" said Hazel. She abandoned her heeled shoes to follow as Martin sped off behind Joe.

It was wooded at the bottom of the hill and as she made her way through the trees she saw Joe, holding Scott's hand, emerge from a large grass-covered hump, presumably a tunnel, just as Martin reached them. Hazel rushed to Scott and scooped him up into her arms as tears of relief poured down her face.

"Are you alright?"

But her pale child didn't answer and Hazel felt him shivering.

"Did someone take you there?" Hazel asked, alarmed that her son was speechless.

Sensing his trauma, Hazel hurried up the hill and straight into the hall with Martin close behind her. Feeling he wouldn't want any fuss around him she remembered seeing a long bench in the reception area, just the other side of the hall. She lowered him on to it. He lay down, still shivering. Martin sat down next to him. Hazel felt his forehead; he was burning up.

"Would you like a drink of water or orange juice, Scott?"

He weakly shook his head in answer. Edwina appeared and asked what had happened. Hazel only said that he'd gone to play down by the train tunnel and had begun to feel ill again. She added that given his high temperature they would probably have to go home.

"Oh Scott, you poor little thing and you were such a great page boy. What a shame." Edwina gave him a kiss then asked Martin, "Can you drop me home, on your way?"

Half an hour later when Scott was no better, Hazel retrieved her shoes and went to apologise to the bride and groom and explained that, as Scott now had a high temperature they should go home, meaning that, sadly, they would miss the evening party. And it did upset Hazel that she had to give preference to her younger son on a day that belonged to her elder son.

Scott did brighten up a little at home and a dose of Calpol lowered his temperature. He did say that a boy with brown hair had carried him down into the tunnel and told him he must stay there. He could say no more than that. The following day he was his normal, smiling self and there were never any signs that the experience had damaged him. Hazel hoped that the rest of his life was so safe and secure that this one negative instance would soon be swallowed by all the positives. Edwina went down with a tummy bug two days after the wedding, confirming Hazel's belief that it wasn't nerves that had caused Scott to be unwell.

Robbie and Annie went to the Isle of Wight for their honeymoon, in a caravan, and took Justine and Tara. Hazel called in to see them when they arrived back home. Robbie and Annie told Hazel about the freezing night-time temperatures and the food poisoning they'd all suffered from (although, maybe it was Scott's tummy bug!) but did say they'd actually had a good time. Hazel then took the opportunity to tell Robbie and Annie exactly what had happened to Scott at the wedding. They had no idea who the brown-haired boy might have been, or how to respond. Undoubtedly, if it had not been her son's wedding, she would have reported it to the police, simply to make them aware that it had happened. She did suggest that, while it may have been the son of one of their friends, it was, hopefully, no more than a childish prank.

That September, when Scott went to the infants school, he befriended Poppy. A pretty little girl with a round face and bouncing black curls. Scott and Walter remained friends and, if Hazel was working on a job, Walter's mum would take Scott back to their house until Hazel was able to collect him. Poppy's mum would obligingly sometimes do the same. Hazel reciprocated by having them to tea on various occasions. At the end of the school year Hazel and Martin attended a parents' evening to discuss Scott's progress. His teacher repeated what they had been told by his final nursery teacher, that Scott was a model pupil. Then she extended this by describing how closely Scott and Poppy supported each other in class. How Scott was immediately able to recognise when Poppy was struggling with something and would offer encouraging advice. His teacher concluded by saying, "If all the boys in the world were like Scott, the world would be a different place!"

They laughed together at this possibility, what else could they do? Surely it was not an unusual remark to make about any kind little boy?

But over the ensuing few days this remark kept jumping into Hazel's thoughts. Even before she fell pregnant, Hazel had told Martin about all that had happened following the misdiagnosis of bronchitis. After Scott was born Kathy mentioned to Martin that she had dreamt that Scott was a special child, although Martin was unable to relay the contents of his mother's dream. In this context it felt astonishing for Scott's teacher to make such a remark. Even Edwina had remarked that Scott was unusual.

"He seems to support old-fashioned values," she had said.

Hazel had not asked her to explain this as she presumed her mother was referring to his quiet, courteous intelligence. Hazel now thought that, regardless of what she may or may not have been told when she was ill, she should consider that, compared to his contemporaries, he was different. Certainly, he appeared to cope with everything he saw on the television with an insight beyond his years.

This line of thinking made no difference to Hazel, however, regarding how she progressed with parenting. Ever since he had started to walk Scott had refused to hold his mother's hand when outside, forcing her to buy a set of reins for him. To Hazel's surprise, Edwina said she had not had any problems getting Scott to hold her hand, when she sometimes collected him from school. He only complained if she didn't walk on the road side of the pavement, because he said she was not doing a good enough job of protecting him from being run over! This showed Hazel how independent her little son was growing.

CHAPTER 27
2000 ◊ The Millennium

The year 2000 loomed with preparations for great revelry. Martin's parents mentioned that there was going to be a big party in their village. Their neighbour would be away visiting her daughter and was very happy for Martin and Hazel to stay in her empty bungalow for the week beginning 30 December. This would allow Scott to enjoy a little party at home with his friends on the afternoon of his birthday on 29 December, followed by an early evening get-together with all his family. Then, at five the following morning they trundled off in the van down to Cornwall. As always, Kathy and Nathan greeted them with coffee followed by a cold lunch before they made themselves comfy in the neighbour's cosy bungalow across the road.

The following morning their plans were overturned. Scott awoke feeling very unwell and with a high temperature. Hazel had brought a bottle of Calpol, which she dosed him with as she made up the sofa with pillows and blankets so he could watch the television if he wanted too. Not that he felt like doing anything other than sleeping. Hazel suspected it might be flu as it had been going around his school. The following day Martin and Hazel both woke with aching limbs and high temperatures. It was a wretched week for them all and they obviously did not attend any celebrations. It was fortunate that Kathy and Nathan could supply them with food, but they never stayed long, not wanting to catch it themselves. Although Scott was beginning to recover by the time they had to leave, Martin and Hazel still felt ill and weak and weren't looking forward to the long drive home. Exactly how they managed it, even with the many service station breaks, is beyond her. They had been dangerously stupid to attempt it.

They returned home on 7 January and were booked to complete a job on 10 January. The client had recently lost her policeman husband to a brain tumour and had wanted to demonstrate to her son, who was visiting her for Christmas, that she was coping by getting the mess in her garden sorted. But she'd only contacted Martin and Hazel at the beginning of December. They already had two other gardens to complete at the time so they had reluctantly agreed to complete the rear garden before Christmas, which involved installing a waterfall feature, with the proviso that they would return after Christmas to plant up the front garden. Hazel wanted to defer the job for a week but Martin was worried that a forecasted freezing spell might delay it even further. He knew that Hazel must not over-exert herself until she was completely recovered but he said all he needed her to do was drop Scott at school and then lay out the plants, ready for him to plant, before going home. He should have been able to do this himself using the plan and it exasperated Hazel that, even with his experience, he was not able to visualise the final size of a plant and would often put some plants far too close together. His argument was that he only ever planted up for immediate impact, such as for Southend's yearly stand at the Chelsea Flower Show or planting up the Civic Centre once a year for 'Mayor Making', in preparation for the new mayor's inauguration. Knowing Hazel would replant until she was happy, he now ensured she always laid the plants out herself.

The morning of 10 January was cold but sunny. Hazel took a dose of a maximum strength cold and flu relief and wasn't feeling too bad. By the time she arrived at the job Martin had got most of the plants out of the van and once she had positioned the plants, exactly as per her plan, he told her to go home. But she could see Martin was still unwell himself. Besides, she wanted to enjoy the sunshine. Hazel told Martin she felt alright and would help him for a while.

She always made sure she wasn't cold in the winter by piling on warm layers over thermals (including thermal long johns). Digging holes, partially filling them with manure, blood, fish and bone, mixed with a little soil before laying in the plant and refilling the hole, always warmed her up within minutes, allowing her to shed at least one layer. They always had a flask of hot water to make tea or coffee, although, if the client was at home, as was the case in this instance, they were offered plenty of extra drinks. They also always had food.

At mid-morning, Martin again told Hazel to go home but she stubbornly continued. She genuinely didn't feel that bad, certainly not compared to the previous ten days. It wasn't until after they'd eaten lunch in the van that she went home. Martin was able to complete the rest of the planting in the afternoon. Hazel was relieved to be home and rested until she collected Scott from school. Then, once dinner had been cooked and eaten and Scott was tucked into bed, she had a bath and went to bed. Followed soon after by Martin.

It was around four or five in the morning that Hazel woke with severe cramp in her left foot. She got up and hobbled downstairs, attempting to clear it. Minutes passed as she walked up and down between the front and back lounges several times. But it was getting worse. Hazel looked down at her foot and saw that her big toe and the next two were bent upwards at a ninety-degree angle. Wondering how on earth her foot had managed to do that, she bent down to try and straighten her toes. A shaft of dizziness shot through her body. Clamping her toes, she crumpled to the floor, her breath coming in fast rasps. Nausea welled up and she was suddenly reminded of how she'd felt just before her seizure. She remembered that she'd told herself that if she ever felt like that again she must not lie down but instead sit on a step out in the fresh air and take some slow deep breaths.

She struggled to her feet, found the key to the back door on the kitchen worktop, unlocked the door and sat out on the step, breathing slowly and deeply. After about ten minutes she began to feel less likely to pass out. She drank some water and went upstairs to wake Martin. She explained what had just happened and said she was too frightened to lie down and wondered whether they should ring for a doctor. Martin, not pleased with his wife for not heeding him when he'd told her to go home, got out of bed and rang the emergency number given by the surgery's answerphone. After taking their details Martin was told a doctor would be there in about an hour. Hazel had on her warm winter dressing gown, but was shivering. Martin got her some warm clothes. Hazel asked if he could get her a scarf from the hall basket as her neck felt cold but as she wrapped it around, her neck felt strangely sensitive and she had to loosen it. Martin put the central heating on and they waited together on the sofa.

They were relieved when the doorbell finally rang. After Hazel explained her previous illness the doctor did a full check, which included testing all her reflexes. He asked whether she knew that she had no reflex in her right ankle, to which Hazel replied that it was due to damage to a disc years ago. The doctor was at a loss as to what Hazel's problem was but suggested she see her own GP first thing in the morning. A couple of hours later Hazel was able to eat a piece of toast with Scott before he got dressed for school.

Martin had managed to get an eight-thirty appointment and dropped Hazel off at the surgery before taking Scott to school, only a short distance away. The effort of getting in and out of the car made Hazel feel very dizzy and ill. As she fumbled her way to the receptionist, she said she thought she might pass out. Someone helped her to a couch in an empty room. The back was raised for Hazel to make herself as comfortable as possible but the dizziness continued. Fortunately, she didn't have to wait long before she was called. She had recently asked to change doctors within the Hadleigh surgery because, despite the surgery promising everyone their own personal GP, the doctor she had originally been assigned to had always been on holiday on the few occasions she had needed to see him. Her present GP was the senior doctor. After hearing Hazel explain her present problem that appeared to follow from the flu she'd had, he checked her breathing and pulse before declaring that she was suffering from anxiety. Hazel was so dumbfounded that she laughed.

"Do you know Dr Clive Dickens, my previous GP from when I lived in Thorpe Bay?"

"Oh yes, I know him. Your previous GP here is a close friend and they used to go sailing together."

"Ah, why am I not surprised?" retorted Hazel, but inside alarm bells were jangling. "Well, you're certainly making me feel anxious now, if you can't think of anything else it might be."

She went on to mention the diagnosis, following warm water treatment, of her overactive balance organs, but to Hazel's further consternation he just swept it aside and said that, no, they don't test balance like that.

"Well, how come a consultant and his registrar both gave the same diagnosis? It must be in my notes."

"No, there's nothing. I'll give you something to help calm you down," he said as he wrote out a prescription.

As she stumbled out to the waiting room to find Martin, she felt a whirling fear engulf her. Now she truly knew what anxiety felt like, although her understanding of it was that it had an irrational cause. Is this how her GP wished her to be viewed? As irrational? She sat in the car while Martin got her prescription. When he returned she told him that she did not believe that anxiety was the correct diagnosis. His comment was, "Well, he's the doctor."

She stared at him. Was she really to be left alone again, without any supportive understanding?

The flu that year had apparently caused an unusual number of ear problems. It seemed to Hazel that whenever she listened to the radio there was further mention of it, as well as a case of an enlarged heart and one of an enlarged brain. Probably none of this is unusual when a virus does its rounds and it may have been that Hazel's sensitivity to such news was heightened. Even more serious at this time was the reporting on Dr Harold Shipman, highlighting how easily a doctor could get away even with murder. It worried Hazel terribly that anxiety could be a great excuse to cover an underlying physical problem. Her dizziness could well be caused by nothing more sinister than a balance issue, just why couldn't her doctor at least consider it?

Hazel's beautiful plateau had crashed. No longer was she lifted above normal life. Now she was desperately trying to find a foothold on a very real, sliding world. Hazel did take the prescribed pills for a couple of days but, as they had all those years previously, they actually made her dizziness and physical illness feel worse. Not continuing them displeased Martin. But she was adamant. Interestingly, when she sat down in front of her speakers in the garden lounge, to allow herself to get lost within some relaxing music, the background beat instantly caused her to feel more nauseous. She lowered the volume but it made little difference. It seemed that the disturbance of musical waves in her ears was making her symptoms worse, because relaxing with her hi-fi, regardless of the type of music, normally completely chilled her out. How could her comforting, well-known music, promote anxiety?

At night she piled pillows behind her head. The memory of that 'pop' at the back of her skull, hung dangerously in her mind and she began to notice that she was now suffering from tinnitus, which within days became loud and constant. Worry and the ringing in her ears were making sleep difficult. Having a husband who was becoming increasingly agitated by the loss of his usually very fit and grounded wife, and who still refused to believe that a doctor could be wrong, in spite of what had previously happened, was possibly the most frightening aspect.

Hazel felt she understood where his anger stemmed from. It had been a very difficult eighteen months for Martin's family. Sue's GP had encouraged her to write about her anorexia, hoping that by delving into her past she might find the reasons behind it. Through this process Sue had slowly written a book. When she showed a draft copy to her parents they were shocked to see that she had cited her grandmother's abuse as the reason for her anorexia.

This was Kathy's mother, Elsie. Kathy and Nathan admitted that one of the reasons they had retired to Cornwall was to put as much distance between them and her as possible. Fortunately, Elsie had remained in her Leigh bungalow. Over the years they had been insidiously trapped by Elsie's dominating character. Kathy's regular weekly migraines meant that she had to retire to a darkened bedroom for at least one day a week, which gave her mother the perfect opportunity to invade the house and take over. Nathan was helpless as he knew that if he interfered it would have repercussions for Kathy. But they had no idea of the mental abuse Sue was getting from her grandmother. The anorexia began when Elsie regularly prodded Sue with the fact that she was getting fat. But Sue believed that the abuse went way back to when she was very young and would go, alone, to stay the night at her grandmother's bungalow and would not be allowed to keep her bedroom door open when she slept. Her grandmother would repeatedly close it if Sue opened it, saying that big girls didn't need to have their door open. She would then threaten Sue that if she told her parents her father would die!

There were many incidents throughout her childhood when her grandmother would force Sue to do things against her will or better judgement and Elsie continued to insist that if her father found out he would die. Sue was a very intelligent child, and one of the very few to achieve a hundred per cent pass mark for the eleven-plus, so Hazel is not sure how Elsie convinced Sue of this. She supposed it would not be difficult to convince her as a small child and then it must have become enmeshed in her psyche. Sue insisted there was evidence in a letter to her from her grandmother in which she threatened her with this while Sue was in hospital to have her tonsils out. A letter Sue apparently hid for years. Although Hazel is not certain that Martin's parents ever saw this evidence. As a forensic scientist for the Metropolitan police Nathan saw many awful child murders and mutilations, which caused him to be over-protective and nervous for his daughter, so he certainly would have been deeply disturbed by Elsie's treatment of her. In the book Sue also mentioned that the instructor who took her for driving lessons had made passes at her and would touch her leg provocatively, then threatened that he would pass a word to the testing officers if she mentioned it to anyone, and she would never pass her test.

However, when Sue gave her parents a copy of the published book it was very different to the draft. It actually said that most of her suffering had been caused by her parents not offering her any security or trying to stop the abuse. As had Martin's apparent ignorance of what was happening, which meant she had no one to turn to. She had also explained that she was aware that Martin and their cousin Tom received very different, favoured treatment from her grandmother. The book totally turned the finger of fault towards her parents and they were utterly devastated. Martin was now their one shining light that proved the family was not completely dysfunctional. But Martin had admitted to Hazel, not long after they married, that it was Hazel who had helped give him confidence. Hazel now realised how fragile his emotional strength was.

Meanwhile, Hazel returned to the doctor a week after her first visit and explained, "The pills made me feel worse and now I've got tinnitus ringing continuously in my ears. And my head feels as though it's been kicked around a football pitch! Please, it has to be more than anxiety."

"Can you run as far as Choice?" he asked – this was a clothes shop about fifty metres from the surgery.

Astounded, Hazel replied, "I can't run. Full stop. I feel so dizzy. Even if I could I would probably be sick."

She then added that listening to music also made her feel nauseous. Surely that meant it did have something to do with her ears and balance.

"Alright, make an appointment at the clinic for a blood test," and he dismissed her.

Five days later, she returned for the result and in a surprised tone he said, "The result shows you do have inflammation. However, it cannot highlight where."

"Well, probably in my head, knowing how it feels. Perhaps somewhere that's linked to my balance. But what do I know?" said Hazel.

"I'll give you a double strength antibiotic, then you can have another blood test in two weeks."

"Thank you," said Hazel as he showed her out.

Martin and Hazel had booked a week away at the end of February in Madeira, with Scott. It was a cheap break and Martin was interested in visiting the Laurisilva, the largest surviving laurel forest in the world. It was an area of outstanding natural beauty and home to a unique variety of plants and animals. Hazel was really hoping the antibiotics would work because in her present state she didn't feel well enough to go. But by the end of the course of antibiotics she felt only marginally less dizzy and was interested to hear the results of her second blood test.

"It is better," said her GP.

Slightly relieved, Hazel said, "My tinnitus is still as loud and I don't feel anywhere near a hundred per cent yet. Do you think I'll be well enough to fly to Madeira in just over a week's time?"

"Oh yes. Get away and relax," he answered.

"Would it be worth taking some Stemetil for my dizziness?"

"You do realise that it is prescribed for psychiatric illnesses? Admittedly in higher doses than you have had."

"Really?" Nothing surprised Hazel. "But it's also used for travel sickness, isn't it?"

He nodded in agreement and wrote her a prescription. As she left, Hazel wondered why he had felt the need to comment on Stemetil's other use and reflected on the tone of voice the doctor had used as he had said 'It is better'. Because she had the impression he was inferring 'than it was'. She should have asked for the exact details, compared to the original result.

Martin's fragility was thrown into focus when, four days after Hazel's first visit to the doctor, an initial free visit was booked for a new couple wanting their garden redesigned. Not knowing how long it would be before Hazel felt well enough to work again, Martin agreed to go. Dealing with the clients had always been Hazel's job, as Martin conceded she was far better at it than he. He took a video of the garden with its old crazy paved patio and filled in most of Hazel's list of questions for the brief. But when he showed this to Hazel there was nothing against an approximate budget. Martin said they were an elderly couple and he didn't think they had that much to spend, which gave Hazel no guideline as to what she could do at all.

"They must want a new patio," stated Hazel.

But Martin said that he didn't think they could afford it. On that assumption Hazel drew up a pencil design that they costed at £1,500.

Unfortunately, the elderly couple were not happy when Martin showed them the initial pencil plan and he visibly shrunk at the outcome. It highlighted that Hazel's strength lay in cultivating a rapport with clients and discovering exactly what they were hoping for; and that an approximate budget was essential. Not once had she had an unhappy client. As yet, they had no work in hand, so it was disappointing. Martin explained to the clients that his wife, who was the designer and would normally have visited, was ill. So Hazel rang them to say that, if they wished, she would make an appointment to call in when she got back from their holiday to look at it all again. They sounded pleased with this and agreed a date.

While Hazel still felt very weak, she looked forward to introducing Scott to flying. For weeks before they went Hazel had described to him what it would be like and how much she really enjoyed it. He knew that his grandfather had been in the RAF so Scott had no fear of becoming one of the many travellers he had excitedly waved at in planes, ever since he was a baby.

Once in the air, Hazel and Scott pointed out all the miniature houses, trees, mountains, boats and white fluffy clouds, as they slid by under them. Martin was amused by such enthusiasm. Hazel was glad to see him smile. She could only hope this holiday might repair the rift that had developed between herself and her husband.

The week before they flew, Madeira had hit an unseasonal high of 22°C. During their week it barely rose above 12°C. Hazel hated being cold, even when she was well, but since she hadn't packed thermals or thick wool jumpers she was cold for the whole week. Martin and Scott couldn't understand it because they were fine.

They'd booked bed and breakfast only and their small apartment didn't have cooking facilities, so Hazel was cheered by the warmth of various restaurants in the evenings. A welcome glass of glowing Madeira wine was given free at the end of every evening meal.

It was raining on the day they booked the excursion to the Laurisilva but at least Hazel was not cold, wrapped up in a hooded waterproof mac and warmed by the effort of some uphill walking, which pushed her strength to its limits. Their guide was a petite, attractive, very knowledgeable young lady. She was impressed by Scott's enthusiasm for the forest and he happily walked alongside her, chattering, as she led their group. She gave him a large piece of paper-white bark to take home.

The sun did shine for their trip to Câmara de Lobos, a pretty fishing village. They enjoyed a meander around the little streets, shops and quayside and had booked a glass-bottomed boat. Knowing it was normally a little colder on the water, Hazel had put on layers of clothing and wore her mac. She still wasn't warm on the boat, but the chill didn't detract from the fascination of watching all the sea life as they chugged around the beautiful coastline.

When they weren't off exploring the surrounding beauty, restricted by Hazel's lack of stamina, they were able to relax and read, stretched out on the loungers on their sheltered little ground-floor patio if the sun was shining. They had direct access to the well-designed area with two swimming pools. The shallow smaller pool was shaped like a large teardrop that wove its way among the rivers and curves of the deeper pool. Several small wooden humped bridges were placed over various parts of the rivers making the attractive area perfect for Scott to play around the edges with his motorised Playmobile boat, filled with family characters. It was too cold for any of them, other than Scott, to wish to paddle.

Their complex was built right on the edge of a hill and the stunning views over Funchal to the ever-changing azure sea partly compensated for the cold. Scott had also brought a few books so was able to cuddle up with whichever parent felt like listening as he read to them.

In spite of Hazel's discomfort with the cold weather, they returned home feeling rested.

Hazel considered that Martin's fear of illness may have been caused by his mother having to shut herself away regularly with her migraines and the presence of his grandmother upsetting his father when she did (even without knowing what was happening to his sister). This fear made it difficult for him to find sympathy when Hazel was ill and he was no different with Scott. Martin was impatient when they didn't recover quickly. The fact that Hazel was sleeping very badly, due mostly to the tinnitus, tended to make her rather hyper. With his migraines, he found it difficult to cope with her bouncy, non-stop chatter and told her so. Whistling was another irritation he couldn't handle. Hazel understood that and attempted not to do it if he was within earshot.

They had been given a tea-making machine as a wedding present and it sat next to their bed. Hazel and Martin took to setting their alarm half an hour earlier than they needed to, to allow them time to wake gently with a welcome brew and a cuddle up to discuss the coming day. Hazel hoped it would help to keep them close, despite their everyday problems. She was becoming a little unsure of the strength of Martin's love, although he assured her of it often enough. Her tinnitus continued and she was sure it was due to damage from inflammation, following her virus. Compared to how ill she had felt, though, the tinnitus was now no more than a nuisance during the day. It was mainly at night that she was unable to keep it from clanging into her mind and, if sleep was eluding her, she would get up for a milky drink and sleep in the spare bedroom to ensure Martin was not further disturbed, knowing a migraine would be the likely result if he were. But she always ensured she was there first thing to have a cup of tea and a cuddle.

Two months after their holiday Hazel was still having to take Stemetil on the days she was working outside. The constant bending up and down as she was planting or clearing gardens still impacted her and brought on a slight, dizzy, nausea. She went back to her GP to ask whether there was a private consultant she could discuss it with, given how her back problems had been helped when she'd taken a similar route.

"Yes, I can arrange for you to see an ENT consultant at the Wellesley Private Hospital," he said.

"Thank you, that's fine," was Hazel's reply.

Her appointment with the ENT consultant was at six-thirty one evening. The Wellesley was the other side of Southend, almost a half-hour drive away, but this was not a problem as Martin was more than able to ensure Scott got to bed on time. After parking and finding the reception she was immediately shown to a small dark room. The consultant had his back to the door as he sat at his desk and he briskly told her to sit down. He remained sitting and Hazel wondered whether he was reading the letter from her GP. When he eventually turned around, he asked her to describe her problem. After explaining the nausea, dizziness and tinnitus, she told him about her business and how, particularly if she was having to climb around in small trees to prune, it was disconcerting and that Stemetil was not curing the problem. She went on to mention the diagnosis from a previous ENT consultant of oversensitive balance organs due to a virus.

"That diagnosis was meaningless," he dismissed, exactly as her GP had. "Will you stand up and walk in a straight line?"

A little bewildered, Hazel said that she could walk in a reasonably straight line right now because she wasn't bobbing up and down planting or doing any of the other things that exacerbated the problem. He ignored her and with a wave demonstrated she should stand. She was able to walk a pretty straight line, as she knew she would. Perhaps she should have faked a wobbly walk!

As she sat down, he said, "It's anxiety."

Hazel attempted to argue and mentioned the blood test that had highlighted inflammation. But he was adamant.

"It's all due to anxiety. Please pay at the desk as you leave."

The cost for the consultation was £100. As Hazel signed the cheque, she was angry with herself for not arranging a consultation privately, without asking for a recommendation from her GP. She was now certain that, whatever her doctor had put in the letter to the consultant, he had not mentioned inflammation because she felt the consultant's mind had already been made up, even before she sat down. Was she being paranoid? Could she add that to her problems? But she was still certain that inflammation had caused the dizziness and that because her GP had left it so long to prescribe antibiotics, she now had permanent tinnitus.

She walked out to the car park and slid into the Tercel. She grabbed the steering wheel for some solid reassurance but didn't start the engine. It was very dark outside, with few cars left in the car park. She was totally alone again. The darkness swirled around and began to seep into her head. She had looked up the correct definition of anxiety as a psychiatric problem, years ago; a state of apprehension and psychic tension occurring in some forms of mental disorder.

This was the second time a virus had caused a serious problem. Suppose it happened a third time. She had no confidence that Martin could cope any better than Trevor had. With anxiety highlighted in her medical notes, would anyone now take her illnesses seriously? And if she were to die of something that hadn't been diagnosed, she was sure no one would get into trouble. Doctors and consultants pulled together to protect themselves. Still prominent in the news was Harold Shipman, who had now been imprisoned for life, but details of his murderous deeds, hidden for such a long period, continued to emerge. Her life, one day, might again be in their hands. These terrifying thoughts were causing her brain to send distress signals to every part of her body. Yes, she thought, terror could kill you. Give you a heart attack.

There had to be something she could do, someone she could speak to. The medical profession was so powerful. Was it to defeat her? As she desperately attempted to slow her breathing, to calm her body, a glimmer of a memory surfaced. She vaguely remembered reading about a Patient Voice group. Well, she was a patient who needed a voice. Finally finding a positive thought, she carefully drove home.

Martin didn't appear to be surprised by the diagnosis – as Hazel had expected. It was almost another six months before the nausea and dizziness went. Although, if she got a cold with catarrh it would surface slightly, for a day or two, as it does to this day. The tinnitus has also remained – no longer a problem, just a part of her.

CHAPTER 28
2001 ◇ The Change

Hazel was forty-seven. She still had regular periods and did not link her tiredness, which was getting more and more difficult to shake off, with the menopause. It was Edwina who suggested the possibility. Hazel did some research online and, indeed, it seemed that progesterone was the first hormone to decline, which often caused tiredness. With the responsibilities of her business, boot sales and young son, not to mention taking Scott, Tara – and sometimes Justine – out for days during the holidays (all things that she so enjoyed), life was not that easy.

Again, it was Edwina who came across reports and research on wild yam cream. It seemed that it worked by encouraging the body to produce its own progesterone. Many women found it helpful. Hazel ordered the cream online. The instructions specified that one should rub a very small amount into a different area of the body three times a day. They suggested starting with an eighth of a teaspoon rubbed, in rotation, into wrists, inner elbows, behind the knees, inner thighs and the stomach. Hazel did exactly as it prescribed and felt a difference overnight. The heaviness that had burdened her was lifting. Within days she felt exactly as she had when she first met Martin.

Two months later it occurred to Hazel that this improvement might mean the chance of another pregnancy. After discussing this with her husband they both concluded that neither of them wanted Hazel, at her age, to become pregnant again and so they should use some sort of protection. She thought the coil would be the best option and booked an appointment at her surgery to have one fitted. She did wonder whether she should book it with her local clinic, then convinced herself not to be paranoid!

When Hazel arrived for the appointment the receptionist advised her that she was seeing Dr Grey. She was pleased, not that she had any experience of him, but he had been there for a while. The regular nurse that she knew and liked was waiting for her. She asked Hazel questions as she filled in a form. Hazel told her about the wild yam cream and how very well it was working to lift the tiredness that she had begun to experience.

Then the doctor entered the room. He was very bouncy and gaily asked Hazel how she was. She wondered, initially, whether he was a little embarrassed to be doing this procedure. He asked her whether she had a preference regarding which coil she wanted fitted. Hazel looked from him to the nurse and back again before admitting that she hadn't known there was a choice.

Dr Grey explained that the new coil was designed to help alleviate the heavy bleeding that could be experienced with older types.

"Oh well," said Hazel. "That's sounds like the best option."

But then the nurse said as she checked in a drawer, "We do have some of the old ones, though."

"Surely the new ones must be best, I would think," replied Hazel. "What exactly is the difference."

"They are made with a more superior material," he answered.

"Well, being newer, they sound like a better option."

Neither the nurse nor doctor made any mention of the fact that the newer ones were impregnated with a progestin hormone. A synthetic steroid hormone with a similar effect to progesterone, as used in the contraceptive pill. Hazel practised her slow, deep breaths as it was fitted. Not pleasant, but it could have been worse. After being told that it was effective immediately, Hazel left.

By the end of the following day, with the coil still feeling a little uncomfortable, Hazel noticed she was feeling tired again. Although, as it had been a busy day, she didn't think too much of it and continued with the eighth of a teaspoon dose of wild yam cream that evening and three times the following day. But three days later she concluded that the yam cream was losing its efficacy. The instructions mentioned the dose might need to be increased over time. So she began to use a quarter of a teaspoon.

The coil continued to feel very uncomfortable. By the end of two weeks she was suffering real pain and knew something wasn't right. She made an appointment with the Southend contraceptive clinic, wishing now that she had listened to the niggling doubt that she'd felt about having the procedure done at her own surgery. During these two weeks, because the effectiveness of the yam cream had faded, she was using half a teaspoon, three times a day but was still not feeling the difference that she had experienced during the first two months of use.

By the time she got to Southend for her appointment the pain from the coil was worryingly intense. As the nurse removed the coil, she inspected it and asked Hazel if she knew it was a Mirena coil.

"No. What does that mean?" asked Hazel.

"It means that it is infused with a progestogen to lower the risk of heavy bleeding. Did you not know this was the one that was fitted? Were you not given a leaflet at the time?"

"No," said Hazel. "Although the nurse did say they had old ones they could fit if I wished, but no one mentioned hormones or gave me a leaflet."

"Who fitted it?"

"Dr Grey."

"That's unusual. He's normally very good. As your cervix seems to be very soft, I suggest I don't fit another yet. And I'll write a letter of complaint to your surgery."

So glad to be relieved of the pain and pleased that a letter of complaint was being sent, Hazel went home. Over the next few hours she was aware of becoming a little disorientated. However, she continued to use the yam cream at the half teaspoon dose, three times a day. By the evening she was sweating.

Kathy and Nathan arrived the following day for a visit of a few days. That morning a thought suddenly occurred to Hazel. It had been during her period when she'd had that seizure and, although she was sure she regularly changed her tampons, should she consider toxic shock as a possible cause? Toxic shock had been quite prominent in the news recently. She'd been a little surprised that first morning at the psychiatric ward to find that her tampon had been removed. Obviously the best thing. Just lucky they saw the blue cord. She mentioned this to Nathan and explained how the nurse had said her cervix was very soft. Did he think it was possible her body was now suffering from some sort of trauma from the coil, as she was feeling quite sick and dizzy? He thought that the possibility couldn't be discounted. Martin said she must stop using the yam cream but Hazel wouldn't believe that could cause her to feel so ill. By the afternoon Nathan agreed Martin should take her to A&E as Hazel was clearly not well. The consultant examined her and said that he could find no sign of an infection around her cervix and suggested she had a virus and should go home and rest. Which she did.

She hadn't improved by the time Kathy and Nathan left two days later so she made an appointment with her GP. He told her to calm down, which by now might have been a reasonable response as Hazel's continued disorientation was upsetting her. He again gave her pills to calm her. And again, she took them. Not only did they not make her feel any better but they made her hands and feet numb. She did listen to Martin's insistence that she stop using the yam cream this time and reduced the dose over a few days, then stopped completely, However, she also refused to take any more of the pills the doctor had prescribed, which made Martin angry.

Still feeling no real improvement, she rang NHS Direct. The nurse listened patiently and made notes while Hazel explained everything. She said she would speak to a doctor and one of them would ring her back. The nurse rang back and told Hazel that she had discussed the matter in depth with the doctor. His conclusion was that things should slowly settle down now but, unfortunately, he was unable to speculate on whether yam cream played a part. The nurse then added that to fit a Mirena coil without giving her a leaflet, or at least informing her that it was impregnated with a progestin hormone, amounted to abuse. Feeling relieved and reassured that she would soon begin to feel better, and somewhat vindicated to hear it was abuse, Hazel went to Martin, who was in the office, to tell him what the nurse had said. As he heard the word abuse, he leapt up from the chair he was sitting in, clutching his head and frantically pulling his hair, shouting, "No, no, no."

He stumbled past Hazel, out of the room. She followed him as he ran down the stairs, still pulling his hair, sobbing audibly. He collapsed into an armchair, cradling his head in his hands, still crying. It was obvious to Hazel then that his sister's abuse had affected him deeply. She went down on her knees in front of him and folded her arms around him.

"I'm really sorry, Martin. I didn't ask for any of this to happen. But to be told I was abused …"

"Just stop, will you? Just stop. I can't take any more. I'm going to have to divorce you, because I'm going to have a breakdown if all this carries on. I don't want to end up like Uncle Ron."

Kathy's brother, an accountant, had had a series of breakdowns. Stunned, Hazel withdrew her arms.

"I hadn't realised it was affecting you so badly."

"I told you to go home after you'd laid out the plants when you had flu and I told you to stop using the yam cream. But you only ignored me. It's driving me mad."

Hazel took his hands. "I'm so very, very, sorry. Please, I promise to listen and do what you want in the future. This is the third thing to happen that's had its root cause with a doctor. I'm going to join the local Patient Voice group. Nothing will happen again. I'll get back to my old strong self. Please. Give me another chance. I love you … Do you still love me?"

"I think so," he replied.

"Then we'll work this out. For Scott's sake we must, as well as our own. I promise we can."

He searched her face, "Alright."

A couple of months later she asked him how he felt. He said things were better, and he continued to say he loved her.

There was light among all the problems. Annie was pregnant again. She'd not been sure about having a third child, particularly as she maintained she could never be a 'stay at home mum'. For her, work, her interaction with people, was vital for her well-being. At the moment, she was working in administration at the hospital but she was hoping to train as a paramedic. But Robbie wanted a son and had persuaded her to have one more go.

A scan showed that it was a boy. His birth in September was joyous. Annie asked Hazel if she would be able to have baby Lucas one day a week, as she was returning to work. Annie's mum would have him the rest of the time. Hazel really wanted to say yes. Martin, knowing what a struggle the year had been for them both, told Hazel it would be ridiculous to lose a whole day each week. Martin's migraines made him incredibly irritable, especially because he suffered not just for the one day but also for a day or two afterwards. Scott was far more adept than Hazel at treading silently around him. She concluded that now was not a good time to add another irritation. Feeling a failure as a grandmother, she sadly explained that she didn't have a spare day every week. It was such a shame she was a young, working grandmother, most were retired or at least part time. Edwina had always been there for her boys, although never for a whole day every week.

Hazel did have Lucas as often as she could. He was a happy, accommodating, beautiful baby and she loved having him. She also continued to have Tara for the odd day during the school holidays and Justine came occasionally. They were all so well-behaved together. If Justine played the bossy elder child (no worse than Hazel had been!) it would cause the odd tear, but it was always easily sorted.

Hazel worked her way through all the local places of interest that she could take them to, including: Watt Tyler's Country Park that had a small steam train; the Butterfly Farm that had a growing collection of animals; Hadleigh Country Park with its rare breeds farm and café; and flying kites at Hadleigh Castle on windy days.

Attempting to keep three or four children in sight at all times wasn't easy and one day Hazel lost Tara when they were at Marsh Farm watching sheep shearing and clambering around the large playground. Hazel had been holding Lucas' hand as he toddled around the baby section. Justine, Scott and Tara were a hundred metres away climbing around the section for older children. Both girls were very pretty, with long dark, glossy hair and big brown eyes. At six, though, Tara was still tiny. And suddenly she vanished. Expecting her to reappear around a climbing frame or from a Wendy house, Hazel took a couple of minutes to panic! After asking Scott and Justine to check every nook and cranny of the playground, Hazel ran around with Lucas in her arms, desperately scanning everywhere. Scott and Justine couldn't find her. Hazel asked them to stay on a bench together while she continued to search. Her heart really pumping with fear, she clutched Lucas tightly. Such a tiny, beautiful, little girl. Easy prey for a predator! Hazel was about to run to find an official when, at the furthest edge of the playground, Hazel caught sight of her dear, cheeky, smiling, little face, coming towards her. Oh, sweet relief and deep breaths.

"I've been here all the time," she said.

'Hiding,' thought Hazel as she put Lucas down to give her a big hug. Hazel was still shaking ten minutes later when she ushered them all into the café for lunch.

There were also longer journeys to Colchester Castle, Mountfitchet Castle and Norman village, with the House on the Hill Toy Museum nearby and, of course, the Science and History museums in London. Hazel never tired of their lively company. They were more like siblings for Scott than nieces and nephew.

Hazel did make time to join the Patient Voice group and was interested to see that her GP was an executive director of the PCT – the local NHS governing body – who championed the group. Belonging to the Patient Voice, who met every fortnight for just a few hours, gave Hazel back a sense of security and strength. It also made her grateful that her problems, unlike those of so many other unfortunate people, were not ongoing. She helped at various venues, handed out leaflets to raise awareness for the group and was able to offer useful suggestions on how to improve conversations between patients and doctors, including ensuring patients carried a card at all times with a constantly updated list of their medications.

Hadleigh Junior School believed in streaming. That meant placing children into classes according to their SATS results. Scott went into the top class. Hazel was now very aware of how competitive he was, which may have helped spur him on to remain within the top five of his class in maths, English and science.

Martin had bought Hazel a mini keyboard as a Christmas present when Scott was three and her son had regularly asked her to teach him to play it. Hazel had enough trouble attempting to play it herself so promised Scott that, as soon as his fingers were long enough, he could have proper lessons. He was six when the mother of a little girl in Scott's class mentioned that they lived next door to a piano teacher and that Lilly had just started lessons. Hazel contacted the lady and, after buying Scott a secondhand training keyboard, he eagerly began lessons. They only lasted half an hour and his teacher Pat was pleased that Hazel wished to stay and listen, partly because she wanted to learn too. Hazel sitting in on the lesson also meant that she could encourage Scott to practice at home as much as Pat expected him to, and he passed Grade I with distinction.

Hazel also wanted Scott to join the Leigh-on-Sea Sea Scout group, as Robbie had, knowing how useful the life skills they taught were. The early groups were now called Beavers. But when she rang Robbie's old troop she was told that it had become so popular that parents put names down almost from birth and there was a long waiting list. The only way they could accept Scott now was if Hazel was willing to become a helper. Hazel didn't hesitate and said that, yes, as she had been a Brownie, a Guide and a Ranger, she would enjoy being a helper. Martin told Hazel that at his first evening at Cubs he had been hit on the head by a football and had refused to go again. But, as Hazel pointed out to her husband, Scott was now quite a confident little boy and she thought he was ready to meet the challenge of some rough and tumble. And anyway, she would be there too.

Hazel had judged her son correctly, he loved it. Hazel befriended another mum whose help had been commandeered in the same way. Her son Ben, who was a little small for his age, became good friends with Scott. Hazel and Liz went on a couple of weekend Beaver camps with the boys and had a lot of laughs. As did the boys. The mums were both careful not to show any preference towards their sons.

Hazel and Martin were now regularly selling plants at Scott's school fêtes, at all the local garden shows and at the Leigh-on-Sea regatta. Hazel thoroughly enjoyed this, particularly as Scott did too. He had made friends with a middle-aged couple who had a regular stall at all the garden shows. They sold outdoor garden games that Scott enjoyed demonstrating. After he helped to pull in interest from many passing families, they gave Scott a brand new box of outdoor darts. It was perfect for their large garden and Hazel and Martin regularly played with Scott, who usually won. The couple gave Scott a new game at each of the shows. After he'd received three expensive games, Hazel told the couple that they really didn't need to do that, but they said he was worth it. They then mentioned that at the following show they were running a competition to find the best player of outdoor garden darts. There would be a trophy for both the best adult and the best junior champions.

Scott had always shown a competitive side when it came to games, especially board games. From snakes and ladders, when he was very young, to his current favourite game, Monopoly. How he had been able to win so often at snakes and ladders aged two and a half, when it was totally a game of chance, dependent on the roll of a dice, was unfathomable to Hazel. Even now, in Cornwall, when he played with his grandparents and parents, he was still guaranteed to win at Monopoly! His grandmother had admitted she gave preference to Scott in her choices. But no one else did. Anyway, he practised outdoor darts with determination because he was certain that another boy, who was also regularly at the garden shows and two years older than him, would win. However, on the day, although it was nail-bitingly close, Scott proudly won the junior trophy. Martin entered for the adult trophy and did reasonably well, but didn't win.

At the end of his first year in the juniors, Scott got a glowing report. He was a delight to have in her class, his teacher said. The one criticism she had, which fortunately she found amusing, was that if he saw another pupil doing something he shouldn't, he would immediately go and tell a teacher. Hazel and Martin were also delighted with such a report, although, the following day Hazel did diplomatically mention that, while it was admirable that he told the teacher if he saw a child doing something he thought was wrong, it was worth him considering whether or not the wrongdoing was going to hurt another child. If it wasn't then it might be better if he did not immediately go to a teacher to report it, because it was possible that he might be nicknamed a 'telltale tit'! He told his mother he understood what she meant.

A few months earlier he had mentioned to his mother that he had to break it off with Poppy.

"She said she definitely never wanted to have children! And I definitely do want to have children, one day."

'Oh, flipping heck. Is this what five-year-olds discuss today?' thought Hazel, but she said, "That's a shame. You've been very fond of each other for a long time. Is Poppy very upset?"

"Not enough for her to change her mind," was his reply.

After the first term of his second year in the juniors, his male class teacher, who Scott particularly liked, left to take over the role of head of computer studies at another school and was replaced by a new male teacher. Within a week Scott came home to report that he didn't like the new teacher. First, because he shouted, which was something Scott deplored. In fact, in his infant classes, if his teacher had raised her voice, even to another child, Scott would cry. Martin would occasionally shout at Scott, which would always elicit tears from his son. The second reason was that the teacher allowed the pupils to get up and wander around and Scott found this very distracting.

At the end of the Easter term Hazel did pop in for a chat with the teacher. His response to Scott's continuing concerns was that Scott needed to make a greater vocal effort within the class. As that seemed totally unrelated, Hazel explained that her son simply didn't react well to a lot of noise and bustle when he needed to concentrate. The teacher just shrugged his shoulders. Unfortunately, the class standard as a whole, did slip that year. Hazel felt she should discuss this with the head. The head had bought a lot of plants from Hazel and Martin at school fêtes so Hazel did not feel uncomfortable mentioning her thoughts on the teacher's methods to a lady she had every respect for. However, the head replied that, while she understood that the teaching style might not suit Scott, it was a modern, freer style that was being more generally adopted. But she thanked Hazel for talking to her.

"Oh well, at least I've made you aware," concluded Hazel.

At the end of the following year the teacher was sacked. Hazel was only saddened that another class had suffered. Fortunately, Scott had pulled back from his unhappy year and was declared a 'Gifted and Talented child' in all academic subjects. Being very modest he tried to play down this label, but did spend a very enjoyable day at Cambridge University listening to a lecture given by Dr Alice Roberts on how, from a recently discovered, local, medieval, mass grave, they had been able to identify, not only the cause of death but also many other health problems that the people had been suffering from.

Martin drove him up to Cambridge as Hazel had a plan she had to complete. Which she was annoyed about, really, because she'd only been to Cambridge once with her father and would have loved the break. She was beginning to feel that work was completely dominating her life, just as migraines were taking over Martin's. On a day out, Martin was guaranteed to get a migraine by lunchtime and would want to go home. It happened during the trip to Cambridge, even though he had spent the day alone just wandering around trying to kill time. This necessitated regular visits to their GP. Because he'd had asthma as a child he was limited on the medication he could take to minimise his suffering. He was now being prescribed a strong painkiller that helped to control the pain but, as he admitted to Hazel, he always felt overly sensitive to the slightest irritation for at least a day after taking it. No improvement there then.

Hazel, as a Patient Voice member, now had a place on the PCT's board of clinical costs and effectiveness. As she'd not had the pleasure of bumping into her own GP at any meetings or functions, she made an appointment to see him. She wasn't ill but wished to make the point that if she ever came to him with symptoms that he put down to anxiety again, when she knew it was incorrect, she would put in an official complaint. She told him that, as she now sat on a PCT board, she might be listened to. She watched with satisfaction as the colour drained from his face. She had battled so long with a loss of confidence in herself that she felt she deserved this sense of vindication. She added that she realised being a doctor was an enormous responsibility and no one was perfect. The odd mistake would be made. All she wanted was to have the doctor apologise for being human.

A year later, when Hazel went to him with an ongoing problem, he did say sorry for feeling he was going up a river without a paddle, but it seemed more like an excuse. Hazel had developed a very unpleasant, weeping rash, all down her back. It had initially been caused by a reaction to hair dye but nothing her doctor prescribed worked. Tea tree oil was the only thing that made even a slight difference, as she'd discovered by herself. She and Michael had inherited the gene that causes premature grey hair and it was depressing that going grey was now her only option. Particularly as she had a much younger husband. Two months on and the rash had not disappeared. It wasn't until her GP was away on holiday that Hazel saw a female GP who prescribed a cortisone cream that cleared it up almost overnight. Why had her GP not offered it? The cost? Was that an issue?

Tiredness, mild hot flushes, problems sleeping, going grey, the dawning of her fifties. Thanks to Martin's migraines, days out relaxing from a business that was so tied up with their home life were non-existent. It was a stark contrast to the deep contentment of their first seven years together.

Hazel wanted to employ a part-time assistant to help with the heavy clearance work and planting, so she could cope with getting up early on Sunday mornings to sell plants (and some Saturdays for shows or fêtes). But Martin insisted that they couldn't afford it.

Martin was still very happy working in his nursery. But cheap plant imports through the Channel Tunnel from Holland were slowly lowering the cost of plants in garden centres, meaning that he had to lower his prices correspondingly. He needed to spend more time in his nursery to produce the same financial result.

He then began to bemoan the fact that Hazel would disappear off to look for bargains at boot sales before all the plants were set out for display and then she'd relax with the Sunday paper while he had to cart all the unsold plants back down to his nursery. Everything started to niggle. Nor was he too happy when, during school holidays, Hazel and Scott spent the day visiting Rachael, as she'd moved to Welwyn. He also felt it was a wasted day when Rachael and Spencer returned to visit them. He didn't dare react when Hazel took Scott, Tara and Lucas out for the day – Justine now preferred to go out with her friends. But Hazel could tell that irritated him too.

It finally became obvious to Martin that producing his own plants was no longer viable. Hazel, who regularly bought plants to make up her plans, had seen the declining prices and, although she made sure that at least a third of the planting she required could be supplied from their nursery, she felt there was very little profit to be made from doing so.

Martin began to explore other options. He had three A-levels: geography, geology and chemistry. His mother had been a teacher and there was a demand for teachers that wasn't being met. He signed up to an entry-level teaching course at a local college. Hazel continued to plan gardens and she and Martin, with the landscaper Luke if necessary, completed them. Martin continued to produce as many plants as before and they continued to sell them exactly as they had but returns from the sales were dropping.

Sue, following the upsetting disclosures in her book, had decided that it was no longer tenable to live with her parents and she had made friends online with a quiet, gentle, Jewish man named Thomas. It transpired that, while training to be a barrister, his nerves had caused him to have a breakdown and he had withdrawn from training and the practice. He was now attempting to write plays online. He was visiting one time when Martin, Hazel and Scott were down for their usual camping holiday in the garden. They had instantly liked this very unassuming, bearded man and thought he was a perfect match for Sue.

Sue's GP was very unhappy when Sue moved to London to live with Thomas, in his mother's house. She believed that Sue had many anger issues with her family that needed to be confronted and resolved first. But Sue was being offered the chance of real happiness and she took it. And it pleased Nathan that now Sue's room was empty he could redecorate it, allowing Hazel and Martin to stay in comfort when they visited (having already turned the lobby into a bedroom for Scott).

Their estate car developed various problems and when the mechanic told Martin the cost of fixing it, they felt it was no longer worth keeping. The bodywork was rusting and, as Scott, at ten, was old enough to get himself about, there was no immediate need for a second vehicle. Their van was still perfectly reliable and cheap to run. Scott did complain that he was seriously uncomfortable in the hard, little middle seat, which made the thought of travelling down to Cornwall very unpleasant, even with the pillows Hazel put in for him. The back was not high enough for his long body and he was unable to rest his head to sleep – although Hazel and Martin did swap around with him to give him a chance of some sleep.

When the mechanic rang to say he had a lovely Toyota Corolla they might be interested in Scott encouraged them to take a look. It was only a small, two-door saloon, not the estate Martin was hoping for. He was going to refuse it but Scott said that he simply was not going to travel down to Cornwall in the van again. So Martin bought it.

Their journey was so beautifully different in this smooth quiet little car that Martin completely missed the M4 turn-off on the M25 in the dark, and had gone almost half way round the M25 again before he realised. Scott, fast asleep in the back, was oblivious. Martin and Hazel laughed about it. It was such an easy car to drive compared to their noisy, thundering van! They both secretly thanked Scott.

Then Kathy and Nathan suggested that, instead of their usual next visit to Cornwall, they should all take a helicopter to the Scilly Isles for a week. They had never been able to face the fear of travelling abroad, neither of them having strong nerves, but they felt the short hop on a helicopter to the Scilly Isles, with Martin's family, would give them a much-needed break.

Travelling by helicopter was a thrilling experience. They were all given ear plugs but, surprisingly, none of them found the heavy beat of the engine and propellers too loud. On the helicopter was a dog in a large cage who appeared very relaxed; it was possibly a regular trip for him.

The weather could have been warmer and drier but their little cottage was neat and cosy. Martin had warned Hazel that she must not do her usual thing of dictating what they did on holiday (this from a man who had said he didn't like to dominate and would rather go along with his wife's wishes!) and she was very happy to take a back seat and let Kathy, Nathan and Martin decide what to do each day. She was just glad to chill out and drift with the mass choice.

On the second but last morning, when Hazel and Martin were drinking their cup of tea in bed, he asked her why she was not joining in with the discussions on what to do each day. There was no pleasing her husband! She reminded him of his warning prior to the holiday, saying she was more than happy to relax and do what pleased everyone. It was now her turn to enjoy not being dominating.

It was though, in all, a wonderful, brilliant holiday.

Back home, Hazel made sure that her increasing unrest had no impact on Scott. Not difficult, as his presence alone would make Hazel's day sunny.

To Scott it seemed a natural option to consider taking the eleven-plus for entry into one of the grammar schools. However, both grammar schools were within Southend borough, not their local borough of Castle Point, meaning Hadleigh Junior School did not coach pupils for the exam. His teachers all agreed, though, that for Scott grammar school was a definite option. Martin and Hazel paid for him to have a few weeks of private tuition to cover the differences in the teaching syllabus.

On the day Martin drove Scott to the nearest grammar school to sit the exam. Scott was reasonably confident. Hazel could only imagine his disappointment when his results failed to grant him entry. Only a few places short. Maths had always been his best subject but this was where, inexplicably, he had failed. Martin and Hazel praised their son though. They knew he had done his best and the maths paper that year was reported to have been particularly hard.

It was a consolation that the best comprehensive school in the area, King John, which catered for an overspill of eleven-plus achievers, was just at the top of their road. During the open day Scott had played a piece of music from memory, which had been impressive enough to draw the attention of the head of music, Mr Bates. On his first day, Scott was pleased to discover that Mr Bates was to be his form teacher.

The majority of Scott's friends went to another local comprehensive, Dean's, that was very sports orientated. Walter and Scott had fallen out over something that Hazel had never got to the root of. And, in an uncomfortable twist, Scott's best friend Aden, also a 'Gifted and Talented' child, who had not initially wanted to sit the eleven-plus and had only been persuaded to by the fact that Scott was, had achieved a slightly higher mark than Scott and was now, a little unwillingly, going to Southend High School. But Scott was not perturbed by a lack of friends. He, like Robbie, would make friends anywhere.

It turned out that Ben, his friend from Beavers, was also attending Scott's new school. Because of Scott's music lessons and Ben's own hobbies, they had not been able to go to Cubs on the same evening, so had lost touch. Ben was pleased that they could renew their friendship and he was joined by a number of friends from his junior school in Leigh. It was natural that Scott became integrated into this group and for that first year all went really well and Scott was happy in the very large, noisy school.

Scott was now a Scout at The Cole Hole in Leigh Old Town. He regularly had the chance to go out sailing and discovered a passion for fighting the wind with sails. Coupled with exciting camps and hikes in Wales and the Lake District, his confidence was really developing.

Then his perfect world was ripped apart.

Martin had taken a part-time post, teaching adults with learning difficulties, at a plant nursery recently opened in Southend by the council for that purpose. He was finding it stressful, which did not help his migraines.

Hazel was still planning gardens and she and Martin continued to do the clearance, turfing and planting together. That and spending two days a week doing the housework, which she'd always hated, was Hazel's life. Her blissful mental plateau, now a distant memory, was replaced by a deep, dark hole. From the brown, muddy floor of this hole Hazel could see the bright blue sky with the odd, fluffy white cloud way above her but she had no idea how she was going to escape. It was too deep. She was sure, though, that she was not clinically depressed. She had no problem getting out of bed in the morning, she didn't cry, and being with Scott and spending time with Robbie and his family still brought her joy. She was confident that she would find a way out. One day. But exactly how eluded her. She still loved Martin but his moods were becoming more difficult to handle and she knew that her unhappiness was not helping him. Unable to sort out her insomnia, and because Martin was likely to get a migraine if he was disturbed in the night, they now slept permanently in separate bedrooms. But still shared their cups of tea first thing in the main bedroom – and sex still featured regularly in their relationship.

One evening Hazel was so tired and drained that she kissed Martin and went to bed early. Lying alone, unable to find a solution to her unhappiness, she decided to attempt a prayer. She closed her eyes and brought her hands together. Then took a few deep breaths to slow and concentrate her mind.

'Please, dear Lord, I'm sorry I've not spoken to you for so long but I'm stuck in a deep, dark hole, unable to see a way out. I know that my being unhappy affects everyone around me but I need your help to show me a way out of this hole. There must be a way. I just can't find it. Please, dear Lord is it possible that you can do that? … Amen.'

The following morning, as she put down her empty cup of tea and snuggled up to Martin, he pulled away. Worried, Hazel asked if he was okay.

"I don't know how to say this but … I don't love you anymore."

She stared at him as a twisting knife shredded her heart. Then it slashed her world to bits. Who was this person in bed with her? Where was her husband who had promised to love and care for her? Where was her life? Scott, oh no, how could his life be plunged into this dread? Wasn't he special? This couldn't be happening to her precious son. Why had God chosen this? Was this how he answered her prayer?

She was frozen in an unrecognisable place, unable to comprehend that Martin, whose apparent religious beliefs ran very deep, could inflict this much pain on her and his son. Apart from that one time, he'd made no attempt to talk to Hazel about his feelings. And he'd still been telling her he loved her!

Martin got up. Hazel knew she must drag herself from their marriage bed. But with those few words she no longer had a marriage. Love wasn't something that could be forced. If Martin's love had gone, then her husband had gone too. She was lost. Totally alone. She should have been prepared. When she had married a man thirteen years younger, she had accepted then that it might not be for life. Why had she allowed that thought to vanish?

She was fifty-three. No spring chicken! But compared to men of her own age, she felt young. They were so wrinkled! The thought of getting together with such a man felt repulsive. But she had wrinkles now and grey hair, and the thought of being with another younger man felt equally wrong. Not that one would want her! She got up. Life was going to continue. Even if she couldn't. She nibbled a bit of breakfast with Scott and waved him off for school from the front door, her heart bleeding for his ignorance of what was about to unfold.

She went to find Martin, upstairs in the office.

"Is there someone else?" she asked.

"No, there's not. It's just that my feelings for you have gone. I'm sorry."

"You'll have to move out then. I can't bear to be around you, knowing you don't love me anymore. You're no longer the man I loved. You'll have to find a flat or something. And soon. I suggest we don't say anything to Scott until you've got something sorted. Have you any idea what this will do to him? I've made sure that you are an equal parent. This will tear his world apart too."

"I know, that's why it's been so difficult to tell you."

They still had a garden to plant up and Hazel had three plans on her drawing board. They had to continue working together and living in the same house for now. But early morning tea in bed or sex would never happen again.

Within a couple of months Martin was offered a full-time teaching job, still teaching adults with learning difficulties. He took the role, which would commence in two weeks They'd completed the planting job and Hazel had finished all the plans. Together they completed all the planting for the first and second plans. For the final one Hazel had to explain to the clients that she would pass the entire garden to Luke to complete. Luke had recently signed a contract to make repairs to a whole new housing estate where the landscaping work had proved to be of an unacceptable quality. Meaning that, in the future, he would be too busy to help Hazel on a permanent basis. She'd actually had enough of the whole business now, though. She was fed up with the rain, fed up with continually muddy tools, fed up with going back to talk clients through all the planting and the maintenance needed, fed up of finding clients enjoying a relaxing glass of wine on their beautiful new patio overlooking their wonderful garden, when she had no time to sit in hers.

An old, established, family-run bookshop in Leigh was advertising for an assistant. Hazel knew the owner from when his son had been at Ridley's Art and Drama school with Robbie, although she knew his wife better. After explaining her love of books and her ability to deal with the public she was offered the job.

Hazel hid her distress from her son but was unable to do so from her husband. Martin, appalled that Hazel continued to display such a vehement need for him to be gone, suggested that, perhaps, he should try to find a way to love her again. That wasn't good enough for Hazel. If his love was gone then hers was smashed to oblivion, the damage done. There was no way back.

After weeks of searching, Martin came across a small one-bedroom flat just off the seafront in Thorpe Bay. A lovely area but expensive. Where would Scott sleep if he stayed, asked Hazel, and why could he not find a flat nearer to Scott's school? Scott would have to take a train to his dad's new flat, which was not easy, as the station was a good forty-five-minute walk from his home and school, and buses went there infrequently. Martin was adamant that this was the flat he wanted. They prepared themselves to tell Scott, together.

Oh, it was awful. Hazel could see all the pain and anguish she had felt reflected in her son. It was as unbearable for her to see it, as it was for him to feel it. She knelt in front of him as he sat speechless, rooted to his chair and she wrapped her arms around him. Martin then rose from his chair and joined Hazel in hugging him, repeating her words that they both loved him very, very deeply and hated that this was happening. That evening when Scott went to bed and Hazel went to kiss him goodnight, he broke into tears. Martin, who always poked his head into his son's bedroom to say good night, also attempted to console him. It took a long time. Martin said Scott could stay with him every weekend. He would get a sofa bed for him to sleep on. It was not enough to quell their son's misery. It would be two weeks before his father moved out.

In the meantime, Hazel said they should go for mediation. It would be cheaper than solicitors. Martin grudgingly agreed to try it. He knew Hazel wanted a sixty per cent share of the house. Her argument being that she had owned a three-bedroom house when they met and that their business had been hers, started and run by her for years before Martin had joined her. And he was younger, with a small pension from his first council job. Their house was meant to be their pension when they downsized. Now she'd have nothing. She had to have a two-bedroom place near Scott's school. And she couldn't be without a garden. As an adult she'd never had to live in a flat; why should she now? His argument against her having more than a fifty per cent share was that he'd had an MR2 that had been worth £20,000, the same as the profit made on the sale of Hazel's house. But that had gone to fund their business vehicle and he had been an equal partner for years.

They had a female mediator. Hazel accepted her forceful manner might not be appreciated but was surprised that the mediator tended to press her with Martin's side of the argument. Finally, though, the mediator went through everything on the premise that Hazel would get what she wanted. Within days, Martin made the decision not to accept mediation, so, after grumbling that he'd wasted his money, he went to a solicitor.

When Martin moved into his own flat on a Saturday he told Scott to wait a couple of weeks before visiting, to allow him to clean and decorate. He promised he would take him out for the day on the following Sunday. Hazel wasn't happy that Scott couldn't help in the flat but Martin wouldn't listen. He said it was not fit for Scott to stay in at the moment. They jointly decided that, as there were still plants in the nursery to sell, Martin would keep the van, after moving out the furniture they'd agreed he could take. The car was best for Hazel.

That Saturday evening Scott was in tears again when Hazel went to kiss him goodnight. She wrapped him in her arms. She explained how devastated she had been when his father had told her he no longer loved her, so she understood how bereft Scott felt now. She said that apart from attempting to become someone else, someone that he might love again, which she knew wasn't possible, there was nothing she could have done to make her son's suffering any less. Scott sobbed that, no, there probably wasn't. And he continued to cry each night, for three heart-wrenching months – except for the two nights a week he stayed with his father. Hazel would drop Scott off for his Friday night Scout meeting in Leigh Old Town, with his weekend bag, and Martin would collect him at the end of the meeting and drop him back Sunday afternoon.

The twisting hurt, the enmity that burnt inside her over the pain Martin had inflicted on Scott, bled deep, swirling with her own distress. And the stress of having to shoulder all the maintenance and worry of their big house, knowing that the flat roofs would soon need replacing, rested with her too. She would eventually have to sell it and look for a smaller alternative. They had put in a new kitchen and a wood-burning stove a couple of years previously, which might make selling their quirky house a little easier. But it was difficult. She couldn't tear Scott from the only home he'd known. Not yet.

Edwina had also been shocked by the apparent suddenness of Martin's declaration and warned her that Scott might consider living with his father rather than with Hazel.

"But, Mum, what can I do? Knowing Robbie's problems with his dad, I brought Scott up to be equally close to us both. I also mentioned to Martin, about a year ago, that I thought a son should slowly and naturally start to move away from the close bond that he had with his mother, by the age of twelve or thirteen, to be closer to his father. I even suggested to Martin that he should look for joint interests in books and films, when Martin said he felt he was emotionally losing his son, about six months ago," Hazel cried. "But then I had no idea this would happen. Although I'm still not sure my suggestion to Martin was wrong. Apart from attempting to disparage his father, which I'm not prepared to do, what do you suggest I do?"

Her mother couldn't offer a solution. Hazel did mention to Scott that he would be unable to live permanently in his father's one-bedroom flat, which Scott, of course, had to agree with. But beyond that there seemed little else to discuss.

Martin's solicitors were pushing for an equal share of the house. Hazel said she was sticking to the mediation agreement. However, they had split their £7,000 savings in half and Hazel decided that she and Scott could use the money to have a completely different holiday at Easter. Somewhere warm. She trawled the internet for cheap destinations. Croatia looked beautiful. Then Hazel came across a hotel in Turkey that was attached to the Aqua Fantasy Water Theme Park, Kusadasi. She showed Scott the enticing photos.

"Oh yes, I'm definitely up for that," he agreed.

Hazel booked it. With money to spare, she then asked Scott what he thought of her buying outdoor table tennis for the garden. He'd said it was great for a laugh at school lunchtimes. But, no, for home he thought a trampoline would be more fun. Hazel attempted to get him to change his mind. At almost thirteen, she thought it likely he would soon lose interest in a trampoline. And, considering his friends would join him for a bounce, it would have to be large and include a safety net, which would be quite expensive. But he was resolute. A trampoline it was. Hazel fitted it together herself while Scott was at Martin's for the weekend. He beamed at his mum when he walked down the garden to find it positioned, hidden from the house, just behind the hedge that divided the garden. With the safety net in place, hopefully, there would be no accidents. Scott and Hazel christened it together, bouncing as high as they could amid helpless laughter as they each unbalanced the other. There would be loads more laughs and Tara and Lucas were young enough to enjoy it for many more years. It was the best buy.

Hazel was glad she now had a holiday to look forward to. The bookshop offered some respite from all the worry at home. Pauline, the manager, although younger than Hazel, as were the other two ladies, was an old-fashioned, fussy stick. Not that thin, but totally unbending. Fair enough, she'd been there a long time and knew exactly how the owner expected the shop to be run. They weren't allowed to sit down, unless they were signing in the daily boxes of new books, and while employees could flick through books, they weren't allowed to read them. But there was a small kitchen with a microwave and drinks and snacks could be consumed in the shop. And learning the rough content of the books and being able to help customers find what they wanted was pleasant enough. She spent her lunch hours wandering around Leigh Broadway, buying a sandwich or pasty and eating it in the library gardens or on the bench in the shop's tiny, back garden. Time drifted by, punctuated about once a fortnight by Edwina meeting her at the shop to walk to one of the many cafés for lunch together.

When Hazel's kitchen had been refitted, the kitchen designer, knowing Hazel had a son who would be using a computer for much of his homework, suggested siting theirs in one corner of the L-shaped kitchen. Then Hazel would be able to help with his homework and keep an eye on what else he might be doing on the computer while she cooked dinner. It worked perfectly and the computer had become an integral part of their life – especially as they would often play games together on it.

When Scott was with his dad, to pass the time Hazel decided to look at the online dating site match.com. Why not? At fifty-three her looks were on the decline but not so much that she felt completely unattractive; and who knew what the ravages of time would produce in a few more years? At least she was now able to add a few gold streaks to blend with her greying hair, without eliciting a rash. After filling in the questionnaire, honestly, a list of men appeared. She skimmed through the details of the few faces that grabbed her. There were two, around her age, who looked interesting. She was aware that not everyone gave a genuine, up-to-date photo or description of their character. But their personal write-ups felt authentic. Tony was blond and tanned with startling blue eyes. He taught maths and PE in a private boys' school and lived in Cheshunt, Hertford. Ian was head of a junior music school and had three daughters he was close to. He actually lived in Hadleigh. But he was laughing in the photo, causing his eyes to narrow into slits which somehow gave him a foxy, untrustworthy air! So much for photographs. Anyway, swayed by Tony's looks Hazel paid the subscription and began conversing with him online.

Wanting to impress Tony at their first meeting, two weeks later, she suggested a meal at The Boatyard restaurant in Leigh Old Town. It was expensive but set in the heart of the old fishing village with expansive views over the estuary and they would be able to have a pleasant stroll afterwards. As a precaution she rang Maggie to let her know exactly where she was going and said she'd ring when she was safely back home. The town and food did impress Tony. The cost didn't, even though Hazel insisted on paying her share. Otherwise, the evening was a success and inviting him in for a coffee afterwards felt natural. After reassuring Maggie, on the phone, that he appeared genuine, a kiss and a cuddle in front of the lit wood-burning stove held promise, but he respected her wish that he sleep in the spare bed that night, before leaving for home the following morning. He was still living with his wife and, although Hazel believed him when he said they were separating, some assurance was needed before she slept with him. Within a few weeks he moved into a newly built, small, two-bed house in Cheshunt. Hazel drove up and spent the night. Sex was acceptable, but that ultimately, was not all Hazel was searching for. No longer needing children, Hazel was looking for a companion to share life experiences with.

Tony's snoring kept her awake. Also, he smoked. As he was tired after work during the week and had paperwork to complete at the weekend, they met up less than once a fortnight. His reluctance to spend money on going out, and his preference for cooking good meals at home, made Hazel feel she should do the same when he visited her when, really, she wanted to go out, even if it was just to the cinema. Their relationship limped along.

The prospect of travelling to Turkey with only Scott as a companion made Hazel slightly apprehensive, which was mainly due to her strange menopausal brain! Hazel now knew why it was aptly named The Change. Until the coil problem, Hazel had rarely, apart from her psychiatric unit experience, questioned her confidence. Now nothing could be relied upon. Certainly not her concentration. She experienced a slight whiff of anxiety each morning when she first awoke, which always disappeared as she got up. She had a waist that showed signs of thickening, forcing her to up the number of back exercises she performed, particularly those that tightened her tummy muscles. At forty, she'd had to reduce her food intake. Now in her fifties, she had to reduce it further – not easy when she loved all food, especially sweet stuff. It was all due to hormones. She refused to give in to middle-aged spread though, and would still wear bikinis on the beach.

Flying from Stansted made the journey easy and Hazel left the car in the long stay car park, from where a bus took them directly to departures. Of course, Scott was hardly a child anymore and was brilliant company. Apart from some earache towards the end of the flight, which settled as soon as they landed, everything went smoothly and a coach drove them to their hotel. After unpacking they went to find lunch. It was a four-star hotel, with two swimming pools. Buffet meals were enticingly laid out in the large food hall and could be eaten under a canopy overlooking the larger pool. They chose soup and a sweet Turkish dessert.

Relaxing on a lounger after their meal while Scott swam, Hazel allowed the warm sun, in a clear blue sky, to soak into her very being, to bathe away all the unhappiness and to disperse all the worry. Seven days of fun and relaxation. The next day they'd experience all the excitement of the water theme park next door, to which they had free access. Later that evening they walked around the complex and the beach it enclosed and found an empty table tennis table. After tracking down bats and a ball from reception they spent a hilarious couple of hours wearing each other out before bedtime.

Hazel's favourite ride in the water park was the one that involved lying on a large rubber ring and bobbing gently down a meandering river of slow-flowing water. But it was exhilarating, and Scott's favourite, to swim in a large lagoon, waiting for the wave machine to push out an enormous heaving sea, then attempt to keep afloat. They were tired by lunchtime and, after enjoying more delicious soup and a salad, they relaxed by the largest pool in the complex, where it was much quieter. Hazel bought a large, clear plastic, water bed for Scott to relax on in the pool while she read her book and dozed.

They booked a trip to Pamukkale where warm, mineral-rich, thermal waters flowed down glistening, pure-white, travertine terraces. It took almost two hours to reach by coach, with a stop midway at a Turkish coffee house. Hazel and Scott managed the thick bitter, brown liquid. A sludge of fine-ground coffee filled the bottom half of their cups. It was an experience to say the least. Even more so was the visit to the toilets. The ladies were simply flat plastic moulded pans lying directly on the ground with a large hole beneath. Astonished, Hazel did manage to squat over it while wondering how many Westerners would refuse.

The coach dropped everyone at the terraces and their driver suggested a stop for lunch at the café there before exploring. Scott found a table and Hazel went to take her purse from her bag. Except it wasn't there. Double checking confirmed it. A sudden sense of desperation. She'd left half of their money in the safe at the hotel, but her credit card was in her purse. Spending hours in the blazing heat and sun without lunch and a drink was not an option. Unable to believe her stupidity, Hazel asked the couple who had sat behind them on the coach whether they could lend her the money for lunch, explaining what had happened.

"Of course, please, what do you need? Take enough to cover a swim in Cleopatra's pool too."

They were very concerned for her. Hazel attempted to ask the café staff whether they knew the coffee house that they had stopped at. It was the only place she could think she might have left it. Finally, someone understood her question and said they would ring them. Scott couldn't believe his mother had lost her purse and he wasn't amused. As they ate, a member of staff informed them that her purse was not at the coffee house.

"Oh well, there's nothing I can do," she said to Scott. "So, let's push it out of our minds and make the most of our time here."

The sparkling white, calcareous terraces were unimaginably stunning. Without sunglasses one could be blinded. The milky blue water in all the terraces was unbelievably warm. It was one thing to see photos of the place but it was totally spellbinding to be there. The loss of her purse did weigh on Hazel's mind but the sheer beauty of Pamukkale surmounted it. Hours later, after they'd absorbed the pureness of the dazzling atmosphere and paddled until their feet wrinkled in the milky warmth, they returned to the café for a drink before finding Cleopatra's Pool (now called Antique Pool). It too was amazingly warm. Sulphurous bubbles rose from depths that were littered with stone columns, felled during an earthquake. As Hazel and Scott floated languidly and swam gently, fascinated by the streams of bubbles, they agreed it was magical. At four o'clock they gathered where the coach had dropped them. It pulled up and the driver jumped down. In his hand was Hazel's purse. She'd left it on her seat! She blamed the menopause. She was so thankful and immediately reimbursed the couple who had saved their day.

Having not lost her money, Hazel decided to hire a car for a couple of days. She'd read that Ephesus, only a few miles away, was the largest, best-preserved Roman city in the world. The coach trips only appeared to spend a few hours there. Scott agreed with his mother that such a place shouldn't be rushed. The hotel provided them with lunch, snacks and drinks. The car allowed them to arrive well before the coaches and they didn't leave until every inch had been explored.

Ephesus transported them back in time. By the sixth century BC this city, with other Ionian cities, had led in culture and science. It had been built around the temple to the powerful Mediterranean goddess Artemis. In Ephesus she reigned not only as Queen of Heaven but as Mother, Healer and Saviour. Even when faced with the onslaught of early Christianity, she could not be deposed. St Paul arrived in Ephesus with the intention of placing the memory of Jesus on her ancient, sacred pedestal. He walked the streets of the city for two years, preaching passionately, until a silversmith, hearing him say that gods were made by man and must not be worshipped, felt his livelihood from the manufacture of silver gods and goddesses was at stake. He rallied his fellow artisans to march to the great amphitheatre. They threatened violence and Paul was forced to leave the city. When Artemis' temple was finally destroyed and Christian churches built on top of her sacred places, reverence for her was so deeply entrenched in the city community that her citizens took the only female character in the new ruling religion of Christianity, the Virgin Mary, and renamed her *Theotokos*, Mother of God. And, although this is still disputed, Mary is believed by many to have been taken by St John to live just outside the city and to have been buried there. St John wrote the fourth book of the New Testament in Ephesus and when he died a basilica was built over his tomb – subsequently replaced by a great church, the remains of which can still be seen.

As Hazel and Scott walked down Harbour Street from the entrance, the great theatre loomed in front of them, Stadium Street led off to the right and the gleaming white Marble Street rose up on the left. It was not difficult to imagine what life there must have been like as Scott and Hazel wandered round the *latrina* (public toilets), with all the closets lined up next to each other without a dividing wall. Further down Marble Street they found the carved footprint in the pavement that pointed to the brothel and followed it to read the story of careful health control, with every facility for washing within its rooms, before climbing the nine great stairs to the tall, imposing, carved beauty of the Library of Celsius.

The Terrace or Slope Houses had been amazingly well-preserved by a landslide and were now partly excavated and covered by a large steel and canvas structure that protected them from the elements. These houses of the rich were further preserved from modern footfalls by glass walkways that stretched over the villas below. Scott was initially very wary of walking on glass with such a long drop underneath. Hazel jumped up and down to show how strong the glass was and he almost forgot his fear as he edged along and absorbed the atmosphere. The walls were full of paintings of gladiators, caricatures, animals and mythological subjects. The floors still showed refined mosaics. Hazel and Scott left with entrenched impressions of a life once lived. Ephesus would not be forgotten by either of them.

They couldn't go to Turkey and not take a boat trip out to the quiet sandy coves that nestled around the coast. Hazel bought two snorkelling sets. They had to grab the chance to view, first-hand, life under the surface. Knowing the boat would stop for a while in deep water to allow everyone to swim made Hazel slightly anxious. Could she and Scott stay afloat indefinitely? It was a relief when she lowered herself down the ladder from the boat and realised that the warm salty sea cradled her naturally on the surface. Along with some of the other boat passengers they enjoyed a languid half hour staring through goggles at brightly coloured fish, some darting at speed, some slowly nibbling among rocks, others gliding in small shoals around a reef. It was utterly absorbing. Then the boat dropped them off at a sandy bay for a couple of hours to snorkel the shallow waters and soak up the sun on the beach.

A visit to a silver factory completed their holiday. Scott had been given spending money by Kathy, Nathan and Edwina. Having spent very little, he bought his mother a stunning turquoise and silver pendant with matching earrings – to thank her for such a wonderful holiday, he said. The holiday had lifted both their spirits and proved that life could still be good.

Unexpectedly, they had to check out the Turkish health service when, on the morning of their departure, Scott woke with earache. A holiday rep immediately organised a taxi to take them to the nearest clinic. It was small but immaculately clean and white and a gentle young male doctor syringed wax from Scott's ear, using a camera fitted to a monitor to show exactly what he was doing. Then he fitted an antibiotic-soaked, cotton wool plug into the ear for the infection, gave him antibiotic pills, some paracetamol tablets and Sudafed liquid. It all worked perfectly for a pain-free trip back to the UK. Guinness welcomed them home with much purring. Having been fed twice a day by their next-door neighbour, he wasn't too cross about their absence. The tortoise was still clomping around the garden, uncaring either way.

The following Sunday Scott met Tony. He was in the kitchen when Scott was dropped home by his father. Within minutes Tony had challenged Scott with a maths question. Hazel squirmed, knowing this would not endear him to her son. She was right. Scott was too polite to say anything to Tony, but told Hazel later that he wasn't that keen on him. That was enough to make Hazel consider where this relationship was going. It wasn't bringing companionship and the constant uncertainty over when she might see him next was actually making her unhappy. She explained this to Tony during his next visit. It saddened him and he told her that he was in love with her. He asked for more time together, but accepted it when Hazel said it was over; she had to move on.

She looked again at Ian's details on match.com. Any father as devoted to his daughters as he clearly was must be worth considering, especially as his interests included cycling, walking, cooking, music and reading. He mentioned *The Kite Runner* by Khaled Hosseini as his latest favourite book, which was one Hazel had enjoyed. She contacted him via email and discovered he was reading *The Island* by Victoria Hislop, another book she had recently read.

It would be ridiculous not to meet when they lived so close. She suggested meeting one evening in Ugo's, a trendy bar in the heart of Leigh, opposite the library. As soon as she entered the bar Hazel saw him sitting towards the back and made her way around the busy tables to reach his. He'd risen and smiled as Hazel removed her jacket, slung it over the back of her seat and sat down. Hazel returned his smile. He was a year younger than her but, with no real signs of wrinkles and only a tiny sprinkling of grey in his head of thick dark hair, he could have been younger. After getting her a drink, they settled into light, chatty conversation, which was not easy among the surrounding noise of music and people. Hazel, though, felt relaxed right from the outset, immediately comfortable with this man.

Through the evening Hazel learnt that, like her, he had finished his first marriage reluctantly. In his case because his wife was psychologically unable to allow penetrative sex. Nowadays, he said, they would most likely have tried counselling. He wanted children so they had agreed to divorce. After an unsuccessful relationship with a journalist who put her career before thoughts of a family, he had met and married his second wife, who had two young daughters from her previous marriage. Their father had moved to Canada and had little contact with his daughters. Ian had willingly filled his absent shoes, continuing when his own daughter was born. Ten years later, when his wife admitted to an affair with the builder who was constructing their extension, he found that their marriage was over too. Ian, as head of the junior department of a London music conservatoire worked every Saturday and Hazel could understand that this may not have been easy for his wife with three children, particularly as she had suffered with post-natal depression following their daughter's birth.

As the bar got busier and noisier, Ian asked if Hazel had eaten. She had, but said she could manage a small meal to keep him company. They strolled down the Broadway to an Indian restaurant, which was quieter, more intimate. Hazel was already experiencing a strange sense of familiarity. Perhaps because he had a similar past to hers. Whatever it was she was delighted when, at the end of the evening, he invited her to meet his daughters. He cooked Sunday dinner each week for them and she was very welcome to join them. The invite extended to Scott.

By now Scott was well into his second year at King John and it was unfortunate when Mr Bates, his form teacher, unexpectedly left at Easter to move on to a higher paid job elsewhere. Then Scott mentioned that there were problems, not directly with him, but among his friends, that he was struggling to resolve. Several weeks later he told Hazel that Ben was accusing him of taking away his friends, which he said was so untrue. He explained that Ben had become moody and difficult and his friends no longer wanted much to do with him. Usual teenage problems. But it upset Scott that he'd been unable to sort things out, particularly as Ben was blaming him. Hazel commiserated with him, but apart from offering to chat to Ben's mum, which Scott declined, she was unable to suggest anything useful.

Hazel still felt cocooned in her own world of stress, which was not making life easy at home for either of them. Scott, who had always been susceptible to colds, had a run of them that winter, even though Hazel bought vitamin tablets and ensured he ate a diet rich in fruit and vegetables. His stomach had also remained sensitive to colds so generally he would still be sick, at least once. This usually meant he would have to be absent from school for a day or so, whenever he had one. As the weather warmed slightly, like most teenagers he thought an unbuttoned blazer over a thin shirt was sufficient clothing for the, still very chilly, mornings. Having just recovered from the latest cold he said goodbye to Hazel one particularly bitter, windy morning and went to leave without his coat.

"Please, put your coat on," Hazel asked. "You can't go down with another cold. Please Scott."

They'd had this argument several times over the last few weeks, with Scott usually, finally, giving in. This time worry and frustration boiled inside Hazel as he ignored her, opened the front door and walked out, slamming the door behind him. Hazel ran across the lobby, pulled the front door open, raised her voice and said, "Well, don't come home until you've had a serious think about this."

Halfway through her sentence, he had turned out of the drive. Hazel was annoyed she'd lost her temper. She so rarely did with Scott, and now was not the best time. Life had become a quagmire of worry. The house was on the market but no one was making a sensible offer and looking after such a large house and garden was really getting her down. Then there was the boredom with her days, standing aimlessly in the bookshop with her feet aching. Sales had been dropping steadily. Another bookshop, incorporating a café, had opened up by the library. It seemed people were reluctant to walk far nowadays and a trek to the far end of the Broadway, just for a book, seemed too much bother.

But there was no excuse to have taken it out on Scott. It bothered her all day as she battered through the housework. Such fun for a Monday, her day off. Scott didn't come home. Knowing her son, Hazel wasn't surprised. By five-thirty it was getting dark and her apprehension was growing. Which friend was he with? He'd had a couple of girlfriends at King John's, among his mix of female friends, but Hazel suspected that he wouldn't burden the mother of his present one by going to hers. It was more likely to be a male friend. Hazel rang Ben's mum.

"Yes," she said. "He's here."

Hazel was so relieved. She drove into Leigh to pick him up.

On the way home he said, "You told me not to come home."

"Oh, Scott, I said not until you'd given it some serious thought and you know how many colds you've had."

"I didn't hear that bit," he said.

387

Hazel didn't force the coat issue again.

It was a respite for them both when they went to Ian's for Sunday dinner. His daughters immediately made them feel welcome and, after some excellently cooked lamb, the girls gathered around their father at the piano. Sitting in close proximity to the instrument, feeling the hammers strike the strings, was enough to pull at Hazel's heart, then, as the sweet, pure sound of the girls' harmonious voices filled the room, tears filled her eyes. She felt drawn to this close family. Scott agreed later that Ian was a far better choice. One he fully approved of.

Scott returned from his next weekend with his father with the information that Martin had met a lady he felt seriously about. Lucy lived in Hitchin, Hertfordshire, with Joshua, her fifteen-year-old son and Elizabeth, her twelve-year-old daughter. Hazel was aware that, unlike Robbie, being an only child did occasionally sadden Scott and, while their house and garden was often full of Scott's friends and relations, there had been a time when she'd seen him sitting alone, on the step of the open French doors, listening to the neighbour's two sons laughing and shouting as they kicked a football around together. Hazel sat down to join him and he confided that he did wish he'd had a sister or brother. Hazel had put her arm around him and apologised, explaining that they had tried but had lost three pregnancies quite early and then it seemed her body decided she was too old and it didn't happen again (discussing yam cream and the menopause with her son didn't feel appropriate!). They were very lucky to have had Scott. Scott did play with the two boys next door, occasionally, but they were fervent footballers, great with a ball, and Scott was not.

A couple of weeks later Scott told Hazel that his father was considering moving up to his girlfriend Lucy's house in Hitchin and he'd asked Scott to go with him, although her house was apparently quite small. Hazel had attempted to prepare herself for the possibility that her son might want to move in with his father but she was not prepared for such a large distance between their two homes. How could Martin consider it? She spent days digesting all the possibilities.

"This a big house. Would his girlfriend consider moving down here if I sold them my share and moved out?" Hazel asked her son.

"I don't think so," he replied. "Joshua and Elizabeth are both happy in their schools and Lucy's parents only live around the corner from them."

Hazel rang Martin and asked him to think about the option.

"We couldn't afford to, even if Lucy wanted it. Living in Hitchin is best for her."

Hazel and Scott had, at various times, discussed the possibility of Scott moving in with his father. Trying to discourage him, Hazel had pointed out that it would not be sensible to change schools in the middle of his GCSE studies. Meaning he had to make the decision to move, either before they began next September or not until he had to consider his AS/A-levels. Scott, hoping to experience the freedom of university life, agreed that his GCSE studies should not be interrupted.

Martin made the decision to move to Hitchin at the end of term. A week before then, Scott was to receive the Chief Scouts Gold award, to be presented by Lord Petre, Lord Lieutenant of Essex, at Ingatestone Hall. It was agreed that Hazel would have Scott that Friday night and take him up to Ingatestone for the ceremony, where Martin would meet them. He would then take Scott home and up to Hitchin the following day to meet Lucy's family. A cloak of foreboding hung around Hazel that day, glorious as it was. Scott, with two other boys and three girls from his troop, proudly joined the small queue to collect his prestigious award. The ceremony was being conducted outside to make the most of the sunshine and the beautiful grounds. Hazel made sure nothing clouded her son's day, but inside she was unable to shake off the knowledge that Martin would do all he could to encourage Scott to move with him to Hitchin.

She wasn't prepared, though, when Martin brought Scott back to her on Sunday evening and told her to sit down. Wasn't prepared to be told that Scott wanted to look at the schools in Hitchin with the intention of moving there. She had presumed Martin would discuss it with her first. Her world tumbled apart as she saw the determination on her son's face. She realised there was nothing she could say; she knew her son. She'd lost him. She swallowed, pushing down her rising tears, not allowing him to witness her grief as she agreed to support his wish. Martin asked whether Hazel would like to visit the schools with them.

"Yes, please," she said.

Again, the awful swirl of tearing emotions. Again, desperately fighting to keep her feet grounded. Later, she diplomatically explained to Scott that his father would have done his best to paint a glossy, rosy picture of life with his new love. Knowing that Joshua played the guitar in a band and that Scott had a wish to join a band. Knowing Scott was fed up tramping the corridors of his large school with upsetting friendship problems. Knowing there was a complete family for him to become part of. Her argument held no conviction. They both knew that.

At least Hazel had Ian in her life now. Although it had only been a matter of months, they fitted together perfectly. There had been no negatives in their relationship at all. They laughed. They loved in time with each other. Everything with Ian felt right.

Hazel made the decision to ring Rouse, owner of the hi-fi company she used to work for, to ask if there was a position for her. He replied that they were about to put new high-end units into production if she was interested. Perfect, as he thought it would only be part time. A week later she joined the company for the second time, for just three days a week.

Following some research and discussion with Scott, Martin had concluded that a small mixed comprehensive with an excellent Ofsted report was worth visiting. Hazel drove up with Scott to meet Martin for an appointment to be shown around the school. She couldn't deny she was impressed by the warm but firm atmosphere it fostered. The large music hall was equipped with lines of keyboards and percussion instruments. Scott would be happy here, she thought. But sadness at the inevitable was soaking her. Having lunch in a nearby pub with Martin and Scott felt weird. Her son was leaving her for a new life. A life she would have no part in. A life she could only orbit around. She would always be there, always be his mother, but would be unable to touch this new world. He was thirteen. Five years as a 'part mother' before university claimed him. Having him only for a weekend, once a fortnight. How could she survive? Was this the antidote for those seven perfect years living on a plateau, that had felt so close to heaven?

Five weeks later, Hazel drove Scott and all he would need for the foreseeable future, up to Hitchin, where Martin was waiting. It was a week before the new school year. That first time was utterly heartbreaking. Waves of searing emotional pain washed over and over as she drove, with tears pouring uncontrollably down her face. She desperately hoped her hair would hide them from Scott. He had plugged his phone into the car's media system and the sounds of Muse, Coldplay and other groups that he had regularly listened to while doing his homework in the kitchen filled the car. Now she thought of the silent and empty kitchen, the silent and empty house she would return to.

After Martin and Scott helped empty the car, Hazel hugged her son and left. The car was so deathly quiet now. Hazel heaved out her anguish with heavy sobs and continued to cry all the way home. She attempted to listen to the radio, but it only saddened her further as she far preferred Scott's choice of songs. They'd all agreed that tomorrow, and each day that Scott was in Hitchin, Hazel would ring at six-thirty in the evening for a chat. A thin thread to cling to.

CHAPTER 30
2008 ◇ An Ending?

With Scott's main residence now in Hitchin, Hazel was no longer able to claim working tax credit because of her low part-time income and Martin withdrew the maintenance he had paid for Scott. To add further financial worry, Martin now insisted she pay him maintenance. Hazel began working four days a week. She missed having spare time to meet up with Maggie and other friends and was now often too tired in the evenings to do more than cuddle up in front of the TV with Ian.

Scott had one final term of Sea Scouts to complete, which meant that for a few months Hazel had him each weekend. After an early meal in Hitchin, Martin brought him down every Friday, about six-thirty, as far as the Summerhills Garden Centre on the A127. Hazel would wait outside in a lane for them to arrive. The traffic was appalling on a Friday but most times she got him to Scouts on time. Saturdays and Sundays, after Hazel allowed Scott to laze in bed until gone eleven sometimes and ensured that he did his homework, were spent together, playing games on the computer, watching films on the television, going out for a walk, having lunch in Sara's tea room in Leigh Old Town, occasionally joined by Edwina. One lunchtime, the tearoom was so full Hazel decided The Peterboat pub was a more appropriate lunchtime venue for a teenage boy. It was opposite Sara's and next to the Cole Hole, Scott's Sea Scout meeting place, and had plenty of wooden tables with a view of Leigh creek and the fishing boats. Sunday dinner was often in the early evening at Ian's house, with one or more of his daughters. Hazel would then drive Scott to meet Martin at South Mimms service station on the M25 – and would cry most of the way home.

Ian was her lifeline. They went for long walks. He fitted their bikes to a roof rack on the car to drive out to cycle on quiet country roads. He cooked Hazel scrumptious meals and took her out to exotic restaurants. He booked a holiday in Spain for the following summer, in a private villa with a swimming pool for them, Scott and Ian's two youngest daughters.

That first Christmas, Scott decided to stay in Hitchin for Christmas Day. His father would bring him down on Boxing Day so he could have his birthday with all of his Essex family.

Hazel, unable to countenance Christmas Day without her youngest son, especially while her eldest still wanted to celebrate the day at his own home, suggested to Ian that they went out walking for the day, taking smoked salmon sandwiches to replace the turkey. Ian agreed and worked out a route around the South Downs. Edwina grudgingly accepted she would enjoy a vegetarian dinner at John's.

Scott did help Hazel decorate a non-drop Christmas tree she had bought a fortnight before, when he was down for the weekend. Ian's daughters all came for Christmas Day evening. So, Boxing Day became Christmas Day for Ian and Hazel, with Scott and Edwina enjoying a second Christmas dinner with them. Hazel invited her whole family, and Ian and his daughters, for a buffet tea on Scott's birthday. It was a great time that made up for the peculiar Christmas.

Then, after months of no one viewing her house, two couples asked to view the same weekend. Both made an offer. The two couples fought it out until Hazel accepted the first to reach the asking price.

There was a semi-detached house in Hadleigh, close to a wood, that Hazel thought she could just afford. It wasn't without problems. The kitchen was very small so the washing machine and tumble dryer had been plumbed into the garage, which had since been pulled down because it was built using asbestos. The washing machine and tumble dryer were left in their original positions but now with a makeshift plastic shed around each one. The washing machine had blown all the fuses in the house while Hazel was viewing! A purpose-built shed or extension would have to be an added expense. It was the only house, apart from one other that had sold quickly, that she had even partially liked in the whole year she had been looking.

The estate agent rang to say a surveyor would be making an appointment to check her house over for the intended buyers. As she put the phone down, her mind began to race. She had thought it would be impossible to: a) find anyone she cared enough about to consider living with again; and b) find someone who would be able and willing to buy out Martin's share of the house. A total impossibility. But then she had met Ian. Having known him for only six months, had she seriously found her one true love? If she'd met him as a teenager, as she had Tim, she was sure they would still be together because he was intelligent, gentle, caring and loved her as she was. They had discussed it in depth. She knew he would have supported her going to university – and their love felt strong enough to have survived separate universities. That weekend she asked Scott how he would feel if Ian moved in with her. Scott confirmed he would be comfortable with it.

That week Hazel swung from feeling it would be good to have Ian move in to being afraid of all the hassle relationships seemed to bring. At work, when she'd completed the high-end orders she would help out in the amplifier department. Lou was supervisor. During Hazel's first week back at the hi-fi company, while waiting for all the required high-end parts to come in, she had sat on a bench facing Lou. It had been impossible for Hazel not to pour out her heart over all that had happened the previous year, because Lou had listened with such empathy. She had experienced an abusive marriage that had been almost impossible to extricate herself from. When she finally did, she lost a son to her ex-husband. Now Hazel turned to Lou and asked,

"What should I do? Ian's such a lovely, dear man."

Having heard how caring Ian was, Lou didn't hesitate to answer.

"Do it," she said. "What, really, do you have to lose?"

Hazel asked Ian what he thought of moving in with her, for a six-month trial, while still keeping his own house. He agreed it was a great idea. Hazel rang the estate agent and explained why she now felt she had to pull out of the sale and to please give her apologies to the buyers. Ian moved in a couple of weeks later, bringing only what he thought necessary for six months. But they knew from the beginning it would work out. It seemed her prayer had finally been answered. Her deep, dark hole had vanished.

She would still cry after leaving Scott at South Mimms to go home with his dad, especially with a twelve-day wait to see him next. But walking through her front door into Ian's arms made it bearable. At least Scott spent a good half of all his school holidays with them. The trampoline was still in place and being used by the grandchildren and Hazel for exercise, sometimes. But the greatest laughter was still when she and Scott attempted to bounce together. Then Ian bought a large shed with heating and lighting to house a table tennis table. It became a great source of amusement as Hazel, Ian and Scott all played at a similar level. Scott would play his mother and Ian separately, and even though Hazel and Ian now played regularly, Scott was able to win at least half the time. It took over from the trampoline in eliciting side-splitting laughter! Scott did confide to Hazel that he felt very comfortable and able to be himself around Ian. Over the years, during holidays in Spain and Crete and in cottages in the Lake District and Cornwall for walking holidays, she was able to watch with amused contentment as Ian and Scott strode off together, way in front of her, deep in conversation.

One warm, sunny day during Scott's summer break, Hazel saw a strange phenomenon. Scott and Hazel were relaxing on loungers in the garden. Scott, in shorts, had taken off his T-shirt. After half an hour of heat Hazel said she'd make them a cold drink and get the sunscreen lotion. From the kitchen window she watched as Scott stood up and stretched. Slim and tall he was on target to reach the six feet two inches predicted at his birth. He turned to walk down the garden. Hazel blinked in shock, not believing what she was seeing. Numerous welts were running across her son's back. Surely, surely, he couldn't have been lashed? But how else could he have got them? When and by whom? Hazel returned to the garden with their drinks and a bottle of sunscreen. As she applied it to her son's back she said,

"Do you know you have welts all down your back?"

"Yes," he replied. "The doctor said they're stretch marks caused by a growth spurt. He said it's not that uncommon."

"Really?" said Hazel, placated by this explanation. "Oh well, together with your third nipple, they certainly make you a little unusual."

And they laughed.

The following summer, Scott's school offered students the chance to undertake a World Challenge in Vietnam. It would be a month-long excursion, described as a 'student-led expedition, an empowering journey for students who are ready to step outside their comfort zones, explore the world and come back forever changed'. Martin's grandmother Elsa had died and left Scott some money. He had every reason to take this brilliant opportunity.

The school organised a BBQ the evening before the group flew out. Martin and Lucy were now married and Hazel drove up to Hitchin and joined Martin and his new family to give their son a grand send-off. It was difficult for Hazel to watch Scott relaxed around them all and then listening as his stepmother discussed with him how he might feel, away for so long, and likening his trip to a TV survival programme they clearly regularly watched and that Hazel knew nothing about. After kissing and hugging his mother hard, Scott promised to stay in touch via Facebook whenever he was able. Apart from experiencing a strange sense of detachment as she glimpsed her son's other life, Hazel drove home feeling incredibly proud that he felt up to the challenge.

Hazel followed his itinerary from Ho Chi Minh City to trekking Dalat and the Central Highlands, initially across agricultural land before a steep ascent into the jungle. Through primary and secondary jungle, pine forests and minor streams, camping with expert guides and helping to prepare tasty evening meals. Then a week helping out in a home for homeless and disabled children whose cheerful resilience amazed Scott. An overnight train to Hanoi, with plenty of time to explore the charming capital. Finishing on a boat around Ha Long Bay. As promised, he did stay in touch via Facebook. Hazel was away on holiday in Crete with Ian for one of the weeks but was able to find cafés that allowed her to check messages and pictures from him.

Scott returned home tired and thinner, with blisters, but wanting to return, to relive his awesome time. He did, indeed, return changed, with a worldly maturity and a desire to continue travelling.

He went on to do well with his GCSEs and decided to study maths, chemistry and physics at A-level. During his final year his school encouraged him to also do an EPQ – an extended project qualification. This involved choosing a topic – preferably, he was told, one that related to one of his A-levels – and, after in-depth research, producing a 5,000-word report. Scott told his mother, during one of their phone chats, that he had decided to do his research on the golden number, 1.6180…, represented by the Greek letter Phi (ø). It is closely related to the Fibonacci sequence and is also called the golden mean, golden ratio, divine proportion and divine section (if you check it out on YouTube you might even find it's been called God's Fingerprint!).

When Hazel read his completed essay, it stirred the depths of her mind. She felt it related to the 'goodness' of nature. Could this be how goodness succeeds? Certainly, it shows how nature can achieve perfection. All beyond her really, though! Scott achieved an A* for it. The essay can be downloaded from www.hazellakeland.co.uk. Understanding the detail is not necessary but being aware of this phenomenon in nature has to be interesting.

After visiting three universities with his mother and two with his father, Scott chose Leicester University, to study physics. Hazel helped him purchase all he would need and drove up to his halls of residence with a full car. Scott arrived with his father and Lucy directly from Hitchin. To make the emotional farewell easier Scott suggested that Hazel arrive after his father and stepmother had left. It was with warm, companionable banter that mother and son unloaded the car and worked out where things should be distributed in the kitchen, or his bedroom. Following cups of coffee, drunk sitting in his new kitchen, it was time for Hazel to leave her son. They hugged and kissed out by the car and Scott turned to begin his new life as his mother drove away. Of course, it was emotional leaving him but neither spilt tears. Hazel mostly felt an enormous pride knowing that Scott would cope well with uni life.

Hazel and Ian spent several weekends in Leicester during those three years, enjoying Scott's company on walks and meals out in pubs and restaurants. Following the discovery of Richard III's remains in a car park there, they followed a trail to various places apparently visited by the king. It was Hazel who helped Scott move all of his belongings at the end of his first year into a house to share with four university friends. She was pleased with the large, sunny, bay-windowed bedroom he had negotiated for himself.

Scott achieved a 2:1 degree in physics, having made the decision to study the computing modules and completed his dissertation on coding, for which he was awarded a first. Both parents, with their respective partners, came together to watch his graduation ceremony. Scott had booked a table for after the ceremony in a Moroccan restaurant he'd been to before. The food was superb and the five of them celebrated together with a heartfelt joy at how life had turned out.

After university, Scott lived for a short while with a girlfriend in Kent. Together they walked 250 miles of the South West Coast path in two weeks to raise money for the RNLI. Scott, not then ready to settle down permanently in a relationship, moved back to live with his mother and Ian for more than six months, much to Hazel's delight. Then, through Michael's son, who held a middle management position in a global insurance company based in the City of London, he was given a six-month trial in their IT department. Within his first six months he was entrusted to go to New York, alone, to entertain clients, for two weeks, not only because of his good IT skills but also because of his excellent social skills. Apparently, these two abilities are not often found together. Two of his best friends from university were also able to find jobs in the City, allowing the three of them to rent a flat together. Where his life will go from here will be his story. At the moment he's just enjoying being twenty-three.

Hazel and Ian married on Christmas Eve 2013. Having previously had four traditional weddings between them, they conferred with their families for approval to run away to marry in the Old Smithy in Gretna Green, their only witnesses a photographer and the women who had arranged the ceremony. They spent the night before and after in a hotel in the Lake District, and on the evening after the perfect ceremony the couple enjoyed singing carols around an open fire with the other guests. So what that the groom slept with the bride-to-be on the night before the wedding? They didn't worry about bad luck. This time it would last forever.

Robbie and Annie are still happily married. Justine is a brilliant mum to a gorgeous and happy four-year-old son. At twenty-one and eighteen respectively, Tara and Lucas have the world at their feet. Guinness the cat, at seventeen years old, blind and with failing kidneys, died in Hazel's arms as the vet gave him a lethal injection. The tortoise still roams the garden for six months of the year and hibernates in a box in the garage during the winter.

◊

As far as helping with the suffering in this world, however, this cannot be the end.

Hazel passed an online course, free to anyone, from the edX learning platform called the Science of Happiness. It is easily accessible by anyone, via a computer, tablet or mobile phone. Or simply visit the website of the Greater Good Science Centre at UC Berkeley, who produced the course, to view all the topics of their research. At work, Hazel offered to lead anyone interested through the course. Eight took up her offer and, while not all attended each week, they reported that it was useful and that Hazel presented it well.

◊

Ultimately, Hazel's hope is that this story will be passed around the globe, to open conversations on how each beautiful and unique child born on this awesome planet might be shown how to reach their potential for happiness, regardless of which religion or culture they may have become saturated with. Hazel believes this can only be achieved through an understanding of goodness. Its presence is everywhere, both within and around us.

Today we can lift children from poverty, and the suffering caused by humanity can be halted because Hazel does feel that God, Allah or the power of the universe suffers with us when we don't. Today we have the power to show all children that one can come close to heaven, even on earth.

We have the global capacity.

Don't we?

To view photographs relevant to Hazel's Story and to download Scott's essay please visit

www.hazellakeland.co.uk

Printed in Great Britain
by Amazon

41778580R00228